NHL

NHL action direct from Canada to your door.
Hockey News – 42 issues per year

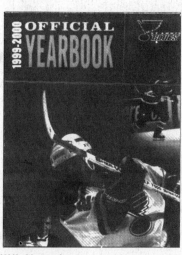

ALSO AVAILABLE: A full range of NHL Magazines,
NHL Match Team Programmes and NHL Team Media Guides, plus many other North
American Sporting Publications. Send for your free list today.

SKATE ATTACK

www.SkateAttack.com   www.E-ClubE.com

www.HockeyBears.co.uk

LONDON HEADQUARTER

Address: 95 Highgate Road, Kentish Tow
London NW5 1TR United Kingdo
Open Mon-Sat 9.30am-6.00p
Sundays and most Bank Holidays 10.00am-2.00p
Enquiries: 020 7485 00C
Mail Order: 020 7267 696

CLUB E: SKATE ATTACK
For the Lowest Prices in the U.K GUARANTEED

FREEPHONE
0800 252 884

THE ICE HOCKEY ANNUAL

2000-01

EDITED AND COMPILED BY STEWART ROBERTS

First published in Great Britain by
Stewart Roberts
The Old Town Hall
142 Albion Street
Southwick
Brighton BN42 4AX

Cover Design by **Channel Graphic Communication**

Digital artwork by **James Mansell**
james_mansell@hotmail.com

British Library Cataloguing-in-Publication Data.
A catalogue record for this book is available from the British Library.

The Ice Hockey Annual 2000-01

ISBN 0-9536410-1-5

The Ice Hockey Annual's official website is at www.graphyle.com/IHA.
Past editions of The Ice Hockey Annual are archived in the Hockey Hall of Fame, London Life
Resource Centre, Toronto, Canada.

Printed in Great Britain by Caldra House Ltd,
23 Coleridge Street, Hove, East Sussex BN3 5AB

CONTENTS

Cover - CHAMPIONS ON PARADE
Clockwise from top left: Captain **Denis Chassé** and coach **Dave Whistle** of *Sekonda* Superleague winners, Bracknell Bees, with the Monteith Bowl; **Scott Stevens,** captain of the New Jersey Devils with the Stanley Cup; **Frank Morris,** captain of the Fife Flyers, with the British National League trophy; Chelmsford Chieftains with the English Premier League trophy.
Photos: Mike Smith/Icepix, Trevor Benbrook, Bruce Jessop/International Hockey Archives, Peter Jones.

ACKNOWLEDGEMENTS

Welcome to the 25th edition of *The Ice Hockey Annual*. There must be some mistake. Try it again. The 25th edition of the Annual.

Yup, that's right, we've been around for longer than, well, you fill in the blanks, we're becoming forgetful now.

A couple of celebratory pieces have been specially written for the occasion - the editor's *Quarter-Century Awards* and a look at some of the young lads who might be playing in Superleague in 25 years' time (only kidding, Ian).

Our super-statsman **Gordon Wade** has compiled an up-to-date register of GB players and we think our designers have come up with a magnificent birthday cover. Hope you agree.

Otherwise, it's the usual mix. As we don't believe it's broke, we ain't thinking of fixing it for at least another 25 years. (**Steve Moria** will have his bus pass by then. Good grief!)

Time for the thank-yous. It's amazing how often we've thanked the same people over the years but it's a pleasure every time.

This is basically a reference book and statistics are what we all like to know, so the afore-mentioned Gordon Wade invariably comes first on the list for his unfailingly accurate Superleague and *Benson and Hedges* Cup stats. Gordon was the official statistician for the league and *Sky Sports* in 1999-2000.

Among his many other duties as the British National League's secretary, **Stan Wiltshire** looks after the league's stats which include the Christmas Cup and the *Benson and Hedges* Plate. **Sue** and **Steve Tomalin** take care of the all the English League's figures.

We've also made great use of the match reports and press releases sent to us every day (it seems) during the season by **Karen French** and **Alyson Pollard** (Superleague) and **Howard Harding** and **Simon Potter** (BNL).

Compiling stats for the many other competitions are **Allan Crow** (the Scottish Cup), **Val Wilkinson** (the GB under-16s), **Alan Moutrey** (the England under-14s) and **Helen Ensor** (women's hockey).

Our photographs were taken by **Mike Smith** of *Icepix*, **Trevor Benbrook, Roger Cook** and **Peter Jones**. Sorry we couldn't find room to use more of your fine efforts, guys. And thanks to all the clubs who sent in their team pics.

We're also grateful to our club reporters who are named on the appropriate page, and to all others who have contributed in ways large and small.

The *Annual's* advertisers have come up trumps again and we hope they find it rewarding to be in this special edition.

Retailers **Skate Attack** have been one of our most loyal customers so North London fans are recommended to get along to the shop in Kentish Town for all their equipment needs.

London fans are also spoilt when it comes to buying hockey books as the **Sportspages** shop in Charing Cross Road is always piled high with them. Fans in Manchester can now enjoy their unrivalled stock, too.

The *Zamboni* people at **Airport and Road Equipment** have been with us for several years as have **Barkers Worldwide Publications**, the sole importers of *The Hockey News of Canada* and other hockey publications and souvenirs.

Hockey sticks and other kit are the speciality of **Miras Sports** while **Flying F Skates** are the people to talk to about, well, skates. Hockey card collectors need look no further than **Armchair Sports** while **Benshaws**, official sponsors of Bracknell Bees, are the distributors of *Virgin Cola*.

We're delighted to welcome several new companies this year. Among the products made by **Terraplas** is the specialist ice covering in the new Nottingham Ice Centre, and **Alexandra Palace** is the home of Haringey Greyhounds, the English League (Div One South) champions.

The Cardiff branch of **Specsavers**, the national chain of opticians, are the official opticians of the Devils.

Whitley Bay's **Richie Crowe** runs **Canadian Imports** which, as the name suggests, brings in equipment from across the pond. **D&P Trophies** supply silverware to the English Ice Hockey Association.

The Annual was printed, as usual, by **Caldra House Ltd**, to whom our especial thanks, along with digital artworker extraordinaire **James Mansell** of *Design Time*. We were particularly fortunate that **Channel Graphic Communications** took an office next to ours just in time to create the wonderful cover design.

Thanks, everyone. Here's to another 25 years. Good grief! **SR**

HONOURS AND AWARDS

HONOURS ROLL-CALL 1999-2000

Sekonda Superleague Playoff Champion
LONDON KNIGHTS
Runner-up
NEWCASTLE RIVERKINGS
Sekonda Superleague
BRACKNELL BEES
Benson and Hedges Cup
MANCHESTER STORM
The Challenge Cup
SHEFFIELD STEELERS
British National League Playoff Champion
FIFE FLYERS
Runner-up
BASINGSTOKE BISON
British National League
FIFE FLYERS
Benson and Hedges Plate
BASINGSTOKE BISON
ntl: **Christmas Cup**
FIFE FLYERS
English Premier League
CHELMSFORD CHIEFTAINS
English Division One (North)
BILLINGHAM EAGLES
English Division One (South)
HARINGEY GREYHOUNDS
Scottish League
SOLWAY (Dumfries) SHARKS
Scottish Cup
FIFE FLYERS
Women's League
NOTTINGHAM VIPERS
Top League Points Scorers
Sekonda *Superleague*
ED COURTENAY, Sheffield Steelers
British National League
CLAUDE DUMAS, Hull Thunder/P'boro' Pirates
English Premier League
MIKKO SKINNARI, Invicta Dynamos
Best Goaltending Percentages
Sekonda *Superleague*
BRIAN GREER, Bracknell Bees
British National League
STEPHEN MURPHY, Fife Flyers
English Premier League
ROLAND BERTRAND, Swindon Chill

BRITISH ICE HOCKEY WRITERS' ASSOCIATION AWARDS

ALL-STAR TEAMS

SEKONDA *SUPERLEAGUE*
First Team

Goal	GEOFF SARJEANT, Ayr	
Defence	CLAUDIO SCREMIN, London	
	ROB STEWART, Bracknell	
Forwards	ED COURTENAY, Sheffield	
	KEVIN RIEHL, Bracknell	
	ROB KENNY, London	

Second Team

Goal	BRIAN GREER, Bracknell
Defence	SHAYNE McCOSH, Sheffield
	NEAL MARTIN, London
Forwards	TEEDER WYNNE, Sheffield
	MIKKO KOIVUNORO, N'castle
	STEVE THORNTON, Cardiff

BRITISH NATIONAL LEAGUE
First Team

Goal	STEPHEN MURPHY, Fife
Defence	RICK STRACHAN, Basingstoke
	TED RUSSELL, Fife
Forwards	RANDY SMITH, Peterborough
	CLAUDE DUMAS, Hull/P'boro'
	RUSSELL MONTEITH, Fife

Second Team

Goal	JOE WATKINS, Basingstoke
Defence	RON SHUDRA, Hull
	NEIL LIDDIARD, Peterborough
Forwards	STEVE CHARTRAND, Solihull
	STEVEN KING, Fife
	JOHN HAIG, Fife

OTHER AWARDS

Best British Defenceman (Alan Weeks Trophy)
STEPHEN COOPER, Nott'ham
Top British Scorer (Ice Hockey Annual Trophy)
TONY HAND, Ayr
Top British Netminder (BIHWA Trophy)
STEVIE LYLE, Cardiff

ALL STARS

above: **Mikko Koivunoro** (Newastle Riverkings) and **Rob Kenny** (London Knights);
below: **John Haig** (Fife Flyers) and **Kevin Riehl** (Bracknell Bees).

photos: Mike Smith/Icepix and PeterJones.

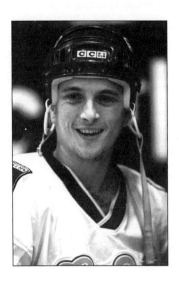 

Player of the Year
ED COURTENAY

THE SEKONDA FACE TO WATCH

At each Superleague game, sponsor Sekonda awarded a watch to the man of the match, with one of these players chosen each month as the Sekonda Face To Watch.

At the end of the season, one of the monthly winners was chosen as the Sekonda Player of the Season.

The winning player was presented with a holiday voucher at a lunch attended by all the monthly winners on the final day of the Sekonda Superleague Playoffs.

THE *SEKONDA* PLAYER OF THE SEASON
ED COURTENAY, Sheffield Steelers

The monthly winners were;

October	ED COURTENAY, Sheffield
November	MARK CAVALLIN, London
December	TONY HAND, Ayr
January	STEVE THORNTON, Cardiff
February	ROB STEWART, Bracknell
March	JIMMY HIBBERT, Newcastle

AWARDS TO OFFICIALS

Micky Curry Memorial Trophy – Most Improved
DAVE CLOUTMAN
Keith Franklin Memorial Trophy - Most Dedicated
GARY PLAISTOW

BRITISH ICE HOCKEY WRITERS' ASSOCIATION AWARDS, contd.

PLAYERS OF THE YEAR

Superleague ED COURTENAY, Sheffield
British Nat'n'l Lge STEPHEN MURPHY, Fife

Sheffield Steelers' forward, **ED COURTENAY**, enjoyed his best season in Britain, leading all Superleague scorers in goals and points ahead of linemates, **Teeder Wynne** and **Dale Junkin**.

Courtenay, 32, was a popular winner, collecting three other individual titles. *Sekonda* made him their Player of the Year as did the Sheffield fans and the Steelers' players, and he was voted on to BIHWA's All-Star team.

The Montreal-born Canadian came to this country in 1997. During his long career in North America he played 44 games with the NHL's San Jose Sharks in 1991-93.

Fife's goalie **STEPHEN MURPHY** was also the first choice of all the voters - writers, players and fans. The 18-year-old enjoyed an outstanding year as Flyers swept a record four trophies.

In only his second term as a senior, the Glasgow-born teenager's save percentage of 93.4 was the best recorded by any netminder in the three seasons of the British National League.

COACHES OF THE YEAR

Superleague DAVE WHISTLE, Bracknell
British Nat'n'l Lge. MARK MORRISON, Fife

DAVE WHISTLE completed a fairy-tale second season as coach by bringing the Superleague title to the London dormitory town of Bracknell.

The quietly spoken 34-year-old from Thunder Bay, Ontario steered Bees to their first ever major trophy against stiff competition from the league's better funded teams.

A Canadian West University All-Star, Dave came to Britain in 1991 and was on four different teams before joining Bees as a player in 1995.

Generally regarded as the architect of Fife Flyers' Grand Slam season, player-coach **MARK MORRISON** modestly disclaims the credit. "I don't believe I'm the greatest coach around, I still enjoy playing too much," he said. "But I do believe the decisions that **Chic [Cottrell]** and I took about players were right for this team."

After seven seasons with Flyers and four as coach, the British Columbian knows his club well. In **Russell Monteith** and **Ted Russell** he found just the men to complement their long serving dual nationals and much envied local talent.

EDITORIAL

The Quarter-Century Awards

As the Annual reaches its quarter-century what better way to celebrate than to look back at the efforts of the many people and organisations who have made important contributions to the growth of the sport in the last 25 momentous years.

Awards have been made in each category, some not too serious as I wouldn't want anyone getting carried away. There's still much work to be done to maintain the enormous progress the game has made.

THE RINK BUILDERS

As you can't have ice hockey without ice rinks, the first award must go the **Sports Council**, as you were then. Your meticulous planning and negotiations with local authorities inspired most of the 27 rinks that were built throughout the UK between 1981 and 1993.

This not only doubled the number of rinks but also laid the foundations on which the sport has been able to build so successfully.

And your award is: **A beautifully crafted begging letter, pleading for UK Sport to do it all over again.**

THE IMPORTS

Here's to you Canadians who came over in the Eighties, in the great days of the three-import rule, and raised the play of the Brits and the level of entertainment.

Too many of you to name individually but I would single out men of the calibre of **Doug McEwen, Steve Moria, Mike O'Connor** and Hall of Fame member **Gary Stefan**.

All of you have made Britain your home, were loyal to one or two clubs, helped to put GB back on the international map, and are a credit to your sport, on and off the ice.

And your award is: **The repeal of the Bosman ruling.**

THE SPONSORS

The governing BIHA was fortunate that *Heineken's* agent, **Ian Wight**, found the sport at the very time when it was starting to pick up in the early Eighties.

STEWART ROBERTS

Heineken and Wight, a member of the Hall of Fame, took the game to Wembley Arena in 1984 with the *Heineken* Championships and helped to guide the progress of the *Heineken* League, our first national league for over 20 years.

Though unfortunately restricted to the Autumn Cup, *Benson and Hedges* have also proved a superb sponsor. You and your agents, **Karen Earl**, deserve honouring just for your mind-bending work on bringing the top two leagues together in one competition each year.

And your award is: **A better known and organised sport than it would have been without you.**

THE NATIONAL TEAM

A lot of hard and too often unpaid work has gone into GB since it was reformed in 1989. Hall of Fame member **Alex Dampier** was the coach who took the team from Pool D in 1990 to Pool A in 1994, and none of us who were in Eindhoven, Netherlands in 1993 will ever forget the thrill of watching GB win promotion to the elite world group. This success alone created huge interest in the sport.

An honourable mention goes to his successor **Peter Woods** who kept the team in touch with the elite nations throughout his five years.

And your award is: **Dampier again in 2000-01, if you'll have us, Damps.**

THE GREAT BRITS

With so few rinks and so much pressure on ice time, it's a wonder anyone in Britain finds time to learn to skate, let alone play hockey. That's not me speaking, by the way, but former Manchester Storm coach, **Kurt Kleinendorst.**

Tony Hand, the only player entirely trained in Britain to be drafted by the NHL, Hall of Famer **Gordon Latto**, the **Cooper** and **Johnson** boys, **Paul Dixon, David Longstaff, Stevie Lyle, Scott Neil, Jim Pennycook, Paul Smith, Ashley Tait, Joe Watkins** and **Jonathan Weaver** have overcome enormous odds to succeed locally and internationally.

And your award is: **Inspiring your countrymen to follow you and, of course, continued selection to the GB team, for those of you still playing.**

THE BRITISH CHAMPIONS

Cardiff Devils under Hall of Famer **John Lawless,** *Sheffield Steelers* and *Murrayfield Racers* under **Alex Dampier** (again), *Dundee Rockets* and *Durham Wasps* under various coaches. All of you captured at least one Grand Slam of titles and became the best known teams in the sport.

And your award is: **An overall British champion again very soon.** (That's as soon as we can find the award. Someone seems to have hidden it.)

ICE HOCKEY SUPERLEAGUE

The young league playing in grown-up arenas has boosted the playing standard in Britain to its highest since the Fifties, and made the rest of the hockey world sit up.

Once you get over your growing pains and stop irritating your elders, your league should be a force to be reckoned with.

And your award is: **This splendid golden globe of an unidentified planet.**

THE REFEREES

Is there a tougher job in sports? Men like **Andy Carson** and **Simon Kirkham** have pushed themselves to keep their standards level with a game that goes on getting harder and faster.

From the early days, let's remember the late **Micky Curry** and **Nico Toemen**, the only Dutchman in the Hall of Fame. In his first five years here, Toemen developed and trained a large cadre of officials.

And your award is: **A small doll in which to keep your pins, wearing a shirt emblazoned 'Coach'.**

THE MAGAZINES

It's never been easy finding out what's happening in this funny old game. Most fans, myself included, would have been lost without the dedicated men who produced, almost single-handedly, the sport's two magazines.

Ice Hockey News Review, under new Hall of Fame member, **Vic Batchelder**, was the first in the field giving us all a comprehensive round-up of events all over the hockey world.

Powerplay is the 'new boy' but **Simon Potter** has published a newsy weekly during the season for a back-breaking eight years.

And your award is: **More readers.**

THE SUPPORTERS

Perhaps you should be the first ones in this list. This sport has had more than its fair share of money troubles over the years and uncounted numbers of you have willingly come to the rescue of your favourite team, digging into your not always deep pockets to keep the sport alive.

And your award is: **The best seat in the house.** (At least, it would be if I owned a rink.)

THE GOVERNING BODIES

The most maligned group of people, sometimes understandably. But having served on a few myself, I know what an extraordinarily difficult task it is trying to run a sport. You'll never be right, gentlemen, but we do need you.

Provided you promise not to be afraid of making a decision and sticking to it, and to love each other in future, you may have an award.

And your award is: **Just one of you in future.**

TELEVISION

Though this fast-moving game is notoriously difficult to capture on camera, Sky Sports, BBC, Channel 5 and others have succeeded in bringing the game, not just to the fans, but also to many folk who didn't realise they were fans.

And your award is: **More viewers.**

YOUTH DEVELOPMENT

The people who should come first in this game, the youngsters, too often seem an afterthought. This award is for the untiring work of all of you who are working to encourage young players.

And your award is: **Wait for it - more young Brits in Superleague.**

And *The Ice Hockey Annual?* Easy. *Our award is:* **More passionate fans like you and more growth in the next 25 years.**

Enjoy your hockey and tell your friends.

Stewart Roberts

August 2000   stewice@aol.com

QUOTES OF THE YEAR

Quick learner, eh?
"I didn't realise it would be this physical." *Chris McSorley*, *London Knights' rookie coach after their first couple of games.*

Stick that stick!
"I'd been using a stick that I've had for a couple of years and I think maybe it was out of goals."
Greg Hadden, of Nottingham Panthers, who scored four goals in two league games and four more in the Continental Cup after changing his stick.

Leap frog
"Hockey here is at a better level than France, a lot more better players, it's quicker, it's better hockey." *Sami Wahlsten, after playing two games for Manchester Storm.*

Happiness challenged
"I challenged my guys. I said to them if there's anyone in this room who isn't happy with our situation, I'd rather have you leave. Well, Rick took me up on it." *Kurt Kleinendorst, Manchester Storm coach, on the departure of forward Rick Brebant.*

Wage cut
"I'd take a pay cut if I knew I was going to be paid." *Jeremy Riehl, after being sacked by Edinburgh Capitals. The Canadian defenceman later returned to the club after agreeing to play for nothing.*

Psst, wanna buy a hockey team?
"...this season's new, sharper image and the success of the team on the ice has turned the Chill into one of the hottest properties on the hockey scene in the UK." *From Swindon Chill's sales prospectus.*

Not greedy then
"Ibiza with FHM's 100 Babes – and my girlfriend, of course." *Russ Plant, Guildford Flames, telling readers of Flames game night programme of his dream holiday.*

Super cosmopolitan league
'...defenceman Rob Donovan, an Irish- American, flew in from Italy this morning...' *Bracknell Bees press release, January 2000.*

Learning to play, Brit-style
"[My ambition to play] was helped by having three imports on each team. You strived to play alongside them and play as well as them. It helped a lot of players to develop. It was the same as wanting to play in the highest league." *Ian Cooper, GB's longest serving player.*

Brotherly love
"He has punched me once or twice and afterwards said he wasn't sure it was me. I suppose he was just doing his job.
"I've always known it was him and I've never punched back. I know better than that. He's still big brother, although there's not much in size, he's actually a bit shorter than me." *'Coops' again, this time while he was with London Knights and brother Stephen was at Nottingham.*

Not so shiney!
"Quick hard shifts and get off the ice, but they were more like slow soft shifts later on." *Shannon (Shinedog) Hope, 37, on coming out of his 18-month retirement with Peterborough Pirates.*

Goon shield
"I feel 6ft, 9ins and 240 pounds playing with those two. No one's going to touch me when they're on the ice!". *Jeff Hoad, the 5ft, 10ins, 183 lbs London Knights forward, on playing alongside hard men Mike Ware and Andy Bezeau.*

Expose the cheaters
"If there are [wage cap] cheaters they should just give them a big fine and expose them. And if they win Superleague they should get the trophy, but everyone would know it was tarnished. Yes, they would have it but that's the way it is." *Kurt Kleinendorst, Storm coach, with his thoughts on how to punish clubs found to have broken Superleague's £500,000 wage cap.*

Goalies ain't what they used to be
"I'd have had trouble scoring against those guys." *Chick Zamick, retired Nottingham superstar centreman, after watching the netminders in action at Panthers' last game at the Ice Stadium.*

With grateful acknowledgements to Ice Hockey News Review, Powerplay, Sky Sports, Manchester Storm's website, Hull Daily Mail.

NEW RINK NEWS

Then four came along at once

STEWART ROBERTS

The Skydome at **COVENTRY** and the long awaited National Ice Centre in **NOTTINGHAM** both opened in April 2000; after almost ten years, in September 2000 there was a new rink in **DUNDEE**; by the end of 2000, the superb Odyssey Arena in **BELFAST** was to be ready.

Four rinks in one year. We have to go back 16 years to the Orwellian year of 1984 to find a 12-month period when so many venues came on stream at once. If you can't remember, they were Lee Valley, Oxford, Telford and Gillingham. Total seating for hockey - 5,000, if you're lucky.

Total capacity for 2000's little beauties? Over 18,000!

We covered Belfast, Coventry and Nottingham last time and there's an update in our *Review of the Season*, but here's the latest on Dundee.

Olympic size ice surface, 2,400 seats and the owners of the £7 million building keen to have ice hockey. No wonder former Dundee Rockets player turned Scottish IHA secretary, **Joe Guilcher,** is over the moon, Brian.

Joe's Tigers, who have had to play all their games away for the last decade, will be entering the new Scottish National League as soon as the rink opens. Then, says Joe, "we'll review the situation at the end of the season to see if we're ready for the BNL."

What's that you say? You're still not satisfied. You want more rinks. No, you're quite right. This quartet brings the total staging ice hockey to 47, including six arenas.

This is laughable for a population of 60 million. It's even worse if you take out the arenas which can only stage pro games and have no time for kids or second teams, let alone pleasure skating. That leaves about one rink for every million and a half people.

From what I'm hearing, though, I'm afraid we're probably going to have pay for this year's good fortune by waiting quite a while for any more.

There's half-a-dozen planned but, as we've learned from bitter experience (eh, Superleague?), these buildings take a long time to go from drawing board to open doors.

Working alphabetically, the first is that much trailed arena in the £240 million Sports Village in **CARDIFF** Bay.

I understand the paperwork is well advanced and everyone involved – local and county authorities – wants to make it happen.

But there's just a small problem with the ground which the engineers say contains, lovely phrase, a 'cocktail of pollutants'. There's a bigger problem with money. Isn't there always? Mainly, no developer has yet come forward to put the whole scheme together.

Lucky Devils have signed a lease at the Ice House then.

Back across the Irish Sea, the Irish government plans to spend 281 million punts (that's about £220 million) on a new sports complex, to be known as Stadium Ireland.

The centrepiece of the project in west **DUBLIN** will be an 80,000-seat national stadium, and the complex will include a 15,000-seat indoor arena. The scheme could be completed by 2005.

Make a nice local rivalry for Giants, eh?

> **AREN'T WE ALL?**
> "I'm, surprised, frankly, with the weather in this country that every city doesn't have a large indoor venue. Even if you didn't have ice hockey you could put so many other things in there." **Colin Ward,** *Bracknell Bees' forward.*

I understand the proposed two-pad rink in **SHEFFIELD** which was mentioned here last year is still on schedule for opening in 2002. With funding from the National Lottery, ice time will be available to all.

WEMBLEY Plc are planning to construct a new £25 million, 20,000-seat arena to replace the existing one, which was built in 1927.

The company got £106 million for the football stadium and, subject to planning, would build the new arena as part of a major leisure and retail 'resort' on part of the 51 acres it owns around the stadium. The existing arena and conference centre would be demolished.

The group is currently talking to two landowners with a further 25 acres next door about building an even bigger complex, but they hope to start the redevelopment early in 2001.

The best hope for new rinks are Planet Ice (See *Review of the Season*) who, even as you read this, are plotting to upgrade some existing buildings and maybe build a couple of new ones.

MORE QUOTES OF THE YEAR

Winning is all Brits want

"What's very important to the British public is that they have a winning team, not the quality of the hockey. It's a totally different attitude to Canada's....Toronto [Maple Leafs] were bad for an awful long time but they filled the rink every single game because they liked the hockey. Here [at Ayr], we're losing fans because we're not winning this year." *Scott Young, Ayr Scottish Eagles.*

Sheffield virgin

"I expect to leave it there as an investment and, hopefully, in ten years' time someone like **Richard Branson** will be coming along and say 'bugger off, here's a few million quid'!" *Darren Brown, the new owner of Sheffield Steelers, on why he purchased the franchise.*

British ice hockey 2000

"I think it's pretty wide open. The style of hockey I played last year [on Team Canada] was way more defensive. Here you can get your breaks and have two-on-ones and breakaways, and I like that." *Casson Masters, of Bracknell Bees.*

"I thought with the big ice surface here in Fife, you'd have a little more time and maybe I'd play a little more finesse. But there's not a lot of room. You have to make quick decisions and play in traffic. It's a lot like in Canada." *Russell Monteith, Fife Flyers' new import.*

"Superleague guys do their job and that's about it, they don't try to do much extra stuff. You're expected to do a bit more in the BNL, perhaps try and rush the puck and be more involved in every play. Try and be in every place at the same time." *Ron Shudra on the differences he's found in moving from Superleague Steelers to the BNL's Hull Thunder.*

"Cam [Law] really needed another year in professional hockey before being ready to step up to the BNL." *Rick Strachan coach of Basingstoke Bison, on releasing the University of Western Ontario defenceman to join North America's Central Hockey League.*

Everything's cool, man

"We had a ten-hour board meeting and everything's fine. The whole thing's on auto-pilot now." *Ken Taggart, chairman of the English IHA, a few days before the English League's Oxford Blades collapsed. (Taggart is an American citizen and lives in Colorado. Yes, really - Ed.]*

Promise?

"I'll be working closely with **Don [Depoe]** to get a good product on the ice, but the team I will leave to him. I will have input but he can tell me where to go." *Glen Meier, on being appointed Director of Hockey Operations with Hull Thunder.*

Lemonade, anyone?

"I don't blame **Colum [Cavilla]** at all. This is the job he wanted and will do for the next 25 years. For us, though, it's terrible. But when life deals you a lemon, you've just got to make lemonade - at the moment, we're swimming in it." *Don Depoe, Hull Thunder's coach, on learning of his goalie's sudden decision to join the Calgary police.*

Honest

"I don't expect to score every game. If I could do that I wouldn't be here..." *Ed Courtenay, Superleague's leading scorer and Player of the Year.*

McQuote

*Just some of the many colourful quotes from London Knights' coach, **Chris McSorley** which kept us reporters chuckling during the season.*

After a hard fought game - "Our hearts were closely attached to our legs tonight."

*On former Boston Bruins' hard man **Darren Banks** after he scored against the Storm:* "Two goals can ruin a tough guy. Remember, when a crusher becomes a rusher, he soon becomes an usher."

Forecasting a physical B&H Cup semi-final series between Knights and local rivals, Bracknell Bees: "Whoever's left standing after the second game will be able to stumble up the street to see who they're going to play next."

On losing the B&H Cup: "I wasn't brought here to kiss a sister, I was brought to take the bride home."

And it's goodbye from him

*We'll miss **Kurt Kleinendorst**, Manchester Storm's only slightly less colourful coach.*

"Their fourth goal was down to us not picking up a late man coming into the zone. I mean I can get my 12-year-old kid to cover something as simple as that, yet I can't get my guys to do it."

After Storm lost three straight games, one in the EHL and two to Bracknell Bees.

BRITS IN AMERICA

Chasing the dream

In pursuit of his dream to play in the NHL, **JONATHAN WEAVER** did what no other British player has ever done before. The 23-year-old from Sunderland played two-thirds of his season in the North American minor leagues.

With seven years of senior hockey behind him, three in Superleague, he was fortunate to be playing for Manchester Storm who had strong links with the NHL's Ottawa Senators. His coach at Storm, American **Kurt Kleinendorst**, encouraged him in his dream, though he warned Weaver that it wouldn't be easy.

He started with a spell in Senators' training camp in September 1999 and received positive reports from the coaching staff. "He showed some good hockey sense. He needs to improve his strength but he didn't embarrass himself."

After five pre-season games with Ottawa's International Hockey League (IHL) team, Grand Rapids (Michigan) Griffins, he returned home to play with Storm before being called up by Mississippi Sea Wolves of the East Coast Hockey League (ECHL). Jonathan played 41 games in America all told, including six playoff games. (See table.)

How good are these leagues? Well, our own Superleague recruits most of their players from them, while the NHL treats the IHL as one of its 'farm' leagues.

So it was interesting that Jonathan told *Ice Hockey News Review*: "I don't know if I'm a better player for my time over there, but I'm cetainly no worse." He acknowledged that the style of play was more physical due to the smaller rinks, but he reckoned that the standard, even in the higher ranked IHL, was "not that much better than in Superleague".

Cetainly the pay was no better. "I was earning probably a little bit more than half as much as in Superleague," he told *IHNR*. Apparently, the real money goes to players who have signed an NHL contract and have been 'sent down' by the big league.

Jonathan knew from what KK told him that he was almost certainly too old, and probably too small at 12-stone and five foot-eleven to win such a contract himself. In any case, Europeans have to be drafted by an NHL team, like **Tony Hand** was, before they can be signed.

But the talented and level headed young man proved himself in a highly competitive environment, enjoyed the experience of playing in a foreign country and learned how to handle playing three games in three nights, five games a week. All of which will stand him in good stead wherever he plays next.

Here are Weaver's complete scoring stats for 1999-2000. You will note that he managed to slip back to Britain between his North American stints to play for his national team in the World Championship, Pool A qualfiers at Sheffield and Eindhoven in November and December.

Weaver's stats 1999-00	GP	G	A	Pts	Pim
Storm - ISL & B&H Cup	11	3	3	6	0
Sea Wolves - ECHL	28	4	17	21	4
Sea Wolves - playoffs	6	1	3	4	0
Vipers - IHL (no playoffs)	7	2	1	3	2
Britain - Pool A Qual.	4	0	0	0	2
Totals	50	10	24	34	8

The big league swoops for Scot

Scot **COLIN SHIELDS**, 20, was drafted by the NHL's Philadelphia Flyers in June 2000, the first British-born player to be selected by the big league since **Tony Hand**, another Scot, in 1986.

We would love to add 'British trained' but apart from learning the basics with his skating-mad family and a handful of games with his dad's Paisley Pirates, Colin's serious hockey education has been in North America.

The Glasgow-born forward set some sort of record by crossing the Atlantic at the tender age of 14 to try and achieve his passionate ambition of playing in the NHL.

Many kids that age fancy playing in the pros but few have the courage or the parental backing to make the dream come true. Colin did and he very nearly has. "You have to go early, you can't wait until you're 16 or 17," Shields told *Ice Hockey News Review*. "The way they play is just too different to change at that age if you want to be successful."

He spent four years in the Canadian junior system before graduating to the North American Hockey League with Cleveland Barons. The NAHL is one of the USA's premier development leagues and a hotbed for college and NHL scouts.

JONATHAN WEAVER

COLIN SHIELDS

Colin's second term with Barons was prolific. He finished as their top scorer and helped them to win the prestigious Detroit junior tournament, the *Compuware* Fall Classic.

He was also wanted at 'home' where he was picked for the GB under-20 side for the third successive year. He was GB's leading scorer in Japan. When he rejoined Barons, the NAHL voted him their player of the month for January and rumours spread that NHL scouts from St Louis Blues were showing interest in him.

So it was a surprise when Philadelphia, one of the NHL's leading clubs, picked him in the annual entry draft in June 2000. Flyers have four years before they must sign him or release him to be a free agent.

Colin will put that time to good use as he has been granted a four-year hockey scholarship by the University of Maine Black Bears.

Maine, the reigning NCAA champions, are one of North America's most renowned hockey colleges - Mighty Duck **Paul Kariya** is their best known graduate - and they only select a very few candidates each year. Shields was one of only four players chosen in 2000.

BACKGROUND

Born East Kilbride, Glasgow, 27 January 1980. Height 6ft, weight 175lb.

Centre/right-wing. 'Smallish but skilled.' *Red Line Scouting Report.*

Father Martin played for GB and Glasgow Dynamos and coached Paisley Pirates 1993-96.

Mother Margaret was a Scottish figure skating champion and later a skating teacher.

COLIN SHIELDS' ROAD TO THE TOP

1994-95 *age 14*	Paisley Pirates (six games). Notre Dame, Sask. -bantam.
1995-96 *age 15*	Paisley Pirates (ten games, 6-1-7). Kitchener, Ont. - midget.
1996-97 *age 16*	Glanbrook, Ont. - won provincial championship, All-Star, Rookie of the Year. GB - World u20 in Romania. GB - European u18 in Romania.
1997-98 *age 17*	Strathroy Rockets (Kitchener) Jr B. GB - World u20 in Estonia.
1998-99 *age 18*	Cleveland Barons (NAHL). USA junior. 55 games 30-30-60.
1999-00 *age 19*	Cleveland Barons - top goals and points scorer, 55 games 46-49-95. *Compuware* Fall Classic (Detroit) - scored championship winning goal. GB - World u20 in Nagano - top scorer.
2000-01 *age 20*	Drafted in 6th round by NHL's Philadelphia Flyers, 195th overall out of 293 players. University of Maine Black Bears, £100,000, four-year scholarship.

STARS OF TOMORROW?

Forwards **Jonathan Weaver** and **Colin Shields** made their mark in the pro game in North America in 1999-2000 after learning some or all of their hockey in this country.

Their experiences, along with those of GB internationals **Tony Hand**, who was drafted by Edmonton Oilers in 1986, and goalie **Stevie Lyle**, prove that there are opportunities for young British trained players to make a name for themselves at the game.

It is equally true, though, that it is more difficult for a Brit to make a impression in ice hockey than in other sports because of the shortage of rinks.

With Superleague discussing ways of introducing an 'apprentices' scheme in 2000-01, however, we may soon hear more about the following players, according to the Annual's reporters.

EDINBURGH CAPITALS
Top talent - **ROSS HAY** netted his first senior goal in 1999-2000. The son of Murrayfield legend, Jock, the Scotland under-19 forward was a consistent junior scorer and improved greatly with Capitals last season.
Ones to watch - **Steven Francey** and Scotland under-19 netminder **Matthieu Davidge**.

FIFE FLYERS
Top talents - Goalie **STEPHEN MURPHY**, 18. (See biography in Fife's section). A GB under-20 international and a key to Flyers' 1999-2000 success has, unfortunately, been lost to the UK as he signed for Omaha Lancers of the junior US Hockey League in the off-season.
PATRICK (Paddy) WARD. The 16-year-old defenceman netted his first goal with Flyers and made his debut with the GB under-16s. A regular choice for the Scottish junior squads, at 15 he attended the IIHF development camp in the Czech Republic.

GUILDFORD FLAMES
Top talents - **TYRONE MILLER**, 17, a GB under-18 defender, played ten games for Flames in 1999-2000. 'Hard hitting and hard working' say scouts.
JASON MOSES, 18, a GB under-18 forward, made his senior debut in 1997-98 and scored two goals for Flames last season.
Ones to watch - **Michael Plenty**, a GB under-18 defender, **Andrew Smith**, a GB under-16 forward, and forward **John Hepburn**, 17, in his second season with Flames.

HULL THUNDER
Top talents - **KARL HOPPER**, 20, played a handful of senior games in 1999-2000 and won a man of the match award.
MATTHEW STREET, 20, a big, bustling forward, is tipped to become a regular with Thunder if his career as a sheet metal worker permits.
Ones to watch - GB under-18 internationals, **Nathan Hunt**, defence, and **Chris Markham**, forward.

MANCHESTER STORM
Top talent - **CHRIS MAIN**, the 18-year-old Altrincham netminder who was drafted in as back-up to **Mark Bernard** when **Frank Pietrangelo** underwent a knee op.
(Storm have no official junior set-up as there is insufficient ice-time in their multi-purpose arena.)

MILTON KEYNES KINGS
Top talent - **JAMES MORGAN**, 17. GB under-20 defenceman who split 1999-2000 between Kings and home town team, Peterborough Pirates. Spent three seasons in Canada and hopes to return there in 2000-01.
Ones to watch - **Michael (Muzzy) Wales**, 17, GB under-18 defender from Gillingham became a regular with Kings in his debut season, though used sparingly. Blueliner **Leigh Jamieson**, 14, was voted the most valuable player at two prestigious junior tournaments *(see photo)*.

NEWCASTLE JESTERS
Top talents - Billingham and GB under-18 defenceman **RITCHIE THORNTON**, 17, was set to be one of Superleague's first 'apprentices' along with his Billingham team-mate **STEPHEN WALLACE**, 16, who was the top scorer for the GB under-16 squad in 1999 and 2000.
One to watch - Sunderland and England under-19 forward **STUART POTTS**.

PAISLEY PIRATES
Top talent - **JAMES CLARKE**, 20, is the first player to break through from Paisley's junior ranks. A bronze medal in the GB under-20 games was a major highlight for the feisty forward who took over 100 minutes in penalties with Pirates.
One to watch - GB under-20 forward **Bryan O'Neil**.

PETERBOROUGH PIRATES
Top Talent - Rushing blueliner **BERNIE BRADFORD**, 14, debuted for the senior team in 1999-2000. Shows good leadership qualities.

ONE FOR THE FUTURE

Milton Keynes junior defenceman, **Leigh Jamieson**, 14, receiving his trophy from your editor as the Most Valuable Player at the English Junior Inter-Conference finals at Hull in May 2000.

Photo: Arthur Foster.

Ones to watch - **Craig Peacock**, 11, the son of former Pirates, Ayr and Nottingham star, **Tim Peacock**. Craig was selected for the England under-14 school of excellence. Goalie **Euan King**, 10, who already shows signs of one day stepping into father Kevin's skates.

SLOUGH JETS

Top talent - Centre/right-wing **MATT FOORD**, 18, was voted Jets' most promising player in his first full season at senior level. He captained the GB under-18 team in their world junior championship 'rehearsal' tournament in France.

Ones to watch - **Adam White**, GB under-18 netminder, made his debut with Jets. **Matt Towalski**, GB under-16 forward, and **Barney Wood**, an England under-14 defenceman.

SOLIHULL BLAZE

Top talent - GB under-20 forward, **JAKE ARMSTRONG** made his debut with Blaze in 1994-95 but played his first BNL games last season. With Basingstoke Bison in 1998-99. **JAMES PEASE**. Armstrong's team-mate on the GB under-20 side in Japan is the club's number one blue line prospect. Voted the team's best young player in 1998-99 and 1999-2000. 'Cool temperament and clever hockey brain' say scouts.

CHELMSFORD CHIEFTAINS

Thanks to sponsors, *Pepsi-Co*, several youngsters have progressed through Chelmsford's junior ranks.

Top talents - In goal **PAUL WILCOX** made his debut in the Millennium Cup and proved to be a reliable backup. On the forward line, **SHAUN WALLIS** scored one of his two Chieftains' goals on his 18th birthday,

Ones to watch - **Carl Ambler**, 13, was given a taste of the big time against the GB under-18 squad, and defenceman **Richard Gunn** appeared on the England under-17 team.

FLINTSHIRE FREEZE

Top talent - **Marc Lovell**, 17, started out just hoping to make it on to the senior squad and ended by playing the full season, scoring 8-9-17, and winning selection to the England under-19 side. 'Has speed, determination, bravery, quick hands and a desire to reach the highest level possible,' says his coach, **Mark Stokes**.

ROMFORD RAIDERS

Top talent - **Ross Jones**, 17, was a regular member of the Raiders, picking up a couple of man-of-the-match awards, in his first full season after joining from Chelmsford, his home town team. Voted most improved player with the under-19 Buccaneers and selected by the GB under-18s.

WHITLEY WARRIORS

Top talent - **Lee Baxter**, 19, finished his first full season in a Warriors' shirt as runner-up in the club's scoring. 'Good hands, a turn of speed and a deadly accurate shot', say the scouts.

ATTENDANCES

OVERALL PICTURE	1999-2000 ATTENDANCE			1998-99	Ave. diff.
	Total	Games	Average	Average	on 1998-99
SEKONDA SUPERLEAGUE					
League	538,132	168	3,203	3,359	Down 4.6%
Challenge Cup Finals	20,640	5	4,128	6,443	(Diff. teams)
Playoffs	75,672	24	3,153	2,857	Up 10.4%
*Playoff Finals	29,752	3	9,917	9,494	Up 4.4%
TOTALS	**664,196**	**200**	**3,321**	**3,461**	**Down 4.0%**
BRITISH NATIONAL LEAGUE					
League and *ntl* Christmas Cup	201,159	198	1,016	940	Up 8.1%
BNL Playoffs (including finals)	36,839	29	1,270	1,226	Up 3.6%
TOTALS	**237,998**	**227**	**1,048**	**971**	**Up 7.9%**
BENSON AND HEDGES CUP					
including Plate and finals	**157,986**	**88**	**1,795**	**1,968**	**Down 8.8%**
TOTALS	**1,057,580**	**515**	**2,053**	**2,063**	**No diff.**
ENGLISH LEAGUE					
Premier Division	50,234	101	497	787	Down 36.8%
Playoffs	3,694	6	616	954	Down 35.4%
TOTALS	**53,928**	**107**	**504**	**776**	**Down 35.0%**
GRAND TOTALS	**1,111,508**	**622**	**1,787**	**1,714**	**Up 4.3%**

* Played at the MEN Arena, Manchester. Only the total for all three games was announced.

THE TOP LEAGUE CROWD-PULLERS			1999-2000 ATTENDANCE			1998-99	
			League	Total	Average+	Average	Changes
1	(1)	Manchester Storm	Super	143,049	6,812	7,414	Down 8.1%
2	(2)	Sheffield Steelers	Super	114,907	5,472	5,502	No diff.
3	(3)	London Knights	Super	65,289	3,109	3,122	No diff.
4	(4)	Nottingham Panthers	Super	52,236	2,487	2,449	Up 1.5%
5	(5)	Cardiff Devils	Super	43,657	2,079	2,313	Down 10.1%
6	(9)	Bracknell Bees	Super	40,846	1,945	1,793	Up 8.5%
7	(6)	Newcastle Riverkings	Super	39,227	1,868	2,236	Down 16.4%
8	(7)	Ayr Scottish Eagles	Super	38,614	1,839	2,044	Down 10.0%
9	(7)	Fife Flyers	BNL	28,038	1,558	1,887	Down 17.4%
10	(10)	Guildford Flames	BNL	26,376	1,465	1,561	Down 6.1%
11	(12)	Basingstoke Bison	BNL	23,719	1,318	1,163	Up 13.3%
12	(11)	Milton Keynes Kings	BNL	19,284	1,071	1,291	Down 17.0%
13	(14)	Hull Thunder	BNL	18,499	1,028	1,094	Down 6.0%

List includes teams that averaged at least 1,000 fans to league games only (excluding playoffs).
Last season's position in brackets.
+ Superleague teams each played 21 home games; British National League (BNL) teams 18 home games.
Figures are based on those shown on the leagues' media information releases.

REVIEW OF THE SEASON

*Editor **Stewart Roberts** goes behind the scenes of another difficult season for the sport in 1999-2000. A bad year for some administrators, a mixed one for the national team, but a vintage one for Superleague's 'goons'.*

A sport of three champs

For the fourth successive season, ice hockey failed to crown an undisputed champion.

It's good to have three distinct levels of play, but each of the sport's main leagues - *Sekonda Superleague*, British National League (BNL) and English Premier League - continued to play to their own rules so no overall British club champion could be crowned.

Bracknell Bees were the surprise Superleague winners. Their four-point victory over Sheffield Steelers was unexpected as they played in one of the league's smallest venues and kept firmly to the £500,000 wage cap.

Their secret was the shrewd recruiting skills of coach **Dave Whistle**, about the only thing that BNL champs, ***Fife Flyers***, had in common with their all-foreign counterparts.

Canadian **Mark Morrison** took Flyers' talented local players and blended in a handful of skilful imports to bring the Kirkcaldy crew their first league title for a decade, as well as three other trophies.

Erskine Douglas's ***Chelmsford Chieftains*** needed only a couple of imports to win the English League, their first title in 13 years.

The only competition to bring together the leading 20 teams in Britain was the *Benson and Hedges* Cup, but it required an excruciatingly complex format to make it work. ***Manchester Storm*** won the Cup while ***Basingstoke Bison*** picked up the consolation Plate.

GB - honour but no glory

Britain's national team played a record 14 full internationals in 1999-2000 as they battled in vain to win promotion to the World A Pool and to qualify for the 2002 Winter Olympics.

Handicapped by poor crowds in Sheffield Arena for the championship push, and by the leagues' refusal to close down during the Olympic bid, **Peter Woods**' team failed by the narrowest of margins to progress in either competition. (See special articles later in the *Annual*.)

Funding was the biggest problem. The team was run by the GB Ice Hockey Board which received grants from Superleague and UK Sport reckoned to be worth over £100,000. But this had to cover the expenses of all Britain's teams, men and women, senior and junior. What's more, the Board reportedly lost a substantial sum on staging the Sheffield games.

BAD NEWS FOR WEMBLEY FANS
'The MEN Arena has won a multi-year contract to stage the finals of the Sekonda Superleague's playoffs.'
Manchester Storm's website, November 1999.

It all totted up until there was nothing left in the kitty for the flagship GB senior squad in the Olympic qualifiers and World Pool B.

The Board's chairman, **David Temme**, resigned in March 2000, complaining about the lack of co-operation he received from the rest of the sport. The national governing body, Ice Hockey UK, took over the running of the team.

The five-year reign of coach Woods also came to an end after 50 games at the helm when his contract was not renewed.

Super troubled league

It was an 'annus horribilis' for Superleague's chief executive, **Ian Taylor**. In only his his second full season, (the league's fourth) his Leicester HQ needed a revolving door to cope with all the comings and goings.

☒ Chairman **David Temme**, the driving force behind the league, resigned out of the blue and Cardiff Devils, the club of which he was president, later admitted they had suffered 'significant losses'.

☒ Director of Sport **Peter Woods** did not have his contract renewed at the end of the season.

☒ Chief referee **Bob Bramah** resigned and his proposed replacement, Finn **Kim Pihl**, declined the post after an interview.

☒ Marketing and events manager **Glen Meier** was released from his contract in mid-season. (He was replaced in the summer by **Suzanne Wells** (marketing) and **Hannah Skinner** (events).)

☒ Several match officials resigned after the league refused to punish coaches who criticised them publicly.

There were other problems:

☒ The chief exec. admitted that "he couldn't prove" that one or two clubs might have broken the league's £500,000 wage cap.

☒ Crowd levels drifted downwards for the third successive season.

☒ No teams progressed in Europe - again.

☒ The league was criticised by the world governing IIHF and the Players Association for failing to develop British-born players to staff the national team.

☒ Although Belfast was finally confirmed in March 2000 as the league's ninth franchise, there was still no news of the Leeds Lasers franchise which was awarded in 1996.

Surely things can only get better, Ian.

Superleague chairman quits

David Temme, probably the most powerful figure in the sport, announced suddenly in March 2000 that he was resigning all his posts with immediate effect.

Welshman Temme was chairman of Superleague and the GB Ice Hockey Board and president of Cardiff Devils. He was replaced as league chairman in May by Manchester Storm's MD, **David Davies**.

At Cardiff, Temme moved across the Celtic Leisure organisation to become chief executive of Cardiff City football club. **Bob Phillips**, a director of Celtic Leisure, took over as boss of the Devils.

A great ice hockey enthusiast, Temme was a co-founder of Superleague with Newcastle's **Sir John Hall**, the first owner of the Newcastle franchise. Hall quit the sport after the league's first season. Both men believed that ice hockey was being held back by an amateurish attitude and they encouraged the major clubs to spend big and to import players on a massive scale.

During Temme's four years at the helm, the league duly splashed out millions on players but sustained such large losses that they were forced to impose a limit on players' wages in the chairman's final season.

Since Superleague's debut in 1996-97, the crowds have gone down by 12 per cent and of the original eight franchises, only three - Ayr, Bracknell and Manchester - have survived unscathed financially.

Temme was a keen supporter of the national team, too, and more money was thrown at GB through the GB Ice Hockey Board, but the squad failed to win promotion or to qualify for the Winter Olympics.

Although Devils were the most successful team on the ice in the league's four seasons, their crowds dipped by 17 per cent over the same period and the club's owners, Celtic Leisure (Cymru) Plc, went out of business. (See next story.)

Their president was keen to see Devils repeat their success on the European stage but his rink was too small for European League competition and the club lost a substantial sum in staging a round of the 1999 Continental Cup.

Temme's successor, David Davies, was also in at the formation of Superleague and is well respected inside and outside the league. But he, too, made an unexpected move in June 2000 when he accepted the post of chief executive of Queens Park Rangers football club.

Davies' appointment does give Superleague a neutral chairman, however, and his business-like and diplomatic approach will hopefully enable the league to move forward.

Devils hit the rocks

In June 2000, Cardiff Devils issued the following brief press release.

'Celtic Leisure (Cymru) Plc has for a number of years operated the Cardiff ice rink and the BT Cardiff Devils ice hockey club.

'This operation has resulted in significant losses over the years culminating with a recent failed rescue attempt by Celtic Leisure (Holdings) Plc.

'The failure of Celtic Leisure (Cymru) Plc will not effect the continued operation of both the Cardiff ice rink and BT Cardiff Devils, as operations will be continued through Celtic Leisure (Holdings) Plc.

'This decision reflects the importance of the future relocation to the new Cardiff Bay Sports Village where ice hockey operations can be put on a more financially sound footing.'

Clarifying the situation, Superleague's chief exec. **Ian Taylor**, confirmed that the ownership transfer was completed before Celtic Leisure (Cymru) Plc failed. That, apparently, made it unnecessary for the new company to pay a franchise fee.

We couldn't possibly comment.

Another press release a few days later confirmed that '**Ceri Whitehead**, until recently General Manager of Cardiff City Football Club, has been appointed as Operations Director at the BT IceHouse.'

Wage cap broken? Who knows?

Rumours persisted after Christmas 2000 that a couple of Superleague clubs had broken the £500,000 wage cap on players' salaries imposed by the league for season 1999-2000.

Ian Taylor, the league's chief executive, could not enlighten us. "It's generally perceived that....it worked and worked well," he told *Ice Hockey News Review* in April. "Was it 100 per cent? We doubt it. Could I prove it wasn't 100 per cent? No," he said.

Mr Taylor had revealed in IHNR in February that 'two cases' were being investigated.

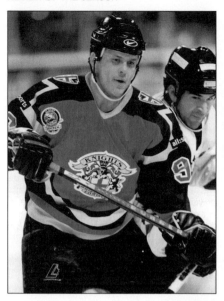

TRADING PLACES

The peerless RICK BREBANT, *left,* was a leading light on three teams - London Knights, Manchester Storm and GB. He joined Knights in mid-season in exchange for London's RYAN DUTHIE who was Knights' top scorer at the time.

Photos: Mike Smith/Icepix.

According to the *Sheffield Star* newspaper, Steelers were one of the prime suspects. But team manager **Dave Simms**, told the paper: "The league has confirmed that we have abided by the rules." But he added, mischievously: "I look forward to seeing whether that is the case across the league.

Superleague has never made public its definition of the wage cap but secretary, **Brian Storey**, told us it relates to the 'costs of players' salaries and benefits in kind, excluding housing costs.' We also understand that cars are excluded from the cap as are payments to the team manager and/or coach.

So, to take a team completely at random, say, just for example, London Knights. The cost of putting their players and coach into luxury apartments on the Thames would not come under the wage cap. Not that we have any reason to believe this happens, but it illustrates one of the many loopholes.

TRADING SYSTEM NEEDED

"One of the problems with our league is that when things go bad our hands are pretty much tied. Our contracts really do tend to favour the players and there is no way to really shake up a group of guys without it costing you a whole lot of money. So you have to be careful."

"In every other league I have been in, you can always shake your team up with a trade. It sends a message that is a wake-up call. But in our league we do not have that opportunity. I would love to see that done here".

Don McKee, *Seffield Steelers' coach.*

Taylor stressed that the league has "a series of preventative measures by which only [a club's] directors can sign contracts and offer employment terms. The directors are responsible for making an affidavit on the gross payments to players."

Martin Weddell, the GM of Bracknell Bees, went so far as to accuse some of his rivals of getting round the cap by allowing players to remain on the payroll of their North American team. He alleged that the British club then paid a nominal fee to the American club for the players' services.

Superleague's new chairman, **David Davies**, had one answer to this. He suggested, in an interview on Storm's website in February 2000, that wage capping "won't really be effective until the players are contracted to the league." But he admitted this was unlikely to happen "until more US owners move in".

Contracts and permits

If Superleague found enough headaches trying to apply the wage cap, that was as nothing compared to the problems of player contracts and work permits.

The ruling in the landmark **Shane Henry** case in July 1999 forced Superleague to remove the 'trial' clause in its player contracts saying that a player's employment can be terminated after one month.

With the backing of the Players Association, Henry, who did not need a work permit (WP) to play here, successfully challenged the clause on the grounds that to insert it only in non-work permit players' contracts constituted race discrimination.

The league had earlier been forced to remove the clause from the contracts offered to work permit players as one of the criteria for issuing work permits is that a contract cannot include a probation clause.

The league's appeal against the ruling was still outstanding in July 2000.

FOR TRANSFER READ LOAN

Hamstrung by the **Shane Henry** ruling, Superleague had to come up with new ways of moving players in and out of clubs. There is no transfer system here as there is in North America with its vast network of teams and leagues.

Storm and Knights proved the most inventive. When **Ryan Duthie** fell out with London's coach **Chris McSorley** a straight swap was arranged with the northern club.

Much travelled veteran **Rick Brebant** had also had a falling out with Storm coach **Kurt Kleinendorst** so the deal suited both parties. Knights' fans took a little longer to persuade as Duthie, a former Canadian national team forward, was London's top league scorer.

But Storm's introduction of a loan clause into **Darren Hurley**'s contract nearly backfired. Early in the New Year, Hurley was told to report to the struggling Newcastle Riverkings within seven days, but when he refused he was suspended without pay.

Both the player and the Ice Hockey Players Association (IHPA) complained that Hurley, who has a British passport and is a GB international had not been given the opportunity to see the full contract. After much haggling over the legal niceties, an auction for the player's services was held between Bracknell Bees and Cardiff Devils and the Devils finally gained his signature.

Superleague agreed that their standard contract for 2000-01 would not contain any loan clause.

WORK PERMITS LIKE SWEETS

Just when we thought the work permit system had settled down, London Knights' coach, **Chris McSorley**, stirred it all up again as he sought to 'improve' his team. Knights' first-year coach decided he could manage without the club's sole British-trained player, **Ian Cooper**, and told the

PLAYOFF RIVALS

London Knights' **CHRIS McSORLEY**, *left*, and **JUKKA JALONEN** of Newcastle Riverkings, both first year coaches in Britain, successfully guided their teams to the final of the *Sekonda* Playoff Championship in Manchester's *MEN* Arena.

Photos: Mike Smith/Icepix.

former Durham Wasp and Cardiff Devil that he "was free to seek employment elsewhere."

Cooper, 31, was Knights' captain in their first season and his gutsy play in the foreigner-dominated league had made him a fan favourite in Docklands. What's more, his 73 caps for GB are the most achieved by any player.

Still, if the coach doesn't want you, there's not much you can do. The trouble was that although Cooper had been 'warned' about his future in

---

PROFIT AND LOSS

Sheffield Steelers expected to make a loss of around £50.000 in 1999-2000, according to club owner, **Darren Brown.** This took into account the extraordinary costs of buying the name and assets of the old club. Without those, Brown believed they might have made a profit.

Martin Weddell, the GM of the league winning Bracknell Bees, said that his club lost £500.000. In order to break even, he added, they would need to sell 5,200 tickets a game. This is the level of crowds attracted by Steelers. Bees' average crowd was 1,945.

November after he missed several games with a shoulder injury, McSorley didn't get round to sacking him until a week before the January registration deadline.

And, according to the player, he gave no reason for his decision.

All was revealed later. Coops' replacement was **Andy Bezeau**, who couldn't be employed as quickly as Knights wanted because his work permit had been held up by the government department.

So it was all down to bureaucratic paperwork then? Not quite. The reason for the delay was that Bezeau, a left-winger only five foot-nine tall, had managed to rack up 3,714 penalty minutes in 509 minor league games in North America. And that didn't include the 1999-2000 season.

The department was scratching its head trying to square that with the work permit criteria which said that WPs should only be issued to players 'who will enhance the sport in the UK and not displace domestic players'.

So how did he get his work permit? Search us. But from what we hear, the government's rule of thumb is to let any sports person have one. Remember **Mike Tyson**?

Darren Banks, another of McSorley's gifted bashers, was allowed to add the games for which he was suspended in North America in order to reach the number required for a WP.

IHPA TAKE ON BLAIR'S BATTALIONS

Not surprisingly, scenarios like this incensed the Ice Hockey Players Association, the players' union, who, like their counterparts in football, are thoroughly fed up with seeing foreigners take over the sport.

The Association's secretary, **Jo Collins**, said: "If the Work Permit scheme goes in the direction which was indicated to us, then there will be no Brits in Superleague in two years' time and maybe only one in the GB team - if it's still around."

The doughty Mrs Collins took the fight all the way to the House of Commons where she was part of a delegation - including the Professional Footballers Association - which gave evidence to a Select Committee looking into the operation of the work permit scheme.

The Select Committee broadly agreed with the arguments put forward and issued a report telling the government so. But **Margaret Hodge**, the Minister of State who looks after these matters, refused to accept the report's findings.

She told the IHPA, who managed to arrange a one-to-one meeting with her, that the government's policy was that when the European Union said 'Jump' they would chorus 'How high?'. No, of course she didn't. But she did say that the government agreed with the Bosman ruling and would not support any moves to change it.

WORLD BODY CRITICISES SUPERLEAGUE

The International Ice Hockey Federation (IIHF), the world governing body of the sport, were sharply critical of our elite league in their January 2000 News Release.

'Great Britain's Ice Hockey Superleague appears to be ineffectual in their attempt to move more British born players through the ranks', they complained.

'Four years ago', they pointed out, the league set a target for the number of British-born players that should be playing, and established a policy for the employment of foreign trained players.

'During the first season, 43 import players [those requiring work permits] participated in the league and that number increased to 53 in the following two seasons.

'This year [1999-2000], the league is likely to exceed that number as clubs are seeking even more imports.

'It is likely that a new import record will be reached by the time of the signing deadline and that the number of British players will drop to the lowest level since the league was established four years ago.

'This will naturally hurt the British national team's chances to ... compete with other national teams for participation in the IIHF World Championship Pool A and Olympic qualification tournaments'.

The reason for the IIHF's concern is not that they are unrepentant old purists. They are keen to see GB compete in the World A Pool as we are a large and weathy Western European nation.

Many of the sport's most successful new countries (Belarus, Latvia, Slovakia for example) are from the poor areas of Eastern Europe and are unattractive to TV and sponsors.

The Bosman decision allowed any player with a European Union (EU) passport to be treated as a citizen of any EU country. Tens of thousands of Canadians can obtain these passports because granny or grandpa, let alone mum or dad, were born in the UK.

But at least that means they can legitimately play for GB (after three seasons). What's irritating the IIHF is that Superleague are not content with this. They are importing players with no connection to this continent at all and who thus need government approval via a work permit to come into Britain.

Such players would have to live and play here long enough to obtain citizenship before they could play for GB. In 1999-2000 there were only 30 Superleague players eligible for GB, which included just eight like Ayr's **Tony Hand** who were actually born and bred here.

Ice Hockey UK

Before you say, Ice Hockey Who K?, this is the organisation that in July 1999 took over from the near-bankrupt British Ice Hockey Association as the sport's national governing body.

The new men were determined not to repeat what they believed were the mistakes of the old lot, especially the bit about being self-elected.

Some 400 groups were involved in electing IHUK's Board of Directors (we're not making this up) with the following being successful:

Jim Anderson, chairman of the Scottish IHA, **John Fisher**, the former acting president of BIHA, **Neville Moralee**, the English IHA's treasurer, **Gary Stefan**, the retired player-manager of Slough Jets, and **Richard Stirling**, the manager of Murrayfield ice rink.

No president or chairman was elected, the board deciding that the five directors should take turns in the hot-seat at their get-togethers.

After several meetings 'to deal with many issues from the past' as their spokesman, **John Fisher**, put it, the Board invited their 'partners' - Superleague, the BNL, and the English and Scottish Associations - to a Summit Meeting in Rotherham. Though hailed as a 'huge success', almost immediately stories came out of bitter infighting.

The meeting was attended by 'all the major decision makers in the sport' including **Ian Taylor,**

Superleague's chief executive, and the league's deputy chairman, **Martin Weddell** of Bracknell Bees. The BNL sent three officials including general secretary, **Stan Wiltshire,** and new general manager, **Gary Stefan**.

The English and Scottish Associations were well represented as was the world governing IIHF who sent their general secretary, **Jan-Ake Edvinsson**.

Afterwards, IHUK confirmed that all parties had agreed that the new body would be responsible for handling the following matters:
- relations with the world governing body, the IIHF, including the national team programmes.
- relations with the domestic sports bodies like the British Olympic Association and the various sports councils.
- all coaching and youth development, in conjunction with the EIHA and SIHA.

In addition, IHUK would provide doping control services, launch a 'PR awareness campaign' and create national teams 'based on indigenous British players'.

They would also be looking for financial contributions from Superleague and the BNL 'to

---

THOUGHT FOR THE SEASON
"The world is run by those who turn up."
Woody Allen

---

supplement those already agreed with the EIHA and SIHA'. On a recommendation from the IIHF, Ice Hockey UK agreed to extend its membership to include representatives of their 'partner' organisations.

Of immediate concern to fans is that the decisions taken in Rotherham meant that IHUK had taken back control of the GB teams from the two-year-old GB Ice Hockey Board.

If IHUK's policy on using 'indigenous players' - that's players born and bred here - is taken literally, this would mean that anyone with a Canadian accent is o-u-t. Where would that leave GB's chances of promotion to the world elite, asked the horrified critics.

Only days after the meeting, **Bob Bramah** resigned as IHUK's chief referee along with their doping control officer, **Jan Stevenson**. Reasons were not given but differences of opinion was understood to be the cause.

■ Bramah's decision to resign became clearer a few days later when Superleague revealed it had been in talks with a Finn, **Kim Pihl**, to take over as the league's chief ref., one of Bramah's tasks.

Ironically, Pihl declined to accept the post as he had expected to be in charge of all Britain's refs, not just Superleague's.

-30-

And coming up on the outside...

The British National League didn't have as torrid a time as Superleague in 1999-2000, but the season was not without the usual batch of clubs teetering on the brink of financial collapse.

Hull Thunder had to be re-financed in mid-season by Sheffield Steelers' owner, **Darren Brown**, and **Peterborough Pirates** sailed close to the wind for much of the second half (see article later).

In Scotland, **Allan Maxwell**, who had kept *Paisley Pirates* in business for four seasons, decided enough was enough at the end of the campaign, but player-manager-coach **Scott Neil** somehow found the capital to keep *Edinburgh Capitals* in the capital.

The league took firm steps in the off-season to avoid any repetition of these problems by instigating an audit of club's finances.

Meanwhile, the league itself continued its quest of becoming as professional as Superleague. It turned itself into a limited company in September 1999 and established an office in Bristol, manned by secretary, **Stan Wiltshire**.

In June 2000 the ubiquitous **Gary Stefan** was appointed General Manager. Stef's main duty is the implementation of the league's Five Year Plan for commercial and youth development.

Working with Stef are Commercial Manager **Lesley Wickham** who was previously with the Basingstoke Bison organisation, and Scottish Junior Development Officer, **Stuart Robertson**, who will carry out a similar role with the league.

Most importantly, the league tied up a partnership with the USA-based telecommunications group, *ntl:* An aggressive, fast-growing organisation (*Microsoft* have a share), *ntl:* is one of only two cable TV companies left in Britain (at the time of writing, anyway). They bought the rights to BBC's flagship football show, *Match of the Day*, in summer 2000.

The main plank of the sponsorship (understood to be worth £75,000) is televising BNL games. *ntl:* showed 15 (recorded) games on their cable TV channel in 1999-2000 and more are expected, possibly via a new *ntl:* sports channel, in 2000-2001.

The *ntl:* connection orginated with Guildford Flames, the first team to have their games shown on the network.

Rare warm-up for Britain

This was GB's most challenging season of the modern era. They were in with a chance of qualifying for both the World A Pool and the 2002 Winter Olympics. *See special articles.*

A second place finish in Pool B in Copenhagen 1999 was enough to put Britain into the World Championship qualifiers. And almost every IIHF

member nation (including Greece and Israel) was eligible for the great Olympic knockout tournament.

With the aid of their six-figure grant from UK Sport, GB pushed the boat out and took on some tough pre-season opposition. In August 1999 they journeyed to the Czech Republic (home of the World and Olympic champs) for a week of play and practice.

Coach **Peter Woods** and his assistant **Paul Heavey** took a squad of 23 on the tour, including, as a pleasant surprise, two under-19s, **Jonathan Phillips** and **David Clarke**.

TOUR PARTY Goal - Joe Watkins BAS, Stevie Lyle CAR, Wayne Cowley (Dayton, ECHL); *Defence* - Mike Bishop AYR, Rick Strachan BAS, Matt Cote BRK, Jason Stone CAR, Stephen Cooper NOT, Scott Campbell LON, Andre Malo, Rob Wilson SHE; *Forwards* - Tony Hand AYR, Mike Ellis, Tony Redmond BAS, Nicky Chinn, Steve Moria (capt), Jonathan Phillips, Merv Priest CAR, Ian Cooper LON, Ashley Tait NOT, David Clarke PET, David Longstaff SHE, Paul Adey (unattached).

RESULTS 15 Aug Znojmo-GB 6-1 (Ellis); 17 Aug Dukla Jihlava-GB 3-0; 18 Aug Sparta Prague-GB 5-0 (abandoned 38 minutes by ref); 20 Aug Ceske Budejowice-GB 5-2 (Moria, Longstaff).

Hockey on the box

Provided you were equipped with all the latest high-tech gadgetry - dish, cable, set-top box and digital doo-dahs - and an endless supply of your favourite poison, you could watch almost every televised hockey game played anywhere in the world. Or so it sometimes seemed.

Sky Sports were there for Superleague and *Benson and Hedges* Cup games, *ntl* covered the British National League, the European League was on *ITV2*, *Channel 5* returned for a second season of NHL coverage and even the BBC found the money for a couple of games.

The Beeb showed their first World Championship game for years in Sheffield Arena with the vital November qualifying game against Kazakhstan on *Sunday Grandstand*. The commentator was Radio Five Live's **Bob Ballard** with former GB captain **Shannon Hope** making his debut as the colourman. Another Radio Five Live man, **Simon Crosse,** did the rinkside interviews.

BBC2's half-hour *Alamo* Challenge Cup final preview in March was reckoned by some to be the best publicity for the sport shown on a terrestrial channel. There were game clips from the semi-finals between Bracknell, Nottingham, Sheffield and London and interviews with the players and coaches. The programme was presented by Crosse and Ballard.

After that, the actual game from London Arena was a bit of a letdown. Delayed by a rumpus in the rugby, this reduced the viewing time to less than that for the preview and the presentation was disappointing.

In the final year of their contract, *Sky Sports* made a number of changes. They dropped their policy of showing live games and went back to a mixture of live games and recorded highlights, a similar format to their first season in 1995-96.

Although a two-hour highlights show was screened on most Tuesday evenings, there were only nine live games in 1999-2000, compared to 28 a year earlier. The choice of Tuesdays rather than Saturdays (Thursday night was hockey night in 1998-99) was seen by many as another blow.

Superleague's chief executive, **Ian Taylor**, told the *Scottish Sun* "Saturday night is a no-go for sport. No one can win against *'Blind Date'*.

The usual turnover of commentators continued. This time the men with the mikes were former player, **Nick Rothwell** (play-by-play), and retired Slough Jets' boss, **Gary Stefan** (colour). Stef proved to be a born TV analyst but Rothwell's manic performance was in complete contrast to the flat-voiced **Steve James** who was in the chair in 1998-99. Nick's impersonation of a Latin-American football commentator was not universally applauded.

In the live games **Dominic Helyer** was back in the presenter's chair with various players and coaches invited to be studio experts.

THE BEST DAILY
NEWS, INTERVIEWS AND
SPEEDY RESULTS SERVICE

ICE HOCKEY CALL

09068-121 109

Calls charged at 60p per minute
IHC, 93 Lee Road, SE3 9EN

For the first time (and, sadly, the last), European Hockey League (EHL) games were shown on British television under a deal done by Superleague on behalf of the IIHF's marketing people, CWL, who held the rights to all EHL games. *Granada* screened all Storm's EHL games on *ITV2* the new channel available via *ONDigital* and *Cable & Wireless* and *Cable London* cable stations.

The coverage was one-hour highlights shown 24 or 48 hours after each match. This was a bit of a let down as three home games had been trailed as being live, and the games in Sweden and the Czech Republic were to have been shown in full.

Again, the personnel were chopped and changed with every game. The shows began encouragingly with two commentators and three front-of-camera

presenters. The anchorman was **Alistair Mann**, a new face to us, with **Beverley Turner** (ditto) talking to the players. The commentators were *Eurosport* refugees, **Paul Ferguson** and **Richard Boprey**, the latter playing hookey from his marketing job with London Knights.

For the second game, in Prague, however, only Boprey and Ferguson appeared, and the later games featured just a voice-over from Mann and one commentator, either Boprey or Ferguson. Expert comment was provided by two players familiar to Storm fans - the injured **Tory Neumeier** and the retired **Brad Rubachuk**.

ntl:'s coverage was restricted to Basingstoke, Guildford and Paisley, the company's only franchise areas in early 2000. A total of 15 games (recorded and shown most nights) were screened on Fridays from 14 January.

Awkwardly, the terms of some of the franchises meant that fans couldn't always see games featuring their own team.

The *Annual* wasn't able to catch any of the games, but we gather that the commentators were the Guildford duo (surprise! - see the piece above on the BNL/*ntl:*partnership) of ex-players **Fred Perlini** and **Andy Sparks**.

Channel 5 were back for a second season of their 'wee small hours' coverage of the NHL, introduced in their London studio by returning Canadian **Todd Macklin** who was joined this season by Cockney **Mark Webster**.

Again the *Annual* failed in its duty to you, dear reader, by failing to watch every game (how much did you pay for this book?) but according to our listings mag., they screened a live game every week, with a two-hour highlights show a couple of days later. The Stanley Cup final was covered in its entirety, as far as we know. Our tape ran out long before the end of some of those marathon OT games.

Talking of late night games, *Channel 4* gave us an entertaining documentary-style programme about the BNL's Peterborough Pirates in the small hours of 5 February 2000.

Shot in early December, the one-hour *Id World* production followed Pirates for a week in a show entitled *Blood on the Ice* [thank you - Ed.] The female interviewer (unnamed) talked to players and officials about their games against Fife (home), Solihull (away) and Guildford (home) and watched them being chased by scantily clad girls for a charity event. (Really!)

Fortunately, the prog. was recorded when Pirates were still riding high in the league despite their financial problems.

We liked **Craig Lindsay**'s reply when he was asked why he liked playing in goal: "They [the out-players] get six-foot guys running them into the

TOP KEEPERS
Ayr Scottish Eagle **Geoff Sarjeant**, *left*, led all goalies in the *Sekonda* Superleague Playoffs,
and **Brian Greer** had the league's best percentage with Bracknell Bees' title winning team.

Photos: Mike Smith/Icepix and Roger Cook.

boards. I only stand in front of a small puck. It's all relative."

■ In July 2000, American comic **Greg Proops** hosted four weekly half-hour shows on *Radio Five Live*, discussing the origins and changes in the sport. The most heavily featured contributor was historian **Martin Harris**, a regular in the *Annual* for many years.

Slap Shot IV - 'The entertainment package'

After a comparatively peaceful 1998-99 season, those fans who love 'goon' hockey were well catered for in 1999-2000. The average penalty minutes per *Superleague* game shot up by a third to a fraction over 40 minutes, the highest in their four seasons. Here's some of the antics:

September was not a season of mellow fruitfulness, more a bellow of uselessness.

Players and, worse, coaches publicly criticised the officials on and off the ice, and when Superleague failed to punish the culprits, two referees resigned and a linesman quit.

The league's only direct response was a letter from their Director of Sport, **Peter Woods,** reminding them that the league has a 'zero tolerance' policy towards abuse of officials.

However, the high profile squealing (see stories below) did prompt the league to call a special meeting in October attended by all the sport's bigwigs: Superleague's chief executive **Ian Taylor,** Ice Hockey UK's president-elect **John Fisher,** their director of officiating **Bob Bramah,** and Woods.

Arising out of this, the league agreed to make adjustments to the video review system and the way games are supervised. The referee would be the first to see any controversial incidents on video, and the practice of having only Woods look at such incidents was discontinued.

The league's only referee supervisor, **John Moore,** who lives in the Home Counties, would receive help with the appointment of Scot **Gordon Pirry.** And regular meetings between Moore, Woods and **Bob Bramah** of Ice Hockey UK were scheduled to ensure, as Woods put it, "that we are all on the same page".

DEVILS TIED IN KNOTS

The troubles had all started with the *B&H* game on 12 September in the House of Steel when Devils were the visitors. An incident-packed game looked like ending in a 3-2 win for Devils when Steelers' **Dale Junkin** was ruled by ref **Jamie Craiper** to have scored the tying goal with three minutes left.

Cue mayhem.

Junkin thought he'd hit the post, Craiper didn't see it nor did his linesmen. The Steelers didn't celebrate. But goal judge **Amanda Evans** turned her light on

and, brave woman, didn't change her mind even under pressure from Devils' injured defenceman, **Aaron Boh,** who raced the length of the rink to confront the goal judge and had to be restrained by rink stewards.

The following article first appeared in Canada's National Post newspaper in November 1999 and is reproduced here with their kind permission.

COACH RESIGNS OVER ORDERS TO MIX IT UP - BRITISH CRAVE HOCKEY FIGHTS

by Alan Adams

A Canadian coaching the Sheffield Steelers of Britain's Superleague said he quit because the management wanted him to replace a skilled player with former NHL goon, **Greg Smyth.**

"The owners felt there wasn't enough of a physical appeal in regards of the entertainment package they wanted for the crowd," **Don McKee** said diplomatically from Waterloo, Ontario. "They wanted some enforcers. They fell that it (fighting) is a valuable part of the entertainment package."

Asked if he was ordered, in his capacity as director of player personnel, to add a fighter to his lineup, McKee said: "Yes, that is what they wanted. If you are bringing in Greg Smyth, then that is what you are bringing in."

Smyth made the headlines last month when he lost his job as an assisstant coach with the St. John's Maple Leafs after he was involved in an altercation with two players on the AHL team at a restaurant in Portland, Maine. What started as a verbal confrontation escalated into a physical one between Smyth and players **Jason Bonsignore** and **David Nemirovsky.** Alcohol was a factor in the fight.

Smyth is a former first round pick of the Philadelphia Flyers. In 229 NHL games, he had four goals and 783 penalty minutes. Three seasons ago he had 353 penalty minutes in 63 games with St. John's.

When Smyth became available, the Steelers' owners wanted his muscle. When McKee refused to sign him, Smyth wound up signing with the London Monarchs (sic).

And in case she hadn't got the message, at the end of the game several Devils' players banged their sticks on the plexi in front of her.

Heavey excused this unattractive behaviour by saying: "It was a very emotional situation" and chuntered on about needing an electronic device to detect whether the puck had crossed the line.

Two weeks later (!), the disciplinary committee (unnamed, as usual) decided that the only person needing punishment was the lovely Boh who was fined £250 and suspended from three games. (He was later released by Devils.)

The bit we like about all this is that a video review conducted by Steelers (if the league did one, they stayed quiet about it) proved that the puck did cross the line and Ms Evans was the only one in the building who was right. (Yawn. That's why we have judges behind the goal).

In revealing this, the *Sheffield Star* quoted Amanda as saying: "The Cardiff players were swearing and spitting at me and threatening me with violence. It was completely unprofessional. I don't know whether I'm going to do this job again, it makes you wonder whether it's worth all the hassle."

THREE OFFICIALS QUIT

The situation worsened a week later when three officials resigned from officiating in Superleague and still the league refused to punish those responsible for their drastic actions.

Craiper's decision came a week after the Boh affair. This time the incident took place in the Cardiff Ice House when Ayr Scottish Eagles were the visitors.

Let Eagles' coach **Jim Lynch** tell us the story of the 2-2 overtime draw. "I don't think I have ever been involved where a team of mine has had 147 penalty minutes. There were 70 minutes solid where we got bombarded by the ref. He said the net came off its hinges when we scored in overtime. It was ridiculous. He was so blatantly biased, it was just disgusting."

He ranted on in this vein at some length in the pages of *Ice Hockey News Review* and the Scottish *Sun* where there was also some wild talk of him threatening to kill Craiper. Lynch denied this bit, of course, insisting: "I don't have any criminal record for attempted murder!"

Jamie was swiftly joined by his fellow stripey **Graham Horner** who was in charge of the Storm-Steelers *B&H* Cup game on the same day, 19 September, which Storm won comfortably 7-3. That wouldn't be why Steelers' coach **Don McKee** found it necessary to exchange pleasantries with the officials in their locker room, would it? Perish the thought.

We were blessedly kept in ignorance of the former headmaster's choice of topic, though we can be fairly certain it wasn't to congratulate the lads on doing a fine job of letting the game flow and keeping the penalties to a minimum (Storm 16, Steelers 18 minutes) despite some hefty hitting.

Horner, whose linesman **Michael Evans** also quit after this verbal assault, wrote a letter of resignation to the league, the gist of which was to tell them to start backing their officials and stop undermining their authority.

SAVE A LIFE - BAN WARE FOR LIFE

London Knights' resident 'goon', **Mike Ware** the Knightmare, was suspended for three games and fined £250 by the league after an unprovoked attack on Nottingham Panther **Curtis Bowen**.

Viewers to *Sky Sports* were treated, if that's the word, to the spectacle of Ware rampaging through a protective screen of his own team-mates to punch Bowen who had earlier collided with London defenceman **Neal Martin.**

Martin, who was also hit by one of his own players in a freakish series of accidents, escaped with whiplash. Ware committed the assault while Martin was being placed on a stretcher. Fortunately, Knights agreed that the league's suspension was too light and Ware missed four games in all.

Our heading, by the way, comes from a Knights' fan who, like many in London Arena, heartily disliked Ware's behaviour.

NO TEARS FOR BRUISER BANKS

Darren Banks, another of London's hard men, went home in February after being told by his club that they wouldn't pay him if he was suspended by the league. Banks, a powerfully built 6ft, 2in forward from Toronto, was one of the more charmless nerks in a team that thinks that sort of thing is clever, as our old mum used to say.

The one-time Boston Bruins' enforcer was thrown out of Knights' game at Ayr on 30 January (major plus game plus gross) by referee **Simon Kirkham** for assaulting one of his linesmen - 'rag-dolling' him as one reporter put it - who was trying to break up a fight between Banks and Eagle **Cam Bristow**.

The club smartly stuck in an appeal so that Banks was able to carry on playing until discipline chief **Peter Woods** could hear the case. But as the multi-titfered Woods' priority was the GB team in Poland, this took two-and-a-half weeks.

Banks, who clocked up 2,649 penalty minutes in 521 games in North America, rewarded his club's quick thinking two days' later in London by getting a minor for showing disrespect to the National Anthem.

Then in Eagles' return game in Docklands less than a week later, his antics reduced Ayr's Lithuanian forward **Dino Bauba** to muttering ruderies under his breath, thus getting himself suspended. Bauba was later exonerated on the grounds that only an linesman had heard the remark. Unless Dino harboured suicidal tendencies that had seemed pretty obvious from the start.

After Banks had joined Port Huron (Michigan) Border Cats in the Central League - his 15th club - Woods suspended him for 12 games and stuck on a £500 fine. As the minor leagues across the water don't acknowledge discipline dished out by foreign circuits like Superleague, the penalties would only be served on Banks' return to Britain.

Here's one punishment we hope never gets administered.

The less goon-ridden BNL had no room for complacency. Their penalties to games ratio of 37 minutes was only a couple of minutes lower than Superleague's.

IT'S NOT WRIGHT

Paisley Pirates' new American coach **Stirling Wright** clashed with referee **Michael Evans** in Pirates' home game against Peterborough on 6 November. The incident came midway through the game after Paisley had gone 5-0 down on a controversial goal.

Wright allegedly threw a punch at the ref, though some witnesses claimed he only pushed the stripey away. The coach was assessed a game misconduct and was later banned for 12 games and fined £100. The ban was changed to six games with six suspended, subject to Wright's good behaviour. He left the UK a few weeks later.

NEW BNL RULES AFTER GALAZZI'S LIFE HAS TO BE SAVED BY OPPOSITION

Basingstoke Bison's **Greg Gatto** was suspended for two years by the British National League after his mid-ice collision with Slough Jet **Mark Galazzi** almost ended in tragedy. (*See our report in the Benson and Hedges Plate final.*)

The incident, in which Galazzi came close to suffering brain damage or worse, highlighted the lack of any regulations by the BNL to ensure that qualified paramedics are available to deal with such emergencies.

The Jets' forward was saved only by Basingstoke's paramedic, **Chris Collins**, whose quick thinking actions kept Galazzi breathing and enabled him to be removed safely to hospital where he recovered.

The league introduced the necessary rules soon afterwards. Gatto left the country to play in North America.

GAME FROM HELL FOR ntl:

The first game shown on the new ntl: cable TV channel, under their partnership agreement with the BNL was disfigured - or enlivened, according to taste - by a 16-player brawl.

The top of the table clash at Basingstoke, a 6-0 win for Bison over Peterborough Pirates, was screened on 14 January. The fracas sarted in the second period with Peterborough 2-0 down when Bison **Michael Knights**, 5ft 11in, lashed out at Pirates' peaceable 6ft 4in player-coach, **Randy Smith**.

The scuffle provoked several bouts of fighting, eventually involving 16 players, including both starting netminders (**Craig Lindsay**, Pirates, and **Joe Watkins**) who met at centre ice for a handbag-throwing session.

Referee **Jamie Craiper** ended the period 59 seconds early and threw eight players out. Knights received a match penalty for fighting and both goalies were handed game misconducts for roughing as were Pirates **Neil Liddiard, Matt Brush** and **James Grimstead**, and Bison **Adam Greener** and **Debb Carpenter.**

Knight and day

The contrast between London Knights' first season and their second was, well, night and day. The team owned by American billionaire, **Phil Anschutz**, won the Playoff Championship after challenging for the league title all year and reaching the final of the *Benson and Hedges* Cup.

Encouraged by the summer appointment of **Chris McSorley** as general manager and coach, 640 fans had bought season tickets by the start of the season compared with just 54 in the whole of their miserable debut year.

McSorley, 38, is an older brother of **Marty McSorley** who spent many years in the NHL as **Wayne Gretzky**'s minder. A hard-nosed player himself, Chris went on to compile a fine coaching record in the International Hockey League (IHL) with Las Vegas Thunder.

Canadian **Brian Jokat** was appointed as the club's chief executive. He enjoyed a varied career as player and coach on both sides of the Atlantic including a spell as GM of Oberhausen in Germany's super league, the DEL. This was not his first time in England. In 1988-89 he played with the Trafford Metros in Altrincham.

Meanwhile, the players were found accommodation about ten minutes' walk from the Arena and training facilities were arranged down the road in Lee Valley, instead of two hours' drive away in Milton Keynes.

Knights began the season with a fighting 1-1 draw with CSKA Moscow, in their heyday the finest hockey team outside North America.

But a lot of the goodwill produced by these events was lost when the win-at-all-costs coach sacked Knights' only native Brit, the popular **Ian Cooper** - right on the trading deadline, too.

Many fans thought McSorley went over the top when he decided to 'toughen up' his team. Even though he had one 'goon', **Mike Ware**, on his roster at the start of the season, he brought over four more whose penalty records in North America nearly went off the Richter scale. (*See stories above.*)

Maybe the coach had something, though. Apart from a piece on the eve of the *B&H* Cup final, almost the only interest in the sport shown by the London *Evening Standard* was a made-up story of **Darren Banks, Greg Smyth** and Ware dressed as *Slapshot*'s Hanson Brothers.

■ Knights tied up an arrangement with English

League champs, Chelmsford Chieftains, in summer 2000 for a summer school and regular coaching sessions throughout the season.

The agreement was achieved through the partnership which Knights' ultimate owners, the Anschutz Corporation, enjoy world-wide with Chieftains' sponsors, *PepsiCo*.

- London suffered another Knight they would rather forget on 23 January 2000 when the Plexiglas supports went missing on the morning of Knights' league game against Nottingham Panthers.

Two games had to be postponed while new supports were brought over from Canada, and Panthers' game five weeks later controversially counted also as the teams' Challenge Cup semi.

As if that wasn't bad enough, the game had been sponsored by West Ham, the East End's biggest football club and Hammers' Canada-born goalie, **Craig Forrest**, not to mention ex-NHLer now **Senator Frank (Big M) Mahovlich** had been asked to drop the ceremonial puck.

Most of the crowd of 5,000, the largest of the season and many of them new to the sport, stayed to watch the game played as a friendly.

It was all horribly similar to London's opening night fiasco in October 1998.

Giant step for Superleague

At last some good news for Superleague! Belfast Giants, the league's second new franchise - after London Knights - was scheduled to start play in December 2000, three years after the franchise was awarded.

Giants' home ice is the state-of-the-art, 7,500-seat (for hockey) Odyssey Arena on Laganside. The arena is part of the £91 million Odyssey entertainment complex which is run jointly by the Sheridan Group, a local property and entertainment company, and the USA-based SMG, who also operate the arenas in London, Manchester and Newcastle, and own Manchester Storm.

The Belfast franchise is owned by two Canadian businessmen. **Robert (Bob) Zeller**, whom hockey fans will remember from his days with Guildford Flames, is a member of the family whose fortune comes from the Zeller chain of stores in Montreal.

His partner is **Albert Maasland**, a former managing director of Deutsche Bank Global Markets who was a hockey goalie at his Canadian college. After leaving the bank, he set up a successful dotcom business specialising in foreign exchange transactions.

Giants' first move was to appoint **Dave Whistle** as coach, a month after the popular Canadian guided Bracknell Bees to the league title. He was

reported to have signed for £60,000 in his first season, as Giants outbid both Bees and Manchester Storm for his services and made him one of the league's highest paid coaches.

Controversially but unsurprisingly, four of Whistle's first six signings were Bees.

Sekonda All-Star Game

The fourth All-Star Game of the modern era was played at Sheffield Arena on 29 December 1999. Superleague sponsors, *Sekonda* backed the latest contest in which the local Steelers beat the All-Stars 10-7.

The first game to feature a club side rather than two select teams pulled in 3,745 fans, a larger crowd than the one at the league's first game in London Arena.

Manchester's **Jeff Jablonski** scored twice for the All-Stars and **Matt Hoffman, Teeder Wynne, Dale Craigwell** and **Dennis Vial** each had a pair for the Steelers.

OFFICIAL CLUB HOTLINES
RAISING FUNDS FOR -
Calls charged at 60p per minute

BASINGSTOKE BISON	09068-800-640
BELFAST GIANTS	09068-800-696
BIRMINGHAM ROCKETS	09068-141-291
BRACKNELL BEES	09068 800-646
CARDIFF DEVILS	**09068-800-636**
AN INDEPENDENT HOTLINE	
COVENTRY BLAZE	09068-888-695
EDINBURGH CAPITALS	09068-121-505
FIFE FLYERS	09068-800-695
GUILDFORD FLAMES	09068-800-689
HULL THUNDER	09068-800-631
INVICTA DYNAMOS	09068-800-675
ISLE OF WIGHT RAIDERS	09068-800-610
MANCHESTER STORM	09068-800-606
NUMBER ONE HOCKEY HOTLINE	
09068-800-616	
MILTON KEYNES KINGS	09068-800-685
NEWCASTLE JESTERS	09068 800-684
NOTTINGHAM PANTHERS	09068-800-660
PAISLEY PIRATES	09068-800-641
PETERBORO' PIRATES	09068-800-628
SLOUGH JETS	09068-800-655
SOLIHULL BARONS	09068-800-686

Gary Moran Covers Ice Hockey
Nottingham NG8 1JB

The other goal scorers were Sheffield's **Greg Clancy** and **Jason Weaver**, and **Tony Hand, Greg Hadden, Claudio Scremin, Yves Heroux** and **Jamie Leach** for the All-Stars.

For the first time, penalty shots were not required to decide the outcome, but Sheffield's **David Longstaff** distinguished himself as the first player ever to disturb the referee (**Mike Rowe**) in an All-Star Game. 'Lobby' was penalised with two minutes for tripping and Jablonski scored his first goal on the resultant powerplay.

In the Skills Competition, Steelers' **Kip Noble** had the Hardest Shot, timed at 89 mph, and Newcastle's **Kim Ahlroos** was the Fastest Skater. Puck Control specialist was London's **Rob Kenny** and best goaltender in the Shoot-out was Sheffield's **Shawn Silver**.

The 20-man All-Star line-up, selected by readers of *Ice Hockey News Review* was:

Stevie Lyle CAR, Mark Bernard MAN; Scott Young AYR, Matt Cote BRK, Darren Durdle CAR, Marc Hussey & Claudio Scremin LON, Eric Dubois NEW, Steve Carpenter NOT; Tony Hand & Yves Heroux AYR, Kevin Riehl & Colin Ward BRK, Rob Kenny LON, Rick Brebant & Jeff Jablonski MAN, Kim Ahlroos & Mikko Koivunoro NEW, Greg Hadden & Jamie Leach NOT.

Coach: Chris McSorley LON.

Selected but injured: Frank Pietrangelo MAN; Vince Boe AYR, Tom Ashe LON, Stephen Cooper NOT; Chris Brant BRK, Steve Moria CAR.

Storm over Europe

For the second successive year, Manchester Storm conducted their pre-season training camp in Europe, entering two competitions in Switzerland.

Up against difficult opposition, Storm lost all their games and coach **Kurt Kleinendorst** said: "We were in a little bit over our heads but the guys handled it really well."

The opening games were in the Coppa Bossi Tournament in the Swiss village of Ambri-Piotta, one of Europe's hockey hotbeds:

Results: 20 Aug HC Lugano-Storm 3-2 (Morin, Gatto); 21 Aug SC Langnau-Storm 3-1 (Allard).

A few days later they were in Zug, Switzerland for the Kolin Cup:

Results: 27 Aug Cologne Haie-Storm 5-2 (Livingston, Allard); 28 Aug EV Zug-Storm 3-2 (Goldman, Brebant), Fribourg-Götteron-Storm 2-1.

Storm sold

Manchester's MEN Arena and the Storm were purchased in off-season 2000 by SMG, the Philadelphia, USA-based international managers of arenas, stadiums and theatres.

Storm are the first ice hockey team to be bought by the company which owns 69 venues around the world. Among them are Newcastle's *Telewest* Arena and London Arena which they co-own with the Anschutz Corporation. SMG also have a management contract to operate Belfast's Odyssey Arena in partnership with the Sheridan Group.

SMG manage two NHL arenas - the National Car Rental Center, the home of the Florida Panthers, and Nassau Veterans Memorial Coliseum on Long Island where the New York Islanders play.

It was not immediately known how the ownership change would affect Storm's connection with the NHL's Ottawa Senators. Storm's previous owners, Ogden Entertainment Services, manage the Corel Center, home of the Senators.

Storm boss and Ogden director, **David Davies**, left to join football club, Queen's Park Rangers, and his number two, **Dave Biggar**, was among those short-listed to replace him.

Finns show faith in Newcastle

Superleague's most star-crossed franchise was saved from almost certain extinction in a remarkable 12-month span ending in August 2000.

Only 48 hours before Riverkings' first game of 1999-2000, wealthy Finnish businessman **Hjallis (Harry) Harkimo** agreed to run the club in partnership with the league.

Harkimo, who is best known for his round-the-world yachting ventures, owns Jokerit Helsinki, one of Europe's richest sports organisations. NHL stars, **Teemu Selanne** and **Jari Kurri** were both Jokerit players before being drafted by the NHL.

Jokerit also made a financial investment in the club (one report said this was 'nearly £170,000') in return for which they were entitled to place a director on Newcastle's board.

GM **Mike O'Connor** was retained by the club, but Finn **Jukka Jalonen** was appointed coach, leaving **Alex Dampier**, the respected former GB coach, as an assistant. 'Damps' later moved to Nottingham Panthers as chief coach.

The changes - and Riverkings' successful playoff run - came too late to prevent a further drop in their crowds which dwindled to an all-time low of 1,868. In their first year, 1996-97, the team had attracted 2,942.

Nevertheless, Harkimo showed great faith in the club's future by taking full control in April 2000. He then persuaded the London-based sporting rights company, the Eye Group, to take a stake and struck a further deal later in the summer when Eye's parent company, Fablon Investments, joined the board.

The new management's first moves were more controversial. The team's name was changed for the third time in five seasons, this time to Jesters. Announcing the change, Newcastle explained that

'Jesters is simply the translation of Jokerit from Finnish to English' and said it was intended to spread the brand name throughout Europe.

According to a survey by the local *Evening Chronicle*, the reaction of the Geordie fans was overwhelmingly against the change. "We did listen to the fans' views about the name but in the end we felt the club needed a fresh start," said Harkimo.

Then **Paul Smith**, the MD of the Eye Group, was confirmed as the club's new chairman. Smith, a former GB international, was a director of Durham Wasps when the team was sold to **Sir John Hall**.

Sir John's Sporting Club ran the Wasps, which was renamed Newcastle Cobras when they moved to the *Telewest* Arena, for three years before pulling out in June 1998 when Superleague took over the club. So the wheel had come full circle, but it did not please some north-east fans.

Smith insisted to the local paper: "We're trying to heal the rifts of the past. If we have a winning team, I'm quite confident we can fill the arena."

* Harkimo, who was rumoured to have shown interest in Manchester Storm when they were up for sale, bought a third European team in July 2000, the ailing Swedish league team, AIK Stockholm.

Panthers lose Adey and Blaisdell

On the eve of the 1999-2000 season, the Nottingham *Evening Post* announced that Panthers' GB international forward **Paul Adey**, 36, had left to go to Milan. He had apparently agreed to take a one-third cut in his wages but he wanted a two-year contract. Panthers' owner, **Neil Black**, was only prepared to offer him one.

"We met his wage demands," said Black, "but we won't agree to his insistence on another two-year deal. We decide to offer players multi-season deals and it is not the other way round." Adey was said to be heartbroken at having to leave. Superleague's reigning top scorer and a veteran of eleven seasons with Panthers - his only British club - signed for Italian club, Saima Milan.

Black explained to fans on the club's website that the delay in opening the new Ice Centre was one of the reasons he had been forced to trim the players' budget, as low as £250,000 according to some reports.

He pointed out that Panthers did not control their own venue and the only way they could increase their income was "to fill all the seats and then raise ticket prices." He added that in 1998-99, "even with record attendances, the wages budget was greater than the gate receipts."

The budget was so tight that the team were reduced to 14 regulars, plus another two who spent much of the time on the sidelines injured.

The situation was too much for coach **Mike Blaisdell** who quit in November, complaining bitterly about unpaid wages, and joined Sheffield

Steelers. Other players were so upset with the club's financial stringency that at one time they threatened to strike.

PANTHERS' LAST GAME

Nottingham Panthers' last game at the 61-year-old Ice Stadium on 22 March 2000 was a memorable occasion.

Though not quite perfect as the Panthers' lost 2-1 to Newcastle Riverkings in overtime, there were presentations to the retiring **Randell Weber** and former stars **Lorne Smith, Les Strongman** and **Chick Zamick.**

Fans were encouraged to help themselves to pieces of the old building and anything that moved or could be torn off was happily carried away by souvenir hunters for up to an hour after the game finished.

Players found themselves signing much of the memorabilia like programmes, seats and even the exit signs, while hundreds of regular supporters poured onto the ice for a commemorative photo.

It was an unfortunate state of affairs, just as Panthers were trying to boost their support to fill the magnificent new Ice Centre. In the off-season, however, the club said they expected to increase their season ticket sales from 700 to 2,000. The new building holds 7,500.

Planet Ice send Blaze to Coventry

We bet **Luke Skywalker** never thought of conquering Coventry with his *Star Wars* Empire, but Planet Ice added the Midlands city to its fast growing empire in April 2000.

The Skydome Coventry became the sixth rink to join the company headed by Greek-Cypriot **Mike Petrouis**. Only a few weeks later Solihull Blaze headed the 20-odd miles east to become the Coventry Blaze.

The £6 million multi-purpose Skydome is in the heart of the city and holds 4,000 people, though only 3,000 for hockey. The seats are arranged in arena style with perfect sightlines and are double the number in the Hobs Moat Road rink. The ice pad is virtually the same size as Solihull's at 56 by 28 metres.

Blaze were due to start playing there in August with their first competitive game in the *Benson and Hedges* Cup on 3 September 2000.

Planet Ice were awarded the contract to run the Skydome after the original operators, Rank Leisure, sold out. Rank had been reluctant to have ice hockey as they felt it would cause too much upheaval.

A couple of months later, Planet Ice added the Basingstoke rink to their portfolio of Birmingham, Gosport, Milton Keynes, Peterborough, and Ryde on the Isle of Wight.

The company are firm supporters of ice hockey which they believe is a key attraction. In addition to operating all seven rinks, they also run three of the teams - the BNL's Basingstoke Bison, and Birmingham Rockets and Isle of Wight Raiders in the English League.

Pirates float, then drown in debt

Peterborough Pirates, one of the first of the new wave of clubs in the early 1980s, suffered through more financial troubles than most of the rest of the sport put together.

We don't have room to go through the whole sorry story, but here's the highlights, if that's the right word.

August 1999 - Peterborough Pirates Plc is successfully floated on OFEX the unreguated stock market. The directors say their total market capitalisation is £887,000. In a private placing, over £170,000 is raised with another £69,000 expected to be contributed by the supporters at 46p a share. The flotation is handled by Brook Corporate Finance.

October 1999 - Coach **Troy Walkington** quits amid reports that he has overspent on players.

December 1999 - After their marketing man is heaved overboard, finance director, accountant **Dane Paul**, walks the plank. "The situation is sufficiently desperate for me to resign," he tells the local paper on Christmas Eve. Trading in the club's shares on OFEX are suspended.

According to *Powerplay* magazine, the club had been losing £2,000 a week. Although crowds were better than in 1998-99, Pirates had budgeted for even more fans. The hoped-for sponsorship had also failed to materialise. (Where have we heard all that before? Pirates' previous owners, Ice Kid, had been wound up in the middle of the 1998-99 season when sponsors, *Omegon*, allegedly failed to pay up.)

February 2000 - Six new directors take over the running of the club.

April 2000 - All the directors, led by MD **Paul Brewster**, tender their resignations and the majority shareholder, **Kevin Tattam**, begins proceedings to wind up the company.

June 2000 - The club appoints a new four-man board of directors, controversially including Brewster. The new company is a wholly owned subsidiary of the old Peterborough Pirates Plc.

July 2000 - The club published figures showing that in the nine months to February, their income was £173,000 while their expenses amounted to £303,000, a loss of £130,000.

We understand that the league have instigated an audit of clubs' books to be carried out in the off-season to avoid scenarios like this in future.

Timberwolves chopped

After recovering from the loss of coach **John Lawless** (difficult) and backer **Ken Crickmore** (not so difficult), everything looked set fair for the re-born Telford team, re-named Timberwolves, in 1999-2000.

It was not to be. The new team boss, **Gabe Gray**, was unable to reach agreement over rental and practice times with the Telford and Wrekin Council who own the rink. The BNL insisted that the club were not in financial trouble. However, Timberwolves were apparently being asked to pay around £30,000 a season in rental, much the same as in 1998-99, and this was not possible within their strict budget.

After losing all six of their *B&H* Cup games, Telford pulled out a few days before their league games were due to begin on 25 September. "We took a risk starting the season without reaching agreement with the council," Gray told the *Guardian*, "and we couldn't get the minimum facilities we needed to keep professional hockey in Telford."

Gray confirmed that all wages had been paid and that sponsors and season ticket holders were to receive refunds. Meanwhile, a rival group, the Telford Ice Hockey Working Party, led by junior coach **Paul Thompson**, hoped to form a new senior team in time for season 2000-01.

But the league vetoed this on the grounds that they had insufficient finance and the group switched its target to 2001-02.

Paul Hands 'em in

Burly Scots defenceman, **Paul Hand**, retired in January 2000 after a lifetime in the sport.

A broken collarbone suffered during the year hastened his decision which came after 18 seasons spent almost entirely with Scottish clubs. He made a couple of stops in Solihull and Peterborough.

Hand, 34, was best known as a member of his home town team, Murrayfield Racers, with whom he played in their glory years. He only left Racers when financial troubles forced them to disband in 1995, an event he called "the saddest day in hockey".

His happiest memories were the three seasons in the mid-Eighties when Racers captured one British Championship and two British League, Premier Division titles. Season 1988-89 was his personal best when he carried off the Alan Weeks Trophy as the Best British Defenceman, a berth on the British All-Star team and three Player of the Year awards. He was capped 18 times for Britain between 1989 and 1992.

Paul spent 11 seasons with Racers where he played alongside - and acted as 'minder' for - his younger brother, Tony. Though he and Tony played for different teams after Racers folded, Paul maintained his feisty reputation.

Back in Edinburgh after four seasons with Paisley Pirates, his last game for Capitals was on 9 January at home to their fierce rivals, Fife Flyers. He was one of three Edinburgh players thrown out of the game!

Despite this, the scaffolder said he was interested in returning to the sport as a referee. What's that they say about poachers and gamekeepers, Paul?!

PAUL HAND'S CAREER
Murrayfield Racers 1982-89, 1991-95; Edinburgh Capitals 1999-2000; Fife Flyers 1989-91, 1995-96; Paisley Pirates 1995-99; Solihull Barons 1986-87; Peterborough Pirates 1989-90.

Seasons	18
Played (league, playoffs, cups)	759
Goals	220
Points	764
Penalty mins	2,156

Britain 1989-92

Championships	4
Games	18
Goals	7
Points	12
Penalty minutes	41

Oxford Blades switch

The Oxford Blades folded early in February 2000 with heavy debts. We understand that the club had problems paying rent for the ice-time, probably because they were paying some players as much as £125 a week, though the English League in which they competed is supposedly a development one.

The Oxford City IHC, which has run the youth programme in the Oxpens Road rink for some years, took over and set up a new senior team in the off-season.

The new team, which will drop down to the league's Southern Conference, will revert to the club's original name of Oxford City Stars and play in the strip of Stanley Cup winners, Dallas Stars. Let's hope this is a good omen

Centenary Varsity Match

Europe's oldest ice hockey rivalry, between Oxford and Cambridge Universities, celebrated 100 years of official competition on 5 March 2000 when the Dark Blues beat the Light Blues 4-2 in the Oxford ice rink.

Daniel Farewell (2) and **Jonathan Finer** scored three times in four minutes in the last period to give Oxford an unassailable 4-1 lead. **John Branch** scored both Cambridge's goals, his first giving his team a 1-0 lead early in the second period which Finer equalised five minutes later.

Finer was selected as the Player of the Game and the Dark Blues 'iron man', **Ian DeArdo,** was their man of the match. Branch took Cambridge's honours.

The winning team received the Patton Cup, named after **Major Peter Patton**, the first president of the BIHA in 1913. Former varsity players, **Charles (Herbie) Little**, 92, and **Hugh Morrison**, 91, crossed the Atlantic for the event and presented the trophy to Oxford's captain **Steve Smith**.

Morrison and Little played on Oxford's Spengler

Cup-winning sides of 1931 and 1932.

There are records of 82 games between the sides going back to 1885. But the 1885 (and 1902) games are believed to have been bandy, so the universities regarded this year's game as marking the centenary of this unique event.

Oxford's victory gives them 54 wins, leaving Cambridge on 24 with two games drawn.

▪ Oxford University also won the Women's Varsity Match, beating Cambridge University 8-2.

Overseas visitors

British clubs entertained three of the world's top teams (outside the NHL) in 1999-2000. Two European club sides visited at the start of the season, and the touring Canadian national team came over for the second time in two years and the third since January 1995.

MALMO REDHAWKS, who compete in the Swedish Elite League, have produced numerous players, notably **Borje Salming** and **Peter Forsberg**. The side that played here included international winger **Tomas Sandstrom** who had just returned to his native country after a 15-year career.

Results: 27 Aug v Nottingham Select 3-8 (Brant, Hadden, Leach), 28 Aug v Cardiff Devils 5-4 (Matulik 2, Sacratini, Moria, Thornton), 29 Aug v Bracknell Bees 0-3.

Did You Know? Malmo's coach in the Fifties was Panthers' legendary **Les Strongman**.

Legendary Russian squad **CSKA Moscow** were coached by **Boris Mikhailov** and starred veteran **Sergei Makarov** both heroes of countless Soviet league and world and Olympic championship winning sides.

Results and goal scorers: 26 Aug v Cardiff Devils 1-4 (Moria); 28 Aug v Sheffield Steelers 3-3 (Courtenay 2, Noble) - CSKA won shoot-out 2-1 (Courtenay); 9 Aug v Peterborough Pirates 3-7 (McEwen 2, R Smith); 31 Aug v London Knights 1-1 (Bultje) - Knights won shoot-out 3-0 (Bultje, Leveque, Wetzel).

UNIVERSITY OF MANITOBA BISON. Ryan Campbell's and **Peter Woods'** old team played at Guildford Flames on 15 December.

Results and goal scorers

Guildford-Manitoba 2-6, Basingstoke-Manitoba 5-3, Milton Keynes-Manitoba 4-8.

(No other details available)

CANADA played three games in Britain during their last tour of Europe before being disbanded in a cost-cutting exercise. (See *International Round-Up.*) Playing 12 games in 16 days, the Canadians went on to meet France (twice), Slovakia (twice) and five Russian Super League clubs.

The 20-man line-up included **Nathan Rempel** ex-Peterborough, and former Newcastle Cobra, **Xavier Majic.** Pirates' **Randy Smith** is a former member of the Canadian team.

British results and goal scorers: 31 Oct at Ayr Scottish Eagles 4-3 (Bauba, Heroux, Bristow, Murano); 2 Nov at Hull Thunder 1-6 (Randy Smith); 3 Nov at Peterborough Pirates 2-7 (Dumas 2).

Canada Joaquin Gage, Jamie Ram; Perry Johnson, Greg Labenski, Wes Jarvis, Troy Stonier, Chris Schmidt, Xavier Majic, Hugo Boisvert, Phillipe Choiniere, Kent Simpson, Nathan Rempel, Curtis Sheptak, Brad Mehalko, Jeff Ulmer, Ryan Mougenel, Peter Allen (capt), Peter Hogan, Rhett Gordon, Ryan Savoia.

Head coach: Tom Renney.

More sponsors like this, please

Fagans, the oldest established equipment suppliers in Britain, sponsored a number of British born and trained players through the world famous brand names of *Bauer* and *Nike*.

Superleague's **Nicky Chinn, Stephen** and **Ian Cooper, Tony Hand, Simon Hunt, David Longstaff, Jason Stone** and **Michael Tasker** all used equipment bearing these brands during the 1999-2000 season, along with the BNL's **Paul Dixon, Steven King** and **Rob Lamey.**

Brand manager **Tom Chant,** explained: "For hockey to really cement itself in Britain, it must offer home grown talent the opportunity to play at the highest level so that youngsters here can identify with British stars and seek to emulate them."

Major Teams 1999~2000

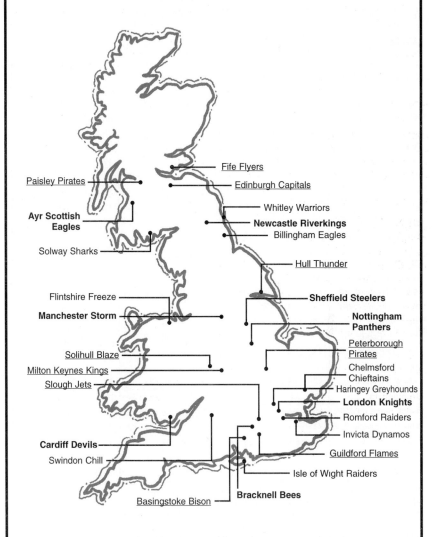

Fife Flyers
Paisley Pirates
Edinburgh Capitals

Whitley Warriors
Ayr Scottish Eagles
Newcastle Riverkings
Billingham Eagles

Solway Sharks

Hull Thunder

Flintshire Freeze
Sheffield Steelers
Manchester Storm
Nottingham Panthers

Peterborough Pirates
Solihull Blaze
Chelmsford Chieftains
Milton Keynes Kings
Haringey Greyhounds
Slough Jets
London Knights
Romford Raiders
Invicta Dynamos
Cardiff Devils
Swindon Chill
Guildford Flames
Isle of Wight Raiders
Bracknell Bees
Basingstoke Bison

Superleague   British National League   English/Scottish Leagues

AYR SCOTTISH EAGLES

PLAYER	SEKONDA SUPERLEAGUE					SEKONDA PLAYOFFS					ALL COMPETITIONS				
Scorers	GP	G	A	Pts	Pim	GP	G	A	Pts	Pim	GP	G	A	Pts	Pim
Shawn Byram	42	17	32	49	108	7	2	2	4	27	57	20	37	57	143
Tony Hand	40	8	35	43	52	7	0	4	4	0	55	11	45	56	52
Yves Heroux	42	18	25	43	92	7	0	0	0	14	57	25	28	53	108
Eric Murano	30	18	15	33	12	7	2	3	5	2	37	20	18	38	14
Cam Bristow (WP)	42	14	16	30	92	7	0	2	2	0	57	14	19	33	104
Jamie Steer	42	16	8	24	16	7	3	1	4	2	57	20	10	30	20
Scott Young	37	7	18	25	127	6	1	0	1	12	51	8	22	30	149
Dino Bauba	33	8	17	25	46	7	0	1	1	8	48	10	19	29	56
Jan Mikel (WP)	41	9	11	20	74	7	0	1	1	8	56	9	17	26	108
Vince Boe	42	5	14	19	60	7	0	0	0	12	57	5	17	22	92
John Varga (WP)	9	3	4	7	10	-	-	-	-	-	17	10	6	16	14
Patric Lochi	42	5	6	11	16	7	1	1	2	0	57	7	7	14	18
Rob Trumbley (WP)	38	3	8	11	72	6	1	0	1	18	52	5	9	14	117
Shayne Stevenson	11	2	8	10	26	7	2	2	4	29	18	4	10	14	55
Iouri Krivokhija (WP)	17	4	6	10	26	7	1	0	1	2	24	5	6	11	28
Louis Dumont (WP)	14	1	4	5	16	-	-	-	-	-	22	2	7	9	24
Mark Montanari	6	2	0	2	18	1	0	0	0	0	13	3	5	8	36
Mike Bishop	17	1	4	5	30	7	0	0	0	4	32	1	6	7	42
Jim Mathieson	34	1	3	4	59	6	0	1	1	8	47	1	5	6	69
Geoff Sargeant (N) (WP)	23	0	4	4	22	6	0	0	0	0	37	0	6	6	24
Ryan Kummu (WP)	18	1	4	5	28	-	-	-	-	-	20	1	4	5	30
Kevin Pozzo 1	3	1	2	3	2	-	-	-	-	-	3	1	2	3	2
Stephen Foster (N)	10	0	0	0	2	1	0	0	0	0	11	0	0	0	2
Dave Trofimenkoff (N) 2	11	0	0	0	2	2	0	0	0	0	13	0	0	0	2
Bench Penalties					14					2					18
TEAM TOTALS	42	144	244	388	1022	7	13	18	31	148	57	182	305	487	1327
Netminders	GPI	Min	SoG	GA	Sv%	GPI	Min	SoG	GA	Sv%	GPI	Min	SoG	GA	Sv%
Geoff Sargeant (WP)	23	1396	739	69	90.7	6	359	206	13	93.7	37	2235	1186	104	91.2
Dave Trofimenkoff 2	11	651	361	38	89.5	2	52	40	7	82.5	13	703	401	45	88.8
Stephen Foster	10	549	270	36	86.7	1	28	13	1	92.3	11	577	283	37	86.9
Empty Net Goals			4	4				0	0				5	5	
TEAM TOTALS	42	2596	1374	147	89.3	7	439	259	21	91.9	57	3515	1875	191	89.8

Back-up Netminders: Pasi Raitanen (Hull Thunder, Peterborough Pirates), Thorsten Apel.
Also played for: 1 Manchester Storm, 2 Paisley Pirates.
Shutouts: Sarjeant - cup: 9 Oct at London Knights (37 saves); playoffs: 18 Mar v Cardiff Devils (34 saves).

All Competitions = Superleague, Playoffs, Challenge Cup and Benson and Hedges Cup

AYR SCOTTISH EAGLES *left to right, back row:* Milan Figala (asst. coach), Vince Boe, Yves Heroux, Ryan Kummu, Jan Mikel, Cam Bristow, Mike Bishop, Eric Murano, Shayne Stevenson, Dainius Bauba, Scott Young, Yuri Krivokhija, Jim Lynch (coach), Mark Montanari; *front row:* Dave Trofimenkoff, Jamie Steer, Tony Hand, Shawn Byram, Geoff Sarjeant, Jim Mathieson, Rob Trumbley, Patric Lochi, Stephen Foster.

Broken wing

RONNIE NICHOL

After a disappointing season, coach **Jim Lynch** reshaped his side, bringing in eleven new players in the summer of 1999. The highlight was the return of Britain's best, **Tony Hand**, to the land of his birth.

Lynch used the *B&H* group match-ups as a 'getting to know you' exercise. Although Eagles were not helped by having four of their opening five games on the road, they gained full points from Newcastle and Nottingham.

Injuries affected the club virtually from day one and influential players **Mark Montanari** and **Ryan Kummu** were hampered early on.

The Cup quarter-finals pitched them in with London and, backstopped by the impressive **Geoff Sarjeant**, they shut out **Chris McSorley**'s troops in the capital. But 24 hours later they were licking some major wounds as Knights embarrassed them 7-0 on Centrum ice.

In that game they lost sharpshooter **John Varga** with a shoulder injury and he quit the club soon afterwards. He was followed by the under-achieving **Louis Dumont** and with Eagles continually blighted by injury problems it was not the happiest of times.

They overcame their troubles, however, and went on a club record-equalling seven-game unbeaten run, helped by the drafting of striker **Eric Murano**. But eventually the lack of numbers told.

Aborted comebacks by Kummu and Montanari failed and **Mike Bishop** and **Jim Mathieson** were the other long term absentees as Eagles iced the minimum bench on many occasions.

The new Millennium brought no change as the outstanding Sarjeant picked up a serious groin injury. With the league wide open, Eagles hung in but the final push was beyond them. A fifth place finish was creditable, though, for a side who had been handicapped by losing over 200 man-games to injuries.

Just before the playoffs, the situation eased. The results improved, especially on the road, and optimism rose that Eagles could be the dark horses for the end-of-season finale.

Sure enough, they slipped in to the finals weekend as runners-up in their group behind Sheffield, knocking out Cardiff and Manchester along the way.

Unfortunately, the season ended in the semi-finals, in overtime to old rivals London, but Lynch was proud of his charges. "It was a good effort to play around .500 hockey with all the problems we faced," he said.

PLAYER AWARDS

Player of the Year   **Vince Boe**

LEADING PLAYERS

Vince Boe *born 23 December 1970.*
Eagles' player of the year had another consistent season on the blueline. He was never flustered, always doing his job quietly and efficiently.

Dubbed 'iron man', he has iced in 252 competitive games for the Centrum club, one short of a perfect attendance.

Tony Hand *born 15 August 1967.*
Britain's finest was as effective a playmaker as ever, setting a new club record for assists in the league season with 35. But he didn't hit the net as often as he or coach Lynch would have liked.

Geoff Sarjeant *born 30 November 1969.*
Despite missing two months through injury, Sarj was named Superleague's first all-star goaltender by the sport's writers.

After taking time to settle he showed class and consistency and was probably the best stickhandler of any goaltender who has played in the league.

FACT FILE 1999-2000

Sekonda **Superleague:** Fifth.
Sekonda **Playoffs:** Semi-finalists.
Benson and Hedges **Cup:** Quarter-finalists.
Challenge Cup: Fifth.

HISTORY

Founded 1996. Previous Ayr clubs were Raiders (1991-92 and 1939-55) and Rangers (1962-65) at Beresford Terrace and Bruins (1974-91, 1969-72, 1966-67) at Limekiln Road.

Leagues Scottish Eagles - Superleague 1996-2000; Raiders - British League 1991-92, 1954-55, Scottish National League 1939-54; Bruins - British League (Premier Div) 1982-91; Scottish National League 1981-82; Northern League 1974-82, 1969-72, 1966-67.

Honours Eagles - 1997-98: grand slam of league, *B&H* Cup, playoffs & *Express* Cup; Bruins - British Championship finalists 1989; Raiders - Scottish National League 1952-53.

BASINGSTOKE BISON

PLAYER	BRITISH NATIONAL LEAGUE					PLAYOFFS					ALL COMPETITIONS				
Scorers	GP	G	A	Pts	Pim	GP	G	A	Pts	Pim	GP	G	A	Pts	Pim
Wayne Crawford	34	25	25	50	46	11	6	2	8	6	63	44	43	87	82
Dru Burgess (I)	36	23	19	42	28	11	3	7	10	4	65	37	44	81	38
Jeff Daniels (I) 4	31	16	35	51	24	11	1	7	8	2	51	26	53	79	32
Mike Ellis	34	23	15	38	26	11	7	7	14	4	63	41	33	74	58
Tony Redmond	36	15	19	34	34	11	4	3	7	10	65	22	23	45	64
Debb Carpenter	17	8	13	21	39	11	4	8	12	12	32	12	24	36	63
Rick Strachan	35	2	13	15	28	11	2	6	8	10	64	10	26	36	48
Mitch Grant (I)	27	7	14	21	10	-	-	-	-	-	40	12	21	33	14
Duncan Paterson (I)	35	7	10	17	64	11	1	5	6	8	64	11	21	32	139
Dwayne Newman (WP) 4	29	0	9	9	26	11	0	2	2	26	47	0	15	15	56
Peter Romeo (I)	12	3	4	7	32	-	-	-	-	-	20	9	5	14	59
Brian Mason 2	7	2	2	4	18	11	4	4	8	8	20	6	6	12	26
Joe Baird	33	1	1	2	20	11	1	1	2	6	59	5	3	8	53
Michael Knights 2	11	0	1	1	35	10	1	0	1	12	27	1	7	8	69
Danny Meyers	35	1	1	2	8	9	0	0	0	4	60	3	4	7	14
Gary N Clark	33	1	2	3	8	11	0	0	0	2	59	1	5	6	14
Mark McGrath (I)	4	1	0	1	10	-	-	-	-	-	13	3	1	4	12
Jake Armstrong 3	9	2	0	2	4	-	-	-	-	-	19	2	2	4	10
Cam Law (I)	2	0	0	0	14	-	-	-	-	-	11	0	4	4	28
Tom Pope	11	0	1	1	0	8	0	0	0	0	23	1	2	3	0
Greg Gatto 1	2	0	2	2	8	-	-	-	-	-	3	0	2	2	10
Joe Watkins (N)	32	0	1	1	27	11	0	0	0	0	61	0	2	2	29
Mark Barrow	33	1	0	1	0	2	0	0	0	0	51	1	0	1	0
Gordon Hester	-	-	-	-	-	-	-	-	-	-	2	0	1	1	2
Alec Field (N)	35	0	1	1	0	11	0	0	0	0	62	0	1	1	0
Adam Greener	30	0	0	0	39	11	0	0	0	0	49	0	0	0	39
Bench Penalties					14					4					26
TEAM TOTALS	36	138	188	326	562	11	34	52	86	118	65	247	348	595	985
Netminders	GPI	Min	SoG	GA	Sv%	GPI	Min	SoG	GA	Sv%	GPI	Min	SoG	GA	Sv%
Joe Watkins	30	1633	722	64	91.1	10	600	253	29	88.5	58	3250	1431	133	90.7
Alec Field	14	527	217	21	90.3	1	60	44	4	90.9	17	640	286	27	90.6
Craig Astill	-	-	-	-	-	-	-	-	-	-	1	10	3	0	100
TEAM TOTALS	36	2160	939	85	90.9	11	660	297	33	88.9	65	3900	1720	160	90.7

Also appeared: Adam Cathcart 10; Chris Vickery 6; Adrian Worship 4; Neil Leary 3; Rick Deadman (N), Ryan Fuller, Joey Greener, David Noakes, Scott Padwick 2; Andy Gorden, Lewis Slade, David Noakes 1.

Also played for: 1 Manchester Storm, 2 Milton Keynes Kings, 3 Solihull Blaze, 4 Telford Timberwolves.

Shutouts: Watkins - cup: 18 Sept v Guildford Flames (25 saves); league: 3 Oct v Slough Jets (15 saves), 20 Nov v Guildford Flames (32 saves), 8 Jan v Peterborough Pirates (22 saves)*, 29 Jan v Paisley Pirates (17 saves)*.
Field - league: 8 Jan v Peterborough Pirates (4 saves)*, 29 Jan v Paisley Pirates (7saves)*.
* shared

All Competitions = league, playoffs, B&H Cup/Plate and ntl: Christmas Cup.

Stampede halted

GRAHAM MERRY

Winning the *Benson and Hedges* Plate, their first major silverware for six years, was the high spot of Bison's successful season.

They also reached two other finals, only to lose to Fife in both the Christmas Cup and the playoff final series.

Rick Strachan moved from captain to player-coach in place of **Don Depoe** and only three Canadians from Depoe's herd remained.

In came former Bracknell Bee **Peter Romeo** joined by rookies to Britain, **Mark McGrath** and **Dru Burgess**, along with defencemen **Cam Law** and **Duncan Paterson**.

Coach of the year from Slough, **Charlie Colon**, joined as bench coach after **Rick Fera**, who Strachan had lined up for the job, decided to stay in Canada.

Strachan also put his faith in British netminding when **Joe Watkins** joined as starting keeper - a gamble in many people's eyes, but one that was richly rewarded.

In the opening *B&H* game, Romeo equalled the club record with five goals in the 11-1 win over Solihull, but he was one of many victims of the injury jinx which hit the team all season.

The first to suffer was McGrath who injured his leg in the fourth league game in Slough and never played for the team again. He joined Law, who had been axed two weeks earlier, on a flight back to North America.

In their place came former Telford duo, **Jeff Daniels** and **Dwayne Newman**, Daniels scoring the vital, late fifth goal in the *B&H* semi in Fife.

However, just when the herd looked ready to stampede, both Newman and captain **Mitch Grant** were injured only a fortnight before the Plate final. Fast replacements were needed and in came **Greg Gatto** and **Brian Mason**.

Slough won the dress rehearsal for the final in Basingstoke 3-1, but a week later in Sheffield Bison turned the tables, despite losing Romeo after 30 minutes.

Wayne Crawford moved from defence to link up with Burgess and Daniels, and the 'BCD' line scored goals as easy as 'ABC'. Their most lethal games were in the Christmas Cup semi-final win over Guildford.

The league season came to a close with further injuries to **Michael Knights**, Watkins and a season-ending one for Grant who was replaced by former London Knight, **Debb Carpenter**.

Mason returned for the playoffs and at home the side were awesome, but once again Fife denied them a further trophy.

PLAYER AWARDS

Player of the Year	**Wayne Crawford**
Most Improved British Player	**Alec Field**

LEADING PLAYERS

Wayne Crawford *born 18 April 1961*

'Reggie' may be a veteran in years but the defender played with the spirit of a 20-year-old, and when he turned attacker he scored some big goals.

Duncan Paterson *born 11 July 1974*

The University of Mantioba defenceman, a summer signing, gave the Bison size at the back as well as showing good offensive skills.

Joe Watkins *born 27 October 1979*

Great positional 'minder, dubbed 'Joe Cool' for his unflappability under pressure. He turned 20 during the season which finished on a dream note with the GB team.

FACT FILE 1999-2000

British National League: Third.
Playoffs: Finalists.
Benson and Hedges:
Won Cup group; won Plate.
ntl: **Christmas Cup:** Finalists.

FRANCHISE HISTORY

Founded 1988 as Beavers. Name changed to Bison in May 1995.
Leagues British National League 1998-2000; Superleague 1996-98; British League, Premier Div 1993-96; British League, Div One 1990-93; English League 1988-90.
Honours British League, Div One & playoffs 1992-93; English League (promotion) playoffs 1989-90.

BASINGSTOKE BISON *left to right, back row:* Alan Parrott (equipment), Adam Greener, Dwayne Newman, Peter Romeo, Duncan Paterson, Gary Clark, Danny Meyers, Michael Knights, Mark Barrow, Dru Burgess, Charlie Colon (coach); *front row:* Joe Watkins, Joey Baird, Rick Strachan, Tony Redmond, Mitch Grant, Mike Ellis, Wayne Crawford, Jeff Daniels, Alec Field.

BILLINGHAM EAGLES

PLAYER	ENGLISH DIVISION ONE NORTH					PLAYOFFS					TOTALS				
Scorers	GP	G	A	Pts	Pim	GP	G	A	Pts	Pim	GP	G	A	Pts	Pim
Paul Windridge	18	25	58	83	49	6	1	15	16	2	24	26	73	99	51
Tom Brown (l)	16	42	22	64	24	6	13	3	16	4	22	55	25	80	28
Martin Lewis	17	27	20	47	28	5	5	2	7	18	22	32	22	54	46
Brian Perry	16	11	22	33	77	6	4	9	13	10	22	15	31	46	87
Steve Wallace	11	18	17	35	4	3	4	1	5	0	14	22	18	40	4
Andrew Fletcher	11	5	20	25	32	6	3	5	8	10	17	8	25	33	42
Simon Hehir	11	6	13	19	8	6	7	5	12	8	17	13	18	31	16
Garry Dowd	15	14	8	22	101	2	0	2	2	0	17	14	10	24	101
Ian Richardson	18	4	16	20	49	6	1	2	3	12	24	5	18	23	61
Liam Thompson	17	6	12	18	18	6	0	2	2	2	23	6	14	20	20
Simon Burns	14	0	15	15	89	3	0	1	1	0	17	0	16	16	89
Richard Thornton	18	1	6	7	2	5	2	3	5	0	23	3	9	12	2
D J Flett	17	3	3	6	4	6	1	1	2	0	23	4	4	8	4
Tom Griffiths	7	2	3	5	0	5	1	1	2	0	12	3	4	7	0
Shaun Black	5	2	5	7	8	-	-	-	-	-	5	2	5	7	8
Craig Bailes	3	1	4	5	2	-	-	-	-	-	3	1	4	5	2
David Maclean	7	1	3	4	0	-	-	-	-	-	7	1	3	4	0
Dale Taylor	8	1	3	4	2	-	-	-	-	-	8	1	3	4	2
John Aisbitt 1	2	1	2	3	0	-	-	-	-	-	2	1	2	3	0
Gareth Crinnion	3	0	2	2	0	-	-	-	-	-	3	0	2	2	0
Phil Pritchard	11	0	1	1	0	6	0	1	1	0	17	0	2	2	0
Martin Lauwers	-	-	-	-	-	3	0	1	1	2	3	0	1	1	2
Scott Ward	3	0	0	0	2	4	0	1	1	0	7	0	1	1	2
Adam Flett (N)	18	0	1	1	2	6	0	0	0	2	24	0	1	1	4
Bench Penalties					2										2
TEAM TOTALS	18	170	256	426	505	6	42	55	97	70	24	212	311	523	573
Netminders	GPI	Min	SoG	GA	Sv%	GPI	Min	SoG	GA	Sv%	GPI	Min	SoG	GA	Sv%
Ricky Hall	3	47	13	1	92.3	1	10	6	0	100	4	57	19	1	94.7
Adam Flett	18	1012	555	72	87.O	6	350	218	26	88.1	24	1362	773	98	87.3
Wesley Fawthrop	1	11	3	1	66.7	-	-	-	-	-	1	11	3	1	66.7
Stephen Fitzpatrick	1	10	2	1	50.O	-	-	-	-	-	1	10	2	1	50.O
TEAM TOTALS	18	1080	573	75	86.9	6	360	224	26	88.4	24	1440	797	101	87.3

Also appeared: Simon Greenwood, Andrew Payne (1L); Andrew Wells (1PO).
Also played for: 1 Sunderland Chiefs.

Shot down by Warriors

TONY BOYNTON

For the second straight season, Eagles swept all before them in the English Division One North and went all the way to the playoff finals, only to go out to fierce local rivals, Whitley Warriors.

In the summer of 1999, many Eagles' fans had expected their team to move up into the English Premier Division but the club's management believed this would be too costly. As Eagles had struggled financially in the past, they couldn't be blamed for being cautious.

There was little doubt, however, that the standard of competition in Division One North forced many fans to choose their games carefully.

Maybe it was because of their domination of the league the previous season that Billingham thought they needed only to turn up to collect the points. In their opening game at Deeside, the Freeze gave them a rude awakening and Eagles went back across the Pennines nursing a 10-4 defeat.

That spurred the team and they returned to their winning ways in their next two games, even though both had to be played on the road as the Billingham rink suffered from its annual problem of being unfit to play on.

It was a month into the season before they returned home, but at least the fans were given plenty to cheer as Eagles crushed Sheffield 13-1. The disparity in the league became all too obvious as Eagles went on to rack up further high scoring victories.

Only one further hiccup blotted 1999 when injuries and work commitments saw an understrength side lose 8-5 in Blackburn.

Eagles' next loss didn't come for another three months by which time they had been crowned league champions. The loss at Whitley Warriors only dented their pride, but in hindsight maybe they should have learned more from that game.

Sadly, the playoffs were a bit of a farce. Although Eagles failed to agree fixture dates with Kingston, they were allowed to go through to the semi-finals. Their only playoff games were two wins over Sunderland.

Basingstoke could not halt Eagles' charge in the semis, their home and away successes earning them a final match-up with Whitley.

Their failure to learn from their league defeat came back to haunt Eagles as Warriors scored a three-goal victory in Hillheads, and Warriors' late surge in the second leg was enough to end Eagles' season long unbeaten home record.

LEADING PLAYERS

Tom Brown born 26 January 1972

Many fans think Tom is Eagles' star 'import'. How else to explain his blistering slapshot and bonecrushing bodychecking. In fact, the forward was born in Glasgow, and his family emigrated to Canada when he was a tot.

Providing a perfect complement to 'Spike' Windridge's silky skills, Tom has been totally committed to Eagles' cause for five seasons. Only the birth of his first child could prevent him from returning.

Adam Flett born 10 February 1980

One of the youngest netminders on the circuit, Adam bore the responsibility of being number one well, with hardly one bad performance.

Eagles' success owed much to his skills and flamboyant style and he looks set to be a fixture with the club, especially as they have no established back-up.

Paul (Spike) Windridge born 11 April 1972

The left winger has been the cornerstone of the team since he broke into the senior ranks in 1989 with the Cleveland Bombers. Once again he carried the captain's mantle well.

He was Eagles' top scorer for the fourth straight year, and his 99 points contained three times as many assists as goals, reflecting his superb playmaking skills.

Though he's had many opportunities to play at BNL level, Paul could not bear to see his home side struggle and continues to pledge his support to Eagles. This dedication makes him a crowd favourite.

FACT FILE 1999-2000

English League Placing: 1st in Div. One North.
Playoffs: Finalists.

CLUB HISTORY

Founded: 1996. The first team in Billingham was Billingham Bombers 1971-82 and 1991-93. Cleveland Bombers played 1982-91 and Teesside Bombers 1993-95.
Leagues: English League 1996-2000; British League, Division One 1994-96 & 1987-90; British League, Premier Division 1990-94 & 1982-87; Northern League 1977-82.

(Eagles made no player awards at the end of the season.)

BRACKNELL BEES

PLAYER	SEKONDA SUPERLEAGUE					SEKONDA PLAYOFFS					ALL COMPETITIONS				
Scorers	GP	G	A	Pts	Pim	GP	G	A	Pts	Pim	GP	G	A	Pts	Pim
Kevin Riehl (WP)	40	27	27	54	22	6	4	3	7	4	58	40	42	82	30
PC Drouin (WP)	40	15	29	44	46	6	2	3	5	10	58	20	39	59	68
Colin Ward	42	18	20	38	16	3	0	1	1	0	57	24	30	54	28
Denis Chassé (WP)	38	18	25	43	100	4	1	3	4	34	50	22	31	53	156
Todd Goodwin (WP)	40	24	19	43	22	-	-	-	-	-	51	28	24	52	22
Paxton Schulte (WP)	39	12	20	32	110	6	3	2	5	4	57	20	30	50	165
Chris Brant	36	14	19	33	55	4	0	3	3	0	52	19	30	49	96
Martin Woods (WP)	42	5	25	30	75	6	1	5	6	16	60	9	38	47	101
Blake Knox	42	10	20	30	60	6	1	2	3	58	60	14	28	42	136
Rob Stewart	42	4	16	20	34	6	3	1	4	4	60	12	22	34	46
Casson Masters	35	11	15	26	12	6	3	3	6	4	45	14	19	33	20
Todd Kelman	42	5	13	18	40	6	1	1	2	2	60	10	21	31	54
Chris Baxter	31	9	7	16	18	6	2	0	2	14	47	13	14	27	69
Shane Johnson (WP)	42	4	13	17	36	6	0	1	1	6	60	5	19	24	60
Adam Smith	32	2	11	13	44	4	1	4	5	2	40	4	17	21	46
Matt Coté	39	2	7	9	12	6	0	0	0	2	55	2	10	12	20
Rick Donovan	12	1	1	2	14	6	0	3	3	10	20	1	4	5	24
Bruno Campese (N)	21	0	3	3	4	3	0	0	0	0	32	0	3	3	8
Brian Greer	22	0	1	1	4	3	0	0	0	2	31	0	1	1	8
Chad Biafore	-	-	-	-	-	-	-	-	-	-	1	0	0	0	0
Bench Penalties					60					2					68
TEAM TOTALS	42	181	291	472	784	6	22	35	57	174	60	257	422	679	1225
Netminders	GPI	Min	SoG	GA	Sv%	GPI	Min	SoG	GA	Sv%	GPI	Min	SoG	GA	Sv%
Brian Greer	22	1321	639	56	91.2	3	190	79	7	91.1	31	1822	878	85	90.3
Bruno Campese	21	1249	618	80	87.1	3	180	91	12	86.8	32	1838	966	124	87.2
Empty Net Goals			2	2				0	0				2	2	
TEAM TOTALS	42	2570	1259	138	89.O	6	370	170	19	88.8	60	3660	1846	211	88.6

Shutouts: Greer - league: 10 Oct at Manchester Storm (28 saves).
Campese - playoffs: 12 Mar v Nottingham Panthers (37 saves).

All Competitions = Superleague, Playoffs, Challenge Cup and Benson and Hedges Cup

BRACKNELL BEES *left to right, back:* Rob Donovan, Martin Woods, Paxton Schulte, Tom Blatchford (trainer); *second:* Kim Creaser (physio), Chris Brant, Todd Goodwin, Rob Stewart, Alan Smith, Shane Johnson, Dave Whistle (coach), Brian Miller (equipment), Gary Montgomery (equipment), mascot; *third:* Chris Baxter, Brian Greer, Bruno Campese, Colin Ward, Denis Chassé, Matt Coté, Blake Knox, mascot; *front:* PC Drouin, Kevin Riehl, Casson Masters. *Photo:* Bob Swann.

High fives in the Hive

JAMIE McDOUGALL

Bees won their first piece of major silverware in some style, capturing Superleague's first championship of the Millennium by playing open, attractive hockey.

Coach **Dave Whistle**'s first priority in the off- season was to re-sign the club's top players and he successfully retained nine, including goalies **Bruno Campese** and **Brian Greer**. But the loss of **Dale Junkin** and **Shayne McCosh** to Sheffield came as a blow.

Bees rebuilt down the middle with **Todd Goodwin**, **Kevin Riehl** and Newcastle's **Blake Knox**. Goodwin and Riehl were explosive offensive threats and Knox was the face-off man.

Shane Johnson, Martin Woods and late signing **Adam Smith** provided the strength needed on the blue line.

> Coach Whistle employed some unorthodox tactics to achieve one of Bees' biggest victories. The team were staring at their fifth consecutive away defeat in Sheffield on 22 January after going 5-3 behind at the end of the second period.
>
> 'Whis' decided it was time for drastic action and stormed across the ice to confront referee **Andy Carson**, accusing him of making bad calls.
>
> He was thrown out for his pains but his shock tactics paid off as the Bees came back and won 6-3 on **Colin Ward**'s OT goal.

In the *Benson and Hedges* Cup, Bracknell won their home games but struggled on the road, something of a team tradition. But when the league campaign began, they soon found themselves on top, with **Denis Chassé, PC Drouin**, Riehl and Goodwin all featuring in the scoring charts.

November brought only two wins, but crucially their only league loss came in overtime. Until that point, their only regulation loss had come against rivals, London Knights, 2-1 at the Hive.

It wasn't until 11 December that Newcastle Riverkings inflicted a second regulation time defeat, again on home ice.

With Bees facing a gruelling schedule of 22 games in an eight-week spell in January and February, Whistle signed offensive defenceman **Rob Donovan** who brought another dimension to their game. But after three games, a knee injury kept him out for three weeks.

He returned to help the team to go back to the top of the league with a 5-1 win over Cardiff, and it soon became clear that their last game against London on 27 February could be the decider.

Drouin netted the winner in a 4-3 Bees' victory, an entertaining game marred by an horrific facial injury to Knights' skipper, **Rob Kenny**.

The playoffs were a sad anti-climax as Bees were drawn against two teams they had struggled against all season, Riverkings and Knights, and the injury-hit side took only three points from the four games.

PLAYER AWARDS

Players' Player	**Kevin Riehl**
Best Forward	**Kevin Riehl**
Best Defensive Player	**Brian Greer**
Coach's Award	**Bruno Campese**
Supporters' Player	**Paxton Schulte**

LEADING PLAYERS

PC Drouin *born 22 April 1974*

If any one player made the difference then it was the French-Canadian left-winger from Quebec. Arguably the league's best puck handler, whenever his team needed a goal during their title run he seemed to be the one who was there to provide it.

Brian Greer *born 15 July 1974*

'Greersy' stepped out of the shadows as Bees' number two goalie, forcing his coach to split the duties between him and Campese.

He had clearly benefited from his colleague's experience as his agility and improved technique helped him to win a sackful of man of the match awards, often stealing the plaudits from Campese.

Adam Smith *born 24 May 1976*

Bees' other defensive blueliner alongside veteran **Matt Coté** was a steadying influence at the back after his arrival halfway through the *Benson and Hedges* Cup campaign.

By the end of the season he was the team's best all-round defenceman but it was only when he played injured during the playoffs that many realised his true value to the side.

FACT FILE 1999-2000

Sekonda Superleague: Winners.
Sekonda Playoffs: 3rd in quarter-final group.
Benson and Hedges Cup: Semi-finalists.
Challenge Cup: Semi-finalists.

FRANCHISE HISTORY

Founded: 1987.
Leagues: Superleague 1996-2000; British League, Premier Div. 1991-95; British League, Div. One 1995-96, 1990-91; English League 1987-90.

CARDIFF DEVILS

PLAYER	SEKONDA SUPERLEAGUE					SEKONDA PLAYOFFS					ALL COMPETITIONS				
Scorers	GP	G	A	Pts	Pim	GP	G	A	Pts	Pim	GP	G	A	Pts	Pim
Steve Thornton	41	26	24	50	14	6	1	4	5	0	57	34	32	66	32
Vezio Sacratini	42	24	26	50	66	6	3	4	7	16	58	30	36	66	104
Steve Moria	42	23	15	38	10	6	2	0	2	4	58	30	20	50	14
Ivan Matulik (WP)	42	13	18	31	38	6	1	1	2	38	58	15	23	38	82
Ian McIntyre (WP)	41	5	22	27	60	6	0	2	2	0	57	8	29	37	114
Daniel Jardemyr	42	8	16	24	61	6	0	0	0	8	57	10	21	31	81
Merv Priest	42	9	16	25	28	6	1	2	3	4	58	10	20	30	44
John Brill (WP)	42	5	11	16	52	6	1	1	2	8	58	7	14	21	72
Darren Durdle	29	4	11	15	18	-	-	-	-	-	39	5	16	21	20
Patrick Lundback	36	4	11	15	47	6	1	3	4	4	52	5	16	21	65
Frank Evans (WP)	36	1	14	15	119	6	1	2	3	16	49	2	19	21	155
Todd Gillingham (WP)	41	5	8	13	171	5	0	0	0	56	56	10	9	19	264
Alan Schuler	34	1	14	15	16	6	1	3	4	4	42	2	17	19	20
Nicky Chinn	39	3	7	10	112	6	0	2	2	4	56	4	11	15	192
Jason Stone	41	3	3	6	54	6	1	0	1	2	56	4	3	7	60
Darren Hurley 1	13	4	1	5	39	5	1	0	1	16	19	5	1	6	55
Saku Eklof	41	0	3	3	18	4	0	0	0	0	55	1	4	5	22
Tobias Ablad	8	0	3	3	2	-	-	-	-	-	10	0	3	3	4
Aaron Boh (WP)	5	0	0	0	12	-	-	-	-	-	12	0	3	3	40
Stevie Lyle (N)	18	0	2	2	2	-	-	-	-	-	23	0	2	2	4
Niklas Barklund	7	0	0	0	8	-	-	-	-	-	15	1	0	1	20
Jonathan Phillips	21	0	0	0	0	2	1	0	1	0	29	1	0	1	0
Derek Herlofsky (N) (WP)	26	0	1	1	0	6	0	0	0	0	37	0	1	1	2
Daniel Wood (N)	-	-	-	-	-	1	0	0	0	0	1	0	0	0	0
Bench Penalties					26					0					36
TEAM TOTALS	42	138	226	364	973	6	15	24	39	184	58	184	300	484	1502
Netminders	GPI	Min	SoG	GA	Sv%	GPI	Min	SoG	GA	Sv%	GPI	Min	SoG	GA	Sv%
Derek Herlofsky (WP)	26	1555	808	80	90.1	6	362	192	16	91.7	37	2217	1198	107	91.1
Stevie Lyle	18	1026	603	66	89.1	-	-	-	-	-	23	1326	738	75	89.8
Daniel Wood	-	-	-	-	-	1	8	2	0	100	1	8	2	0	100
Empty Net Goals			3	3				0	0				3	3	
TEAM TOTALS	42	2581	1414	149	89.5	6	370	194	16	91.8	58	3551	1941	185	90.5

Back-up Netminder: Matt van der Velden (Invicta Dynamos & Romford Raiders).
Also played for: 1 Manchester Storm.
Shutouts: Lyle - cup: 30 Oct v Manchester Storm (20 saves).
Herlofsky - league: 9 Jan v London Knights (32 saves);
playoffs: 12 Mar v Manchester Storm (25 saves).

All Competitions = Superleague, Playoffs, Challenge Cup and Benson and Hedges Cup.

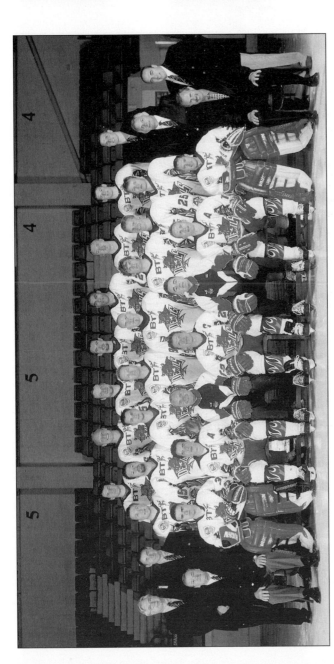

CARDIFF DEVILS *left to right, back row:* Vezio Sacratini, Steve Thornton, Saku Eklof, Merv Priest, Ian McIntyre, Jason Stone, Jonathan Phillips, Rob Britton (equipment); *middle row:* John Jones (sponsor), Jason Ellery (equipment), Nicky Chinn, Todd Gillingham, Aaron Boh, Darren Durdle, Daniel Jardemyr, John Brill, Patrick Lundback, Niklas Barklund, Bob Phillips (director), Andy French (manager); *front row:* David Temme (president), Stevie Lyle, Steve Moria, Peter Ekroth (asst. coach), Ivan Matulik, Paul Heavey (coach), Frank Evans, Derek Herlofsky, Paul Guy (director).
Insets: top - Darren Hurley, bottom - Alan Schuler.

Photo: Richard Murray.

Hindmost season

ANDREW WELTCH

A season which began with wholesale changes of playing staff ended with a major departure at management level. Club chairman **David Temme** left suddenly during the playoffs to become chief executive at Cardiff City AFC.

It was a disappointing season by any standards, and particularly by those which the Devils had set over their 14-year history, with seventh place in the Superleague marking their lowest finish in any division.

Pre-season signings came from far and wide, with new faces from the Swedish, Italian, German, Danish, Austrian, American and East Coast leagues, while local youngster **Jonathan Phillips** was called up from 'farm team' Cardiff Rage, bringing Devils' Welsh contingent to four.

Out went defencemen **Kip Noble** (to Sheffield), **Martin Lindman** (to the German DEL) and **Brent Pope** (to Nottingham), and forwards **Mario Simioni** (Danish League), **Mike MacWilliam**, who retired, and long-time favourite **Doug McEwen** (back to Peterborough).

The campaign started well enough with a 6-2 win over eventual league champions Bracknell, in a game which saw veteran **Steve Moria** score four points to pass the 1,500 mark for the club.

But the bad news soon centred around the new arrivals: within a month **Niklas Barklund** was released and replaced by ex-Ayr defenceman **Alan Schuler** who went on to have a superb season.

Then **Aaron Boh** was let go for 'disciplinary reasons', **Darren Durdle** suffered a long-term shoulder injury and **Patrick Lundback** was suspended.

Assistant coach and junior development chief **Peter Ekroth** returned home to Sweden. All this, and it was still only December.

Cardiff had briefly held fourth place but were more often in the wrong half of the table, and the new millennium did nothing to improve matters.

Despite efforts to boost a struggling squad, **Darren Hurley** was the only new name to arrive before the transfer deadline, while **Troy Walkington** came from Peterborough to fill Ekroth's vacancy.

As the season wound down, netminder **Stevie Lyle** was sidelined by injury, and a 3-1 home defeat by Bracknell condemned the Welsh club to an all-time low league finish.

Off the ice, there was confirmation that Devils' new arena looked set to go ahead. But the club were likely to spend another two or three full seasons in their city centre rink before moving into the long-awaited 8,500-seat facility in the capital's Bay area.

PLAYER AWARDS:

Player of the Year	Stevie Lyle
Players' Player	Vezio Sacratini
Away Player of the Year	Alan Schuler

LEADING PLAYERS

Steve Lyle *born 4 December 1979*

Cardiff's home-grown netminder had another great season for his club and country, backing up an often overstretched Devils' defence in a campaign curtailed by injury.

Steve Moria *born 3 February 1961*

The veteran forward proved he can still compete with the best. He had a flying start to the season, passed the landmark of 1,500 club points and finished as Devils' third highest scorer.

Vezio Sacratini *born 12 September 1966*

The little man performed wonders in a big man's league and was particularly impressive after returning from Italy's successful Pool A playoff campaign.

FACT FILE 1999-2000

Sekonda **Superleague:** 7th.
Sekonda **Playoffs:** 3rd in quarter-final group.
Benson and Hedges **Cup:** Semi-finalists.
Challenge Cup: 7th.

FRANCHISE HISTORY

Founded 1986.
Leagues Superleague 1996-2000; British League, Premier Div. 1989-96; British League, Div. One 1987-89; British League, Div. Two 1986-87.
Honours Superleague Playoff Champions in 1999; League and Championship winners in 1993-94, 1992-93, 1989-90; League winners in 1996-97; *Benson and Hedges* Cup winners 1992.

CHELMSFORD CHIEFTAINS

PLAYER	ENGLISH PREMIER LEAGUE					PLAYOFFS					ALL COMPETITIONS				
Scorers	GP	G	A	Pts	Pim	GP	G	A	Pts	Pim	GP	G	A	Pts	Pim
Andy Hannah	23	23	25	48	26	4	5	4	9	6	33	35	37	72	34
Duane Ward (I)	19	31	17	48	32	4	2	5	7	2	30	39	32	71	34
Darren Cotton	22	20	20	40	4	4	4	4	8	0	33	35	31	66	8
Jon Cotton	23	17	9	26	24	4	1	4	5	4	34	27	22	49	32
Karl Rogers	21	5	16	21	16	4	1	4	5	6	30	8	26	34	26
Jamie Randall	21	4	6	10	4	4	0	1	1	0	32	8	13	21	4
Jake French	23	6	11	17	20	4	0	1	1	0	32	7	14	21	28
Billy Price	23	4	5	9	8	4	1	1	2	0	34	10	9	19	10
Craig Metcalf (I)	23	5	4	9	26	3	0	3	3	2	33	9	10	19	30
Carl Greenhous	21	4	6	10	12	3	0	0	0	0	31	8	11	19	22
Kevin Conway 1	8	6	6	12	6	4	3	3	6	0	12	9	9	18	6
Shaun McFadyen 2	12	3	6	9	12	4	2	2	4	8	22	5	11	16	36
Richard Whiting	20	5	3	8	26	4	2	0	2	0	29	11	3	14	28
Peter Morley	23	1	6	7	38	4	0	0	0	2	34	2	10	12	52
Craig Britton	23	0	4	4	26	4	0	0	0	0	34	2	6	8	32
Tari Suwari	21	1	2	3	2	2	0	0	0	0	29	3	2	5	10
Simon Smith (N)	22	0	2	2	12	4	0	0	0	2	33	0	4	4	18
Shaun Wallis	7	1	0	1	0	2	0	0	0	0	13	2	1	3	0
Jonas Stenmark (I)	4	1	1	2	4	-	-	-	-	-	4	1	1	2	4
Daniel Oliver	21	0	0	0	0	4	0	0	0	0	31	1	1	2	20
Johan Vikstrom (I)	4	1	0	1	0	-	-	-	-	-	4	1	0	1	0
David Heavey	2	0	1	1	2	-	-	-	-	-	2	0	1	1	2
Ross Mackintosh	1	0	0	0	0	-	-	-	-	-	3	0	1	1	0
Richard Gunn	9	0	0	0	0	2	0	0	0	0	13	0	1	1	2
Andrew Clements	7	0	1	1	0	3	0	0	0	0	14	0	1	1	2
Brian Biddulph	2	0	0	0	25	1	0	0	0	0	3	0	0	0	25
Bench Penalties					0					2					4
TEAM TOTALS	23	138	151	289	341	4	21	32	53	34	34	223	257	480	454
Netminders	GPI	Min	SoG	GA	Sv%	GPI	Min	SoG	GA	Sv%	GPI	Min	SoG	GA	Sv%
Simon Smith	22	1307	733	77	89.5	4	240	116	10	91.4	32	1813	1026	105	89.8
Paul Wilcox	2	67	43	5	88.4	-	-	-	-	-	5	221	108	14	87.0
Carl Ambler	1	6	4	2	50.0	-	-	-	-	-	1	6	4	2	50.0
Empty Net Goals			1	1									1	1	
TEAM TOTALS	23	1380	781	85	89.1	4	240	116	10	91.4	34	2040	1139	122	89.3

Also appeared: Stuart Coleman (21L), Richard Gunn (9L, 2PO), Ricky Lamey (4L), John Fisher, Tighe Ransom (2L).

Also played for: 1 Hull Thunder, 2 Invicta Dynamos.

Shutouts: Smith - Playoffs: 18 Mar at Invicta Dynamos (32 saves).

All Competitions = league, playoffs and Millennium Cup.

CHELMSFORD CHIEFTAINS *left to right, back row:* Kevin Reed (centre manager), Craig Britton, Duane Ward, Craig Metcalf, Peter Morley, Tari Suwari, Andy Hannah, Shaun McFadyen, Erskine Douglas (coach); *middle row:* Jon Cotton, Kevin Conway, Darren Cotton, Richard Gunn, Billy Price, Shaun Wallis, Dan Oliver, Jamie Randall; *front row:* Paul Wilcox, Sylvian Clifford (director), Richard Whiting, John Blundell (director), Carl Greenhous, Kyle Whitehill (*PepsiCo* franchise director), Jake French, Ollie Oliver (director), Karl Rogers, John Sherrington (director), Simon Smith.

Lucky 13 brings Grand Slam

IVOR HOBSON

In their lucky 13th campaign, Chelmsford struck gold winning the Grand Slam of English Premier League and playoffs plus the Millennium Cup.

After 12 seasons with only an Autumn Trophy to show for their efforts, Chieftains lost only four of their 23 league games and five of 34 in all. With only two defeats on the road, their away form was even more imposing.

Coach **Erskine Douglas** made a shrewd signing in netminder **Simon Smith** from Guildford Flames who became a cornerstone of the team's success.

Returning to Chelmsford were **Craig Britton** from Milton Keynes and **Carl Greenhous**, while among the eight newcomers were Invicta's **Jamie Randall** and **Darren Cotton**, the latter renewing his partnership with brother Jon.

The blow of losing Swedish imports, **Jonas Stenmark** and **Jonas Vikstrom**, after only five games was softened considerably by the signing of former Tulsa Oiler centreman, **Duane Ward**, who ended as the club's top goal scorer.

In first place in the league after winning their opening five games, Chelmsford stumbled to two straight defeats at home, including a 5-1 loss to Swindon who took over at the top of the table on 3 October.

The team recovered and players came and went, but Invicta Dynamos' defenceman, **Shaun McFadyen**, signed and stayed.

Douglas' last big signing was completed on the transfer deadline when left winger, **Kevin Conway**, joined the squad. The one-time GB international made his presence felt immediately with a wrap-around goal 86 seconds into his opening game at Romford on 30 January.

Chieftains qualified comfortably for the final of the Millennium Cup with only one loss, at home to the Isle of Wight. But they travelled to Swindon with some trepidation as Chill had been one of their most difficult opponents.

Sure enough, Swindon took an early two-goal lead but they were no match for the rampant Ward who hit back with five to lead Chieftains to a 10-7 triumph.

Two weeks later, Chelmsford clinched their first ever league title with an impressive 8-3 win on the Isle of Wight.

In the playoffs, Chieftains demolished Dynamos in the first leg at Gillingham 7-0 and cruised to a 14-6 aggregate victory. Another come-from-behind win at Swindon in the final set up a 7-4 two-leg triumph and an historic treble.

PLAYER AWARDS

Players' Player	**Duane Ward**
PepsiCo International *Player*	**Simon Smith**
Supporters' Player	**Duane Ward**

PepsiCo International *for Special Contribution*
Richard Whiting/Jamie Randall/Billy Price

LEADING PLAYERS

Kevin Conway *born 13 July 1963*

A year earlier the Sault St Marie, Canada native had been playing Superleague hockey with Newcastle. He came to Chieftains from Hull Thunder and added much needed skill and experience in the all-important final stretch.

Simon Smith *born 31 July 1979*

The Chatham, Kent-born netminder was a key presence, pulling off many impressive saves and finishing runner-up in the table only to Swindon's former Canadian pro, **Ronald Bertrand.**

Duane Ward *born 20 February 1976*

The club's leading goal scorer with 33, the Ontario-born centreman was unquestionably their player of the season. A great puck handler who reminded many fans of former Chieftain great, **Alexi Kuznetzov.**

FACT FILE 1999-2000

English League: 1st in Premier Division.
Playoffs: Champions.
Data Vision **Millennium Cup:** Winners.

CLUB HISTORY

Founded: 1987.
Leagues: English League 1997-2000 and 1988-93; British League, Div One 1993-96; British League, Div. Two 1987-88.

THANKS, ESTHER

Defenceman **Richard Gunn** appeared on the BBC show *That's Life* in 1988 as an aspiring three-year-old who decided he wanted to play ice hockey for the Chelmsford Chieftains.

He realised his dream in the autumn of 1999.

EDINBURGH CAPITALS

PLAYER	BRITISH NATIONAL LEAGUE					PLAYOFFS					ALL COMPETITIONS				
Scorers	GP	G	A	Pts	Pim	GP	G	A	Pts	Pim	GP	G	A	Pts	Pim
Steven Lynch	36	24	25	49	26	6	5	2	7	8	54	38	32	70	48
Iain Robertson	36	18	27	45	42	6	1	3	4	2	54	21	42	63	66
Neil Donovan (I)	28	19	14	33	39	-	-	-	-	-	40	27	25	52	51
Kyle Edwards (I)	37	13	28	41	46	6	3	2	5	0	54	19	33	52	54
Tony Malm (I)	22	12	10	22	4	-	-	-	-	-	31	20	14	34	16
Craig Wilson	31	5	16	21	38	6	2	1	3	12	47	13	21	34	60
Alan Hough	30	5	13	18	20	6	2	5	7	4	46	8	21	29	38
Jeremy Riehl	29	8	8	16	14	-	-	-	-	-	41	13	13	26	51
Angelo Catenaro (I)	31	0	14	14	92	6	0	4	4	16	47	1	25	26	141
Jason Heywood (!)	13	5	9	14	18	-	-	-	-	-	21	8	16	24	64
Steven Flockhart	24	3	4	7	36	3	0	0	0	4	35	5	4	9	46
Ryan Boyd (I)	18	1	4	5	22	-	-	-	-	-	27	3	5	8	61
Neil Abel	29	0	2	2	12	6	2	3	5	2	39	2	6	8	16
John Fisher	4	0	1	1	29	-	-	-	-	-	10	2	4	6	57
Scott Plews	27	0	3	3	128	3	0	0	0	25	39	0	6	6	179
Wayne Maxwell 2	13	2	0	2	24	-	-	-	-	-	19	2	1	3	28
Richie Lamb	3	1	1	2	2	4	0	1	1	0	7	1	2	3	2
Ross Hay	22	1	2	3	2	3	0	0	0	0	31	1	2	3	2
Paul Hand	6	0	0	0	20	-	-	-	-	-	13	0	2	2	75
Scott Neil	7	1	0	1	14	3	0	0	0	0	13	1	0	1	14
Matthieu Davidge (N)	35	0	1	1	0	6	0	0	0	0	53	0	1	1	0
David Beatson	22	0	0	0	8	3	0	0	0	16	30	0	0	0	28
John Finnie (N)	36	0	0	0	44	6	0	0	0	4	54	0	0	0	54
Bench Penalties					10					0					14
TEAM TOTALS	36	118	182	300	690	6	15	21	36	93	54	185	275	460	1165

Netminders	GPI	Min	SoG	GA	Sv%	GPI	Min	SoG	GA	Sv%	GPI	Min	SoG	GA	Sv%
John Finnie	33	1868	1117	151	86.5	6	344	243	34	86.0	50	2791	1692	224	86.8
Matthieu Davidge	9	294	207	40	80.7	1	16	10	2	80.0	15	451	281	53	81.1
Ryan Ford	1	6	4	1	75.0	-	-	-	-	-	1	6	4	1	75.0
TEAM TOTALS	36	2168	1328	192	85.5	6	360	253	36	85.8	54	3248	1977	278	85.9

Also appeared: Alan Plews 7; Laurie Dunbar (1) 4; Steven Francey, Raymond Mills 2; Craig Docherty, Gary Hughes, Ian MacFarlane 1.

Also played for: 1 Paisley Pirates, 2 Fife Flyers.

All Competitions = league, playoffs, B&H *Cup/Plate and* ntl: *Christmas Cup.*

Cat's Caps collapse

NIGEL DUNCAN

Angelo Catenaro breezed into Murrayfield in the summer of 1999 intent on raising his considerable profile even higher and helping Capitals back to the top.

The popular player, who helped Ayr Eagles to claim Superleague's Grand Slam, looked to be the answer to Capitals' prayers.

The success-starved fans, who had suffered as their heroes struggled near the foot of the table in previous seasons, drooled as Catenaro's champions soared into third place.

Then, sadly, the cracks began to show. Cash troubles forced the team to cut players including much-hyped former Sheffield Steelers' hit-man, **Jason Heywood.**

Then Edinburgh satellite TV dealer, **Raymond Lumsden**, one of the club's most ardent fans and a long-term benefactor, resigned as a director leaving **Scott Neil** in the hot-seat.

Neil, a former captain of the now defunct Murrayfield Racers, and the man who conceived the Capitals, soldiered on admirably, with Catenaro calling the shots on the ice.

With dogged determination, Neil ran the club day-to-day, took on the bench coaching duties, and even made a shock playing comeback, as Catenaro, troubled by knee problems, continued to cajole his men on the ice.

But all the efforts were in vain and Capitals continued to slide down the British National League table. They also failed to make an impact in the Christmas Cup and were spectators as Fife and Paisley contested the Scottish Cup.

Words also flew as defenceman **Jeremy Riehl**, who had played for free for several months, was jettisoned during an acrimonious dispute over his commitment to the team.

Then **Neil Donovan** walked out to join a club in North America and there were injuries galore. **Alan Hough** was sidelined over Christmas and New Year, and **Tony Malm** was ruled out for the season with a cheekbone injury which required surgery. He later took over as bench coach.

But despite the desperate disappointment, there was a nugget in the consistent form of **Steven Lynch**, the former Ayr, Fife and Paisley target-man.

His efforts were rewarded nationally with inclusion in the Writers' All-Star team and locally by him pocketing both the clubs' end-of-season awards. His partnership with **Iain Robertson** and **Craig Wilson** could provide the basis for next season's side.

PLAYER AWARDS

Player of the Year	Steven Lynch
Players' Player	Steven Lynch

LEADING PLAYERS

Steven Lynch born 14 August 1976
Left-winger was a consistent scorer despite his team's difficult year. His inspiration helped to keep spirits up in the dressing-room despite the awful run of defeats.

Iain Robertson born 2 June 1969
The centreman on Lynch's line maintained pressure on his team-mate in the points-gathering stakes and refused to allow set-backs and disappointments to interfere with his play.

Craig Wilson born 6 December 1974
The third man on the Green Line (so-called for the colour of their training bibs) provided an ideal foil for Lynch and Robertson. He worked hard to win the puck and gained his reward with a string of rave notices and a number of goals.

FACT FILE 1999-2000

British National League: Eighth.
Playoffs: Fourth in quarter-final group.
Benson and Hedges: Runners-up in Cup group; knocked out in first round of Plate.
ntl: Christmas Cup: Quarter-finalists.
Scottish Cup: Knocked out in qualifying round.

HISTORY

Founded: 1998. Known as Murrayfield Royals 1995-98 and 1952-66, Edinburgh Racers 1994-95 and Murrayfield Racers 1966-94.
Leagues: Capitals - British National Lge 1998-2000; Royals - British National Lge 1997-98, Northern Premier Lge 1996-97, British Lge, Div One 1995-96, British Lge 1954-55, Scottish National Lge 1952-54; Racers - British Lge, Premier Div 1982-95, Northern Lge 1966-82.
Honours: See *The Ice Hockey Annual 1998-99*

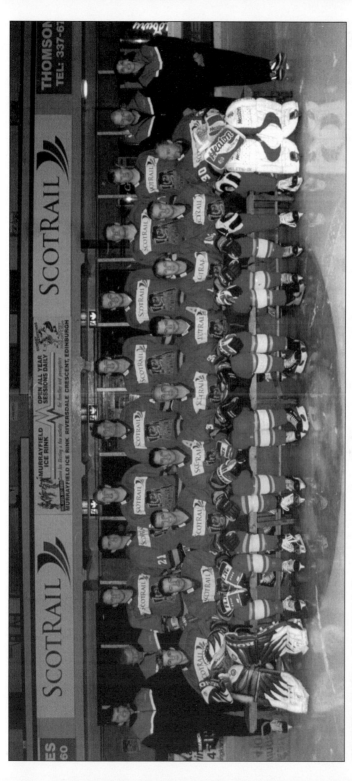

EDINBURGH CAPITALS *left to right, back row:* Scott Neil, *(unidentified)*, Tony Malm, Jeremy Riehl, David Beatson, Neil Abel, Alan Hough, Colin Wilson, Scott Plews, Ross Hay, *(two unidentified); front row:* Matthew Davidge, Iain Robertson, Neil Donovan, Ryan Boyd, Angelo Catenaro, Steven Lynch, Kyle Edwards, Steven Flockhart, John Finnie.

FIFE FLYERS

PLAYER	BRITISH NATIONAL LEAGUE					PLAYOFFS					ALL COMPETITIONS				
Scorers	GP	G	A	Pts	Pim	GP	G	A	Pts	Pim	GP	G	A	Pts	Pim
Russell Monteith (WP)	36	36	32	68	6	11	15	14	29	4	65	66	61	127	24
Todd Dutiaume (I)	35	28	35	63	48	11	9	9	18	4	64	46	61	107	74
John Haig	35	17	36	53	24	11	3	9	12	6	63	27	59	86	36
Frank Morris	36	16	29	45	60	11	7	17	24	18	64	28	56	84	117
Ted Russell (WP)	36	5	38	43	60	11	2	11	13	12	65	15	64	79	106
Mark Morrison (I)	33	14	26	40	18	11	5	5	10	18	59	36	38	74	52
Steven King	32	16	22	38	32	11	8	8	16	6	56	34	40	74	88
David Smith	32	19	10	29	8	11	2	5	7	12	60	28	21	49	38
Dean Edmiston	31	10	16	26	36	11	0	7	7	22	56	15	33	48	76
Andrew Samuel	32	3	4	7	10	11	1	2	3	14	60	8	12	20	71
Derek King	35	2	1	3	42	10	1	2	3	0	62	3	11	14	54
Gary Wishart	33	5	3	8	10	9	1	1	2	0	59	7	6	13	20
Andrew Finlay	36	2	5	7	4	11	0	0	0	2	64	4	9	13	14
Bill Moody (I)	15	3	3	6	6	11	3	1	4	8	28	6	5	11	14
Daryl Venters	23	0	2	2	6	-	-	-	-	-	39	2	4	6	14
Kyle Horne	35	0	3	3	8	11	0	0	0	0	61	0	5	5	18
Paddy Ward	17	0	0	0	2	3	0	0	0	0	32	1	0	1	2
Stephen Murphy (N)	35	0	0	0	4	11	0	1	1	0	61	0	1	1	4
Ricky Grubb (N)	34	0	1	1	2	11	0	0	0	0	62	0	1	1	2
Bench Penalties					4					0					12
TEAM TOTALS	36	176	266	442	390	11	57	92	149	126	65	326	487	813	836
Netminders	GPI	Min	SoG	GA	Sv%	GPI	Min	SoG	GA	Sv%	GPI	Min	SoG	GA	Sv%
Stephen Murphy	30	1774	954	63	93.4	11	660	378	24	93.7	53	3146	1693	116	93.1
Ricky Grubb	7	386	235	24	89.8	-	-	-	-	-	14	754	409	43	89.5
Empty Net Goals			2	2				0	0				3	3	
TEAM TOTALS	36	2160	1191	89	92.5	11	660	378	24	93.7	65	3900	2105	162	92.3

Also appeared: Liam Grieg 7, Derek Downie (N), Wayne Maxwell, Ray Mills, Andrew Moffat (N) 3.

Shutouts: Murphy - league: 28 Nov at Slough Jets (26 saves), 30 Jan v Basingstoke Bison (23 saves); playoffs: 11 Mar v Hull Thunder (25 saves).

All Competitions = league, playoffs, B&H Cup/Plate and ntl: *Christmas Cup.*

FIFE FLYERS *left to right, back row:* David Smith, Derek King, John Haig, Ted Russell, Kyle Horne, Paddy Ward, Daryl Venters; *middle row:* Gary Reidy (stick boy), Alan Wishart (equipment), John McKean (doctor), Dean Edmiston, Andy Samuel, Todd Dutiaume, Bill Moody, Russell Monteith, Gary Wishart, Steven King, Andy Finlay, Allan Anderson (coaching team), Allan Crow (press officer), Alistair Cameron (commercial manager); *front row:* Ricky Grubb, Chic Cottrell (asst coach), Tom Muir (director), Frank Morris, Mark Morrison, John Waring (director), Jack Wishart (director), Stephen Murphy.

High Flyers

ALLAN CROW

If Fife Flyers' Diamond Jubilee season was memorable, then what followed was magnificent.

A British National League playoff victory in March 1999 was the catalyst for the most successful season in the club's long history - four trophies, a handful of all-star honours, and enough highlights to make a movie, never mind a video.

Flyers won their first national league title since 1991-92, lifted the *ntl:* Christmas Cup, and then turned that double into a treble with a second consecutive BNL playoff championship.

They also managed to find space in the trophy cabinet for their fifth Scottish Cup. Only the *Benson and Hedges* Plate eluded their grasp - they were beaten semi-finalists after winning their group in the Cup.

Canadian player-coach **Mark Morrison** and his Scottish assistant **Chic Cottrell** took 19 diverse individuals and moulded them into a team which played fast, skilful and disciplined hockey.

MORRISON'S CLUB RECORD

For Morrison the reward was a post-war club record equalling third Coach of the Year title from the BNL and the hockey writers, while his men dominated the post-season honours.

Netminder **Stephen Murphy** cleaned up at every level after a superb rookie season in which the 18-year-old out-performed every goalie in the league. At the other end stood forward **Russell Monteith**. He didn't so much break **Fred Perlini's** club record of 26 powerplay goals as shatter it with 38, a figure which may stand the test of time.

Flyers also got huge seasons out of their key players. **Frank Morris** and **Ted Russell** were immense on defence, **John Haig** again topped the British points scorers, and a revitalised **Dean Edmiston** played his best hockey in years.

But it was Steven King who best summed up the spirit in the camp by playing through two of the BNL final games with a double broken jaw.

Apart from that, Flyers, who played more games than even the Superleague teams, were fortunate at avoiding injuries, with 16 of their 19 regulars fit to ice in just about every game.

Cottrell, by the way, had a unique way of celebrating each victory. He seized the game puck, drilled a three-inch nail through it and hammered it into a wall in the dressing-room.

They remain as a tribute to arguably the greatest Flyers team ever.

PLAYER AWARDS

Player of the Year (Mirror of Merit)
Stephen Murphy
Supporters' Club Player Of the Year
Stephen Murphy
Players' Player **Stephen Murphy**
Most Improved Player **Andy Finlay**

LEADING PLAYERS

Frank Morris born 22 March 1963
One of the BNL's outstanding D-men, the 13-year veteran seems to get better with every passing season.

Stephen Murphy born 11 December 1981
The teenager is the youngest goaltender to make his mark on the senior game since Stevie Lyle. Like the Welshman, Stephen's strengths are his positioning and quick reflexes.

Ted Russell born 7 May 1971
A key defence signing from Peterborough whose precision passing gave the powerplay a new dimension. Lapped up the ice time.

Allan Crow has produced a *Fife Flyers' Yearbook* containing a complete 50,000-word summary of Flyers' 61st season in 1999-2000.

Within its 100 pages are profiles of all the Flyers and results and match reports from each of their BNL league and Cup games.

It's available for £10 plus £2 p&p from **Alistair Cameron** at the Fife Ice Arena

---

FACT FILE 1999-2000

British National League: Winners.
Playoffs: Champions.
Benson and Hedges: Won Cup group; Semi-finalists in Plate.
ntl: Christmas Cup: Winners.
Scottish Cup: Winners.

CLUB HISTORY

Founded: 1938.
Leagues: British National League (BNL) 1997-2000; Northern Premier League (NPL) 1996-97; British League 1982-96, 1954-55; Northern League (NL) 1966-82; Scottish National League (SNL) 1981-82, 1946-54, 1938-40.
Major Honours: British Champions 1985. *Leagues:* BNL 1999-2000; NPL 1997-98, 1996-97; British Lge, Div. One 1991-92; NL 1976-78; SNL 1951-52, 1939-40. *Playoffs:* BNL 1999-2000, 1998-99. *Autumn Cup:* 1978, 1976, 1975; Scottish - 1950, 1948. *Scottish Cup:* 2000, 1999, 1998, 1995, 1994.

FLINTSHIRE FREEZE

PLAYER	ENGLISH DIV ONE NORTH					PLAYOFFS					TOTALS				
Scorers	GP	G	A	Pts	Pim	GP	G	A	Pts	Pim	GP	G	A	Pts	Pim
Mark Stokes	17	28	31	59	14	3	3	6	9	14	20	31	37	68	28
Peter Founds	15	16	21	37	48	3	3	3	6	4	18	19	24	43	52
Simon Wedd	16	11	13	24	8	3	1	0	1	4	19	12	13	25	12
Alan Steele	14	5	6	11	18	3	3	4	7	6	17	8	10	18	24
Marc Lovell	17	8	8	16	16	3	0	1	1	2	20	8	9	17	18
Aaron Davies	16	6	10	16	68	3	0	1	1	8	19	6	11	17	76
Jason Titmuss	15	8	6	14	10	2	0	0	0	0	17	8	6	14	10
Phil Brook	7	8	5	13	2	-	-	-	-	-	7	8	5	13	2
Mike Murray (I)	5	6	4	10	44	1	0	1	1	25	6	6	5	11	69
Mark Hobson	15	3	4	7	16	2	0	1	1	2	17	3	5	8	18
Paul Richardson	4	2	6	8	8	-	-	-	-	-	4	2	6	8	8
Richard Amos	14	1	7	8	12	2	0	0	0	0	16	1	7	8	2
Danny Compton	8	3	1	4	0	3	0	0	0	0	11	3	1	4	0
Steven Fellows	12	1	3	4	8	-	-	-	-	-	12	1	3	4	8
Andrew Hughes	10	0	3	3	30	3	0	0	0	33	13	0	3	3	63
Dave Clancy (N)	15	0	2	2	31	3	0	0	0	2	18	0	2	2	33
Matthew Gilday	4	1	1	2	0	-	-	-	-	-	4	1	1	2	0
Alan Founds	9	1	1	2	0	3	0	0	0	0	12	1	1	2	0
James Hussaney	6	1	0	1	4	-	-	-	-	-	6	1	0	1	4
Dan Wilkinson	1	0	1	1	4	-	-	-	-	-	1	0	1	1	4
Wayne Whitby 1	4	0	1	1	0	-	-	-	-	-	4	0	1	1	0
Robert Hill	13	0	1	1	0	3	0	0	0	2	16	0	1	1	2
Neil Hynes	3	0	0	0	10	-	-	-	-	-	3	0	0	0	10
Michael Clancy (N)	15	0	0	0	4	3	0	0	0	4	18	0	0	0	8
Bench Penalties					4					0					4
TEAM TOTALS	17	109	135	244	359	3	10	17	27	106	20	119	152	271	455
Netminders	GPI	Min	SoG	GA	Sv%	GPI	Min	SoG	GA	Sv%	GPI	Min	SoG	GA	Sv%
Matt Compton	2	62	33	3	90.9	-	-	-	-	-	2	62	33	3	90.9
Dave Clancy	14	730	558	59	89.4	2	80	81	6	92.6	16	810	639	65	89.8
Michael Clancy	5	228	171	24	85.9	3	100	88	11	87.5	8	328	259	35	86.5
TEAM TOTALS	17	1020	762	86	88.7	3	180	169	17	89.9	20	1200	931	103	88.9

Also appeared: Pete Olsson (11L, 3PO), Gary Shaw (11L), Tony Melbourne (2L), Brian Jackson (1L).
Also played for: 1 Blackburn Hawks.

Warming up youth

NEIL MACDONALD

The Freeze enjoyed more than their fair share of ice capades in their second season in the English Division One North, when they finished two places lower than in their first year.

National call ups, threats of expulsion from the league and problems with players leaving were all on the agenda for coach **Mark Stokes**.

Under his guidance, a young team had reached the playoffs in their first year, so that was the immediate target to try and match.

With the nucleus of the same side they started well, winning four of their first six games, including victories over the division's top sides, Billingham and Whitley Bay.

From then on teams began to clamp down on the Freeze and wins were hard to come by - just four more in the next 12 games.

Injuries and absenteeism also began to take their toll, particularly in defence where captain and talisman **Paul Richardson** left because of travelling difficulties, and **Stevie Fellows** picked up a back injury that kept him out from Christmas onwards.

Stokes was also hampered in the crucial run-in by an elbow injury that left him skating through the pain barrier.

Without the finances to buy in established replacements, he turned to the burgeoning youth section and unearthed potential gems in teenagers **Alan Founds, Aaron Davies** and **Rob Hill**. Davies and **Marc Lovell** were later selected for national squads.

The youngsters grew up quickly in the first team, but matches continued to go against the Freeze until the final game of the regular season against Nottingham Lions which became winner-take-all.

Although he was playing with virtually one arm, Stokes inspired his team to a 15-3 blow-out win, scoring five goals and three assists, and Freeze claimed the final playoff spot.

But the dream died almost as soon as it started. At the end of the first period of the first playoff game against Whitley, the score was 3-1 when a brawl erupted as both teams left the ice.

Freeze player **Mike Murray** was arrested by police although assault charges were later dropped. Not surprisingly the team lost heart and surrendered tamely 13-2.

But they won back their self respect and buried a hoodoo when they beat bogey team Altrincham Aces home and away. Controversially, they decided not to travel for the return against Warriors, despite threats of being thrown out of the league; they escaped with a 5-0 forfeit.

PLAYER AWARDS

Player of the Year	**Simon Wedd**
Most Improved Player	**Marc Lovell**
Rookie of the Year	**Aaron Davies**

LEADING PLAYERS

Dave Clancy *born 9 September 1978*
Netminder Dave soaked up shots like a sponge does water and saved 89.4 per cent of efforts in the league season. Made the position look easy.

Pete Founds *born 26 August 1977*
Captain Pete led by example using his speed and agility to make countless outside breaks to set up a shot or be on the end of a scoring move.

Mark Stokes *born 12 August 1966*
The Canadian player-coach enjoyed another excellent year. Despite being double and triple teamed at times, his stickhandling and shooting ensured he led the squad in goals and assists.

FACT FILE 1999-2000

English League placing: 6th in Div. One North.
Playoffs: 2nd in group B.

CLUB HISTORY

Founded: 1998. The previous club was Deeside Dragons 1975-89 & 1991-96.
Leagues: Freeze - English Lge, Div. One North 1998-2000. Dragons - English Lge North 1994-96, English Conference 1991-94; British Lge, Div. One 1987-89 & 1983-85; British Lge, Div. Two 1985-87 & 1982-83; English Lge North 1981-82; Midland Lge 1978-81, Southern Lge 1975-78.
Honours: Dragons - English Conference 1993-94, Welsh Cup 1988-89.

FLINTSHIRE FREEZE *left to right, back row:* Peter Olsson, Robert Hill, Richie Amos, Alan Founds, Andrew Hughes, Mike Murray, Matty Compton, Alan Steele, Steven Fellows, Mark Stokes; *front row:* Dave Clancy, Simon Wedd, Jason Titmuss, Peter Founds, Marc Lovell, Aaron Davies, Michael Clancy.

GUILDFORD FLAMES

PLAYER	BRITISH NATIONAL LEAGUE					PLAYOFFS					ALL COMPETITIONS				
Scorers	GP	G	A	Pts	Pim	GP	G	A	Pts	Pim	GP	G	A	Pts	Pim
Karry Biette (I)	36	23	37	60	63	6	4	6	10	30	51	32	48	80	105
Barcley Pearce	34	23	32	55	48	6	2	3	5	24	50	29	42	71	96
Pete Kasowski (I)	36	26	27	53	30	6	5	2	7	14	50	33	33	66	48
Derek DeCosty (I)	35	24	23	47	32	6	6	3	9	4	51	33	29	62	44
Ryan Campbell	35	18	25	43	40	6	3	2	5	8	51	27	32	59	56
Chris Crombie (I)	34	23	13	36	54	6	1	1	2	20	50	29	18	47	125
Rick Plant	36	13	18	31	36	6	1	1	2	6	52	16	24	40	48
Paul Dixon	31	5	20	25	16	6	0	6	6	6	46	6	30	36	30
Robert Lamey	36	10	13	23	14	6	0	1	1	4	48	10	15	25	20
Tom Brown (I)	34	4	9	13	34	6	2	0	2	2	44	7	11	18	44
James Manson	36	3	10	13	48	6	0	3	3	18	52	3	15	18	76
Ian Cooper 2	7	1	8	9	14	6	1	4	5	6	13	2	12	14	20
Gary D Clarke 3	15	2	3	5	4	-	-	-	-	-	21	4	4	8	6
Simon Howard	36	1	5	6	48	6	0	0	0	4	52	2	5	7	62
Russ Plant	29	3	2	5	2	-	-	-	-	-	39	3	3	6	4
Andrew Einhorn (I)	14	0	2	2	39	6	0	3	3	8	24	0	5	5	85
Lee Cowmeadow 3	7	1	1	2	2	6	0	2	2	0	16	1	3	4	2
Jason Moses	15	2	1	3	2	3	0	0	0	0	22	2	1	3	2
Dominic Hopkins 1	25	0	1	1	0	-	-	-	-	-	31	0	3	3	4
Stan Marple	7	1	0	1	8	-	-	-	-	-	10	2	0	2	14
Patrick Flanagan	11	0	1	1	0	-	-	-	-	-	14	1	1	2	2
Mark McCoy 1	-	-	-	-	-	-	-	-	-	-	6	0	2	2	2
Jamie Organ (N)	36	0	0	0	2	6	0	1	1	0	52	0	2	2	2
John Hepburn	4	1	0	1	0	-	-	-	-	-	6	1	0	1	0
Tyrone Miller	6	0	0	0	2	-	-	-	-	-	10	0	0	0	2
Bench Penalties					4					2					10
TEAM TOTALS	36	184	251	435	542	6	25	38	63	156	52	243	338	581	909
Netminders	GPI	Min	SoG	GA	Sv%	GPI	Min	SoG	GA	Sv%	GPI	Min	SoG	GA	Sv%
Jamie Organ	35	2031	947	91	90.4	6	365	169	19	88.8	51	2963	1395	146	89.5
Jamie Thompson	4	141	50	6	88.0	-	-	-	-	-	5	174	67	7	89.5
Empty Net Goals			1	1				0	0				1	1	
TEAM TOTALS	36	2172	998	98	90.1	6	365	169	19	88.7	52	3137	1463	154	89.5

Also appeared: Grant King (N) 8, Adam Franks 5; James Clark, Simon Lavis 2; Rory Alexander, David Alexander, Tom Boney, Simon Griffith, Ben Hammond, Michael Plenty, Vicky Robins (N), Michael Simmons, Matt Thornhill 1.

Also played for: 1 Slough Jets, 2 London Knights, 3 Milton Keynes Kings.

Shutouts: Organ (7) - league: 25 Sept v Peterborough Pirates (19 saves), 23 Oct v Edinburgh Capitals (30), 31 Oct v Slough Jets (16), 5 Dec v Slough Jets (25), 13 Feb at Paisley Pirates (33), 20 Feb v Peterborough Pirates (24); playoffs: 19 March v Slough Jets (18).

All Competitions = league, playoffs, B&H Cup/Plate and ntl: Christmas Cup.

GUILDFORD FLAMES *left to right, back row:* Adrian Jenkinson (trainer), Derek DeCosty, Simon Howard, Gary Clarke, Pete Kasowski, Tom Brown, Jason Moses, Rick Plant, Rob Lamey, James Manson, Russ Plant, Malcolm Norman (managing director); *front row:* Jamie Organ, Ryan Campbell, Chris Crombie, Stan Marple (coach), Karry Biette, Mike Urquhart (asst. coach), Paul Dixon, Barcley Pearce, Jamie Thompson.

Flickered out

This was the season when the high-spending Flames narrowly failed to light up the British National League.

What made it so frustrating for **Stan Marple**'s crew was the way they came so close to glory before flickering out. They improved their league position by one place, finishing as runners-up to the all-conquering Fife Flyers. With late signing, **Ian Cooper**, from Superleague's London Knights, they were determined to make a go of it in the playoffs.

By then, success in the season's last competition was their only chance of silverware. In a disastrous start to the campaign, Flames not only failed to retain the *Benson and Hedges* Plate but were knocked out of the Cup in the first round after gaining only one point on the road.

Perhaps the team needed longer to settle after **Terry Kurtenbach**'s retirement and the loss of imports **Kirk Humphreys** and **Mark McCoy**. Marple's key signings were English defender **Paul Dixon** from Superleague Newcastle and Basingstoke's heavy hitting Canuck, **Chris Crombie**.

Sure enough, by the time the *ntl:* Christmas Cup rolled round, Flames were able to squeeze past Hull Thunder, thanks to club stalwart **Ryan Campbell**. His second tally at Hull less than three minutes from time in the second leg was enough to put them in the semis.

But nagging doubts that this might not be Flames' year set in when they outshot Bison at home in the first leg only to crash 7-2 to their rivals who got four goals from **Wayne Crawford**.

Their league chances still looked good, though. They were three points behind leaders Peterborough with three games in hand and the only other threat came from those Flyers.

By early February, Flames had inflicted their second defeat on Fife in the Spectrum and were top of the table by two points from the Scots.

The crunch game came on 12 February in Kirkcaldy where Flames had lost 5-1 in November. This time they held on for a 2-2 draw with three minutes left...then collapsed horribly to lose 5-2.

Even more upsetting was being knocked out of the playoffs on a three-way tie-break.

Many personal milestones were achieved during the year: **Pete Kasowski** and **Derek DeCosty** scored their 100th goals, Marple coached his 100th game and Campbell scored his 500th assist.

PLAYER AWARDS

Player of the Year	**Paul Dixon**
Player's Player	**Paul Dixon**
Best British Player	**Paul Dixon**
Supporters Club Player	**Derek DeCosty**
Sportsmanship Award	**Tom Brown**

LEADING PLAYERS

Karry Biette *born 24 February 1973*

Flames' captain was a leader on and off the ice as well as being the club's top points scorer. An ex-Superleague player with Ayr who first came to Britain in 1996-97 with Swindon IceLords.

Derek DeCosty *born 4 January 1968*

The American returned for the third time in four seasons and enjoyed another impressive, high scoring campaign. The highlight came on 26 February when he scored six goals and seven points against Paisley at the Spectrum.

Paul Dixon *born 4 August 1973*

The former Superleague defenceman was a fan favourite from the start, and remained that way until he almost made a clean sweep of the club's awards. He was rewarded with a place on the GB team in the World Championships.

FACT FILE 1999-2000

British National League: Runners-up.
Playoffs: Quarter-finalists.
Benson and Hedges Cup: 3rd in group.
ntl: Christmas Cup: Semi-finalists.

HISTORY

Founded: 1992.
Leagues: British National League (BNL) 1997-2000; Premier League (PL) 1996-97; British League, Div. One 1993-96; English League 1992-93.
Honours: BNL and Playoffs 1997-98, PL 1997-98, *B&H* Plate 1998-99.

HARINGEY GREYHOUNDS *left to right, at the back:* Zoran Kozic, Gary Organ, Jamie Hirst, Martin Garwood, Phillip Myers, Steve Fullan, Victor Somfaleanu, Simon Cruickshank, Bradley Beck-Hill, Ian Clark, Octavian Sersea, Deavon Clayton, Gary Dodds, Harvey Wroe (club secretary); *in the middle:* Kevin Grey, Brian Clark, Steve Clements, Paul O'Neill, Tom Clark, Alan Graichen, Jan Bestic, Kwabina Oppong-Addai; *in front:* Rob Sheldrake, Dave Robb, Dean Birrell *(behind glove).*

HARINGEY GREYHOUNDS

PLAYER	ENGLISH DIVISION ONE SOUTH					PLAYOFFS					ALL COMPETITIONS				
Scorers	GP	G	A	Pts	Pim	GP	G	A	Pts	Pim	GP	G	A	Pts	Pim
Zoran Kozic (I)	7	28	9	37	12	3	0	2	2	61	18 ·	39	25	64	75
Kevin Gray	14	9	10	19	16	5	2	1	3	39	27	19	18	37	61
Victor Somfaleanu	14	13	16	29	4	4	2	3	5	10	21	16	20	36	41
Rasmus Edmund (I)	6	10	7	17	4	-	-	-	-	-	13	20	13	33	8
Octavian Sersea	14	6	9	15	22	6	6	4	10	8	26	14	17	31	36
Gary Dodds	16	7	8	15	16	6	1	7	8	10	30	11	16	27	30
Steve Fullan (I)	9	4	8	12	8	5	4	1	5	16	22	8	19	27	61
Phillip Myers	13	4	7	11	18	5	4	2	6	38	26	9	11	20	84
Kwabina Oppong-Addai	15	4	8	12	117	3	1	1	2	16	23	7	11	18	157
Jan Bestic	15	2	8	10	0	6	3	1	4	6	27	6	10	16	6
Michael Linsley	6	4	6	10	4	-	-	-	-	-	13	5	10	15	8
Paul O'Neill	15	1	11	12	8	5	0	1	1	4	26	1	14	15	20
Gary Organ	15	1	4	5	47	4	1	2	3	2	26	3	8	11	55
Ian Clark	16	1	1	2	8	6	2	3	5	10	30	3	6	9	20
Brian Clark	13	2	5	7	22	6	0	1	1	22	22	2	7	9	46
Steven Clements (N)	16	0	0	0	0	6	3	3	6	2	27	3	3	6	2
Thomas Clark	14	2	1	3	6	6	0	2	2	2	28	2	4	6	8
Sam Mager	12	1	3	4	74	2	0	1	1	6	14	1	4	5	80
Simon Cruickshank	10	1	2	3	4	6	0	2	2	29	18	1	4	5	33
Bradley Beck-Hill	5	3	1	4	25	-	-	-	-	-	7	3	1	4	25
Jamie Hirst	8	0	1	1	2	2	0	0	0	2	13	1	2	3	4
Deavon Clayton	13	0	2	2	8	6	0	0	0	22	26	0	3	3	52
Rob Sheldrake (N)	16	0	1	1	6	6	0	0	0	2	32	0	2	2	10
Dean Birrell	5	0	0	0	24	3	0	0	0	4	12	0	0	0	30
Bench Penalties					8					4					14
TEAM TOTALS	16	103	128	231	469	6	29	37	66	315	30	174	228	402	966
Netminders	GPI	Min	SoG	GA	Sv%	GPI	Min	SoG	GA	Sv%	GPI	Min	SoG	GA	Sv%
Steven Clements	6	233	130	18	86.1	3	114	67	7	89.5	12	487	284	37	86.9
Rob Sheldrake	14	693	362	38	89.5	5	246	132	21	84.1	25	1259	696	100	85.6
Amy Johnson	-	-	-	-	-	-	-	-	-	-	20	20	13	4	69.2
TEAM TOTALS	16	*926	492	56	88.6	6	360	199	28	85.9	30	1766	993	141	85.8

Also appeared: Alan Graichen (7L), Martin Garwood (4L), Daniel Wright (1L).

* Game against Bracknell Hornets was abandoned.

All Competitions = league, playoffs and Millennium Cup.

ALEXANDRA
PALACE

HOME OF THE
HARINGEY GREYHOUNDS
ICE HOCKEY CLUB
1999/2000 English Division One South Champions

* Ice Skating Sessions Daily *
* Disco Sessions *
* Children's Birthday Parties *
* Adult and Children's Skating
Courses *
* Arcades * Cafeterias *
* Kiddies Kingdom Inflatables *

'NORTH LONDON'S PREMIER ICE SKATING FACILITY'

Alexandra Palace, Alexandra Palace Way,
Wood Green, London N22 7AY
Tel: 020 8365 2121
www.alexandrapalace.com

One goal enough for title

MARTIN BENTLEY

Three years of hard work for coach **Dave Robb** finally came to fruition when Haringey Greyhounds were crowned English League South champions. A one-goal victory over fierce rivals, Basingstoke Buffalo, brought the club the first piece of silverware in their ten-year history.

With former Chelmsford junior, **Tom Clark**, the only addition to the previous year's squad, 'Hounds got off to a slow start with two defeats by Buffalo, their only meaningful rivals.

The season didn't catch fire until Dane **Rasmus Edmund** and Croatian **Zoran Kozic** joined in October. Both had played at a high level in their native countries and they linked with **Kevin Gray** to form the most powerful scoring line in the reformed club's short history.

Though Edmund returned home at Christmas, the team remained inspired with **Victor Somfaleanu** and **Octavian Sersea** providing able support for Kozic and Gray. In the rather truncated division, Greyhounds had two more chances against Buffalo and if they were both wins, 'Hounds would go top.

THRILLING BATTLE

A 6-2 victory at Basingstoke in November brought the aggregate scores level after three meetings, leaving the all-important game to be played on 13 February in Alexandra Palace.

In a thrilling, seesaw battle, a crowd of 1,050 saw Greyhounds trail 3-1 after the first period, then fight back to triumph 8-7, with **Paul O'Neill** scoring the winning goal in a heart-stopping final period. After that, it was just a matter of winning the remaining game at home to Slough which they did comfortably a couple of weeks later.

The playoff programme was almost an anti-climax as Greyhounds breezed through their group to set up a semi-final clash with Whitley Warriors. The Londoners travelled north optimistically but found themselves up against faster, bigger, and considerably more physical opposition. Two bad-tempered encounters resulted in an 18-5 aggregate defeat to bring Haringey's momentous season to an end.

In addition to their league duties, Greyhounds also entered the Millennium Cup, which gave them an opportunity to test themselves against Premier League opposition. With the Kozic-Edmund-Gray line in full flight, they turned in creditable showings against Swindon and Romford, most notably in a controversial 5-4 home defeat by Raiders.

PLAYER AWARDS

Most Valuable Player	Octavian Sersea
Best Forward	Zoran Kozic
Best Goalie	Rob Sheldrake
Most Improved Player	Ian Clark

LEADING PLAYERS

Kevin Gray born 29 April 1968

Lively Glaswegian who has been top British scorer in each of his two seasons as a Greyhound. Joined the club in the summer of 1998 following spells with Chelmsford and Stevenage.

Zoran Kozic born 5 February 1970

The crowd-pleasing forward from Belgrade, who lives and works in London, joined the club in October 1999 and made an immediate impact. His playmaking and goal scoring were one of the chief reasons for Greyhounds' success.

Phil Myers born 26 October 1967

Team captain has been with the club right from the start in 1990, racking up over 200 appearances. Hard-working third line winger who can also take a turn on defence.

FACT FILE 1999-2000

English League Placing: Division One South winners.

Playoffs: Semi-finalists.

Data Vision Millennium Cup: 2nd in group.

CLUB HISTORY

Founded: 1990. (Haringey Racers were Alexandra Palace's senior team in 1990-92).

Leagues: English League 1994-2000; English Conference 1991-94; English Div. Three 1990-91.

Honours: English Div. One South 1999-2000.

HULL THUNDER

PLAYER	BRITISH NATIONAL LEAGUE					PLAYOFFS					ALL COMPETITIONS				
Scorers	GP	G	A	Pts	Pim	GP	G	A	Pts	Pim	GP	G	A	Pts	Pim
Ron Shudra (I)	35	18	32	50	26	6	2	6	8	2	53	26	46	72	34
Slava Koulikov	31	21	25	46	10	-	-	-	-	-	42	25	38	63	22
Anthony Johnson	26	13	22	35	40	6	4	6	10	10	34	19	28	47	52
Jason Tatarnic (I)	25	10	17	27	66	6	2	3	5	16	43	17	30	47	118
Steve Brown	35	8	24	32	41	6	3	3	6	14	53	16	30	46	61
Stephen Johnson	34	7	19	26	60	6	1	4	5	8	50	11	30	41	78
Scott Stephenson (I) 3	22	5	21	26	10	-	-	-	-	-	34	11	28	39	14
Claude Dumas 3	16	16	16	32	16	6	2	4	6	2	22	18	20	38	18
Steve Morden (I)	35	19	9	28	96	6	3	1	4	16	45	22	14	36	112
Kevin Conway 1	13	8	8	16	6	-	-	-	-	-	20	12	16	28	6
Anthony Payne	22	8	9	17	58	5	1	3	4	10	29	10	13	23	68
Tom Watkins 3,6	30	5	8	13	43	6	2	4	6	0	40	7	13	20	43
Daniel Grandqvist (I) 3	10	2	8	10	6	6	2	4	6	4	16	4	12	16	10
Esa Nurmi (I)	10	1	3	4	10	-	-	-	-	-	20	4	11	15	12
Mark Pallister 5	13	1	5	6	22	-	-	-	-	-	23	3	8	11	44
Mark Florence	36	5	3	8	12	6	1	0	1	4	54	7	3	10	22
Ian Defty	29	0	9	9	16	6	0	1	1	8	47	0	10	10	28
Paul Thompson	12	0	5	5	8	-	-	-	-	-	22	2	7	9	26
Norman Pinnington 4	4	1	6	7	0	-	-	-	-	-	5	2	6	8	0
Chris Kelland	6	0	4	4	10	6	0	3	3	22	12	0	7	7	32
Simon Greaves	35	1	2	3	12	6	0	2	2	0	53	2	4	6	16
Dan Carney (I)	4	0	2	2	0	-	-	-	-	-	4	0	2	2	0
Matt Street	2	0	0	0	0	-	-	-	-	-	6	1	0	1	0
Colum Cavilla (I) (N)	17	0	1	1	6	-	-	-	-	-	19	0	1	1	6
Pasi Raitanen (N) 2,3	18	0	1	1	0	-	-	-	-	-	28	0	1	1	2
Karl Hopper	6	0	0	0	4	-	-	-	-	-	6	0	0	0	4
Chris Hobson	10	0	0	0	0	-	-	-	-	-	19	0	0	0	14
Chris Bailey	20	0	0	0	24	-	-	-	-	-	32	0	0	0	28
Bench Penalties					16					0					18
TEAM TOTALS	36	149	259	408	618	6	23	44	67	116	54	219	378	597	888

Netminders	GPI	Min	SoG	GA	Sv%	GPI	Min	SoG	GA	Sv%	GPI	Min	SoG	GA	Sv%
Colum Cavilla (I)	17	1005	547	38	93.1	-	-	-	-	-	19	1125	611	45	92.6
Gavin Armstrong 4, 6	-	-	-	-	-	6	352	193	20	89.6	6	352	193	20	89.6
Pasi Raitanen 2, 3	14	795	467	60	87.1	-	-	-	-	-	22	1279	711	87	87.8
Chris Douglas	9	375	193	34	82.4	1	12	5	1	80.0	12	507	253	38	85.0
Empty Net Goals			0	0				1	1				1	1	
TEAM TOTALS	36	2175	1207	132	89.1	6	365	6	22	89.0	54	3263	1769	191	89.2

Also appeared: Bobby McEwan 14, Andy Steel 4, Darren Blades, Paul Wallace 1.
Also played for: 1 Chelmsford Chieftains, 2 Ayr Scottish Eagles, 3 Peterborough Pirates,
4 Milton Keynes Kings, 5 Solihull Blaze, 6 Telford Timberwolves.
Shutouts: Cavilla - league: 23 Jan at Edinburgh Capitals (31 saves), 29 Jan at Slough Jets
(17 saves), 26 Feb at Basingstoke Bison (34 saves).

All Competitions = league, playoffs, B&H Cup/Plate and ntl: Christmas Cup.

A game of one period

CATHY WIGHAM

If football's a game of two halves and ice hockey's a game of three periods, what were Hull Thunder's efforts in 1999-2000?

About half a game.

Maybe that's harsh considering that the Hull club had two new owners after the debt-ridden Kingston Hawks collapsed in February 1999.

As usual, close season hopes sprang eternal with newly arrived Basingstoke coach **Don Depoe** building what was billed as a title contending squad.

Unfortunately, wannabe league winners need continuity and cash, something that rarely emerged from the magic roundabout of personnel changes and mid-season financial problems.

After an optimistic *B&H* Cup group start, Thunder twice lost narrowly to Bison in the Challenge Round, blew a four-goal first leg lead to Slough in the Plate and then struggled for league consistency.

Inside five weeks Finn **Esa Nurmi** quit over a contractual dispute, **Chris Hobson** left for the Jets, a shoulder injury ruled out leading scorer **Jason Tatarnic** until Christmas, and **Mark Pallister** and **Kevin Conway** were released 'in the long term interests of the club'.

Telford's pre-season pullout, the *B&H* defeats which cost Thunder extra home gates, and Ice Hockey UK's failure to provide officials for a home game which clashed with GB's Sheffield internationals, combined to put the club on the brink.

They were rescued in December by Sheffield Steelers' owner, **Darren Brown**, whose financial clout ushered in the season's second period.

This produced more personnel changes, led by the replacement of goalie **Pasi Raitanen** with **Colum Cavilla** from Superleague Manchester and the signing of the high scoring **Claude Dumas** from Peterborough.

This did the trick as Thunder beat every team to finish fourth, picking up 30 points from their last 18 games, after managing only 17 from their opening 18.

The playoff semis beckoned, right? Wrong. Just as Cavilla's arrival had sparked the victory streak, his sudden departure for the Calgary police wrecked Thunder's playoff dreams and they bowed out at the group stages.

It was a devastating third period.

PLAYER AWARDS

Player of the Year	**Ron Shudra**
Best Forward	**Jason Tatarnic**
Best Defenceman	**Ron Shudra**
Most Improved Player	**Tom Watkins**
Spirit of the Game	**Ron Shudra**

LEADING PLAYERS

Steve Brown *born 31 March 1965*

No fuss, no frills and still one of the best defenders in the league. He played consistently game in, game out and was the cornerstone of the Thunder's often under-manned blueline.

Colum Cavilla *born 7 November 1973*

Full marks on the ice. Although regularly outshot, Thunder oozed confidence with match winner Cavilla between the sticks.

But no marks for staying power. He arrived in mid-December and quit after the last league game virtually blowing the club's playoff chances.

Ron Shudra *born 28 November 1967*

'Rocket' Ron impressed fans with his professional approach and ability to buckle down to BNL life after the more rarefied atmosphere of Superleague Sheffield.

FACT FILE 1999-2000

British National League: 4th.

Playoffs: 3rd in group.

Benson and Hedges: First in Cup group; knocked out in first round of Plate.

ntl: **Christmas Cup**: Quarter-finalists.

HISTORY

Founded: February 1999. First club in Hull was Humberside Seahawks 1988-96 (known as Humberside Hawks 1993-96). Second club was Kingston Hawks 1996-99 (briefly Hull City Hawks 1998-99).

Leagues: Kingston - British National Lge 1997-99, Premier Lge 1996-97; Humberside - British Lge, Premier Div. 1991-96, British Lge, Div. One 1989-91, English Lge 1988-89.

Honours: British League, Div. One 1990-91; English League 1988-89.

HULL THUNDER *left to right, back row (standing):* Glen Meier (GM), Jan Musil (doctor), Bobby McEwen, Chris Kelland, Jason Tatarnic, Daniel Grandqvist, Karl Hopper, Simon Greaves, Steve Morden, Claude Dumas, Ian Defty, Tom Watkins, Anthony Payne, Slava Koulikov, Vanessa Brown (physio), Don Depoe (coach); *front row:* Colum Cavilla, Mark Florence, Steve Brown, Anthony Johnson, Ron Shudra, Stephen Johnson, Chris Douglas.

Photo: Arthur Foster.

PLAYER	ENGLISH PREMIER LEAGUE					PLAYOFFS					ALL COMPETITIONS				
Scorers	GP	G	A	Pts	Pim	GP	G	A	Pts	Pim	GP	G	A	Pts	Pim
Mikko Skinnari (I)	24	17	34	51	6	2	0	1	1	0	34	34	44	78	10
Kyle Dolman	23	22	13	35	38	2	1	0	1	0	33	31	23	54	44
Mike Kindred	24	19	17	36	42	2	0	1	1	2	34	23	24	47	56
Elliot Andrews	24	11	17	28	24	2	2	0	2	0	31	16	20	36	30
Sean Clement	21	7	13	20	26	2	0	2	2	4	30	10	24	34	36
Henrik Schonberg (I)	24	7	11	18	18	2	0	0	0	0	33	8	18	26	22
Phil Chard	24	8	9	17	18	2	0	1	1	0	33	12	13	25	34
Ola Wallen (I)	20	4	11	15	49	2	2	1	3	0	29	8	16	24	53
Kevin Parrish	22	3	3	6	18	2	0	0	0	2	32	7	12	19	38
Dave Stevens 3	7	6	9	15	0	2	1	1	2	4	9	7	10	17	4
Mike Dumka (I)	14	1	2	3	42	1	0	0	0	16	23	8	7	15	80
Andy Martin	19	2	4	6	47	2	0	0	0	2	26	4	8	12	51
Shaun McFadyen 1	8	6	3	9	12	-	-	-	-	-	8	6	3	9	12
Phil Donovan	15	1	0	1	32	-	-	-	-	-	23	4	4	8	38
Stephen Howard	2	0	1	1	12	-	-	-	-	-	7	4	3	7	49
Paul Slaughter	21	3	0	3	18	2	0	0	0	0	25	3	0	3	18
Richard Hodge	2	0	0	0	0	-	-	-	-	-	6	0	3	3	0
James Whitehouse	-	-	-	-	-	-	-	-	-	-	1	2	0	2	0
Greg Hales	2	0	0	0	0	-	-	-	-	-	4	0	2	2	0
Andy Gillon (N)	19	0	0	0	31	-	-	-	-	-	27	0	0	0	31
Bench Penalties					26					0					26
TEAM TOTALS	24	117	147	264	465	2	6	7	13	30	34	187	234	421	632
Netminders	GPI	Min	SoG	GA	Sv%	GPI	Min	SoG	GA	Sv%	GPI	Min	SoG	GA	Sv%
Matt van der Velden 2	-	-	-	-	-	2	120	111	14	87.4	2	120	111	14	87.4
Murray Tester (I)	20	1156	699	94	86.5	-	-	-	-	-	26	1485	914	121	86.8
Ian Rowlands	2	66	51	12	76.5	-	-	-	-	-	3	126	85	15	82.3
Andy Gillon	5	218	154	32	79.2	-	-	-	-	-	7	309	177	36	79.7
TEAM TOTALS	24	1440	904	138	84.7	2	120	111	14	87.4	34	1920	1176	172	85.5

Also appeared: Scott Hughes (6L, 2PO); Peter Korff (1L, 1PO).
Also played for: 1 Chelmsford Chieftains, 2 Romford Raiders, 3 Oxford Blades.
All Competitions = league, playoffs and Millennium Cup.

INVICTA DYNAMOS *left to right, back row (standing):* Alf Carle (trainer), Kevin Parrish, Dave Stevens, Kyle Dolman, Ola Wallen, Sean Clements, Henrik Schoberg, Mikko Skinnari, Scott Hughes, Richard Hodge, Mike Dumka, Phil Donovan; *front row:* Murray Tester, Andy Martin, Mike Kindred, Elliot Andrews, Phil Chard, Paul Slaughter, Andy Gillon.

Photo: Lorraine Hodge.

Inconsistent

ANDY BRADLEY

This was a frustrating season for Invicta Dynamos and their loyal supporters.

The campaign began with only seven opponents in the English Premier League and this was reduced to a forlorn and inadequate programme when Oxford Blades and Cardiff Rage withdrew in mid-season.

Though Dynamos ended fourth in the final standings - one place higher than the year before - with only five teams remaining in the league, this was also next-to-bottom.

Player-coach **Sean Clement** was in little doubt that a lack of consistency cost his team a higher placing.

"One night we would be a match for anyone - the best team in the league - and on another we would suffer a disappointing defeat," he reflected. "We suffered a poor run of results around Christmas, but I was pleased with our form in the last few months."

A flurry of pre-season activity improved the depth of Invicta's squad with five players added to the roster - **Henrik Schonberg, Ola Wallen, Paul Donovan, Shaun McFadyen** and Canadian netminder, **Murray Tester**.

CASH INJECTION

A subsequent injection of cash following a sponsorship deal with double-glazing company, *Supreme-O-Glaze*, boosted the club's budget and provided the funds to acquire **Dave Stevens** from Oxford.

Early results were mixed but three particular matches in October gave an indication of what Invicta could do at their best. These encounters featured an exciting 5-5 draw with league leaders, Chelmsford, a 7-2 victory at Romford (the first of three road wins for the Dynamos over the Essex club) and a 9-3 home triumph over the Isle of Wight.

From an early stage it was obvious that Chelmsford were on course for the title, with the Isle of Wight holding off the challenge of Swindon and Invicta for the runners-up spot.

Dynamos suffered a major blow when netminder Tester sustained a season-ending injury and they were unable to clamber higher than fourth.

The governing EIHA permitted the club to borrow Romford goalie **Matthew van der Velden** for the playoffs, but this wasn't enough to prevent their elimination by the league-winning Chieftains in the playoff semi-finals.

PLAYER AWARDS

Players' Player	Kyle Dolman
Supporters' Player	Murray Tester
Best Forward	Mikko Skinnari
Best Defenceman	Sean Clement
110 Per Cent Player	Kyle Dolman
Clubman of the Year	Sean Clement

LEADING PLAYERS

Sean Clement born 26 February 1966

Vastly experienced and cool Canadian defenceman who returned to the Ice Bowl from Slough in 1998. Only missed a few games after being appointed player-coach.

Mikko Skinnari born 14 September 1975

Slightly built finisher with good hands and the ability to score from unlikely angles. In his second season in Gillingham, the Finn was the league's leading points scorer.

Murray Tester born 23 June 1978

Young Canadian netminder who faced a baptism of fire on his debut in this country. Played in two-thirds of Dynamos' games and excelled in most of them.

FACT FILE 1999-2000

English League: 4th in Premier Division.
Playoffs: Semi-finalists.
Data Vision Millennium Cup: 3rd in group.

CLUB HISTORY

Founded: 1997. Club known as Medway Bears 1984-97.
Leagues: English League (Premier Div.) 1997-2000, 1991-92 & 1984-86; Premier League 1996-97; British League, Div. One 1986-91 and 1992-96.
Honours: English League & (promotion) playoffs 1991-92; British League, Div. Two 1985-86.

ISLE OF WIGHT RAIDERS

PLAYER	ENGLISH PREMIER LEAGUE					PLAYOFFS					ALL COMPETITIONS				
Scorers	GP	G	A	Pts	Pim	GP	G	A	Pts	Pim	GP	G	A	Pts	Pim
Luc Chabot	23	20	22	42	24	2	0	0	0	0	33	31	54	85	24
Johan Larsson (I)	22	28	18	46	140	2	0	0	0	2	30	39	25	64	170
Peter Nyman (I)	19	4	33	37	29	1	0	0	0	0	26	8	48	56	31
Jani Saartama (I)	23	21	11	32	96	2	1	0	1	0	32	35	17	52	102
Andy Pickles	23	5	17	22	36	2	0	0	0	0	33	15	29	44	40
Richard Hargreaves	23	8	9	17	73	2	2	0	2	0	33	23	20	43	77
Andreas Ost (I)	24	14	8	22	22	2	0	0	0	0	32	20	20	40	22
Chad Brandimore (I)	12	16	20	36	16	2	0	1	1	22	14	16	21	37	38
Scott Carter	21	3	12	15	43	2	0	1	1	0	31	10	27	37	49
Joachim Johnsson	21	8	9	17	18	2	0	0	0	0	30	12	14	26	32
Tony Blaize	24	3	6	9	58	2	0	0	0	0	33	10	11	21	91
Johan Jonsson (I)	18	2	3	5	70	2	0	0	0	0	28	9	10	19	70
Bobby Brown 1	12	1	7	8	107	-	-	-	-	-	18	4	11	15	113
Daniel Giden	21	0	0	0	0	2	0	0	0	0	31	7	4	11	4
Steve Gannaway	22	1	6	7	20	2	0	1	1	2	32	2	9	11	22
Paul Sanderson	13	0	0	0	4	-	-	-	-	-	20	5	5	10	4
Michael Hargreaves	24	0	1	1	20	2	0	0	0	0	34	3	6	9	45
Jason Coles	2	6	2	8	0	-	-	-	-	-	2	6	2	8	0
Andy Johnston	14	1	1	2	0	2	0	0	0	0	24	3	5	8	0
Sean Kelso (I)	7	0	1	1	32	2	0	2	2	6	9	0	3	3	38
Craig Wynn (N)	24	0	3	3	6	2	0	0	0	2	34	0	3	3	8
Damon Larter	-	-	-	-	-	-	-	-	-	-	1	1	1	2	0
Norman Pinnington	8	0	1	1	28	2	1	0	1	10	10	1	1	2	38
Steve Slater	3	0	1	1	20	-	-	-	-	-	3	0	1	1	20
Bench Penalties					12					0					24
TEAM TOTALS	24	141	191	332	874	2	4	5	9	44	34	260	347	607	1062
Netminders	GPI	Min	SoG	GA	Sv%	GPI	Min	SoG	GA	Sv%	GPI	Min	SoG	GA	Sv%
Toby Cooley	2	80	54	10	81.5	-	-	-	-	-	6	320	127	13	89.8
Craig Wynn	23	1360	838	91	89.1	2	120	54	8	85.2	29	1720	1043	116	88.9
Empty Net Goals			2	2				-	-				3	3	
TEAM TOTALS	24	1440	894	103	88.5	2	120	54	8	85.2	34	2040	1173	132	88.7

Also appeared: Matt Brennen (3L), Andrew Goddard (2L).
Also played for: 1 Swindon Chill & Sheffield Scimitars.
All Competitions = league, playoffs and Millennium Cup.

Playoffs on different Planet

JOHN HAMON

Raiders finished as runners-up in the English Premier League, a dramatic improvement from seventh a year earlier, but a disastrous playoff run left their huge band of supporters restless.

Raiders were delighted that Finn **Jani Saartama**, was back in the line-up after making a full recovery from a broken wrist. Their leading scorer the previous season, he was in the top five points scorers again at the end of this one.

Also back in the fold was their Canadian skipper, **Scott Carter**, and Swede **Joachim Johnsson**. Raiders signed six Scandinavians in all, almost as many as Superleague's Newcastle.

Last year's player-coach, Swede **Peter Nyman,** decided this time to concentrate on playing and Canadian scoring ace, **Luc Chabot** from Solihull, agreed to take on the dual role. His first signing was Peterborough defender, **Andy Pickles**.

With new owners, Planet Ice, in charge of the team and with sponsorship from the local IOW *County Press* newspaper, hopes were high of a good campaign.

BIG CHIEFS' RIVALRY

After only four league defeats, Raiders were challenging table-topping Chelmsford at Christmas-time. Indeed, Chieftains were the only side to win on the Island in the league.

But after the mid-season break, their form dropped alarmingly. Added to this, they suffered badly from the EIHA's decision to wipe out the results of the collapsed Cardiff and Oxford teams.

Raiders had chalked up nine of their victories against these clubs and the lost points cost them more dearly than it did their biggest rivals, Chelmsford and Swindon.

With so few clubs left, it was inevitable that the Raiders would make the playoffs but controversy surrounded their semi-final clash with Swindon. The Wiltshire side claimed that their ice pad needed work on it, forcing the first leg to be played on the Island.

But it made little difference as Raiders had no answer to Chill's superior play and they suffered a very disappointing 5-1 defeat at the Planet Ice arena. With nothing more than pride to play for in the return, Raiders held on for a 3-3 draw, but it was not enough.

Their overseas contingent was held to one goal and Englishman **Richard Hargreaves**, 21, ended as top scorer with two of their four tallies.

PLAYER AWARDS

Player of the Year/Best Forward	Johan Larsson
Players' Player	Andreas Ost
Best Defenceman	Peter Nyman
Most Improved Player	Richard Hargreaves

LEADING PLAYERS

Scott Carter *born 24 October 1971*

The Canada-born defenceman played with 100 per cent commitment and was always trying to rally his troops.

Andy Pickles *born 9 August 1973*

The much travelled Bournemouth-born defender was almost back at home when he came to the Island from Peterborough. A steadying influence on his new team.

Jani Saartama *born 10 February 1977*

Back for his second season, the flying Finn scored over 50 points in all competitions to finish in the club's top five scorers.

FACT FILE 1999-2000

English League: 2nd in Premier Division.
Playoffs: Semi-finalists.
***Data Vision* Millennium Cup**: 2nd in group.

CLUB HISTORY

Founded: 1999. Club founded in 1991 as Solent Vikings, known as *Wightlink* Raiders 1992-99.
Leagues: English League 1991-2000.
Honours: English League winners 1993-97.

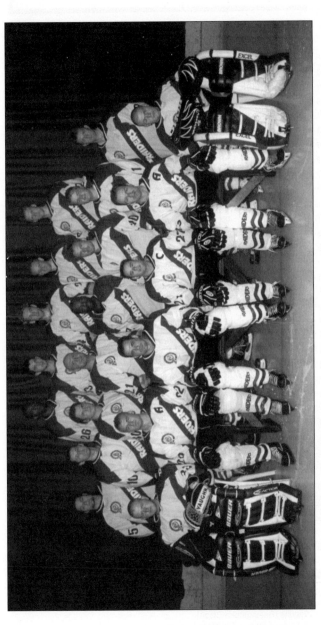

ISLE OF WIGHT RAIDERS *left to right, back row:* Tony Blaize, Michael Hargreaves, Richard Hargreaves, Andy Johnston, Johan Jonsson; *middle row:* Johan Larsson, Paul Sanderson, Jani Saartama, Peter Nyman, Bobby Brown, Andreas Ost, Daniel Giden, Steve Gannaway; *front row:* Craig Wynn, Andy Pickles, Luc Chabot, Scott Carter, Jo Johnsson, Toby Cooley.

LONDON KNIGHTS

PLAYER	SEKONDA SUPERLEAGUE					SEKONDA PLAYOFFS					ALL COMPETITIONS				
Scorers	GP	G	A	Pts	Pim	GP	G	A	Pts	Pim	GP	G	A	Pts	Pim
Claudio Scremin	40	7	26	33	18	8	3	8	11	6	60	14	44	58	32
Rob Kenny	39	17	23	40	63	-	-	-	-	-	50	26	29	55	79
Mark Bultje	39	7	20	27	66	8	5	6	11	6	56	14	31	45	74
Jeff Hoad	41	16	18	34	28	8	2	3	5	12	61	19	25	44	58
Todd Wetzel	33	11	11	22	22	8	4	4	8	12	52	20	19	39	46
John Byce (WP)	29	11	18	29	6	6	1	4	5	4	39	14	25	39	10
Rick Brebant 1	19	9	14	23	32	8	3	8	11	10	28	13	22	35	42
Marc Hussey (WP)	39	6	13	19	58	7	3	6	9	2	57	11	22	33	66
Paul Rushforth	20	5	14	19	48	7	5	2	7	8	34	12	20	32	70
Ryan Duthie 1	21	6	15	21	16	-	-	-	-	-	30	9	18	27	20
Tom Ashe	37	5	11	16	48	8	0	5	5	2	51	5	21	26	62
Neal Martin	39	6	10	16	24	8	3	2	5	0	54	9	13	22	24
Greg Burke	39	5	9	14	72	8	1	2	3	4	59	7	13	20	92
Tim Murray (WP)	40	1	10	11	26	8	0	3	3	2	60	2	17	19	34
Darren Banks (WP)	23	8	2	10	101	-	-	-	-	-	26	8	4	12	117
Mike Ware	26	6	2	8	90	8	0	1	1	8	44	8	4	12	162
Andy Bezeau (WP)	11	1	5	6	44	8	2	2	4	29	20	3	8	11	102
Jeff Johnstone 1	7	2	2	4	2	-	-	-	-	-	11	4	4	8	4
Ian Cooper 2	18	3	4	7	51	-	-	-	-	-	26	3	5	8	53
Brent Cullaton (WP)	4	1	1	2	2	-	-	-	-	-	10	4	3	7	8
Barry Nieckar (WP)	18	2	0	2	143	8	2	2	4	10	27	4	3	7	153
Shawn Wansborough	11	0	2	2	57	5	3	2	5	2	17	3	4	7	59
Scott Campbell 1	10	0	2	2	18	-	-	-	-	-	19	1	2	3	30
Jens Nordin	-	-	-	-	-	-	-	-	-	-	5	0	2	2	6
Trevor Robins (N) (WP)	26	0	1	1	2	7	0	1	1	0	44	0	2	2	4
Mark Cavallin (N)	21	0	1	1	2	1	0	0	0	0	24	0	1	1	2
Guy Leveque	-	-	-	-	-	-	-	-	-	-	1	0	0	0	2
Greg Smyth	9	0	0	0	42	-	-	-	-	-	9	0	0	0	42
Bench Penalties					26					2					44
TEAM TOTALS	42	135	234	369	1107	8	37	61	98	119	62	213	361	574	1497

Netminders	GPI	Min	SoG	GA	Sv%	GPI	Min	SoG	GA	Sv%	GPI	Min	SoG	GA	Sv%
Mark Cavallin	21	1117	511	47	90.8	1	60	27	5	81.5	24	1285	586	57	90.3
Trevor Robins (WP)	26	1451	711	77	89.2	7	443	183	13	92.9	44	2516	1178	116	90.2
Empty Net Goals			1	1				0	0				1	1	
TEAM TOTALS	42	2568	1223	125	89.8	8	503	210	18	91.4	62	3801	1765	174	90.1

Back-up Netminders   Gavin Armstrong (Milton Keynes Kings),
Craig Lindsay (Peterborough Pirates), Simon Smith (Chelmsford Chieftains),
Joe Watkins (Basingstoke Bison).

Also played for:
Shutouts: 1 Manchester Storm, 2 Guildford Flames.
Robins - cup: 11 Sept at Sheffield Steelers (28 saves); league: 10 Oct at Ayr
Scottish Eagles (26 saves), 6 Feb v Ayr Scottish Eagles (19 saves).

All Competitions = Superleague, Playoffs, Challenge Cup and Benson and Hedges Cup.

LONDON KNIGHTS *left to right, back row:* Rick Brebant, Jeff Hoad, Andy Bezeau, Mark Bultje, Liam Mellor (equipment); *middle row:* Neal Martin, Greg Burke, Tim Murray, Marc Hussey, Mike Ware, Barry Nieckar, Shawn Wansborough, Todd Wetzel, Tom Ashe; *front row:* Trevor Robins, John Byce, Rob Kenny, Chris McSorley (GM/coach), Scott Rex (asst. coach), Claudio Scremin, Paul Rushforth, Mark Cavallin.

Slap Shot-on-Thames

STEWART ROBERTS

Knights won their first major trophy, reached the final of a second and the semi-finals of a third. In only their second season, they challenged for league honours all year long, only to finish fourth, just two points out of the runners-up spot.

They brought in charismatic coach, **Chris McSorley**, who recruited a roster studded with guys whose 'Slap Shot' antics could fill pages of the *Police Gazette*. Yet still the crowds failed to come and watch Superleague's 'flagship' team.

Only two Saturday games was one problem, scoring goals was another. Knights hit the target less often than any other team bar the last place Newcastle Riverkings, and on some nights the hockey should have been sponsored by *Horlicks*.

McSorley's late appointment contributed to this as the Las Vegas-based Canadian had little time to put together a team - goalie **Mark Cavallin** was the only returnee - to suit the unique style of British hockey: European sized rinks and North American style play.

But the intense coach signed up a team of winners. That's his trademark.

First was the *B&H* Cup. After a shaky 2-2-2 start and a 1-0 shutout at home by Ayr, Knights won their next three games to reach the final against reigning league champs, Manchester Storm. Though it was his first British final, McSorley was mortified at losing to his old adversary, **Kurt Kleinendorst**, even though it took a shoot-out to settle matters.

He took small but swift revenge by signing Storm's **Rick Brebant**, scorer of the winning penalty shot. The feisty forward went on to tally 13 goals in 28 games with Knights, the second best scoring percentage on the squad.

There was a catch, though. **Ryan Duthie**, Knights' top marksman at the time, went to Storm after falling out with his coach.

The league title was lost in a wild game at bitter rivals, Bracknell Bees, on 27 February. Worse still, their best player, **Rob Kenny**, was struck in the face by a team-mate's shot which injured him so badly he was out for the rest of the season.

McSorley had brashly forecast on the eve of the *B&H* final that Knights would win all four trophies. Knocked out of the Challenge Cup by the surprising Nottingham Panthers, there was only the Playoffs left now.

The league's most penalised team cleaned up their act in the post-season, losing only their opening game - to Bees - and when they reached the final they comfortably overcame the amazing Riverkings to capture their first ever silverware.

Controversial stick measurements, stolen Plexiglas supports, the sacking of the team's one Brit, **Ian Cooper**, who was on 999 major league

points at the time. Special 'Wind-up **Paxton Schulte** Nights', big leads chucked away, injuries galore with **Jeff Hoad** the Iron Man, playing in 61 of Knights' 62 games.

All great stories, but we've only room to give you the briefest of highlights. Like most of the capital's media, sadly.

PLAYER AWARDS

Most Valuable Player	**Neal Martin**
Players' Player	**Rob Kenny**
Best Defenceman	**Claudio Scremin**
Unsung Hero	**Jeff Hoad**

LEADING PLAYERS

Rob Kenny *born 19 October 1968*

No one there will forget the scene when the New York Irishman from the Bronx skated calmly off the Bracknell ice despite having his face caved in by a booming slapshot.

A NY Rangers' draft pick, captain Kenny epitomised Knights' fighting spirit and might have been their leading scorer except for this injury.

Neal Martin *born 8 September 1975*

Blueliner who went about his task with little fuss but great effectiveness. Member of the 1992-93 Sault Ste Marie Greyhounds when they won the Canadian junior championship.

Claudio Scremin *born 28 May 1968*

The former San Jose Shark was one of the smoothest and cleverest Canadian defencemen to grace these shores in recent times. Tough, too, as he competed in the Playoff final with a badly bruised leg and stopped a puck with his head.

FACT FILE 1999-2000

Sekonda Superleague: 4th.
Sekonda Playoffs: Winners.
Benson and Hedges Cup: Finalists.
Challenge Cup: Semi-finalists.

FRANCHISE HISTORY

Founded: 1998.
League: Superleague 1998-2000.
Honours: Superleague Playoffs 1999-2000.

MANCHESTER STORM

PLAYER	SEKONDA SUPERLEAGUE					SEKONDA PLAYOFFS					ALL COMPETITIONS				
Scorers	GP	G	A	Pts	Pim	GP	G	A	Pts	Pim	GP	G	A	Pts	Pim
Jeff Jablonski (WP)	42	24	9	33	38	6	0	2	2	2	59	32	17	49	44
Jeff Tomlinson	37	5	30	35	41	2	0	0	0	2	50	9	33	42	45
Mike Harding	42	9	17	26	34	6	1	0	1	6	59	16	22	38	44
Norm Krumpschmid	40	11	13	24	56	6	0	4	4	2	57	14	22	36	66
Dave Livingston	42	6	20	26	24	6	1	2	3	12	59	9	26	35	48
Blair Scott	40	10	15	25	76	6	1	1	2	2	57	13	21	34	100
Rick Brebant 1	18	8	12	20	20	-	-	-	-	-	29	11	23	34	30
Pierre Allard	42	8	14	22	14	6	1	2	3	4	59	12	21	33	20
Kelly Askew (WP)	38	16	12	28	16	6	2	0	2	2	49	18	13	31	20
Kevin Hoffman (WP)	39	7	16	23	18	6	2	1	3	4	53	9	19	28	24
Kris Miller (WP)	39	7	9	16	26	6	1	2	3	8	56	8	20	28	44
Jeff Johnstone 1	30	7	18	25	12	6	1	0	1	12	37	8	19	27	24
Darren Hurley 3	21	7	9	16	20	-	-	-	-	-	32	13	12	25	32
Ryan Duthie 1	20	4	15	19	14	6	1	4	5	6	26	5	19	24	20
Mike Morin	42	9	8	17	20	6	0	0	0	4	59	12	10	22	26
Alexei Lozhkin (WP)	17	6	11	17	2	6	0	3	3	6	23	6	14	20	8
Troy Neumeier (WP)	8	0	2	2	2	-	-	-	-	-	18	2	8	10	12
Greg Gatto 2	11	2	1	3	16	-	-	-	-	-	21	4	5	9	53
Rob Robinson (WP)	41	1	6	7	36	5	0	1	1	0	57	1	8	9	38
Jonathan Weaver	7	2	3	5	0	-	-	-	-	-	11	3	3	6	0
Sami Wahlsten 5	19	2	3	5	6	-	-	-	-	-	20	2	4	6	8
Arttu Kayhko	15	1	4	5	2	6	1	0	1	0	21	2	4	6	2
Scott Campbell 1	21	2	2	4	57	-	-	-	-	-	22	2	3	5	59
Kevin Pozzo 4	10	1	2	3	8	-	-	-	-	-	11	1	2	3	10
Frank Pietrangelo (N)	19	0	0	0	12	-	-	-	-	-	28	0	2	2	12
Sami Siltavirta	10	0	1	1	2	5	0	0	0	0	15	0	1	1	2
Mark Bernard (N)	30	0	1	1	8	6	0	0	0	0	38	0	1	1	8
Bench Penalties					8					8					22
TEAM TOTALS	42	155	253	408	588	6	12	22	34	80	59	212	352	564	821

Netminders	GPI	Min	SoG	GA	Sv%	GPI	Min	SoG	GA	Sv%	GPI	Min	SoG	GA	Sv%
Mark Bernard	30	1635	802	75	90.6	6	389	226	16	92.9	38	2144	1077	99	90.8
Frank Pietrangelo	19	910	439	59	86.6	-	-	-	-	-	28	1465	672	77	88.5
Empty Net Goals			4	4				0	0				4	4	
TEAM TOTALS	42	2545	1245	138	88.9	6	389	226	16	92.9	59	3609	1753	180	89.7

Back-up Netminders: Chris Main (Altrincham Aces), Colin Downie (Blackburn Hawks).
Also played for: 1 London Knights, 2 Basingstoke Bison, 3 Cardiff Devils, 4 Ayr Scottish Eagles, 5 Newcastle Riverkings.
Shutouts: Pietrangelo - cup: 29 Oct v Cardiff Devils (23 saves), 30 Oct at Cardiff Devils (27 saves).
Bernard - league: 2 Oct at Nottingham Panthers (31 saves), 3 Mar v Newcastle Riverkings (25 saves).

All Competitions = Superleague, Playoffs and Benson and Hedges *Cup.*

Kurtain comes down

PETER COLLINS

Dreams of retaining the Superleague title evaporated as injury and discontent broke up the Storm and indirectly led to the end of an era.

Losing the influential **Dave Morrison** and **Brad Rubachuk** was always going to be hard, and although London Knights **Greg Gatto** and **Mike Harding**, along with netminder **Mark Bernard** from Bracknell and **Dave Livingston** and **Norm Krumpschmid** from Austria were drafted in, things just weren't the same.

The campaign started well with the team breezing through the *B&H* qualifying round 5-1-0, and their indifferent start to both Superleague and the EHL being more than compensated for by reaching the *B&H* final.

Sheffield were dumped out of the Cup quarters 9-8 by a Darren Hurley hat-trick in the second leg after the first leg had ended 6-6. Then against Cardiff in the semis, netminder Frankie Pietrangelo recorded back-to-back shutouts (4-0 home and 0-0 away) to set up a mouth-watering clash with London in the final.

BEGINNING OF THE END

The rest of the league knew the roof was leaking in the Storm Shelter when coach Kleinendorst dropped his first choice netminder Pietrangelo at the end of January.

In their first game with Bernard replacing Frankie, Storm crashed 10-2 at Bracknell, one of their worst ever defeats.

The strangest thing, though, was KK's decision to go to Nottingham and watch the Panthers, saying he feared his dislike of the Bracknell rink might rub off on his players. It was an awkward night for his deputy, **Daryl Lipsey.**

Kleinendorst returned home to North America at the end of the season after three years at the helm.

And what a game it was. Tied 3-3 after overtime, and with only **Rick Brebant** netting from the first eight shooters, it was up to Pietrangelo to stop the Knights' fifth shot for victory. He didn't disappoint and the club claimed its first ever knock-out trophy.

But it was to prove the highlight of the campaign. From January to the season's end Storm were probably the best team in Superleague, but their inability to beat either eventual winners, Bracknell (going 1-5-0 and suffering a humiliating 10-2 defeat in their final meeting) or London (until the very last game) proved decisive.

Losing captain **Troy Neumeier** to injury early on and then every other defencemen at one time or another affected the team badly. Pietrangelo's knee injury was covered by the excellent form of back-up Bernard, but **Jonathan Weaver** left to try his luck in North America.

With Gatto already shown the door, Brebant announced at Christmas he wanted out and was traded to London for **Ryan Duthie**. Hurley and **Sami Wahlsten** were both gassed while defenceman **Kevin Pozzo** was binned for disciplinary reasons.

Scott Campbell and **Jeff Johnstone** along with Finnish defensive duo, **Arttu Kayhko** and **Sami Siltavirta**, and the impressive Belorussian forward, **Alexei Lozhkin**, were drafted in. But the damage had already been done.

PLAYER AWARDS

Player of the Year	Mark Bernard
Players' Player	Mark Bernard
Best Defenceman	Blair Scott
Best Forward	Pierre Allard
Road player	Pierre Allard
Unsung hero	Mike Morin

LEADING PLAYERS

Pierre Allard *born 19 August 1972*
A pain to play against with his intense work rate and aggression, Montreal-born 'Frenchie' was always popping up to net the important goals.

Mark Bernard *born 1 February 1969*
A starting netminder at any other club, 'Barnyard' stepped up when it mattered and emerged as the fans' favourite with his acrobatic approach to his job.

Mike Morin *born 20 July 1971*
The 'play-anywhere' guy every team needs. A winger, he played every out-field position and will surely pop up in goal before too long. A true unsung hero.

FACT FILE 1999-2000

Sekonda **Superleague**: 3rd.
Sekonda **Playoffs**: Quarter-finalists.
Benson and Hedges **Cup**: Winners.

FRANCHISE HISTORY

Founded: 1995.
Leagues: Superleague 1996-2000; British League, Div. One 1995-96.
Honours: *Benson and Hedges* Cup winners 1999-2000; Superleague champions 1998-99, British League Division One champions 1995-96.

MANCHESTER STORM *left to right, back row:* Julia Trevor (physio.), Jeff Jablonski, Jeff Johnstone, Sami Siltavirta, Blair Scott, Rob Robinson, Arttu Kayhko, Mike Harding, Kris Miller, Mike Morin, Scott Campbell, Kevin Hoffman, John Crawley (equipment); *front row:* Frank Pietrangelo, Norm Krumpschmid, Dave Livingston, Alexei Lozhkin, Kurt Kleinendorst (GM/coach), Jeff Tomlinson, Daryl Lipsey (asst manager/coach), Pierre Allard, Ryan Duthie, Kelly Askew, Mark Bernard.
Photo: Kevin Bailey

MILTON KEYNES KINGS

PLAYER	BRITISH NATIONAL LEAGUE					ALL COMPETITIONS				
Scorers	GP	G	A	Pts	Pim	GP	G	A	Pts	Pim
Nick Poole	36	18	28	46	53	48	24	42	66	55
Derek Higdon	36	25	17	42	22	47	31	25	56	28
Dan Prachar	36	14	14	28	26	48	16	18	34	30
Rob Coutts	36	4	24	28	40	48	6	25	31	54
Gary D Clarke 2	17	15	8	23	10	23	17	13	30	14
Greg Randall	35	10	10	20	14	48	15	12	27	18
Marc Twaite	21	10	7	17	45	27	14	8	22	55
Justin Bekkering (I)	35	0	11	11	112	47	2	14	16	130
Dean Campbell	35	4	7	11	4	47	6	7	13	8
Norman Pinnington 4	12	2	3	5	24	20	3	6	9	98
Mark Mackie	18	2	5	7	10	24	2	7	9	12
Lee Cowmeadow 2	18	0	8	8	10	22	1	8	9	14
Mike Galati (I) 1, 6	12	4	3	7	12	12	4	3	7	12
Brian Mason 3	7	0	4	4	6	13	1	5	6	10
James Morgan 5	17	1	5	6	57	19	1	5	6	63
Mark Hazlehurst 6	29	0	3	3	109	34	1	4	5	129
Michael Wales	27	2	1	3	10	32	2	2	4	10
Simon Ferry	10	1	3	4	14	10	1	3	4	14
Ross Mackintosh 5	18	1	1	2	10	24	1	2	3	10
Michael Knights 3	7	0	2	2	6	13	0	2	2	41
Steve Howard (I)	6	1	0	1	10	6	1	0	1	10
Dan Markham	23	0	1	1	6	34	0	1	1	10
Gavin Armstrong (N) 4, 6	30	0	1	1	2	36	0	1	1	2
Bench Penalties					6					8
TEAM TOTALS	36	114	166	280	618	48	149	213	362	835
Netminders	GPI	Min	SoG	GA	Sv%	GPI	Min	SoG	GA	Sv%
Chad McLeod (I)	2	125	87	11	87.4	8	485	290	35	87.9
Gavin Armstrong 4, 6	29	1711	1060	154	85.5	35	2076	1263	178	85.9
Stuart Spells	7	332	181	36	80.1	7	332	181	36	80.1
Empty Net Goals			1	1				1	1	
TEAM TOTALS	36	2168	1329	202	84.8	48	2893	1735	250	85.6

Also appeared: Mark Krater 8; Jason Earl, Allan Sutton 5; Adam Todd,
Ben Williams 3; Leigh Jamieson, Paul Jamieson, Darren Elliott,
Kieron Goody, Colin Pritchard, Paul Sample 2; Ryan Blackwood,
Mark Conway, Lee Featherstone, Latham French, Lee Gadseer,
Richard Munnelly, Paul Price, Rob Rausa, Elliott Wade, Matt Woollard (N) 1.

Also played for: 1 Paisley Pirates, 2 Guildford Flames, 3 Basingstoke Bison, 4 Hull Thunder,
5 Peterborough Pirates, 6 Telford Timberwolves.

All Competitions = league, B&H *Cup/Plate and* ntl: *Christmas Cup.*

MILTON KEYNES KINGS *left to right, back row:* Pete Nolan *(physio)*, Marc Twaite, Dean Campbell, Michael Wales, Simon Ferry, Justin Bekkering, Mike Galati, Greg Randall, Gary Clarke, Dan Markham, Mark Hazlehurst; *front row:* Gavin Armstrong, Nick Poole, Rob Coutts, Derek Higdon, Dan Prachar, Stuart Spells.

Photo: Perry Sports Photography.

Kings for a month

PAUL BROOKMAN

What looked like being an 'annus horribilis' - to borrow an aptly royal expression - turned into an 'annus optimisticus' a month from the end of the season.

In the second year following their rebirth, Kings moved up from the English League to the British National League. For much of the time it looked like a leap too far, despite coach **Mark Mackie** assembling a squad with plenty of BNL experience.

But it took until the eve of the season before he recruited former Chelmsford Chieftain netminder, **Chad MacLeod**, and then the dual national lasted just a month before he asked to be released. Luckily for Kings, former MK favourite **Gavin Armstrong** became available after the demise of Telford Timberwolves.

Telford were the only team Kings defeated in a poor *Benson and Hedges* group campaign and this was followed by a dismal start to the league. Only two points from the first 13 games - both from overtime losses - told the tale and it wasn't until mid-November that Kings won for the first time, beating old rivals Solihull Blaze 4-3.

> Kings signed a two-year deal worth 'tens of thousands of pounds' *with Pharmacia & Upjohn*, the 12th largest pharmaceutical company in Britain whose UK headquarters is in Milton Keynes.
> *Powerplay*

By then Mackie had axed the talented **Michael Knights**, veteran captain **Brian Mason** and giant Canadian **Steve Howard**. In their place came youngsters **James Morgan** and **Paul Sample**, plus ex-Fife Flyer, **Lee Cowmeadow**.

Sample lasted less than a fortnight before returning to Canada while Cowmeadow was dismissed by the club in November for failing to inform them of a drink-driving charge, an allegation of which he was subsequently cleared.

Rob Coutts took over as captain in the first step of what was to be a meteoric rise up the ranks. There was more hope for Kings when they reached the semi-finals of the *ntl:* Christmas Cup, but they lost to Fife.

Back in the league the poor form continued with only two wins in 26 matches. Mackie resigned and Coutts, who had been appointed assistant two weeks before, took over.

The transformation was almost immediate. Kings won three of their last ten games and lost five more by a single goal, finishing the season with their first maximum point weekend which lifted them off the bottom of the table.

PLAYER AWARDS

Players' Player	Derek Higdon/ Nick Poole
Most Valuable Player	Gavin Armstrong
Best Defenceman	Justin Bekkering
Coach's Award	Dean Campbell
Clubman of the Year	Rob Coutts
Most Improved Player	Dan Markham

LEADING PLAYERS

Rob Coutts *born 18 March 1967*

Kings' most reliable defenceman really began to shine on and off the ice once he took over as captain and was then promoted to player-coach.

Derek Higdon *born 11 August 1966*

He brought a wealth of experience when he joined Kings after five years with Slough Jets. With Poole, he finished the season as assistant coach to Coutts.

Nick Poole *born 11 July 1973*

The team's top scorer joined Kings from Superleague's London Knights. Always popular with the fans, he doubled up his playing role with that of director of junior development.

FACT FILE 1999-2000

British National League: 9th.
Playoffs: Did not qualify.
Benson and Hedges Cup: 3rd in group.
ntl: Christmas Cup: Semi-finalists.

HISTORY

Founded: 1990. Rink closed 1996-98.
Leagues: British National League 1999-2000; English League (Premier Div) 1998-99, 1990-91; British League, Premier Div 1994-96; British League, Div One 1991-94.
Honours: English Cup 1998-99; British League, Div. One 1993-94.

NEWCASTLE RIVERKINGS

PLAYER	SEKONDA SUPERLEAGUE					SEKONDA PLAYOFFS					ALL COMPETITIONS				
Scorers	GP	G	A	Pts	Pim	GP	G	A	Pts	Pim	GP	G	A	Pts	Pim
Mikko Koivunoro	40	13	39	52	46	7	1	5	6	4	55	17	49	66	52
Iiro Jarvi	41	14	28	42	51	8	2	2	4	4	51	16	31	47	55
Kim Ahlroos	41	14	18	32	4	4	0	0	0	2	53	14	25	39	6
Joel Poirier (WP)	38	11	12	23	50	8	4	3	7	6	52	19	16	35	78
Hilton Ruggles	42	12	7	19	34	8	0	5	5	8	58	16	14	30	48
Glen Mulvenna	38	8	7	15	10	8	2	1	3	0	51	10	12	22	12
Mikael Tjallden	34	3	11	14	26	8	1	3	4	4	50	6	16	22	38
Teemu Numminen	38	9	5	14	14	8	4	0	4	2	48	14	7	21	16
Eric Dubois (WP)	35	5	8	13	42	8	0	4	4	2	45	6	13	19	44
Darby Walker	34	6	5	11	81	5	3	0	3	0	47	10	7	17	99
Clayton Norris (WP)	40	4	9	13	172	8	0	4	4	46	50	4	13	17	230
Shaun Johnson	33	2	9	11	8	8	1	3	4	2	47	4	12	16	16
Juha Lampinen	36	2	9	11	32	8	0	0	0	6	52	3	10	13	44
Jari Eerikainen	36	0	5	5	2	8	0	0	0	24	52	2	6	8	26
Jussi Eloranta	22	2	3	5	12	8	2	0	2	6	30	4	3	7	18
Tomi Makela	36	3	3	6	16	7	0	0	0	0	50	3	4	7	16
Michael Tasker	11	1	0	1	0	-	-	-	-	-	19	3	2	5	4
Anthony Johnson	8	0	0	0	2	-	-	-	-	-	16	1	4	5	4
Dan Carney	9	0	3	3	2	-	-	-	-	-	14	0	5	5	2
Hakan Galiamoutsas	8	1	1	2	0	7	0	2	2	4	15	1	3	4	4
Sami Wahlsten 1	8	1	1	2	2	8	0	2	2	6	16	1	3	4	8
Roni Mesikammen	35	1	2	3	111	-	-	-	-	-	39	1	2	3	117
Sami Mettovaara	9	1	1	2	27	-	-	-	-	-	9	1	1	2	27
Jim Hibbert (N)	23	0	1	1	0	8	0	1	1	16	35	0	2	2	16
Marco Rantanen (N)	23	0	1	1	0	-	-	-	-	-	27	0	1	1	0
Patrick Fox	-	-	-	-	-	-	-	-	-	-	6	0	0	0	2
Bench Penalties					46					2					50
TEAM TOTALS	42	113	188	301	790	8	20	35	55	144	58	156	261	417	1032
Netminders	GPI	Min	SoG	GA	Sv%	GPI	Min	SoG	GA	Sv%	GPI	Min	SoG	GA	Sv%
Jim Hibbert	23	1251	578	80	86.2	8	508	211	18	91.5	35	1999	913	115	87.4
Marko Rantanen	23	1294	606	91	85.0	-	-	-	-	-	27	1534	747	115	84.5
Empty Net Goals			6	6				2	2				8	8	
TEAM TOTALS	42	2545	1190	177	85.1	8	508	213	20	90.6	58	3533	1668	238	85.7

Back-up Netminders: Stephen Wall (Sunderland Chiefs), Chris Salem.
Also appeared: Don Dunnigan (3).
Also played for: 1 Manchester Storm.

All Competitions = Superleague, Playoffs, Challenge Cup and Benson and Hedges Cup.

Last is best

DAVID HALL

The Millennium season finally gave hope to the troubled Newcastle franchise. Against the odds Riverkings made it to the Championship final and just as importantly, they acquired the sound financial backing of Finnish giants, Jokerit.

Jokerit's partnership with club owners, Superleague, came only days before the first puck was due to drop and when the team hit the ice, they did little to inspire their loyal band of followers. The hastily put together collection of North Americans and Finns struggled to come to terms with the physical aspect of the league.

On the good nights they were great - two wins away to eventual champions Bracknell were testimony to that - but on most occasions they were distinctly ordinary and it showed in the final league standings. The one bright spot was the line of **Iiro Jarvi**, **Kim Ahlroos** and **Mikko Koivunoro**. The latter set a new Superleague record of 39 assists, a remarkable achievement in a side that scored only 113 times.

But coach **Jukka Jalonen** - brought in by the new owners to succeed **Alex Dampier** - had insisted all along that come the playoffs, his team would be hard to beat. Few had agreed at the start of the season but Riverkings were indeed transformed as goalie **Jimmy Hibbert**, a summer signing from Sheffield, became almost impossible to pass and confidence began to flow through the side.

A home draw with Bracknell and an overtime defeat in London was a reasonable start, and when Bracknell were dumped on their own ice for the third time in the season, the once seemingly impossible task of reaching the Manchester finals looked achievable.

Back-to-back victories over Nottingham sealed Riverkings' surprising appearance at the *MEN* and in perhaps the most incredible game of the competition, they put out hot favourites Sheffield in the semis, their first victory over Steelers since November 1998.

Shaun Johnson, the only Brit left on a roster that had featured five the previous season, netted the breakthrough goal with 2.02 remaining, sparking off a bout of scoring that ended with Newcastle 3-1 victors.

After matching London for the opening period of the final, Riverkings ran out of gas. Their cause wasn't helped by a controversial illegal stick call by Knights which, as Jalonen pointed out: "Just isn't something we would consider in Finland."

PLAYER AWARDS

Player of the Year	Joel Poirier
Player's Player	Joel Poirier
Defenceman of the Year	Clayton Norris
Best Forward	Mikko Koivunoro
*Petri Rautiainen Memorial Trophy	

LEADING PLAYERS

Iiro Jarvi born 23 March 1965

Koivunoro called him "the greatest player I have ever played with" and the former NHL forward didn't disappoint. Where Newcastle might have been if not for his presence is almost unthinkable.

Shaun Johnson born 22 March 1973

A big fan favourite, Johnson also endeared himself to the coaching staff with his spirit and tenacity. Being recalled to the GB squad for the world championships was no less than the Durham-born forward deserved.

Mikko Koivunoro born 12 November 1971

Playmaker extraordinaire, 39 assists for a bottom of the table side says it all about this super Finn. His unerring ability to find a team-mate was a huge bonus for coach Jalonen.

FACT FILE 1999-2000

Sekonda **Superleague**: Eighth.
Sekonda **Playoffs**: Finalists.
Benson and Hedges **Cup**: Quarter-finalists.

FRANCHISE HISTORY

Founded May 1998 when Ice Hockey Superleague Ltd purchased the franchise from The Sporting Club. The Sporting Club created the franchise in May 1995 when they purchased the Durham Wasps (founded 1947) from liquidators. Team was renamed Newcastle Cobras in August 1996 when franchise moved to Newcastle Arena.

Leagues *Riverkings* - Superleague 1998-2000, *Cobras* - Superleague 1996-98, *Durham Wasps* - British League, Premier Div 1982-96; Northern League 1966-82.

Honours *Wasps* - See *The Ice Hockey Annual 1998-99.*

NEWCASTLE RIVERKINGS *left to right, back row:* Kim Ahlroos, Jari Eerikainen, Hilton Ruggles, Teemu Numminen, Mikko Koivunoro, Shaun Johnson, Roni Mesikammen; *middle row:* Steven Wall, Juha Lampinen, Darby Walker, Iiro Jarvi, Clayton Norris, Tomi Makela, Mikael Tjallden, Joel Poirier, Sami Metovaara, Eric Dubois, Tim Blake (equipment), Ken Swinburne (player co-ordinator); *front row:* Jim Hibbert, Mike O'Connor (GM), Glen Mulvenna, Jukka Jalonen (coach), Marko Rantanen.

NOTTINGHAM PANTHERS

PLAYER	SEKONDA SUPERLEAGUE					SEKONDA PLAYOFFS					ALL COMPETITIONS				
Scorers	GP	G	A	Pts	Pim	GP	G	A	Pts	Pim	GP	G	A	Pts	Pim
Jamie Leach (WP)	42	17	29	46	18	6	2	3	5	12	59	23	37	60	36
Greg Hadden	36	22	18	40	10	6	1	2	3	8	52	28	25	53	30
Marty Flichel (WP)	38	17	23	40	82	5	1	0	1	8	47	18	25	43	94
Brent Bobyck	37	6	23	29	32	3	1	1	2	0	51	10	29	39	40
Ashley Tait	42	11	21	32	34	6	0	0	0	2	58	13	24	37	44
David Struch (WP)	42	8	16	24	22	6	1	0	1	0	59	12	22	34	30
Calle Carlson	39	14	13	27	24	5	0	0	0	2	54	16	16	32	28
Curtis Bowen	36	6	15	21	98	6	0	2	2	12	47	7	18	25	141
Steve Carpenter	30	4	17	21	114	6	0	1	1	44	43	5	20	25	176
Graham Garden	38	7	13	20	82	2	0	1	1	6	50	7	16	23	173
Steve Roberts	30	9	10	19	16	6	1	1	2	2	38	10	11	21	18
Aaron Cain (WP)	39	9	9	18	78	6	0	1	1	2	56	9	11	20	86
Brent Pope	42	2	10	12	90	6	0	0	0	4	59	3	11	14	104
Stephen Cooper	42	2	8	10	22	6	0	0	0	4	59	2	12	14	40
Randall Weber	36	4	3	7	4	6	0	0	0	0	51	4	5	9	4
Jason Mansoff (WP)	13	2	3	5	4	6	0	1	1	0	21	2	4	6	6
Simon Hunt	15	0	1	1	22	3	0	0	0	0	27	2	1	3	46
Marcus Adolfsson	5	0	2	2	10	-	-	-	-	-	10	1	2	3	12
Jordan Willis (N) (WP)	40	0	2	2	6	6	0	0	0	2	55	0	2	2	8
Marc Levers	-	-	-	-	-	-	-	-	-	-	2	0	0	0	0
Paul Moran	-	-	-	-	-	-	-	-	-	-	3	0	0	0	0
Jarkko Kortesoja (N)	6	0	0	0	0	-	-	-	-	-	10	0	0	0	0
Bench Penalties					18					4					24
TEAM TOTALS	42	140	236	376	786	6	7	13	20	112	59	172	291	463	1140
Netminders	GPI	Min	SoG	GA	Sv%	GPI	Min	SoG	GA	Sv%	GPI	Min	SoG	GA	Sv%
Jordan Willis (WP)	40	2344	1211	141	88.4	6	362	193	26	86.5	55	3214	1676	200	88.1
Jarkko Kortesoja	6	213	112	22	80.4	-	-	-	-	-	10	365	186	33	82.3
Empty Net Goals			2	2				0	0				3	3	
TEAM TOTALS	42	2557	1325	165	87.5	6	362	193	26	86.5	59	3579	1865	236	87.3

Shutouts: Willis - league: 18 Sept v Cardiff Devils (28 saves), 20 Nov v Newcastle Riverkings (28 saves), 5 Feb v Bracknell Bees (44 saves).

All Competitions = Superleague, Playoffs, Challenge Cup and Benson and Hedges Cup.

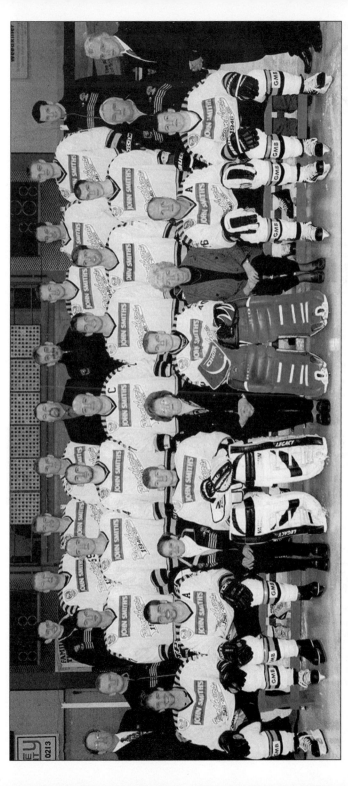

NOTTINGHAM PANTHERS *left to right, back row:* Adam Goodridge (equipment), Steve Roberts, Stephen Cooper, David Struch, Simon Moor (marketing), Glyn Childs (merchandising), Greg Hadden, Brent Bobyck, Marty Flichel, Dan Webster (physio); *middle row:* Alex Dampier (coach), Matt Elliott (physio), Calle Carlsson, Brent Pope, Aaron Cain, Jamie Leach, Curtis Bowen, Jason Mansoff, Ashley Tait, Pete Hunt (equipment), Gary Moran (GM); *front row:* Randall Weber, Steve Carpenter, Sarah Longden (office), Jordan Willis, Pat Maltby (office), Jarkko Kortesoja, Bernice Sansom (secretary), Graham Garden, Simon Hunt.

Photo courtesy Nottingham Evening Post

A season of two coaches

MICK HOLLAND

Failing to make the playoffs, reaching just one final compared to last season's three and struggling at the foot of the Superleague table signified a miserable closing of the century for the fans of Nottingham Panthers.

But not many of the faithful can look back and complain they had been undersold. The season hadn't always been like that.

The prospect of a £40 million, state-of-the-art, 7,000-seat arena for season 2000-01 brought with it the belief that Panthers would end their 54-year reign at the old Ice Stadium with a bang.

Unfortunately, just ten ineffective games into the league season, long-serving coach **Mike Blaisdell** walked out for arch-rivals Sheffield, claiming breach of contract and lack of financial backing.

Struggling with a four-man defence and a rebuilt team, things looked bleak. Then came the return of an old face as coach **Alex Dampier** arrived from Newcastle and brought the smiles back to the supporters' faces. As a bonus he also master-minded some titanic tussles as Panthers ensured a memorable end for the famous stadium.

'DAMPS' CREATES TEAM SPIRIT

Getting to work immediately with reputably the cheapest squad in the league, Damps admitted the players were better than he thought, with much of the commitment problem down to simple dressing room spirit.

Panthers had 11 new faces, including local boy **Ashley Tait**, who returned after two years in Hull, and sharp-shooter **Steve Roberts**, back from his season-long shoulder injury. But it wasn't until mid-January that Damps brought in the player who had been promised for so long when **Jason Manson** came to bolster the flagging backline.

With the forwards failing to hit the target with any regularity, it was the defence - plus goaltender **Jordan Willis** - who were the mainstays of Panthers' resurgence. At one stage they couldn't win a thing on the road but at their old building, they became the 'comeback kings', winning games that seemed beyond them.

That spirit took them to a Challenge Cup final against all the odds after remaining unbeaten in two memorable semi-final games against future championship winners, London.

But with injuries again biting hard, they didn't win another game - and that cup final defeat by Blaisdell's Sheffield was perhaps inevitable.

PLAYER AWARDS

Most Valuable Player	Jordan Willis
Players' Player	Jordan Willis
Supporters' Player	Calle Carlsson
Manager's award	Graham Garden
Coach's trophy	Curtis Bowen
Most consistent player	David Struch
Most entertaining player	Brent Bobyck
Most improved player	Ashley Tait
Gary Rippingale Memorial Trophy	Aaron Cain

LEADING PLAYERS

Calle Carlsson born April 2, 1972

The genial Swedish defenceman made a tentative start to his first year in Britain but his eye for goal, particularly on the powerplay, made him a great favourite.

Ashley Tait born August 9, 1975

Back with his hometown club, he grew in stature after GB duty in November and went from strength to strength. Was also a stand-out for the national side in Poland.

Jordan Willis born February 28, 1975

When he signed, the Panthers' website was inundated with e-mails from his Baton Rouge Kingfish 'fan club' wishing the goalie well. He didn't let them down, coming up with many match-winning games.

Panthers' fan **Mick Chambers** is compiling a massive 200-page statistical guide to the club covering every season right from the first one in 1946-47.

The book will be ready in time for Christmas so contact Mick now at spik1999@yahoo.co.uk. Tel: 0115-914-5255.

FACT FILE 1999-2000

Sekonda **Superleague**: Sixth.
Playoff Championship: 4th in qr-final group.
Benson and Hedges **Cup**: Quarter-finalists.
Challenge Cup: Finalists.

FRANCHISE HISTORY

Founded 1946. Re-formed 1980. Club suspended operations 1960-80. Purchased by Aladdin Sports Management in 1997
Leagues Superleague 1996-2000; British Lge (BL) (Premier Div) 1982-96 and 1954-60; English Nat Lge (ENL) 1981-82 and 1946-54; Inter-City Lge 1980-82.
Honours British BL Champions 1989; League - BL 1955-56, ENL 1953-54 and 1950-51; Autumn Cup winners 1998, 1996 & 1994 (B&H), 1991, 1986, 1955.

PAISLEY PIRATES

PLAYER	BRITISH NATIONAL LEAGUE					ALL COMPETITIONS				
Scorers	GP	G	A	Pts	Pim	GP	G	A	Pts	Pim
Chris Jamieson (l)	34	31	19	50	16	40	37	28	65	47
Matt Beveridge (l)	34	14	34	48	12	43	18	41	59	18
Robert Chalmers 4	36	10	5	15	42	44	15	10	25	48
Jim McLean (l)	36	6	15	21	14	44	7	18	25	45
John Downes	36	10	9	19	12	44	12	11	23	14
Mike Galati (l) 1, 5	19	9	7	16	26	21	11	9	20	26
Jesse Hamill	30	3	11	14	135	36	5	12	17	172
James Clarke	28	6	5	11	101	33	9	6	15	111
Bryan O'Neil	35	2	9	11	18	43	4	10	14	24
Todd Mallette (l)	4	0	6	6	6	10	2	11	13	8
Ian Simpson	34	5	3	8	2	42	5	4	9	2
Laurie Dunbar 3	34	1	6	7	18	38	2	7	9	30
Craig Nelson (l)	11	1	8	9	38	11	1	8	9	38
Lucas Miller (l)	10	1	5	6	18	10	1	5	6	18
Sean Kelso (l) 5	19	1	4	5	67	21	1	5	6	85
John Robertson	9	0	0	0	18	15	1	3	4	22
Ken Shadlock (l)	20	0	0	0	14	28	1	3	4	43
Lee Mercer	34	0	3	3	62	42	0	4	4	84
Joe Eagan (WP)	17	1	2	3	68	17	1	2	3	68
Mike Rees (l)	3	1	1	2	0	3	1	1	2	0
Dave Trofimenkoff (N) (l) 2	26	0	2	2	16	34	0	2	2	16
Robert Henderson	26	0	1	1	57	34	0	2	2	59
Graeme Lester	12	1	0	1	0	16	1	0	1	25
John Churchill	3	0	1	1	0	3	0	1	1	0
Colin Grubb (N)	8	0	1	1	0	8	0	1	1	0
Damian Orr (N)	35	0	0	0	2	43	0	0	0	2
Bench Penalties					28					30
TEAM TOTALS	36	103	157	260	790	44	135	204	339	1035
Netminders	GPI	Min	SoG	GA	Sv%	GPI	Min	SoG	GA	Sv%
Dave Trofimenkoff (l) 2	25	1480	1123	135	88.0	33	1894	1412	170	88.0
Colin Grubb 4	6	373	275	43	84.4	6	373	275	43	84.4
Damian Orr	10	284	225	41	81.8	13	350	268	50	81.3
John Russell	1	33	23	6	73.9	1	33	23	6	73.9
Empty Net Goals			1	1				1	1	
TEAM TOTALS	36	2170	1647	226	86.3	44	2650	1979	270	86.3

Also appeared: John Wilson 16; Colin Connor 8; Phillip Connor 6; John Denovan, Murray Johnstone, Gordon Nelson 2; Reggie Connor, Gordon Langford (N), David Spence 1.

Also played for: 1 Milton Keynes Kings, 2 Ayr Scottish Eagles, 3 Edinburgh Capitals, 4 Solway Sharks, 5 Telford Timberwolves.

All Competitions = league, B&H *Cup/Plate and* ntl: *Christmas Cup.*

Rookies save the ship

GEORGE SEYMOUR

While nobody was under any illusion that this campaign was going to be easy, for Pirates to finish rooted to the foot of the table for the second successive season was a setback.

But the blow was softened by the club's policy - announced in April 1999 - that they would embark on a three-to-five-year plan to develop young British talent.

The season started with a new coach, a crop of younger imports and some raw Scottish talent. **Stirling Wright** came in with a brash enthusiasm which nevertheless made everyone pull together. Sadly, after an incident with official **Michael Evans** at a home match against Peterborough in early November, Wright was banned for 12 games, though on appeal this was reduced to six plus six suspended.

With hindsight, this was the beginning of the end for Wright in the Paisley hot seat as the relationship between players and coach deteriorated from then on. After an 11-0 mauling at the hands of Guildford in the middle of February, the players had a meeting with club chairman **Allan Maxwell** which resulted in Wright's immediate release.

IMPORTS DRIFT AWAY

Of the imports who began the campaign in Pirates' colours only four remained at the season's end while no fewer than 13 in all iced for Pirates.

By contrast, **John Robertson**'s early departure was the only change all season in the young Scottish contingent who grabbed the chance to prove their worth in a BNL side.

Laurie Dunbar reversed the close-season flow from Paisley to Edinburgh and several youngsters competed in a limited number of games. The most unfortunate was **Graham Lester** who succumbed to a back injury in October which ended his season.

The greatest improvement was shown by **Robert Henderson, Bryan O'Neil, James Clark** and **Robert Chalmers**. Indeed, the last three named went to Japan with the GB under-20 side and returned with a bronze medal.

None of the others disgraced themselves: each and every one gave of his best. That the club finished bottom was more to do with a lack of experience than a lack of talent.

PLAYER AWARDS

Atlantic Telecom *Player of the Year*   Jim McLean
Supporters' Club Player   Jim McLean
Most Improved Player   James Clark/Robert Henderson
Patricia Warner Friendship Trophy   Jim McLean

LEADING PLAYERS

Chris Jamieson *born 28 August 1975*
Outstanding import forward and club captain who helped out with coaching at the end of the season. Fifty points is a creditable tally especially when achieved with the bottom club.

Jim McLean *born 28 October 1973*
All-round good guy who gave 100 per cent effort and deservedly scooped most of the awards with his solid defensive displays.

Dave Trofimenkoff *born 20 January 1975*
For the second year running Pirates brought an excellent netminding talent to the country who saved the team on numerous occasions. Sadly, he left in January to fulfil his ambitions with Superleague Ayr.

FACT FILE 1999-2000

British National League: 10th.
Playoffs: Failed to qualify.
Benson and Hedges Cup: 3rd in group.
ntl: Christmas Cup: Failed to qualify.

HISTORY

Founded: Current team in 1992, original team at the East Lane arena 1946-70. Known as Mohawks 1966-77, playing games at Glasgow's Crossmyloof rink after East Lane closed.
Leagues: British National Lge 1997-2000, Northern Premier Lge 1996-97, British Lge, Div. One 1993-96, Scottish Lge 1992-93 & 1996-97, Northern Lge (NL) 1971-77 & 1966-70, Scottish Lge (SL) 1962-65, British Lge (BL) 1954-60, Scottish National Lge (SNL) 1946-54.
Honours: *Pirates* - Scottish Cup 1996-97; BL 1958-59; SNL and Scottish Autumn Cup 1953-54; SNL & playoffs 1950-51; Scottish Autumn Cup 1947-48. *Mohawks* - NL 1968-69; Grand Slam of Icy Smith Cup, NL, Spring Cup and Northern Autumn Cup 1967-68; NL 1966-67; SL 1964-65.

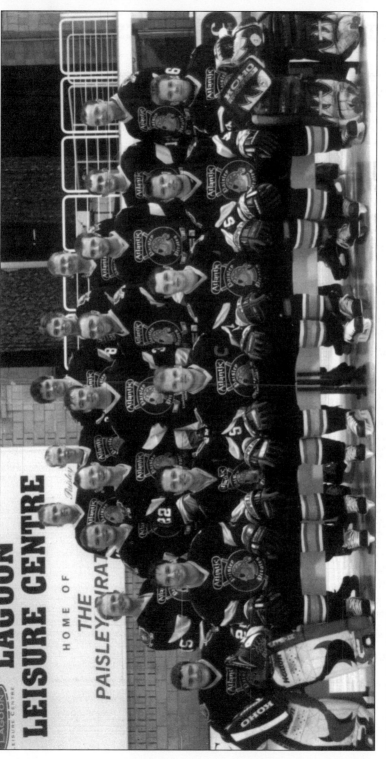

PAISLEY PIRATES *left to right, back row:* Lucas Miller, John Wilson, Murray Johnstone, Gordon Nelson, Robert Chalmers; *middle row:* Iain Simpson, Lee Mercer, Robert Henderson, Craig Nelson, James Clark, Bryan O'Neil, Laurie Dunbar, Graham Lester; *front row:* Damian Orr, Joe Egan, Matt Beveridge, Jim McLean, John Downes, Chris Jamieson, Colin Grubb.

PETERBOROUGH PIRATES

PLAYER	BRITISH NATIONAL LEAGUE					PLAYOFFS					ALL COMPETITIONS				
Scorers	GP	G	A	Pts	Pim	GP	G	A	Pts	Pim	GP	G	A	Pts	Pim
Randy Smith	36	43	44	87	30	8	9	10	19	24	57	62	74	136	81
Claude Dumas 1	25	23	40	63	38	-	-	-	-	-	38	37	49	86	46
Doug McEwen	31	23	24	47	46	8	2	14	16	30	52	31	46	77	94
David Clarke	35	19	22	41	81	8	8	3	11	40	55	33	36	69	153
Junji Sakata (WP)	27	15	25	40	10	-	-	-	-	-	40	23	35	58	12
Matt Brush (WP)	27	16	12	28	39	-	-	-	-	-	39	19	16	35	114
Jimmy Andersson (I)	27	3	22	25	26	-	-	-	-	-	40	4	29	33	32
Neil Liddiard	33	4	18	22	66	7	1	4	5	51	53	7	23	30	149
Daniel Grandqvist (I) 1	23	6	18	24	50	-	-	-	-	-	35	9	20	29	89
Andrew Milne (I)	22	8	12	20	181	-	-	-	-	-	34	10	13	23	238
Shannon Hope (I)	3	1	1	2	6	8	5	5	10	34	11	6	6	12	40
Jason Porter	36	0	7	7	42	8	0	0	0	29	57	0	9	9	101
Ross Mackintosh 3	8	3	3	6	10	8	1	1	2	10	16	4	4	8	20
Scott Stephenson (I) 1	6	2	3	5	0	8	1	2	3	12	14	3	5	8	12
Matt Williams	18	1	4	5	30	-	-	-	-	-	29	2	5	7	62
James Morgan 3	9	1	2	3	20	6	0	3	3	68	15	1	5	6	88
James Grinstead	36	1	3	4	49	8	0	0	0	26	57	2	3	5	93
Todd Bidner	-	-	-	-	-	5	2	1	3	39	6	2	1	3	39
Jon Oddy	6	1	0	1	20	3	0	2	2	0	9	1	2	3	20
Grant Hendry	36	1	0	1	8	8	1	0	1	0	57	2	0	2	8
Tom Watkins 1, 4	4	0	1	1	0	-	-	-	-	-	6	0	2	2	0
Craig Lindsay (N) (I)	27	0	2	2	29	-	-	-	-	-	40	0	2	2	31
James Ellwood	7	0	0	0	0	6	0	1	1	0	13	0	1	1	0
Lewis Buckman	31	0	0	0	0	8	0	1	1	0	52	0	1	1	4
Jason Buckman	15	0	0	0	2	8	0	0	0	0	25	0	0	0	2
Daniel Wilson	32	0	0	0	2	-	-	-	-	-	43	0	0	0	2
Bench Penalties					18					0					22
TEAM TOTALS	36	171	263	434	805	8	30	47	77	363	57	258	387	645	1505
Netminders	GPI	Min	SoG	GA	Sv%	GPI	Min	SoG	GA	Sv%	GPI	Min	SoG	GA	Sv%
Craig Lindsay (I)	27	1574	828	76	90.8	-	-	-	-	-	40	2322	1166	114	90.2
Pasi Raitanen 1, 2	6	361	297	28	90.6	8	465	317	34	89.0	14	826	614	63	89.7
David Whitwell	9	227	143	23	84.0	1	20	16	5	68.8	12	279	165	28	83.0
Empty Net Goals		1	1				0	0				1	1		
TEAM TOTALS	36	2162	1269	128	89.9	8	485	333	39	88.3	57	3427	1946	205	89.5

Also appeared: Jon Fone 19; James Bennett 10; Frazer Hendry, Sonny Thompson 4; James Homewood, James Moore (N) 3; Bernie Bradford, Russell Coleman 1.

Also played for: 1 Hull Thunder, 2 Ayr Scottish Eagles, 3 Milton Keynes Kings, 4 Telford Timberwolves.

All Competitions = league, playoffs, B&H Cup/Plate and ntl: Christmas Cup.

PETERBOROUGH PIRATES

Seasick

STEVE JUDGE

The season will be remembered for three farewells - two tearful, the other rocking the club to its foundations.

Troy Walkington was first to go in October. Now there are plenty around the British National League scene who are not too enamoured of 'Mad Dog's demeanour. But he gained the admiration of Pirates' fans for his decision to sacrifice himself rather than his players when news broke that the Pirates were sailing in financially choppy waters.

His departure was followed by the team's semi-final exit at the hands of Slough in the *Benson and Hedges* Plate.

Randy Smith was sworn in as the new coach and the team, despite taking heavy pay cuts, set off on a nine-game winning streak. Even back-to-back defeats at home to Fife and in Solihull were forgotten with December victories over championship rivals, Guildford and Fife.

Channel 4's cameras were filming a documentary on the team when Flames were smashed 7-3, and Pirates produced their best performance of the season next day in Kirkcaldy, walloping the eventual champions 6-1.

EVERY GAME LIKE THE LAST ONE

Then on Christmas Eve, of all days, the club's financial director resigned and every game in January was tipped as being the club's last.

After a mass clear-out of imports, the fans rallied round, and home games were treated to cup final-like atmospheres.

The supporters' efforts away from the rink raised around £15,000 in under a month, allowing the team to see out the season.

Supporters' Club chairman **Paul Brewster** and seven cohorts formed the new board of directors, and former Pirates' star and Cardiff Devils legend, **Shannon Hope**, came on board to help the cause.

Finnish netminder **Pasi Raitanen**, Hull's Canadian **Scott Stephenson**, Aussie **John Oddy** and **Ross Mackintosh** bolstered the bench and, against the odds, Pirates qualified for the playoff semi-finals.

After difficult quarter-final games, featuring a disastrous weekend in Scotland and a penalty shoot-out defeat at home to Thunder, Basingstoke awaited in the last four, but their depth proved too much for Pirates to handle.

When veteran Randy Smith announced his retirement after Pirates failed to win the series on home ice, it was the end of an era in every way.

PLAYER AWARDS

Player of the Year	Randy Smith
Clubman of the Year	Doug McEwen
Best British Player	Neil Liddiard
Best Young Player	Lewis Buckman
Maggie MacFarlane Award	Doug McEwen

LEADING PLAYERS

Lewis Buckman born 19 May 1983
A cool young English forward who isn't afraid to use his body. Has the knack of finding the killer pass and being in the right place at the right time in front of the net. Nephew of former Pirates' star, **Kevin King**.

Neil Liddiard born 7 May 1978
Outstanding defenceman on and off the puck. No one works harder or is more willing to put his body on the line for his team.

Shone while playing alongside Swedish imports Andersson and Grandqvist, and helped to hold the team together after they left. Fully deserved his GB call-up.

Doug McEwen born 2 October 1963
Skated through teams with such grace that passing figure skaters turned green with envy. At other times he was a one-man penalty killing machine, ragging the puck magnificently.

How the evergreen forward didn't make it onto an All-Star team ranks alongside the disappearance of Shergar as a great sporting mystery.

FACT FILE 1999-2000

British National League: 5th.
Playoffs: Semi-finalists.
Benson and Hedges: 2nd in Cup group; semi-finalists in Plate.
ntl: Christmas Cup: Quarter-finalists.

HISTORY

Founded: 1982.
Leagues: British National Lge 1997-2000; Premier Lge 1996-97; British Lge, Div One 1995-96, 1986-87, 1982-85; British Lge, Premier Div 1987-95, 1985-86.
Honours: Christmas Cup 1999; British Lge, Div. One playoffs 1987-88; British Lge, Div. One 1986-87, 1984-85.

-107-

ROMFORD RAIDERS

PLAYER	ENGLISH PREMIER LEAGUE					ALL COMPETITIONS				
Scorers	GP	G	A	Pts	Pim	GP	G	A	Pts	Pim
Jaakko Komulainen (I)	23	15	21	36	12	31	25	32	57	14
Danny Marshall	21	11	14	25	10	29	20	30	50	18
Timo Kauhanen (I)	13	6	18	24	6	18	8	33	41	8
Janì Lehtovaara (I)	22	9	10	19	24	30	20	14	34	32
Jani Mertanen (I)	10	7	8	15	6	12	7	9	16	6
John Fisher	14	3	4	7	70	21	5	11	16	94
Richard Tomalin	12	4	3	7	39	20	6	9	15	102
Alexei Eskine (I)	13	7	3	10	35	17	8	5	13	35
Daniel Cabby 2	13	1	2	3	12	18	6	7	13	18
Jon Beckett	11	1	3	4	8	19	5	4	9	18
Marten Furubom (I)	13	1	2	3	14	17	4	4	8	18
Barry Smith	10	2	1	3	2	15	4	3	7	2
Glen Moorhouse	11	1	1	2	2	17	3	4	7	10
Dan Wright	17	1	2	3	0	23	3	4	7	0
Ben Pitchley	22	1	5	6	103	24	2	5	7	109
Brian McLaughlin	1	0	0	0	0	7	2	4	6	14
Carson Lewis (I)	10	3	2	5	4	10	3	2	5	4
John Robertson	12	1	4	5	36	12	1	4	5	36
Ross Jones	13	2	1	3	2	18	2	2	4	2
Ken Shadlock (I)	12	2	1	3	27	12	2	1	3	27
Jon Main	7	0	0	0	24	15	2	1	3	42
Darren Botha	13	0	0	0	0	18	1	1	2	6
Matthew van der Velden (N) 1	14	0	1	1	4	21	0	2	2	4
Kevin Lake	3	0	1	1	2	3	0	1	1	2
Anthony Leone	7	0	1	1	4	7	0	1	1	4
Russell Bishop	8	0	1	1	2	11	0	1	1	27
Nathan Lawrence (N)	18	0	0	0	27	23	0	0	0	27
Bench Penalties					50					2
TEAM TOTALS	23	78	109	187	547	31	139	194	333	681
Netminders	GPI	Min	SoG	GA	Sv%	GPI	Min	SoG	GA	Sv%
Pasi Kolehmainen (I)	8	448	292	34	88.4	8	448	292	34	88.4
Matthew van der Velden 1	14	776	542	79	85.4	7	1162	754	104	86.2
Nathan Lawrence	5	149	77	13	83.1	7	213	101	21	79.2
Adam Noctor	1	7	4	1	75.O	2	37	20	2	90.O
TEAM TOTALS	23	1380	915	127	86.1	31	1860	1167	161	86.2

Also appeared: Paul Hume (9L); Joel Hume (5L); Tom Looker, Scott Wright (4L),
   Jason Knight (2L); Chris Goddard, Liem LeHuyen (1L).
Also played for: 1 Invicta Dynamos, 2 Oxford Blades.
All Competitions = league and Millennium Cup.

ROMFORD RAIDERS *left to right, back row:* Timo Kauhanen, Glenn Moorhouse, Jon Main, Jon Beckett, John Fisher, Jani Lehtovaara, Brian McLaughlin, Stuart Low, Jaakko Komulainen; *middle row:* Justin Andrew (equipment), Liem LeHuyen, Jani Mertanen, Anthony Leone, Ross Jones, Tom Looker, Barry Smith, Russell Bishop, Nathan Lawrence, Scott Wright; *front row:* Adam Noctor, Darren Botha, Ben Pitchley, John Wright (manager), Danny Marshall, Robert Spalenka (coach), Richard Tomalin, Dan Wright, Matt van der Velden.

ROMFORD RAIDERS

The more things change...

MICK CAHILL

Despite wholesale changes down Rom Valley Way, Raiders' season ended in under-achievement and bitter disappointment.

For the second successive year, a controversial EIHA ruling played a part in Romford's failure to make the playoffs.

Before a puck was dropped, **Alan Bishop** had resigned as team boss to be replaced by **John Wright** and a new support committee. Reports of increased sponsorship prompted high expectations, but in reality Raiders operated with the smallest budget outside of Cardiff Rage.

New coach **Robert Spalenka** had offered **Shaun McFadyen** a role as assistant coach, but had to change direction when McFadyen was unable to agree a deal and went to rivals, Invicta.

On opening night Raiders went down only narrowly to Chelmsford and their new Finnish net-minder, **Pasi Kolehmainen**, looked an able replacement for the retired **Mikko Nurminen**.

A win over a full-strength Oxford and a draw against the Isle of Wight augured well, but Kolehmainen's displays became more erratic and he went from hero to zero before being released.

KNOCKED OUT OF CUP

The deal to sign **Matt van der Velden** from Invicta as a replacement hit a snag and Raiders stumbled at home to Oxford in the Millennium Cup with an off-form **Nathan Lawrence** in goal. The 8-4 defeat cost Raiders a place in the final.

Money worries haunted the club until Christmas and it was some achievement to continue playing competitive hockey, if not consistently so. By January the roster had lost five regulars along with the injured **Scott Wright**.

A playoff place still looked achievable but the team were hit by the homeward return of high scoring Finn, **Jani Mertanen**, and the retirement of his compatriot, **Timo Kauhanen**, after one injury too many.

Six players were brought in but only imports **Ken Shadlock** and returnee **Alexei Eskine** brought much to the party, although local boy **Daniel Cabby** was a welcome addition.

The EIHA's decision to discount all games involving the Oxford and Cardiff clubs cost Raiders 12 points, another blow as Rage were the only side that they had consistently beaten.

By the end, experienced blueliner **Glen Moorhouse** had gone and **Richard Tomalin**, their best local forward, had retired shortly after returning from serious injury.

PLAYER AWARDS

Players' Player	Jaakko Komulainen
Coach's Player	Danny Marshall
Supporters' Player	Jaakko Komulainen
Top Defenceman	Jani Lehtovaara
Top Forward	Danny Marshall
Most Improved Player	Ross Jones

LEADING PLAYERS

Daniel Cabby born 4 July 1979
After some years flitting around the leagues, the forward returned to the club where he had been a junior. He made an immediate impact with his 100 per cent commitment and hockey brain.

Danny Marshall born 14 May 1977
Centreman replaced injury victim **Richard Tomalin** as skipper and became Romford's most influential player. His hard work and silky stick-handling produced consistently outstanding displays.

Matt van der Velden born 21 August 1979
Some eyebrows were raised when Raiders snapped up the young Rugby-born netminder, but Vandy was a reliable and sometimes match-winning last line of defence.

FACT FILE 1999-2000

English League: 5th in Premier Division.
Playoffs: Did not qualify
Data Vision Millennium Cup: 2nd in group.

CLUB HISTORY

Founded: 1987.
Leagues: English League 1995-2000, 1989-90; British League, Div One 1990-94 and 1988-89; British League, Div Two 1987-88. Withdrew from Div One midway through 1994-95 for financial reasons.
Honours: British League, Div Two 1987-88.

SHEFFIELD STEELERS

PLAYER	SEKONDA SUPERLEAGUE					PLAYOFF CHAMPIONSHIP					ALL COMPETITIONS				
Scorers	GP	G	A	Pts	Pim	GP	G	A	Pts	Pim	GP	G	A	Pts	Pim
Ed Courtenay	42	32	38	70	38	7	4	1	5	2	61	43	46	89	42
Teeder Wynne (WP)	40	28	31	59	18	7	2	3	5	0	58	35	42	77	22
Dale Junkin (WP)	42	20	36	56	24	7	1	3	4	2	61	23	42	65	34
Jason Weaver	42	20	15	35	76	7	3	6	9	39	61	31	27	58	135
Shayne McCosh (WP)	41	8	37	45	22	6	2	2	4	2	59	11	44	55	32
Greg Clancy (WP)	37	14	20	34	40	7	2	6	8	2	56	21	30	51	48
David Longstaff	40	12	24	36	32	7	2	7	9	14	59	14	36	50	52
Kip Noble	42	7	29	36	12	7	2	3	5	4	61	9	36	45	24
Dan Ceman	42	16	13	29	34	7	4	2	6	14	61	23	18	41	56
Dale Craigwell (WP)	25	7	18	25	0	7	0	6	6	2	35	9	26	35	2
Rob Wilson	29	5	16	21	60	7	3	0	3	4	48	8	18	26	98
Matt Hoffman	42	6	8	14	68	7	1	3	4	20	61	9	15	24	128
Kayle Short (WP)	42	3	10	13	46	6	0	2	2	10	60	4	15	19	66
Scott Allison	21	4	6	10	18	7	1	3	4	8	31	7	10	17	34
Derek Laxdal (WP)	18	3	3	6	20	-	-	-	-	-	27	5	6	11	24
Andre Malo	34	0	8	8	6	6	0	0	0	2	52	0	10	10	16
Mark Matier	36	0	6	6	40	6	0	1	1	6	52	0	10	10	54
Dennis Vial	26	2	5	7	82	7	0	1	1	10	36	2	7	9	96
Tommy Plommer	36	1	5	6	58	7	0	0	0	12	55	1	5	6	96
Grant Sjerven (WP) (N)	27	0	3	3	2	5	0	0	0	0	43	0	4	4	2
Frank LaScala	9	0	2	2	8	-	-	-	-	-	18	0	3	3	10
Shawn Silver (N)	17	0	1	1	2	3	0	0	0	10	22	0	1	1	12
Bench Penalties					8					2					10
TEAM TOTALS	42	188	334	522	714	7	27	49	76	165	61	255	451	706	1093
Netminders	GPI	Min	SoG	GA	Sv%	GPI	Min	SoG	GA	Sv%	GPI	Min	SoG	GA	Sv%
Shawn Silver	17	979	536	58	89.2	3	166	78	3	96.2	22	1225	652	64	90.2
Grant Sjerven (WP)	27	1567	821	94	88.5	5	285	160	12	92.5	43	2497	1359	141	89.6
Empty Net Goals			3	3				2	2				6	6	
TEAM TOTALS	42	2546	1360	97	88.6	7	451	240	17	92.9	61	3722	2017	211	89.5

All Competitions = Superleague, Playoffs, Challenge Cup and Benson and Hedges Cup.

Still hungry for more

SETH BENNETT

A season of change at Broughton Lane saw Sheffield Steelers retain the Challenge Cup, finish Superleague runners-up and make it to the Playoff Finals weekend. But it was still not good enough for their success-hungry management.

After the uncertainty of the 1998-99 season, the club went into liquidation in the close season and reformed under the guidance of local businessman, **Darren Brown**.

Brown retained the services of team manager **Dave Simms** and coach **Don McKee** who put together a team loaded with offensive talent, led by the off-season signings of Bracknell pair, **Shayne McCosh** and **Dale Junkin**.

But when Steelers hosted the Continental Cup in October they played as inconsistently as they would for the rest of the season, failing to qualify for the next round despite beating the favourites from Omsk.

Later in the month, an horrendous 10-2 league defeat in Bracknell led to McKee parting company with the team he built, though he had already signed **Dale Craigwell** and ex-NHL tough guy **Dennis Vial**.

Steelers responded to the change with a 10-1 Bonfire Night blow-out of Nottingham under the leadership of captain **Rob Wilson**. Amazingly, it was **Mike Blaisdell**, the coach of their arch-rivals, who took over McKee's post. When **Derek Laxdal** also quit to join his old boss as his assistant in the American WPHL, the gap was filled by **Scott Allison** who returned to the Steel City after a nightmare three months in Germany.

Steelers pressed hard in the league, with **Ed Courtenay** in record breaking form, along with linemates **Teeder Wynne** and Junkin. But it was the second unit of **Greg Clancy**, **Jason Weaver** and **David Longstaff** who shone come playoff time.

Steelers' solid performance in the *Alamo* Challenge Cup final brought 'Blaiser' his first victory in a Sheffield v Nottingham cup final.

With the playoffs the only trophy left, Steelers felt they had a great chance against the league's wooden spoon winners, Newcastle Riverkings, they couldn't find a way to beat their ex-goaltender, **Jimmy Hibbert**.

Although Blaisdell brought Sheffield an exciting new style of run-and-gun hockey, lack of commitment to defence cost them the league.

Two long serving Steelers, fan favourite **Tommy Plommer** and reliable defenceman **Andre Malo**, retired at the end of the season.

PLAYER AWARDS

Player of the Year	Ed Courtenay
Players' Player	Ed Courtenay
Coach's Player	Tommy Plommer
Best Road Player	Grant Sjerven
Services to the Community	Greg Clancy

LEADING PLAYERS

Ed Courtenay *born 2 February 1968*
Always deadly around the net, in his third season with the club the ex-NHLer topped the league in goals and points and linked brilliantly with linemates **Teeder Wynne** and **Dale Junkin**.

Shayne McCosh *born 27 January 1974*
Dubbed 'Bish-bosh' for his hard hitting play, the defenceman who joined Steelers from Bracknell Bees was also a skilled playmaker whose 37 assists was one of the league's best totals.

Teeder Wynne *born 6 December 1973*
Moved up to the club's first line alongside Courtenay and Junkin, he enjoyed a productive season, his first full one with the club after contracting glandular fever in Russia in 1998.

FACT FILE 1999-2000

Sekonda **Superleague:** Runners-up.
Playoff Championship: Semi-finalists.
Benson and Hedges **Cup:** Quarter-finalists.
Challenge Cup: Winners.

FRANCHISE HISTORY

Founded 1991. Franchise purchased from liquidators in 1999 by consortium led by **Darren Brown**.

Leagues Superleague 1996-2000; British League, Premier Div 1993-96; British League, Div One 1992-93; English League 1991-92.

Honours Challenge Cup 1999-2000 & 1998-99, Superleague Playoff Championship 1996-97, British League and Championship 1995-96, 1994-95.

SHEFFIELD STEELERS *left to right, back row:* Mike Blaisdell (coach), Garry Crookes (equipment), Dave Doherty (equipment), Ed Courtenay, Dennis Vial, Paul Turner (bench asst.), Mark Matier, Teeder Wynne, Dale Craigwell, Andy Akers (equipment); *middle row:* Kayle Short, Andre Malo, Scott Allison, David Longstaff, Shane McCosh, Kip Noble, Dave Simms (GM); *front row:* Jason Weaver, Grant Sjerven, Dan Ceman, Rob Wilson, Matt Hoffman, Greg Clancy, Shawn Silver; *on ice:* Tommy Plommer (with Challenge Cup), Dale Junkin.

SLOUGH JETS

PLAYER	BRITISH NATIONAL LEAGUE					PLAYOFFS					ALL COMPETITIONS				
Scorers	GP	G	A	Pts	Pim	GP	G	A	Pts	Pim	GP	G	A	Pts	Pim
Joe Stefan	36	28	18	46	78	6	2	2	4	14	55	34	32	66	104
Nick Cross	35	20	23	43	76	6	1	2	3	45	53	25	31	56	163
Richard Little	28	11	17	28	48	6	2	3	5	8	44	15	22	37	62
Adam Lamarre (I)	35	7	23	30	86	6	1	0	1	8	53	9	27	36	114
David Heath	35	8	12	20	20	6	2	0	2	10	53	14	15	29	61
Jason Kendall	32	6	14	20	144	4	1	1	2	8	49	9	18	27	174
Jason Reilly	36	4	13	17	67	6	0	0	0	4	55	7	15	22	87
Perry Pappas (I)	8	4	4	8	35	-	-	-	-	-	17	7	7	14	74
Ian Pound	36	1	7	8	58	6	0	0	0	10	55	2	12	14	78
Mark McCoy 1	10	6	5	11	6	-	-	-	-	-	13	6	6	12	6
Richard Gallace (N)	36	0	12	12	40	6	0	0	0	0	55	0	12	12	44
Adam Bicknell	32	1	4	5	10	6	0	1	1	0	47	3	7	10	14
Mark Galazzi	16	1	3	4	8	6	1	0	1	2	29	5	4	9	10
Matt Foord	32	1	4	5	24	6	0	1	1	6	50	3	6	9	36
Rob Cole	25	4	3	7	0	-	-	-	-	-	38	5	3	8	0
Warren Rost	23	2	3	5	90	6	0	0	0	14	34	3	4	7	122
Danny Farren	34	4	2	6	22	6	0	0	0	2	51	4	2	6	26
Scott Moody	33	0	3	3	16	6	1	0	1	2	50	2	4	6	30
Dominic Hopkins 1	11	1	2	3	14	6	0	0	0	0	17	1	2	3	14
Russell Stevens	13	0	0	0	6	5	0	0	0	0	24	1	0	1	6
Stuart Tait	5	0	0	0	4	-	-	-	-	-	14	0	0	0	6
Bench Penalties					12					2					16
TEAM TOTALS	36	109	172	281	864	6	11	10	21	135	55	155	229	384	1247
Netminders	GPI	Min	SoG	GA	Sv%	GPI	Min	SoG	GA	Sv%	GPI	Min	SoG	GA	Sv%
Adam White	4	159	57	4	93.0	-	-	-	-	-	4	159	57	4	93.0
Richard Gallace	34	2010	951	95	90.0	6	370	180	20	87.8	53	3164	1544	147	90.4
Empty Net Goals			1	1				0	0				2	2	
TEAM TOTALS	36	2169	1009	100	90.1	6	370	180	20	88.9	55	3323	1603	153	90.5

Also appeared: Charlie May (N) 3; Tommy Brooks (N) 2; Trevor Cogan, Kevin Murphy, Owen Murphy 1.

Also played for: 1 Guildford Flames.

Shutouts: Gallace - *B&H* Plate: 20 Oct at Peterborough Pirates (35 saves); league: 11 Dec v Paisley Pirates (15 saves).

All Competitions = league, playoffs, B&H Cup/Plate and ntl: Christmas Cup.

SLOUGH JETS *left to right, back row:* David Heath, Russell Stevens, Danny Farren, Matt Foord, Rob Cole; *middle row:* Adam Bicknell, Nick Cross, Scott Moody, Ian Pound, Richard Little, Adam Lamarre, Mark Galazzi; *front row:* Adam White, Perry Pappas, Joe Stefan, Jason Kendall, Jason Reilly, Richard Gallace.

Just happy to be here

DICK BELLAMY

After a nail-biting off-season with everyone wondering if there would be a Slough Jets team at all, the 1999-2000 campaign was a particularly satisfying one, with Jets reaching a cup final against the odds.

Withdrawal of local authority funding left the club fearing that the English League was their best option, but this unwanted choice was narrowly averted after their supporters came to the rescue.

Their pledges, plus some concessions wrung from the council, enabled the club to return to the British National League.

Unfortunately, the decision came after coach **Charlie Colon** had moved down the M3 to Basingstoke. Leading forward, **Joe Stefan**, stepped up to be player-coach.

Perry Pappas, the league's player of the year, committed himself, goalie **Richard Gallace** and defenceman **Adam Lamarre** returned, too, and the team began to take shape.

Jason Kendall was appointed captain and the new team management recruited several players from the under-19s including **Matt Foord** and **Russell Stevens**. The most experienced additions were returnees **Ian Pound** on defence and forward **Richard Little** who came back after a two-year break from the game.

Against expectations, Jets reached the final of the *Benson and Hedges* Plate at Sheffield, but they lost heavily to Bison and it was a turning point for the club in other important ways.

Mark Galazzi suffered a near-fatal injury in the game and around this time Pappas had to undergo reconstructive surgery on a career-threatening knee injury.

The Canadian could not be replaced due to a problem with his injury insurance and the club's tight budget, and the team were less competitive in the second half of the season.

Ex-Guildford and Hull import **Mark McCoy** joined for two months until January when another Flame, **Dominic Hopkins**, signed on. *Sky* TV presenter **Nick Rothwell** signed, too, but he never made an appearance.

Jets were knocked out of the *ntl*: Christmas Cup at the quarter-final stage by Milton Keynes, a defeat which was hard to explain as Kings were bottom of the league at the time.

A respectable league finish put Slough in the playoffs, but they were drawn in a group with powerhouses, Guildford and Basingstoke, and a vastly improved Solihull. It proved too much for a team that had struggled to score goals all season.

PLAYER AWARDS

Players' Player	Richard Gallace
Coach's Award	Richard Gallace
Captain's Award	Ian Pound
Player of the Year	Adam Lamarre
*British Player of the Year	Jason Reilly
Most Promising British Player	Matt Foord

*Chosen by the Supporters' Club

STEF'S No. 17 RETIRED
Gary Stefan, Jets' all-time highest scorer, manager and sometime coach, who retired in 1999, was presented with his no. 17 shirt at the club's annual Awards Dinner/Dance in April 2000.

LEADING PLAYERS

Matt Foord *born 9 September 1981*
High Wycombe-born Matt is equally at home on right-wing or at centre. He was voted Jets' most promising young player after stepping up from the under-19 squad.

Adam Lamarre *born 7 June 1974*
The Canadian University defender played a major role in his second year with Jets. Relishes making forward runs and getting among the points.

Jason Reilly *born 8 January 1971*
Londoner in his fifth season at the Hangar. His total commitment to the team set a great example to Jets' young players.

FACT FILE 1999-2000

British National League: Sixth.
Playoffs: 3rd in quarter-final group.
Benson and Hedges: 2nd in Cup group; Plate finalists.
ntl: Christmas Cup: Quarter-finalists.

HISTORY

Founded: 1986.
Leagues: British National Lge 1997-2000; Premier Lge 1996-97; British Lge, Premier Div 1995-96; British Lge, Div One 1986-95.
Honours: British National League 1998-99; *Benson and Hedges* Plate 1997-98; British League, Div One 1994-95 (and Playoffs), 1993-94 (south), 1989-90.

SOLIHULL BLAZE

PLAYER	BRITISH NATIONAL LEAGUE					PLAYOFFS					ALL COMPETITIONS				
Scorers	GP	G	A	Pts	Pim	GP	G	A	Pts	Pim	GP	G	A	Pts	Pim
Steve Chartrand	36	34	31	65	30	8	3	8	11	2	52	46	47	93	32
Anthony (AJ) Kelham (I)	33	30	35	65	4	8	5	4	9	4	49	41	44	85	12
Mike Shewan	36	12	32	44	6	8	4	5	9	8	52	19	47	66	18
Blake Sorensen (I)	34	16	21	37	38	8	6	6	12	8	50	27	37	64	54
Mike Tasker	24	17	21	38	32	8	2	3	5	6	34	20	25	45	38
Jason Coles	32	18	12	30	60	8	4	2	6	8	46	26	17	43	84
Nate Leslie (I)	36	5	20	25	88	8	0	4	4	20	52	5	26	31	124
Hakan Klys (I)	30	5	14	19	12	8	1	4	5	4	40	6	19	25	18
Mark Pallister 1	20	5	10	15	26	8	1	2	3	10	28	6	12	18	36
Kurt Irvine	33	5	7	12	156	8	1	4	5	2	49	6	12	18	200
Boe Leslie (I)	15	7	1	8	55	-	-	-	-	-	23	9	3	12	57
Jake Armstrong 2	28	1	5	6	24	8	0	5	5	6	38	1	11	12	30
Mattias Soderstrom (I)	35	1	8	9	52	4	0	0	0	4	47	1	9	10	68
Perry Doyle	33	0	4	4	94	8	2	1	3	12	49	3	5	8	126
James Pease	34	1	5	6	10	8	0	2	2	2	50	1	7	8	16
Gareth Owen	33	2	2	4	72	8	1	0	1	0	49	3	2	5	74
Don Breau	21	1	2	3	4	8	0	1	1	0	37	1	4	5	6
Barry Hollyhead (N)	36	0	2	2	2	8	0	1	1	0	52	0	4	4	4
Rob Eley	35	1	0	1	2	8	0	0	0	0	51	1	0	1	4
Stephen Doyle (N)	33	0	0	0	18	-	-	-	-	-	41	0	1	1	20
Neil Adams	34	0	1	1	2	5	0	0	0	0	47	0	1	1	8
Shaun Yardley	13	0	0	0	2	1	0	0	0	0	18	0	0	0	2
Bench Penalties					34					4					60
TEAM TOTALS	36	161	233	394	823	8	30	52	82	100	52	222	333	555	1091
Netminders	GPI	Min	SoG	GA	Sv%	GPI	Min	SoG	GA	Sv%	GPI	Min	SoG	GA	Sv%
Barry Hollyhead	20	1123	610	82	86.6	8	483	249	31	87.5	32	1848	973	132	86.4
Stephen Doyle	18	1048	570	88	84.6	-	-	-	-	-	22	1293	714	119	83.2
Empty Net Goals			2	2				1	1				3	3	
TEAM TOTALS	36	2171	1182	172	85.4	8	485	251	32	87.3	52	3141	1690	254	85.0

Also appeared: Tom Ayers (N) 10; Eike Gilbert 7; Andrew Howarth 4; Andrew Hughes 3, Tom Iveson 1.
Also played for: 1 Hull Thunder, 2 Basingstoke Bison.
Shutouts: Hollyhead - playoffs: 19 Mar v Basingstoke Bison (17 saves).

All Competitions = league, playoffs, B&H Cup/Plate and ntl: *Christmas Cup.*

Out in a Blaze of glory

TONY MACDONALD

The previous year's English League champs proved to be no pushovers at the higher level of the British National League.

Although missing out on silverware, the West Midlands side played an entertaining brand of hockey and reached the playoff semi-finals before succumbing to treble winners, Fife Flyers.

A big cash injection from a major company had been expected to boost the club's promotion. But amid uncertainty over the team's future in Solihull, as they pondered a move to Coventry's new Skydome, the sponsorship launch was scrapped. The name of the backer remained a mystery all season.

Despite that hiccup, coach **Paul Thompson** and manager **John Doyle** recruited well on a realistic budget. Key players returning included top scorers **Steve Chartrand** and **A J Kelham**, talented goalie **Stephen Doyle**, feisty forward **Kurt Irvine** and hard-hitting **Perry Doyle**.

New arrivals included Telford-trained cageman **Barry Hollyhead**, who enjoyed a fine campaign, along with experienced blue-liners, **Mike Shewan**, **Jason Coles** and young Swede, **Mathias Soderstrom**.

Up front were three Canadians, **Boe** and **Nate Leslie** from Switzerland, and speedy **Blake Sorenson** who soon became a fans' favourite.

Despite finishing bottom of their B&H Cup group, an opening league victory at Peterborough proved the team could compete on the road. But a string of defeats was blamed on defensive frailties, forcing coach Thompson to shore his back line with highly rated Swede, **Hakan Klys**, and much travelled Brit, **Mark Pallister**. The arrival of **Michael Tasker** from Newcastle added extra scoring punch.

The results improved, despite a rising penalty tally as the team fell foul of the men in stripes on more than one occasion.

Although a shoot-out loss to Milton Keynes quickly ended their interest in the ntl: Cup, Solihull played .500 hockey over the last 17 league games to finish in a creditable seventh place, ending with a surprise home win over champions, Fife.

The side Blazed their way into the playoff semi-finals with memorable victories over Slough, Guildford and Basingstoke, but their hopes finally expired in two straight losses to the Flyers, although only the width of a post prevented overtime in Game Two at home.

As the final hooter sounded, 1,320 fans were left to wonder whether they had witnessed the team's final act at Hobs Moat Road.

PLAYER AWARDS

Players' Player	Mike Shewan
Supporters' Player of the Year	Mike Shewan
Coach's Award	James Pease
Most Improved Player	Kurt Irvine
Best Young Player	James Pease

LEADING PLAYERS

Steve Chartrand born 8 January 1969
Now virtually a legend among the Blaze faithful, the stylish French-Canadian proved he has lost none of his class. Almost a decade since making his Solihull debut, he terrorised opposing cagemen to average almost a goal a game.

Anthony 'AJ' Kelham born 30 March 1974
Always a threat to opposing defences, the speedy Canadian adapted easily to the pace of the BNL and finished joint fourth in league scoring alongside Chartrand.

Mike Shewan born 11 April 1973
An astute signing from Superleague Newcastle, his classy blueline performances made him a favourite with the fans. No slouch in attack either, he blasted five goals in eight games during Solihull's impressive playoff run.

FACT FILE 1999-2000

British National League: Seventh.
Playoffs: Semi-finalists.
Benson and Hedges Cup: 4th in Cup group.
ntl: Christmas Cup: Failed to qualify.

HISTORY

Founded: 1997. Previous Solihull clubs: Barons 1965-97, Vikings 1970-74.
Leagues: Blaze - British National League 1999-2000; English Lge 1997-99. Barons - Premier Lge 1996-97; British Lge, Div. One/Two 1993-96 & 1982-86; English Lge 1991-93; British Lge, Premier Div. 1986-91; Inter-City Lge 1978-82; Southern Lge 1972-78. Vikings - Southern Lge 1970-74.
Honours: Blaze - English League, Premier Div. 1998-99, 1997-98; Barons - English League 1992-93; British Lge, Div. One 1985-86, Div. Two 1983-84; Southern League 1977-78.

SOLWAY SHARKS *left to right, back row:* Chris Black, Jamie Creighton, John Ballentyne, Ryan McBride, Chris Gracie, Scott Webster, Gordon Whyte, Colin Freeman; *front row:* Cameron Currie, Andy Patrick, John Churchill, Michael Brunton, Gordon Langford, Ross Edgar, Scott Edgar, Jamie Thomson, Gary Carruth.

SOLWAY SHARKS

Just when Raiders thought it was safe...

IAIN YEOMAN

The Dumfries-based Sharks successfully retained their Scottish League title by six points from Murrayfield Raiders.

Joint coaches **Martin Grubb** and **Stuart Wilson** worked well to keep their 1998-99 championship team on the winning trail after losing the services of three players in the off-season, notably 49-goal scorer and GB under-21 forward **Robert Chalmers** who was snapped up by Paisley Pirates.

When the season got underway **Richie Lamb** departed to Raiders and there was the usual crop of injuries with on-form captain **Ross Edgar** out for six weeks with a dislocated shoulder.

Their fortunes changed when former Dumfries Vikings skipper **Gordon Whyte** returned from Blackburn Hawks along with **Jamie Thomson**, and Kilmarnock Avalanche's **Ryan McBride** added a new dimension in attack. **John Churchill**'s late return brought the team up to strength and Sharks were again the team to beat.

Then a run-in with the authorities left their title aspirations hanging by a thread. The Scottish IHA docked the team four points for allegedly icing Whyte before his paperwork was complete.

The next battle to overcome was the loss of netminder **Colin Grubb** on loan to Paisley but fortunately, while he was enjoying a taste of the big time, **Gordon Langford** filled in successfully.

The league race went right to the wire with Ayr Bruins and Murrayfield chasing Sharks, and Perth Panthers not far away, either.

It was Panthers who knocked out Sharks in the Cup semi-final as Solway played arguably their worst game of the season.

Kirkcaldy Kestrels beat Paisley Mohawks in the other semi and went on to lift the trophy, so it was some consolation for Sharks when they later beat Kestrels by two goals in their own rink in the final of the Hockey UK tournament.

FACT FILE 1999-2000

League Placing: Scottish League winners.
Playoffs: Semi-finalists.
Border League: Last.

PLAYER AWARDS 1999-2000

Players' Player	Gordon Whyte
*Player of the Year	John Ballentyne
Coach's Award	John Ballentyne
*Best Defenceman	John Ballentyne
*Most Improved Player	Chris Black
* Awarded by the Supporters' Club	

Scottish League & Playoffs, Border League

Scorers	GP	G	A	Pts	Pim
Martin Grubb	23	30	27	57	18
Michael Brunton	26	14	9	23	75
John Ballentyne	15	15	7	22	20
Chris Black	24	9	10	19	61
John Churchill	7	5	10	15	10
Scott Webster	20	5	8	13	129
Ryan McBride	6	9	3	12	4
Gordon Whyte	20	5	6	11	6
Ross Edgar	19	2	9	11	24
Chris Gracie	23	5	5	10	54
Andy Patrick	21	8	1	9	73
Jamie Thomson	18	4	4	8	138
Cammy Currie	15	2	6	8	39
Scott Edgar	26	1	5	6	30
Jamie Creighton	23	2	2	4	58
Colin Freeman	20	0	2	2	28
Gary Carruth	23	1	0	1	36
TEAM TOTALS	26	117	114	231	803

Netminders	GPI	Mins	SoG	GA	Sv%
Colin Grubb	14	750	386	30	92.2
Gordon Langford	17	810	446	51	88.6
TEAM TOTALS	26	1560	832	81	90.3

CLUB HISTORY

Founded: 1998. Previous club was Dumfries Border Vikings 1993-98.
Leagues: Sharks - Scottish League 1998-2000; Vikings - British Lge, Div. One 1993-96.
Honours: Sharks - Scottish Lge 1998-2000; Vikings - Autumn Trophy 1995-96.

SWINDON CHILL

PLAYER	ENGLISH PREMIER LEAGUE					PLAYOFFS					ALL COMPETITIONS				
Scorers	GP	G	A	Pts	Pim	GP	G	A	Pts	Pim	GP	G	A	Pts	Pim
Lamonte Polet (I)	23	27	18	45	6	4	5	3	8	0	35	45	35	80	20
Darcy Cahill	22	15	25	40	172	4	4	4	8	6	33	25	48	73	247
Ken Forshee (I)	24	13	12	25	34	4	0	2	2	0	36	27	30	57	58
Ryan Mair (I)	17	8	13	21	209	2	0	0	0	0	26	21	21	42	281
Magnus Josefsson (I)	23	8	13	21	49	4	2	1	3	0	33	17	21	38	51
Sean Tarr (I)	22	4	11	15	97	4	0	2	2	8	34	6	19	25	109
Michael Smith	24	5	5	10	6	4	0	0	0	0	36	9	7	16	8
Jeff Sinnott (I)	20	0	4	4	6	4	1	1	2	0	32	2	12	14	14
Alan Armour	23	1	7	8	130	4	0	0	0	2	33	2	10	12	138
Richard Wojciak	17	2	0	2	12	-	-	-	-	-	25	7	4	11	16
Robin Davison	5	1	3	4	18	-	-	-	-	-	6	1	6	7	20
Drew Chapman	7	1	2	3	18	4	0	0	0	6	15	1	6	7	40
Rob Johnston	10	0	1	1	4	4	0	4	4	6	21	1	6	7	35
Peter Nilsson (I)	12	1	2	3	2	-	-	-	-	-	18	2	4	6	2
Ady Smith	22	0	1	1	2	4	0	0	0	0	34	2	4	6	4
Ronald Bertrand (I) (N)	21	0	3	3	14	4	0	0	0	2	34	0	5	5	18
Chris McEwen	17	1	1	2	0	-	-	-	-	-	24	2	2	4	18
Marc Gariss (I)	16	1	0	1	94	4	0	0	0	0	27	2	2	4	129
Adam Andrews	20	0	1	1	0	3	0	0	0	0	31	0	2	2	4
Wayne Fiddes	3	1	0	1	0	-	-	-	-	-	3	1	0	1	0
Bobby Brown 1	7	1	0	1	14	2	0	0	0	0	9	1	0	1	14
Myles Peppin (I)	5	0	1	1	4	-	-	-	-	-	5	0	1	1	4
Bench Penalties					22					4					28
TEAM TOTALS	24	90	123	213	925	4	12	17	29	34	36	174	245	419	1258
Netminders	GPI	Min	SoG	GA	Sv%	GPI	Min	SoG	GA	GAA	GPI	Min	SoG	GA	Sv%
Ronald Bertrand (I)	21	1241	924	90	90.3	4	240	189	11	94.2	33	1885	1326	122	90.8
Jamie Thompson	3	154	91	9	90.1	-	-	-	-	-	3	154	91	9	90.1
Ben Knock	3	45	44	11	75.O	-	-	-	-	-	5	101	66	15	77.3
Lee Lansdowne	10	0	0	0	0	4	0	0	0	0	1	20	11	0	100.o
Empty Net Goals			1	1									1	1	
TEAM TOTALS	24	1440	1060	111	89.5	4	240	189	11	94.2	36	2160	1495	147	90.2

Also appeared: Andrew Shurmer (14L, 4PO, 8C); John Reynolds (3L); Mike Kellond, Andy McGurk (2L); Russell Cowley, Kevin Doherty (1L).
Also played for: 1 Isle of Wight Raiders & Sheffield Scimitars.
Shutouts: Bertrand - league: 5 Feb v Romford Raiders (35 saves).

All Competitions = league, playoffs and Millennium Cup.

Chill out on the road

PHIL JEFFERIES

In the third year of the Chill era at the Link Centre, owner **Mike Kellond**'s clear intent was to get some silver into their barren trophy cabinet.

After losing players to neighbouring Oxford, Kellond revamped his side into one which was almost unrecognisable from the previous season's. Returning import, **Darcy Cahill**, took over as player-coach and brought in new boys **Miles Peppin** and **John Reynolds** from Canada, **Peter Nilssen** from Sweden and no-nonsense defenceman **Marc Garris** from San Diego, California.

After a narrow victory at home to Invicta in the opening game, Chill failed to beat Oxford on the road next day. This was a problem which would plague the Chill throughout the season. Worse was to follow the next weekend when goalie **Jamie Thompson** suffered a serious leg injury in a first period tangle at Gillingham and the Chill crashed to a heavy defeat.

The diagnosis on the former Player of the Year was poor and Chill were forced into swift action. **Ron Bertrand**, recently with the Austin Ice Bats, flew in as cover, and he was joined on the flight from Timmins, Ontario by imposing forward **Ryan Mair**. Mair replaced the disappointing Reynolds who had been cut from the squad early on.

Bertrand was a revelation and soon took over the mantle of the league's top netminder, while Mair found his way to the top end of both the scoring and the penalty minutes charts.

After Chill added the scoring potential of **Lamonte Polet**, their home form was impressive. But away from the Link, apart from a stunning 5-1 victory at champions-elect Chelmsford, results were less flattering. Despite this, Chill briefly topped the table prior to Christmas and reached the final of the *DataVision* Millennium Cup, though they lost to Chieftains on home ice.

Despite uncertainty over the future of the side, as Kellond put up the 'for sale' signs, there were more changes after Christmas. Pepin returned to Canada and **Bobby Brown** added to his growing resumé of clubs by joining Swindon.

Inconsistency continued to frustrate and the league season finished with Chill in third place, but in a playoff spot. A surprise victory at Ryde in the semi-final set them up for another final.

Once again they met Chelmsford, and once again they suffered a loss on home ice. A fighting draw at the Riverside, however, brought Chill their second runners-up medals of a mixed campaign.

PLAYER AWARDS

Player of the Year	Ron Bertrand
Players' Player	Ron Bertrand
Best Forward	Lamonte Polet
Best British Forward	Mike Smith
Best Defenceman	Sean Tarr
Best British Defenceman	Adam Andrews
Most Improved Player	Adam Andrews
Team Spirit	Ian Smith
Dedication	Ken Forshee/Mike Smith

LEADING PLAYERS

Ron Bertrand *born 15 January 1972*
Impressed straight from the off and soon took over as the club's number one goalie and one of the best in the league. The Canadian's transitional play earned him extra praise, along with a few assists.

Darcy Cahill *born 19 August 1970*
In his second season, the six-foot Canadian took on the dual role of player-coach after obtaining his level two coaching certificate. Finished at the head of the league scorers but also topped the penalty minutes.

Ryan Mair *born 15 December 1976*
The six-foot Canadian forward's hard hitting style and booming slap shot soon put him among the league's leading scorers, although he also found himself near the top of the 'sinners' list.

FACT FILE 1999-2000

English League: 3rd in Premier Division.
Playoffs: Finalists.
Data Vision Millennium Cup: Finalists.

CLUB HISTORY

Founded: 1997. The town's team was known as Wildcats from 1986 to 1996 and IceLords in 1996-97.
Leagues: Chill - English League 1997-2000; IceLords - Premier League 1996-97; Wildcats - British League, Div One 1986-96.

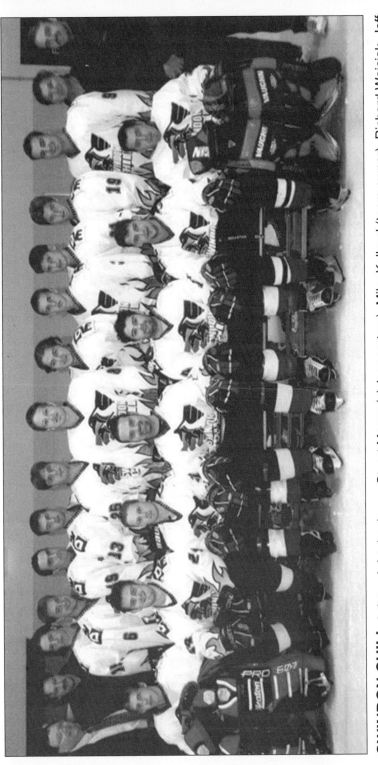

SWINDON CHILL *left to right, back row:* Stuart Morse (club secretary), Mike Kellond (team owner), Richard Wojciak, Jeff Sinnott, Marc Garris, Mike Smith, Magnus Joseffson, Lamonte Polet, Adam Andrews, Chris McEwen, Adi Smith, Andrew Shurmer, Drew Chapman, Ian Smith (equipment), Phil Jefferies (shareholder); *front row:* Ben Knock, Sean Tarr, Ken Forshee, Darcy Cahill, Alan Armour, Ryan Mair, Ron Bertrand.

WHITLEY WARRIORS

PLAYER	ENGLISH DIVISION ONE NORTH					PLAYOFFS					TOTALS				
Scorers	GP	G	A	Pts	Pim	GP	G	A	Pts	Pim	GP	G	A	Pts	Pim
Simon Leach	14	39	42	81	48	7	18	13	31	16	25	58	58	116	90
Lee Baxter	17	18	21	39	12	7	11	9	20	16	30	30	33	63	30
Andrew Carter	17	14	21	35	43	4	6	7	13	14	27	23	30	53	59
Karl Culley	18	17	15	32	18	7	9	7	16	8	31	27	23	50	28
Stuart Lonsdale	16	15	14	29	24	7	7	8	15	16	29	25	25	50	42
Paul McGinnety	17	5	18	23	55	6	2	10	12	18	29	8	30	38	83
Darren Taylor	14	12	22	34	69	1	0	1	1	27	21	12	23	35	124
Paul Sample	13	11	14	25	16	4	0	0	0	2	17	11	14	25	18
Kevin Bucas	14	6	10	16	78	6	1	6	7	16	26	7	16	23	100
Bobby Bradley	16	5	9	14	69	5	0	1	1	39	27	7	10	17	110
Simon McGinnety	10	6	6	12	14	2	0	4	4	4	18	6	10	16	22
Steve Winn	15	4	10	14	67	-	-	-	-	-	19	4	10	14	79
Paul Willis	13	1	8	9	42	4	1	2	3	47	21	2	10	12	95
Daniel Ord	13	2	3	5	55	6	3	0	3	49	19	5	3	8	104
Andrew Clish	6	0	1	1	10	6	2	5	7	28	12	2	6	8	38
Scott Taylor	11	2	0	2	0	2	2	2	4	4	13	4	2	6	4
Trond Gundersen (I)	4	3	1	4	0	-	-	-	-	-	4	3	1	4	0
Paul Massam	9	1	3	4	4	2	0	0	0	2	11	1	3	4	6
Brian Dunn	12	0	1	1	0	7	0	3	3	4	24	0	4	4	4
Paul Miller	2	2	1	3	0	-	-	-	-	-	5	2	1	3	0
Paul Graham	6	0	0	0	0	4	1	1	2	2	10	1	1	2	2
Pete Wynn	2	0	1	1	16	-	-	-	-	-	2	0	1	1	16
Chris Taylor	18	0	1	1	4	7	0	0	0	2	31	0	1	1	6
Anthony Markham (N)	15	0	0	0	6	7	0	0	0	22	28	0	0	0	28
Bench Penalties					2					2					6
TEAM TOTALS	18	163	222	385	652	7	63	79	142	340	31	238	315	553	1106
Netminders	GPI	Min	SoG	GA	Sv%	GPI	Min	SoG	GA	Sv%	GPI	Min	SoG	GA	Sv%
James Latimer	-	-	-	-	-	-	-	-	-	-	1	3	4	0	100
Rory Dunn	3	92	16	1	93.7	-	-	-	-	-	3	92	16	1	93.7
Gordon Ford	5	211	135	17	87.4	2	45	31	2	93.5	7	256	166	19	88.5
Anthony Markham	14	777	352	41	88.3	7	375	203	21	89.7	27	1509	840	112	86.7
TEAM TOTALS	18	777	352	41	88.3	7	420	234	23	90.2	31	1860	1026	132	87.1

Also appeared: Paul Ditchburn 6; Neil Bainbridge 5; Lee Forrest, Martin Gamsby, Mark Good, Ray Haslam 3; Dale Howey, Paul Matthews 2; Steve Downey, O J Good, Joe Stamp, Adam Winter 1.

All Competitions = league, playoffs and Benson and Hedges *Cup.*

WHITLEY WARRIORS *left to right, back:* Dave Shearer (equipment), Andrew Carter, Peter Winn (coach), Paul Willis, Paul Sample, Darren Taylor, Andrew Clish; *middle:* Paul Towns (asst coach), Stephen Winn, Paul Graham, Paul McGinnety, Stuart Lonsdale, Neil Bainbridge, Gordon Ford, Michael Winn (manager); *front:* Kevin Bucas, Bobby Bradley, Simon Leach, Lee Baxter, Bryan Dunn, Martin Gamsby, Scott Taylor; *on ice:* Chris Taylor, Anthony Markham, Daniel Ord, Karl Culley.

25-year trophy famine broken

DAVID HALL

Warriors' English League Division One playoff championship was their first major trophy since their Northern League title in 1975.

Coach **Peter Winn** had said at the beginning of the season: "We want that cup more than anything else," and his experienced side didn't let him down.

The campaign began with six defeats, but what glorious defeats. Edinburgh, Fife and Paisley had nothing bad to say about the Warriors as they made their first *Benson and Hedges'* appearances in four years and weren't embarrassed in any of them. Their best result was a 5-2 home defeat by Paisley.

Despite that showing, the league season didn't start the way Whitley wanted. After opening with a ridiculous 25-1 home win over Bradford, they were forced onto the road for six weeks while the Hillheads rink played host to Newcastle Riverkings and Superleague.

Two draws from the next four games was not the kind of reward the coach was looking for, either, though the 7-7 tie at Kingston in October was a thriller.

Trailing by four with 3.41 minutes remaining, **Stuart Lonsdale** and **Paul McGinnety** brought Warriors back to 5-7. Jets called a time-out, then Winn responded with a break for Warriors.

His team-talk was the more effective as Lonsdale scored his second at 59.04. Warriors pulled their netminder at 59.32 looking for the equaliser which came from **Andrew Carter** at 60 minutes dead, according to the timekeeper. Fortunately for Warriors, the ref. insisted that the puck had crossed the line before the hooter sounded.

After a 4-3 reverse in Nottingham in late November, Whitley suffered only three more defeats all season - all on nights when the bulk of the squad was made up of under-19s and under-16s because of senior work commitments.

Then they breezed through the playoffs against Altrincham and Flintshire, winning all three games. It might have been four, but Flintshire refused to travel for the second match after trouble in Wales when Winn was struck in the head by a stick. The offending player was taken away by the police and charged with assault.

Haringey were brushed aside in the semi-final and defending champions Billingham were beaten in the final. The playoff silverware was Whitley's first since their 1992 Scottish Cup.

PLAYER AWARDS

*Player of the Year	Karl Culley
*Player of the Playoffs	Paul McGinnety
Hillheads' Player of the Year	Stuart Lonsdale
*awarded by the Supporters Club	

LEADING PLAYERS

Simon Leach *born 3 August 1974*
Topped Warriors' scoring in a spectacular return to Hillheads after three years. The delight on his face when he lifted the playoff trophy showed how much the club means to him.

Stuart Lonsdale *born 16 November 1977*
The heart of Warriors' engine room, as likely to be helping the defence as scoring an important goal. The playoff success was especially sweet as he was one of five players to join Whitley from Sunderland who had lost out to Billingham in the 1999 final.

Anthony Markham *born 1 November 1977*
Described by his coach as the best netminder in the English League, he proved it with a goals against average around the three mark. Picked up two Gold Awards in the *Benson and Hedges* Cup.

FACT FILE 1999-2000

English League: 2nd in Division One North.
Playoffs: Champions.

CLUB HISTORY

Founded: 1956. Known as Newcastle Warriors in 1995-96, playing part of the season in Newcastle's *Telewest* Arena.
Leagues: English League 1997-2000; Northern Premier League 1996-97; British League, Premier Division 1982-96; Northern League 1966-82.
Honours: English League, Div One playoffs 1999-2000; Scottish Cup 1992; Northern League 1973-75; Icy Smith Cup 1972-73 & 1973-74.

LEAGUE ORGANISATION

Organised ice hockey in 1999-2000 was divided into three leagues, each run independently of the other.

The eight-team **Superleague** is a commercial organisation run under the auspices of a limited liability company, Ice Hockey Superleague Ltd (ISL), with each member club having a director on the ISL board.

The players are professionals recruited worldwide but mostly from North America. There was a £500,000 wage limit on players' salaries, and team rosters were limited to 20 skaters plus two netminders.

A proportion of the league's players require work permits (WP) and the guidelines on the origin and number of WP players are agreed annually between Superleague, the Dept of Employment (overseas labour section), the governing body, Ice Hockey UK, and the Ice Hockey Players Association (GB).

For 1999-2000, the guidelines were that this category of players should not exceed one-third of a team's roster with the remainder holding European Union passports.

North Americans should have played in a league at East Coast Hockey League (ECHL) level or above; Europeans must have played on a team from a country which competed in World A Pool the previous season.

The second tier **British National League** (BNL), which comprised ten teams, had an agreement that at least 50 per cent of each team's playing strength (16 players and two goalies, plus two under-19s) must be British trained and eligible to play for the national team. The league used only seven WP holders. The cap for players' wages was set at £100,000.

The **English League** (EL), which is run by the English Ice Hockey Association, comprises a wide range of clubs, from the virtually amateur to those with budgets as large as the smaller BNL clubs. The teams with the most ice time and largest budgets competed in the Premier Division with the remainder playing in one of the two regional Division One conferences.

Many teams iced overseas players (but only one WP holder), the number depending only on a club's finances. The wage cap in the Premier Division was around £65,000 per team.

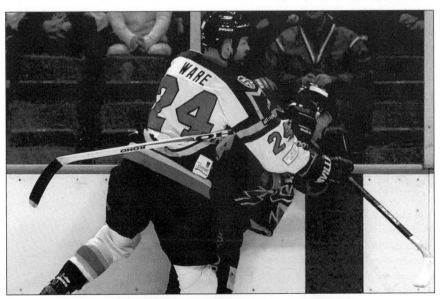

BETWEEN A ROCK AND A HARD MAN
London Kinghts' enforcer, **MIKE WARE**, crunches another victim on the boards.
photo: Mike Smith/Icepix

SEKONDA **SUPERLEAGUE**

FINAL STANDINGS

	GP	W	L	D	OL	GF	GA	Pts	Pct.
(5-4) **Bracknell Bees** BRK	42	24	15	3	5	181	138	56	66.7
(6-6) **Sheffield Steelers** SHE	42	24	16	2	2	188	155	52	61.9
(2-1) **Manchester Storm** MAN	42	23	17	2	3	155	138	51	60.7
(/-8) **London Knights** LON	42	23	16	3	1	135	125	50	59.5
(1-5) **Ayr Scottish Eagles** AYR	42	17	20	5	4	144	147	43	51.2
(4-3) **Nottingham Panthers** NOT	42	18	21	3	1	140	165	40	47.6
(3-2) **Cardiff Devils** CAR	42	17	21	4	2	138	149	40	47.6
(8-7) **Newcastle Riverkings** NEW	42	11	31	0	2	113	177	24	28.6

Positions of teams tied on points are decided by the number of wins.
Pct *Percentage of points gained to points available.*
Note 1 *If score tied at the end of normal time, teams played ten minutes' sudden-death overtime. Overtime winner received two points (W) and loser one (OL). If neither team scored, each received one point (D).*
Note 2 *Figures in brackets are last two seasons' league positions.*

LEADING SCORERS

excluding playoffs	GP	G	A	Pts	Pim
Ed Courtenay SHE	42	32	38	70	38
Teeder Wynne SHE	40	28	31	59	18
Dale Junkin SHE	42	20	36	56	24
Kevin Riehl BRK	40	27	27	54	22
*Mikko Koivunoro NEW	40	13	39	52	46
Steve Thornton CAR	41	26	24	50	14
Vezio Sacratini CAR	42	24	26	50	66
Shawn Byram AYR	42	17	32	49	108
Jamie Leach NOT	42	17	29	46	18
Shayne McCosh SHE	41	8	37	45	22

Record for assists in one season

FAIR PLAY

Team Penalties	GP	Pim	Ave
Manchester Storm	42	588	14.0
Sheffield Steelers	42	714	17.0
Bracknell Bees	42	784	18.7
Nottingham Panthers	42	786	18.7
Newcastle Riverkings	42	790	18.8
Cardiff Devils	42	973	23.2
Ayr Scottish Eagles	42	1022	24.3
London Knights	42	1107	26.4
LEAGUE TOTALS	168	6764	20.1

LEADING NETMINDERS

excluding playoffs	GPI	Mins	SoG	GA	Sav%
Brian Greer BRK	22	1321	639	56	91.2
Mark Cavallin LON	21	1117	511	47	90.8
Geoff Sarjeant AYR	23	1396	739	69	90.7
Mark Bernard MAN	30	1635	802	75	90.6
Derek Herlofsky CAR	26	1555	808	80	90.1

Qualification: 840 minutes

SIN-BIN

Player Penalties	GP	Pim	Ave
Barry Nieckar LON	18	143	7.94
Darren Banks LON	23	101	4.39
Clayton Norris NEW	40	172	4.30
Todd Gillingham CAR	41	17	4.17

OFFICIAL SUPERLEAGUE WEBSITE
www.iceweb.co.uk

POWERPLAY

Powerplay percentages	Adv.	PPG	Pct.
Sheffield Steelers	216	52	24.1
Manchester Storm	200	44	22.O
Nottingham Panthers	231	44	19.O
Cardiff Devils	202	37	18.3
Newcastle Riverkings	194	35	18.O
Bracknell Bees	200	32	16.O
Ayr Scottish Eagles	189	28	14.8
London Knights	180	25	13.9
LEAGUE TOTALS	1612	297	18.4

Adv. - times with man advantage
PPG - powerplay goals scored
Pct. - percentage of goals scored to powerplays.

IT WUZ LIKE THIS, 'ARRY

"I've nothing against Nicky Chinn. He didn't do anything to me. It just happened. I don't know whether I hit him in the helmet or in the head." Chris Baxter of Bracknell Bees, on fracturing his left hand on the Welshman.
IHNR.

TOP POWERPLAY POINTS SCORERS

Ed Courtenay SHE 15; Steve Thornton, Vezio Sacratini CAR 9; Jamie Leach NOT; Teeder Wynne & Dale Junkin SHE 7.

PENALTY KILLING

Penalty killing percentages	TSH	PGA	Pct.
Sheffield Steelers	200	29	85.5
Cardiff Devils	227	36	84.1
Ayr Scottish Eagles	223	40	82.1
London Knights	224	42	81.3
Manchester Storm	150	29	80.7
Bracknell Bees	204	41	79.9
Newcastle Riverkings	204	42	79.4
Nottingham Panthers	180	38	78.9
LEAGUE TOTALS	1612	297	81.6

TSH - times shorthanded
PGA - powerplay goals against

TOP SHORTHANDED GOAL SCORERS

Todd Goodwin BRK, Steve Thornton, Vezio Sacratini CAR, Iiro Jarvi NEW 2.

Giant killers

Bracknell Bees' league championship was the clasic giant-killing sports story as the small budget team toppled their more glamorous, big arena rivals to win their first Superleague title.

Much of the credit must go to second year coach, **Dave Whistle**, whose recruitment and man management skills created a rounded side that could score, defend and mix it with the best the opposition could offer.

Mike Blaisdell at runners-up **Sheffield Steelers**, on the other hand, was handicapped by having to coach a team which had been assembled by **Don McKee**, a man with a very different philosophy.

Steelers led the league for long spells and their first line topped the league scoring, a first in Superleague history. But defence was just a word they'd heard someone talking about.

London Knights, in only their second year and under a new coach, **Chris McSorley**, also topped the league for several weeks. But they never found a potent scorer and overdid the rough housing.

Defending title-holders **Manchester Storm** made wholesale player changes and lost their chemistry of the previous season. Goalie **Frank Pietrangelo** was particularly distracted by the internal problems.

Ayr Scottish Eagles, too, struggled to recapture their glory days of two seasons before. They failed to make the best use of the talents of Scotland's own great playmaker, **Tony Hand**, who they'd captured from Sheffield.

Nottingham Panthers' hopes of leaving the venerable Ice Stadium in a blaze of glory were dashed by a tight budget and a falling out between the owner and coach Blaisdell.

They brought in **Alex Dampier**, Britain's most successful coach, but even he couldn't turn their fortunes round. But their home record in regulation time (15-4-2) was the league's best.

It was the end of an era at **Cardiff Devils** as their president **David Temme** resigned and the club's finances crumbled. Though these traumatic events didn't happen until the season was over, or nearly over, the strains were apparent all year long and Devils' seventh place finish was their worst ever.

The troubled **Newcastle Riverkings** were kept afloat with Finnish help on and off the ice and forward **Mikko Koivunoro** set a league record for most assists in a season. But they won only seven games in the Telewest Arena and finished last for the second time in three years.

RESULTS CHART

	AYR	BRK	CAR	LON	MAN	NEW	NOT	SHE
AYR	*****	5-6 6/11	2-2ot 17/10	6-3 12/12	1-4 23/10	3-2ot (4) 30/10	7-2 5/12 CC	5-2 26/9
SCOTTISH	*****	4-2 8/1 CC	3-1 7/11 CC	1-3 19/12 CC	3-3ot 21/11 CC	7-1 26/12 CC	4-4ot 1/2	6-3 28/11 CC
EAGLES	*****	2-3ot 26/2 (18)	4-5ot (11) 15/1	3-2 30/1	4-6 3/1	5-3 20/1	2-4 17/2	2-8 27/2
BRACKNELL	5-2 3/10 CC	*****	4-5ot (1) 26/9	1-2 24/10	4-3 17/10	3-4ot (8) 5/12 CC	8-2 19/9	10-2 31/10
BEES	5-4 19/2	*****	3-2 23/1 CC	2-3 28/12 CC	5-2 27/11 CC	5-7 11/12	6-3 12/12 CC	4-5ot (6) 21/11 CC
	3-4 5/3	*****	5-1 15/2	4-3 27/2	10-2 29/1	6-1 6/2	7-3 2/1	3-2 16/1
CARDIFF	2-2ot 19/9 CC	6-5ot CC (11) 13/1	*****	5-3 3/10	4-5 25/9	5-2 28/11	8-3 21/11	1-4 10/10
DEVILS	7-4 27/1	3-5 24/2	*****	5-0 9/1	7-5 26/12	2-1 22/1	5-3 19/12	4-5ot (9) 12/12 CC
	1-3 20/2	1-3 4/3	*****	6-5 17/2	4-1 27/2	4-1 3/2	7-2 30/1	2-5 6/2
LONDON	2-1ot (5) 4/11 CC	3-3ot 28/11	6-1 14/10	*****	4-2 7/11 CC	1-3 19/9	5-3 26/9	5-4 5/10
KNIGHTS	1-4 21/12	1-4 27/12 CC	3-1 20/11 CC	*****	4-3ot 1/2 (17)	2-1ot (7) 2/12 CC	3-1 13/1 CC	3-2 17/10 CC
	5-0 6/2	3-3ot 3/2	1-1ot 16/12	*****	1-3 5/3	7-2 6/1	1-4 29/2+	5-7 18/11
MANCHESTER	4-6 2/12	0-2 10/10	4-2 2/1 CC	2-5 6/11	*****	5-2 26/9 CC	5-2 28/11 CC	7-3 19/9
STORM	4-2 28/12 CC	4-4ot 19/11 CC	5-2 20/1	3-4ot CC (14) 16/1	*****	3-1 30/1	3-1 6/2	5-2 22/12 CC
	5-4ot (16) 23/1	6-4 9/1	5-2 2/3	2-3 20/2	*****	4-0 3/3	5-3 25/2	3-2 17/2
NEWCASTLE	2-4 27/11 CC	2-3 18/9	2-5 2/10	2-3 31/10*	3-2ot (3) 24/10*	*****	4-3ot (2) 17/10*	1-3 3/10
RIVERKINGS	4-3 26/1	2-4 19/12 CC	2-4 22/12 CC	2-3 21/11 CC	3-5 17/11	*****	3-7 9/1	1-6 2/1 CC
	2-4 16/2	6-4 12/2	6-2 16/1	3-4 19/2	4-2 12/12 CC	*****	6-4 5/3	1-5 23/1
NOTTINGHAM	3-3ot 25/9	5-4ot CC (13) 15/1	4-0 18/9	2-1 27/11 CC	0-4 2/10	2-3 6/11	*****	3-1 16/10
PANTHERS	6-3 18/12 CC	3-2 26/1	4-3 8/1	2-5 3/1	7-6 11/12	6-0 20/11	*****	3-2 27/12 CC
	2-3 22/2	4-0 5/2	2-1ot 26/2 (19)	5-4ot (20) 4/3	4-2 22/1	8-7 20/2	*****	2-2ot 29/1
SHEFFIELD	4-1 2/10	5-6ot(15) 22/1 CC	3-3ot 6/11	4-2 18/9	4-5ot 6/1 (10) CC	4-3 25/9	4-3 30/10	*****
STEELERS	7-5 11/1 CC	3-6 30/1	7-4 27/11 CC	7-3 15/1 CC	5-3 27/1	9-3 15/12 CC	10-1 5/11 CC	*****
	4-3 3/3	8-5 20/2	7-2 19/2	5-8 12/2	1-3 5/2	6-5 31/12	3-2 26/12	*****
	AYR	**BRK**	**CAR**	**LON**	**MAN**	**NEW**	**NOT**	**SHE**

SEKONDA SUPERLEAGUE

NOTES ON RESULTS CHART
Second figure is date of game.
CC - *Points also counts towards Challenge Cup.*
*played at Whitley Bay
+also counted as Challenge Cup semi-final. League game on 23 January postponed due to stolen Plexiglas supports.

OVERTIME GAME WINNERS

(1)	CAR	Thornton (Evans)	69.00
(2)	NEW	Jarvi	61.07
(3)	NEW	Koivunoro (Ahlroos, Jarvi)	65.50
(4)	AYR	Young (Murano, Heroux) pp	69.55
(5)	LON	Kenny (Duthie, Martin)	66.29
(6)	SHE	Junkin (T Wynne, Courtenay)	61.03
(7)	LON	Martin (Scremin) pp	64.35
(8)	NEW	Numminen (Ahlroos, Norris)	63.04
(9)	SHE	Craigwell	62.19
(10)	MAN	Allard (Krumpschmid, Miller)	60.36
(11)	CAR	Sacratini pp	60.40
(12)	CAR	Chinn (Stone, Priest)	67.08
(13)	NOT	Bowen (Garden, Cain)	63.15
(14)	LON	Byce (Kenny, Brebant)	65.04
(15)	BRK	Ward	61.46
(16)	MAN	Lozhkin (Duthie, Robinson)	61.30
(17)	LON	Byce (Brebant, Martin)	61.26
(18)	BRK	Schulte	61.21
(19)	NOT	Pope (Tate)	61.30
(20)	NOT	Flichel (Roberts, Carpenter)	60.57

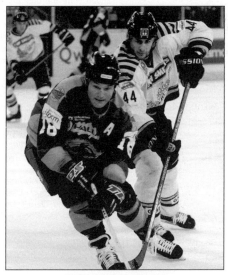

THE CHALLENGE

Sheffield Steeler **Dennis Vial** *left* is hooked by **Aaron Cain** of Nottingham Panthers in the *Alamo* Challenge Cup final at London Arena.

PLAYOFFS

All eight teams qualified for the Sekonda Superleague Playoff quarter-finals.

The teams were divided into two sections with the teams finishing the league in 1st, 4th, 6th and 8th place going into Group A and the others into Group B.

Each team played the others in its group home and away; the two leading teams in each group qualified for the semi-finals˜ where the winner of one group faced the runner-up in the other.

The semi-finals and final were played over one weekend at the Manchester Evening News Arena.

QUARTER-FINAL STANDINGS

Group A	GP	W	L	D	OL	GF	GA	Pts
London Knights	6	5	1	0	0	28	14	10
N'Castle Riverkings	6	3	2	1	2	14	12	9
Bracknell Bees	6	3	2	1	0	22	19	7
Nott'ham Panthers	6	0	6	0	1	7	26	1
Group B								
Sheffield Steelers	6	4	0	2	0	26	14	10
Ayr Scottish Eagles	6	2	3	1	1	12	19	6
Cardiff Devils	6	2	3	1	0	15	16	5
Manchester Storm	6	1	3	2	1	12	16	5

QUARTER-FINAL RESULTS

Group A	BRK	LON	NEW	NOT
Bracknell Bees	-	2-9	3-4	4-0
London Knights	3-5	-	3-2ot (2)	5-1
N'castle Riverkings	2-2ot	1-2ot (3)	-	3-1
Nott'ham Panthers	1-6	3-6	1-2ot (4)	-
Group B	AYR	CAR	MAN	SHE
Ayr Scottish Eagles	-	3-0	3-2	2-3ot (1)
Cardiff Devils	7-2	-	3-0	4-4ot
Manchester Storm	1-1ot	2-1	-	5-5ot
Sheffield Steelers	6-1	5-0	3-2ot (5)	-

Overtime Winners

(1) SHE Ceman (Wynne)   61.55
(2) LON Wetzel   66.24
(3) LON Bezeau (Brebant, Hoad)   69.57
(4) NEW Eloranta (Jarvi, Koivunoro)   61.46
(5) SHE Hoffman (Ceman, Short)   69.11

Riverkings come of age

The biggest upset of the *Sekonda* Superleague Playoffs was the performance of Newcastle Riverkings who had finished a long way last in the league. First, they took two points off the undefeated Knights in overtime. Three periods was too brief to settle the result either at home or away.

As OT wound down in the *Telewest* Arena, fans wondered which coach would pull their goalie. Although London weren't desperate for points, their coach **Chris McSorley** loves this gamble. But it was **Jukka Jalonen** of Riverkings who blinked first and pulled **Jim Hibbert** even though they had one priceless point in the bag. The move backfired with Knights **Andy Bezeau** netting the winner three seconds from time.

Next night in Bracknell, Riverkings chalked up their first win of the playoffs in - of all places - Bracknell, the home of the league champs. No OT, either, with Riverkings leading the lacklustre Bees 4-2 from **Glenn Mulvenna**'s goal at 37.38 until **Kevin Riehl** scored a consolation for Bees on a powerplay with 15 seconds remaining.

What made this win even more satisfying for the north-east club was that it put both teams on five points and left Riverkings needing only to beat the struggling Panthers - which they did twice - to make it to the Manchester semis.

The competition in group B was not nearly as close as league runners-up Sheffield Steelers romped through the quarter-finals. **Mike Blaisdell**'s squad were the only unbeaten team at this stage, though four of their six games went into overtime.

A typical Steelers' battle came in their own rink on the second weekend against Manchester Storm. With the score 1-1 with less than three minutes left a defensive error let in **Pierre Allard** to give Storm the lead.

Greg Clancy tied it up again 83 seconds from time and it needed a last-minute effort from **Kevin Hoffman** in overtime for Steelers to squeak the win and stay on top of their group.

This was also the story of Storm's playoffs as they could only draw at home the next night when Ayr took them into overtime. Two of Storm's three losses were by one goal.

That was the only time Eagles managed a point on the road, though their away record was not as disastrous as Cardiff Devils who failed to win a single game away from the Ice House.

PLAYOFF SEMI-FINALS

MEN Arena, Manchester
Saturday 1 April 2000

NEWCASTLE RIVERKINGS	3 (0-0-3)
SHEFFIELD STEELERS	1 (0-0-1)

First Period
No scoring.
Pims: Riverkings 4, Steelers 2.
Second Period
No scoring.
Pims: Riverkings 2, Steelers 2.
Third Period
1-0 NEW Johnson (Ruggles, Norris)   17.58
2-0 NEW Poirier (Norris, Hibbert) eng 19.20
2-1 SHE Courtenay (Craigwell)   19.42
3-1 NEW Walker (Mulvenna) eng   19.56
Pims: Riverkings 2, Steelers 12 (Longstaff 2+10 checking from behind).
Shots on Goal
Hibbert NEW   9-8-9 26   save percentage 96.1
Sjerven SHE   9-5-8 22   save percentage 95.4
Man of the Match: Hibbert NEW.
Referee: Moray Hanson.
Linesmen: Andy Allsop, Alan Craig.
Attendance: 8,000 approx.

AYR SCOTTISH EAGLES	1 (0-0-1)
LONDON KNIGHTS	2 (1-0-0)

First Period
0-1 LON Bultje (Hussey)   1.42
Pims: Eagles 31 (Stevenson 5+game), Knights 27 (Bezeau 2+5+game).
Second Period
No scoring.
Pims: None.
Third Period
1-1 AYR Steer pp   12.55
Pims: Eagles 2, Knights 2.*Overtime*
1-2 LON Bultje (Hussey, Nieckar)   6.41
Pims: None.
Man of the Match: Sarjeant AYR.
Referee: Simon Kirkham.
Linesmen: Simon Norcott, Matt Thompson.
Attendance: 9,918.

PLAYOFF FINAL

MEN Arena, Manchester
Sunday 2 April 2000

NEWCASTLE RIVERKINGS	3 (2-0-1)
LONDON KNIGHTS	7 (2-2-3)

First Period
1-0 NEW Walker (Johnson)   2.46
1-1 LON Wetzel (Bultje, Burke)   6.42
1-2 NEW Walker (Tjallden, Johnson) pp 10.32

2-2 LON Brebant (Rushforth, Byce) pp 15.55
Pims: Riverkings 4, Knights 2.
Second Period
2-3 LON Rushforth (Byce)   2.42
2-4 LON Rushforth (Scremin, Hussey) pp 11.37
Pims: Riverkings 6, Knights 8.
Third Period
2-5 LON Rushforth (Scremin, Robins)   1.55
2-6 LON Bultje (Martin, Scremin)   11.01
3-6 NEW Poirier (Dubois, Jarvi) pp   14.12
3-7 LON Bultje (Ashe) sh   16.00
Pims: Riverkings 0, Knights 6.
Man of the Match: Rushforth LON.
Referee: Andy Carson.
Linesmen: Matt Folka, Paul Staniforth.
Attendance: 8,500 approx.

THE FINAL FOUR

LONDON KNIGHTS
Mark Cavallin, Trevor Robins; Marc Hussey, Tim Murray, Tom Ashe, Neal Martin, Claudio Scremin, Greg Burke, Mike Ware; John Byce, Jeff Hoad, Mark Bultje, Andy Bezeau, Barry Nieckar, Paul Rushforth (capt), Todd Wetzel, Rick Brebant.
Head Coach: Chris McSorley.
Asst Coach: Scott Rex.

NEWCASTLE RIVERKINGS
Jim Hibbert, Marko Rantanen; Eric Dubois, Juha Lampinen, Jari Eerikanen, Tomi Makela, Mikael Tjallden, Hakan Galiamoutsas; Kim Ahlroos, Shaun Johnson, Mikko Koivunoro, Iiro Jarvi, Sami Wahlsten, Jussi Eloranta, Clayton Norris, Darby Walker, Glenn Mulvenna (capt), Joel Poirier, Teemu Numminen, Hilton Ruggles.
Manager: Mike O'Connor.
Coach: Jukka Jalonen.

AYR SCOTTISH EAGLES
Geoff Sarjeant, Dave Trofimenkoff; Scott Young, Mike Bishop, Vince Boe, Iouri Krivokhija, Jan Mikel; Tony Hand, Jamie Steer, Mark Montanari, Cam Bristow, Shawn Byram (capt), Shayne Stevenson, Eric Murano, Yves Heroux, Patric Lochi, Dino Bauba, Rob Trumbley.
Manager: Ken McLeod.
Coach: Jim Lynch.

SHEFFIELD STEELERS
Grant Sjerven, Shawn Silver; Rob Wilson (capt), Shayne McCosh, Andre Malo, Mark Matier, Kip Noble, Kayle Short, Dennis Vial; Ed Courtenay, Scott Allison, Tommy Plommer, Matt Hoffman, Teeder Wynne, David Longstaff, Dan Ceman, Greg Clancy, Dale Junkin, Dale Craigwell, Jason Weaver.
Manager: Dave Simms.
Coach: Mike Blaisdell.

LEADING SCORERS

all Playoff games	GP	G	A	Pts	Pim
Mark Bultje LON	8	5	6	11	6
Rick Brebant LON	8	3	8	11	10
Claudio Scremin LON	8	3	8	11	6
Marc Hussey LON	7	3	6	9	2
Jason Weaver SHE	7	3	6	9	39
David Longstaff SHE	7	2	7	9	14
Todd Wetzel LON	8	4	4	8	12
Greg Clancy SHE	7	2	6	8	2
Paul Rushforth LON	7	5	2	7	8
Kevin Riehl BRK	6	4	3	7	4
Joel Poirier NEW	8	4	3	7	6
Vezio Sacratini CAR	6	3	4	7	16

FINNS ARE GENTS

"We have a gentlemen's agreement in Finland that you don't do such things. I don't like it. I don't use those tactics - but this was **Chris' [McSorley]** choice. *Riverkings' coach* **Jukka Jalonen,** *on his rival coach calling an illegal stick on* **Clayton Norris** *in the final.*

LEADING NETMINDERS

all Playoff games	GPI	Min	SoG	GA	Sv%
Geoff Sarjeant AYR	6	359	206	13	93.7
Trevor Robins LON	7	443	183	13	92.9
Mark Bernard MAN	6	389	226	16	92.9

Qulaification 180 minutes

FAIR PLAY

Team Penalties	GP	Pim	Ave
Manchester Storm	6	80	13.3
London Knights	8	119	14.9
Newcastle Riverkings	8	144	18.0
Nottingham Panthers	6	112	18.7
Ayr Scottish Eagles	7	148	21.1
Sheffield Steelers	7	165	23.6
Bracknell Bees	6	174	29.0
Cardiff Devils	6	184	30.7

SIN BIN

Player Penalties	GP	Pim	Ave
Todd Gillingham CAR	5	56	11.20
Blake Knox BRK	6	58	9.67
Denis Chassé BRK	4	34	8.50

Knights stick it to Riverkings

Chris McSorley's aggressive tactics had made his London Knights the league's most feared opponents during the season. But when they won the Playoffs - their first major title - with smart, skilful play, not to mention one of the lowest penalty totals, they could add respect.

But McSorley himself remained controversial to the end as he couldn't resist using his much despised tactic of making an illegal stick call against Newcastle Riverkings, Knights' upstart challengers in the final.

The call came as Knights were trying to establish their superiority on the well-coached Riverkings in the middle of the second period. **Jukka Jalonen**'s men were down 3-2 when **Sami Wahlsten** was called for slashing.

With the two-man advantage, **Paul Rushforth** scored the second goal of his hat-trick and though Newcastle held on until early in the last session, McSorley's master plan succeeded in snuffing out their fire.

"I know you don't make a lot of friends with such calls, but that's hockey," said McSorley in reply to the criticisms. "We had the lead and just needed to grab some momentum."

DEFENCES ON TOP

While the fans enjoyed ten goals in the final, the semis were the more familiar professional display of defences grinding out a draw. Apart from **Mark Bultje**'s unscripted second-minute goal against Ayr on Saturday evening, all the goals in both games came in the later stages.

Ayr forced Knights into overtime before Bultje's winner. "I just wanted to get it over with and get to bed, ready for the big game tomorrow," grinned the Dutch-Canadian.

The flurry of goals in the Steelers-Riverkings shocker all came in a wild last 2.02 minutes and coach **Mike Blaisdell** was duly shocked and subdued afterwards. "Newcastle were exceptional," he said. "They controlled the neutral zone. We under-estimated them."

Jimmy Hibbert's goaltending as well as Jalonen's patient coaching were the main contributors to the biggest upset in a major trophy game that Steelers have suffered since they lost 12-1 to Cardiff Devils in the 1994 Wembley final. Steelers had beaten Newcastle six times in six league and *B&H* Cup games.

- *Sky Sports* covered all three games for the fifth successive year.

- Knights' All-Star defender, **Claudio Scremin**, played the final with a badly bruised leg, then caught a puck behind the ear. "That took your mind off your leg," quipped a heartless reporter in the press conference afterwards.

CHALLENGE CUP

A made-for-TV competition with highlights of the final and, briefly, the semi-finals shown on BBC2's Sunday Grandstand.

One round of nominated Superleague games counted as the qualifying round of the Cup. (See Superleague Results Chart).

The leading four teams qualified for the semi-finals with first meeting fourth and second playing third, over home and away legs.

The Cup's destination was decided at London Arena in a one-game final which was sponsored by car rental group, Alamo.

QUALIFYING ROUND STANDINGS

	GP	W	L	D	OL	GF	GA	Pts
London Knights	14	10	4	0	0	35	34	20
Bracknell Bees	14	7	6	1	4	57	48	19
Sheffield Steelers	14	8	6	0	2	77	56	18
Nott'ham Panthers	14	8	6	0	0	55	61	16
Ayr S. Eagles	14	6	6	2	1	50	43	15
Manchester Storm	14	6	6	2	1	55	52	15
Cardiff Devils	14	6	7	1	1	48	47	14
N'castle Riverkings	14	2	12	0	1	28	64	5

all games counted towards Superleague points.

SEMI-FINALS

First leg

29 Feb	LONDON - NOTTINGHAM	1-4*

Scorers: LON Brebant;
NOT Garden (2), Roberts,
Carlsson.

2 Mar	SHEFFIELD - BRACKNELL	1-2

Scorers: SHE Allison;
BRK Drouin, Brant.

Second leg

7 Mar	NOTTINGHAM - LONDON	3-3

Scorers: NOT Hadden (2), Leach;
LON Ware, Brebant, Rushforth.

PANTHERS win 7-4 on aggregate

9 Mar	BRACKNELL-SHEFFIELD	4-8

Scorers: BRK Chasse, Woods,
Stewart, Schulte; SHE Craigwell 2,
Hoffman 2, Weaver 2, Allison,
Courtenay.

STEELERS win 9-6 on aggregate
* also Superleague game.

PAST WINNERS

1999	Sheffield Steelers (at Sheffield).	
1998	*Ayr Scottish Eagles (at Newcastle).	

* competition sponsored by The Express.

FINAL

London Arena
Sunday 26 March 2000

NOTTINGHAM PANTHERS	1 (1-0-0)
SHEFFIELD STEELERS	2 (2-0-0)

First Period
1-0 NOT Hadden 8.15
1-1 SHE Courtenay (McCosh, Wynne) 10.07
1-2 SHE Weaver (Longstaff, Sjerven) pp 14.41
Pims: NOT 8, SHE 6.
Second Period
No scoring.
Pims: NOT 6, SHE 8.
Third Period
No scoring.
Pims: NOT 2, SHE 6.
Shots on Goal:
Willis   NOT   11-12-8 31   (save percent. 93.55)
Sjerven SHE   11-10-9 30   (save percent. 96.66)
Men of Match: Willis NOT, Short SHE.
Referee: Andy Carson.
Linesmen: Koenen, Westney.
Attendance: 6,602.

Willis' brilliance not enough

In front of the largest crowd in London Arena all season, Sheffield Steelers retained the Challenge Cup by the narrowest of margins from their old rivals, Nottingham Panthers.

Steelers' high-powered offence only twice found a way past the injury-hit Panthers, led by an inspired **Jordan Willis** in goal.

The very different approaches of the teams made for some entertaining, end-to-end hockey which was spoiled in some eyes by over-zealous refereeing from **Andy Carson**.

"The penalties disrupted the flow," complained Steelers' coach, **Mike Blaisdell**. "We knew they had injuries and we wanted to go at them."

Blaiser couldn't complain about the crowd, though. "They were like an extra player, it was like being at home," he said as around 4,000 Steelers' fans roared their team on.

The final moments were spoiled when the chanting crowd drowned Carson's whistle for offside with 3.1 seconds left. The clock ran down to zero, the fireworks flashed and banged and a blizzard of coloured paper made further play impossible.

The teams eventually agreed to take a face-off in Panthers' end and allow the clock to tick off the final seconds officially.

Nottingham's skipper, **Jamie Leach**, explained: "As there was only one chance in a billion that we would score, I said let's drop the puck so we don't end a great game in a fiasco."

ALL-TIME SUPERLEAGUE RECORDS

LEAGUE STANDINGS

1996-2000	S	GP	W	L	D	OL	GF	GA	Pts.	Pct.
Cardiff Devils	4	154	89	56	9	10	589	460	197	64.0
Manchester Storm	4	154	85	60	9	9	575	495	188	61.0
Sheffield Steelers	4	154	79	63	12	9	594	524	179	58.1
Ayr Scottish Eagles	4	154	76	63	15	9	568	513	176	57.1
Nottingham Panthers	4	154	78	68	8	5	535	545	169	54.9
Bracknell Bees	4	154	72	74	8	11	589	604	163	52.9
London Knights	2	84	33	45	6	5	249	308	77	45.8
Newcastle Riverkings	4	154	48	100	6	10	454	618	112	36.4
Basingstoke Bison	2	70	16	47	7	9	232	318	48	34.3

LEADING SCORERS

1996-2000	S	GP	G	A	Pts.
Dale Junkin SHE/BRK	4	154	65	110	175
Vezio Sacratini CAR	4	144	70	96	166
Tony Hand AYR/SHE	4	145	41	24	165
Ed Courtenay SHE	3	108	81	78	159
Ivan Matulik CAR	4	150	73	82	155
Greg Hadden NOT	4	137	77	69	146
Steve Thornton CAR	4	130	59	83	142
Steve Moira CAR	4	150	71	66	137
Jamie Leach NOT/SHE	4	134	62	75	137
Paul Adey NOT	3	104	58	75	131

LEADING NETMINDERS

1996-2000	S	GPI	MINS	SOG	GA	Sav%
Rob Dopson AYR	1	28	1674	885	66	92.5
Derek Herlofsky CAR	3	68	4077	2041	177	91.3
Frank Pietrangelo MAN	2	57	3192	1497	132	91.2
Trevor Robins NOT/LON	4	101	5866	3188	290	90.9
Geoff Sarjeant AYR	1	23	1396	739	69	90.7
Stevie Lyle CAR	4	66	3847	2011	189	90.6

BRITISH NATIONAL LEAGUE

FINAL STANDINGS

		GP	W	OW	L	OL	GF	GA	Pts	Pct
(6-5)	**Fife Flyers** FIF	36	28	1	7	0	176	89	58	80.5
(1-3)	**Guildford Flames** GUI	36	26	1	7	2	184	98	56	77.8
(/-2)	**Basingstoke Bison** BAS	36	23	2	11	0	138	85	50	69.4
(3-6)	**Hull Thunder** HUL	36	20	3	12	1	149	132	47	65.3
(4-4)	**Peterborough Pirates** PET	36	22	1	13	0	171	128	46	63.9
(7-1)	**Slough Jets** SLO	36	19	0	14	3	109	100	41	56.9
(/-/)	**Solihull Blaze** SOL	36	13	1	20	2	161	172	30	41.7
(9-8)	**Edinburgh Capitals** EDI	36	9	1	25	1	118	192	21	29.2
(/-/)	**Milton Keynes Kings** MIL	36	4	1	28	3	114	202	13	18.1
(5-9)	**Paisley Pirates** PAI	36	4	1	30	1	103	226	11	15.3

Pct. *Percentage of points gained to points available.*
Note 1. *All games were played to a decision. If score tied at end of normal time, teams played five minutes' sudden-death overtime. If still no winner, the decision was made on sudden-death penalty shots. The winning team in overtime or after penalty shots (OW) received two points and loser (OL) one.*
Note 2. *Penalty shots are not included in the above table.*
Note 2. *Figures in brackets are last two seasons' league positions.*
Hull Thunder *previously competed as Kingston Hawks.*

LEADING SCORERS

	GP	G	A	Pts	Pim
Claude Dumas HUL/PET	41	39	56	95	54
Randy Smith PET	36	43	44	87	30
Russell Monteith FIF	36	36	32	68	6
Steve Chartrand SOL	36	34	31	65	30
A J Kelham SOL	33	30	35	65	4
Todd Dutiaume FIF	35	28	35	63	48
Karry Biette GUI	36	23	37	60	63
Barcley Pearce GUI	34	24	32	56	48
Pete Kasowski GUI	36	26	27	53	30
John Haig FIF	35	17	36	53	24
Jeff Daniels BAS	31	16	35	51	24

FAIR PLAY

Team Penalties	GP	Pim	Ave
Fife Flyers	36	390	10.83
Guildford Flames	36	542	15.05
Basingstoke Bison	36	562	15.61
Milton Keynes Kings	36	618	17.17
Hull Thunder	36	618	17.17
Edinburgh Capitals	36	670	18.61
Paisley Pirates	36	790	21.94
Peterborough Pirates	36	805	22.36
Solihull Blaze	36	823	22.86
Slough Jets	36	864	24.00
LEAGUE TOTALS	180	6682	18.56

LEADING NETMINDERS

	GPI	Min	SoG	GA	Sv%
Stephen Murphy FIF	30	1774	954	63	93.4
Colum Cavilla HUL	17	988	507	35	93.1
Joe Watkins BAS	30	1631	722	64	91.1
Craig Lindsay PET	27	1573	828	76	90.8
Jamey Organ GUI	35	2030	948	92	90.3

SIN-BIN

Player Penalties	GP	Pim	Ave
Andrew Milne PET	22	181	8.23
Kurt Irvine SOL	33	156	4.73
Scott Plews EDI	27	126	4.66

OFFICIAL BNL WEBSITE
www.britnatleague.co.uk

PAST WINNERS

1998-99	**Slough Jets**
1997-98	**Guildford Flames**

LEAGUE AWARDS

Player of the Year	Stephen Murphy FIF
Players' Player	Stephen Murphy FIF
Defenceman of the Year	Ron Shudra HUL
Netminder of the Year	Stephen Murphy FIF
Coach of the Year	Mark Morrison FIF

ALL-STARS

Goal	Stephen Murphy FIF
Defence	Ron Shudra HUL
	Adam Lamarre SLO
Forwards	Russell Monteith FIF
	Claude Dumas HUL/PET
	Randy Smith PET

BRITISH ALL-STARS

Goal	Stephen Murphy FIF
Defence	Paul Dixon GUI
	Neil Liddiard PET
Forwards	Steven Lynch EDI
	John Haig FIF
	Nick Cross SLO

Super soaraway Flyers

Fife Flyers', the sport's oldest club, celebrated their 61st season by winning the British National League and collecting the lion's share of the league's individual awards.

Flyers, who were formed in 1938, have captured many Scottish and northern titles, but the only other national trophy in their cabinet is the Division One silverware from the *(Heineken)* British League in 1991-92.

This is more a comment on the structure of the sport than on the consistently fine performances of the fiercely patriotic Scots side. They were especially proud this season of the recruiting job carried out by their Canadian coach, **Mark Morrison**.

Flyers have a long tradition of producing talented local players, and the high standard of imports which Morrison signed meant that they could manage most of the season with only five overseas players, the fewest of any BNL team.

Add to this the awesome netminding of Dundee-born **Stephen Murphy**, 17, and good fortune with injuries, and Flyers enjoyed one of their best ever campaigns.

Guildford Flames, reputedly the league's richest members, had been expected to set the place alight and they did for much of the season. But **Stan Marple**'s crew lacked the all-important team chemistry to bring them victory.

In a competitive league where there was little to choose between the top five, *Basingstoke Bison* also failed to find that necessary extra spark. **Charlie Colon** and **Rick Strachan**, two veterans of the British game, shared the coaching duties and

signed promising young English netminder, **Joe Watkins**. The previous season's runners-up also boasted one of the league's largest overseas player contingents but, despite **Wayne Crawford**'s scoring records, Bison lacked consistent fire power.

Hull Thunder had the league's most potent attacker in leading scorer **Claude Dumas**, a Superleague goalie in **Colum Cavilla**, and an All-Star defender in **Ron Shudra**. But the first two only joined the unsettled and import-heavy squad in mid-season after Thunder's finances had been boosted by new owner, **Darren Brown**.

Peterborough Pirates were unsettled for most of the season as the supposed re-financing of the club mostly failed to trickle down to the coach and his players. After coach **Troy Walkington** quit, popular forward **Randy Smith** added the duties to his sharp shooting role.

Defending champions *Slough Jets* had a satisfying campaign finishing in mid-table after almost failing to reach the starting line after the local authority slashed their financial backing.

Joe Stefan, brother of retired player-manager Gary, carried on the family line at Slough as he added the coaching to his playing duties. Jets were second only to Fife in their limited use of non-British trained players.

The return of *Solihull Blaze* after two seasons in the English League was also considered a success, though they owed much to the super scoring exploits of **Steve Chartrand** and **AJ Kelham** who tallied 40 per cent of Blaze's goals.

ONE CLUB - THREE SAVIOURS

Coach **Paul Thompson** also recruited well on defence where he signed former Superleague blueliner **Mike Shewan**.

Milton Keynes Kings and their coach **Mark Mackie** found the going harder after a similar 'promotion' from the English League. Results improved after Mackie was replaced by defenceman **Rob Coutts** in mid-season, but not enough for Kings to rise above ninth place.

Charismatic former Superleague defender, **Angelo Catenaro**, was seen as the saviour of *Edinburgh Capitals* - until he fell out with the team's other saviour, backer **Raymond Lumsden**. After hitting third place in the early going, Capitals, now under their third messiah, forward-director-coach **Scott Neil**, slipped all the way down to eighth.

Paisley Pirates, the league's third Scottish club, limped their way through the second half of the season, beset by financial restrictions and a similar internal dispute. This time new American coach **Stirling Wright** didn't see eye-to-eye with an official as well as his club and he was sacked in February.

RESULTS CHART

	BAS	EDI	FIF	GUI	HUL	MIL	PAI	PET	SLO	SOL
BAS	*****	7-2 15/1	1-4 16/10	3-0 20/11	6-2 25/9	2-1 7/11	4-2 9/10	6-0 8/1	1-0 2/10	6-1 27/12
	*****	9-2 19/2	1-4 13/2	3-1 22/1	0-3 26/2	6-3 5/2	4-0 29/1	5-3 6/2	1-3 27/11	4-2 22/2
EDI	5-3 17/10	*****	1-6 7/11	4-3 24/10	1-6 31/10	3-1 14/11	6-3 3/10	2-4 21/11	4-5 26/9	3-8 28/11
	2-3ot (H) 20/2	*****	2-8 9/1	3-7 19/12	0-2 23/1	4-10 27/2	5-4 12/10	7-4 30/1	3-6 13/2	3-8 6/2
FIF	4-1 18/12	6-4 13/11	*****	5-1 6/11	5-1 9/10	5-4 30/10	3-1 16/1	2-3 20/11	6-5 25/9	7-1 27/11
	3-0 30/1	9-5 22/1	*****	5-2 12/2	4-5 8/1	9-2 29/1	10-2 19/2	1-6 11/12	3-1 26/2	8-1 5/2
GUI	3-2 26/9	6-0 23/10	4-3 10/10	*****	6-6ot (2) 16/10	7-1 28/11	5-3 13/11	6-0 25/9	1-0 31/10	12-5 3/10
	1-1ot (3) 12/12	6-4 29/1	5-3 23/1	*****	5-3 6/2	9-3 9/1	14-1 26/2	5-0 20/2	6-0 5/12	6-2 18/12
HUL	2-8 5/12	4-2 10/10	3-2 26/9	4-5 7/11	*****	6-5 3/10	4-3ot (C) 28/11	4-9 17/10	4-3 21/11	2-6 15/1
	3-1 27/2	4-6 12/12	4-5 24/10	3-2ot (E) 5/2	*****	5-2 9/2	11-3 9/1	4-2 13/2	3-1 30/1	2-1 20/2
MIL	3-5 10/10	4-5ot 6/11	1-7 5/12	3-4 27/11	3-5 23/10	*****	5-5ot (1) 25/9	1-6 2/10	1-3 17/10	4-3ot (B) 13/11
	4-5ot (F) 12/2	6-4 20/11	3-4 22/2	2-10 8/1	4-6 16/1	*****	8-4 6/2	2-5 31/10	2-3 20/2	7-5 26/2
PAI	1-5 24/10	4-2 27/11	4-6 21/11	5-8 17/10	3-5 2/10	5-3 26/9	*****	2-10 7/11	1-4 10/10	5-6 23/10
	2-11 19/12	7-4 5/2	1-7 20/2	0-11 13/2	3-6 22/1	7-6 30/1	*****	1-5 12/12	1-3 27/2	3-8 8/1
PET	7-2 29/10	5-3 9/10	2-3 4/12	1-3 1/10	5-3 12/11	11-1 19/11	8-3 16/10	*****	3-2ot (A) 22/10	6-7 24/9
	2-7 4/2	6-3 12/2	1-5 15/1	7-3 10/12	9-5 26/11	5-4 18/2	6-2 6/11	*****	5-2 7/1	7-5 27/1
SLO	4-2 3/10	2-4 16/10	0-1ot (D) 28/11	3-2 15/1	4-2 20/11	6-1 9/10	6-3 30/10	2-3 23/10	*****	4-2 6/11
	2-3 16/1	5-2 8/1	3-6 6/2	2-4 19/2	0-5 29/1	5-1 23/1	3-0 11/12	3-5 18/12	*****	2-2ot (4) 12/2
SOL	2-5 21/11	3-4 2/10	2-4 17/10	4-5 4/11	1-5 19/12	5-1 24/10	8-3 31/10	6-9 10/10	4-5 7/11	*****
	2-5 9/1	8-4 16/1	6-3 27/2	4-6 30/1	6-7ot (G) 19/2	12-2 13/2	6-5 23/1	5-2 5/12	3-6 22/1	*****
	BAS	EDI	FIF	GUI	HUL	MIL	PAI	PET	SLO	SOL

Second figure is date of the game

OVERTIME GAME WINNERS

(A) David Clarke (Granqvist, Sakata) PET   61.33
(B) Prachar (Randall, Morgan) MIL   62.34
(C) Stephen Johnson (Payne, Brown) HUL   64.34
(D) Samuel (Smith) FIF   62.16
(E) Tatarnic (Grandqvist) HUL   62.10
(F) Ellis (Redmond, Carpenter) BAS   60.18
(G) Dumas (A Johnson, Payne) HUL   63.23
(H) Daniels (Burgess) BAS   63.07

GAME WINNING PENALTY SHOTS

(1) Chris Jamieson PAI
(2) Barcley Pearce GUI
(3) Dru Burgess BAS
(4) A J Kelham SOL

Note
Score in table is result after overtime

PLAYOFFS

The top eight BNL teams qualified for the playoffs. In the quarter-finals the teams were split into two groups of four with the teams finishing 1st, 4th, 5th and 8th in the league going into group A and the others into group B.

The top two teams in each group qualified for the semi-finals with the winner of one group playing a best-of-three series against the runner-up in the other group. Home ice advantage went to the top team in each group.

The winning semi-finalists competed for the title in a best-of-five final series, with the home ice advantage going to the team that finished highest in the league.

QUARTER-FINAL STANDINGS

Group A	GP	W	OW	L	OL	GF	GA	Pts
Fife Flyers	6	5	0	1	0	37	13	10
P'boro' Pirates	6	3	0	1	1	25	29	7
Hull Thunder	6	2	1	3	0	23	22	6
E'burgh Capitals	6	1	0	5	0	15	36	2
Group B								
Bas'stoke Bison	6	4	0	2	0	19	18	8
Solihull Blaze	6	3	1	2	0	24	22	8
Guildford Flames	6	3	1	2	0	25	19	8
Slough Jets	6	0	0	4	2	11	20	2

Teams tied on points separated first by wins in normal time, then by away wins in normal time. Table excludes penalty shots.

QUARTER-FINAL RESULTS

Group A	EDI	FIF	HUL	PET
Edinburgh Capitals	-	1-2	2-3	6-2
Fife Flyers	12-2	-	5-0	10-2
Hull Thunder	9-1	4-5	-	4-6
Peterboro' Pirates	8-3	4-3	3-3ot (2)	-
Group B	BAS	GUI	SLO	SOL
Basingstoke Bison	-	4-2	3-2	5-4
Guildford Flames	4-3	-	5-0	7-4
Slough Jets	2-4	2-2ot (1)	-	2-3
Solihull Blaze	4-0	6-5	3-3ot (3)	-

GAME WINNING PENALTY SHOTS

1	Karry Biette	GUI
2	Claude Dumas	HUL
3	Mike Shewan	SOL

SEMI-FINALS

Best-of-three series

25 Mar	Basingstoke-Peterborough	6-3
	Fife-Solihull	5-2
26 Mar	Peterborough-Basingstoke	2-4
	Solihull-Fife	4-5

Basingstoke and Fife win two games to nil.

FINALS

Best-of-five series

Game One, Kirkcaldy, 1 April 2000

FIFE FLYERS	6 (1-2-3)
BASINGSTOKE BISON	3 (0-1-2)

First Period
1-0 FIF   Monteith (Haig, Russell)   pp 11.22
Pims: Fife 2, Basingstoke 2.
Second Period
2-0 FIF   Smith (Haig, Morrison)   5.38
2-1 BAS   Mason (Carpenter, Ellis)   7.23
3-1 FIF   Morrison (Haig, Smith)   12.16
Pims: Fife 2, Basingstoke 2.
Third Period
4-1 FIF   Morrison (Morris, Haig)   5.07
4-2 BAS   Carpenter (Burgess)   6.17
5-2 FIF   Dutiaume (D King)   10.24
6-2 FIF   Morrison (Russell, Morris)   pp 14.00
6-3 BAS   Carpenter (Ellis, Baird)   16.14
Pims: Fife 4, Basingstoke 4.
Shots on Goal
Murphy FIF   8-16-10 34   *save percentage:* 91.2
Watkins BAS 14-10-12 36   *save percentage:* 83.3
Referee: Graham Horner.
Linesmen: Evans, Fraser.
Attendance: 1,653

Game Two, Basingstoke, 2 April 2000

BASINGSTOKE BISON	1 (1-0-0)
FIFE FLYERS	2 (1-1-0)

First Period
1-0 BAS Carpenter (Burgess, Mason)   pp 14.18
1-1 FIF S King (Dutiaume, D King)   16.37
Pims: Basingstoke 0, Fife 2.
Second Period
1-2 FIF   Moody (Haig, S King)   14.11
Pims: Basingstoke 2, Fife 2.
Third Period
No scoring.
Pims: Basingstoke 4, Fife 4.
Shots on Goal:
Watkins BAS   5- 9-10 24   *save percentage:* 91.7
Murphy FIF   17-15-13 45   *save percentage:* 97.8
Referee: Dave Cloutman.
Linesmen: Tottman, Gosden.
Attendance: 1,280

ALL BRITS

Four of the brightest home-grown talents in the British National League: goalies **Joe Watkins** (Basingstoke Bison and GB) *top left* and the league's top netminder **Stephen Murphy** (Fife Flyers) *top right*; defenceman **Neil Liddiard** (Peterborough Pirates and GB) *below left* and GB forward **Ian Cooper** *below right* who joined Guildford Flames from Superleague's London Knights.

photos: Mike Smith/Icepix and Peter Jones.

Game Three, Kirkcaldy, 7 April 2000

Grand Slam for Mark's Marvels

FIFE FLYERS	2 (1-0-1)
BASINGSTOKE BISON	1 (0-0-1)

First Period
1-0 FIF   Monteith (Morris)   pp 3.32
Pims: Fife 8, Basingstoke 10.
Second Period
No scoring.
Pims: Fife 2, Basingstoke 6.
Third Period
1-1 BAS   Daniels (Ellis, Carpenter)   46.51
2-1 FIF   Dutiaume (Morris, Russell)   pp 48.59
Pims: Fife 0, Basingstoke 2.
Shots on Goal
Murphy FIF   18-14-21 53   *save percentage:* 98.1
Watkins BAS 14-6-6 26   *save percentage:* 92.3
Referee: Graham Horner.
Linesmen: Evans, Fraser.
Attendance: 2,344

FIFE FLYERS champions
three games to nil.

THE FINALISTS

FIFE FLYERS
Ricky Grubb, Stephen Murphy; Frank Morris (capt),
Ted Russell, Bill Moody, Derek King, Kyle Horne;
Todd Dutiaume, Russell Monteith, Steven King, Mark
Morrison, John Haig, Gary Wishart, Dean Edmiston,
Andy Samuel, David Smith, Andy Finlay, Liam Grieg,
Paddy Ward.
Manager: Chic Cottrell.   *Coach:* Mark Morrison.

BASINGSTOKE BISON
Alec Field, Joe Watkins; Rick Strachan, Brian
Mason, Adam Greener, Michael Knights, Tony
Redmond, Dwayne Newman, Duncan Paterson;
Mike Ellis (capt), Dru Burgess, Jeff Daniels, Tom
Pope, Joey Baird, Danny Meyers, Gary Clark, Debb
Carpenter, Wayne Crawford.
Bench coach: Charlie Colon.   *Player-coach:* Rick Strachan.

LEADING PLAYOFF SCORERS

	GP	G	A	Pts	Pim
Russell Monteith FIF	11	15	14	29	4
Frank Morris FIF	11	7	17	24	16
Randy Smith PET	8	9	10	19	24
Todd Dutiaume FIF	11	9	9	18	4
Steven King FIF	11	8	8	16	6

LEADING PLAYOFF NETMINDERS

	GPI	Min	SoG	GA	GAA
Steven Murphy FIF	11	660	378	24	93.6
G Armstrong HUL	6	352	193	20	89.6
Pasi Raitanen PET	8	465	317	35	89.0

Qualification: 120 minutes

Fife Flyers captured the first Grand Slam of British
National League titles by sweeping Basingstoke
Bison in three games to add the playoff
championship to their league and *ntl:* Christmas Cup
trophies.

Flyers first won the playoffs last season in a
one-game victory over Slough Jets. Bison also lost
out to Fife in the Christmas Cup final.

Apart from the opening playoff final game in
Kirkcaldy, there was little to choose between the
sides, with Bison either tying or trailing by a single
goal for much of games two and three.

But they led only once in 180 minutes of play and
that lasted for only a couple of minutes early in game
two.

One major difference was super saver **Stephen
Murphy**, the teenaged Scots netminder who
outplayed his English opposite number, **Joe (Cool)
Watkins**, in all three contests. Murphy stopped all
bar one of Bison's 53 shots in game three.

The other was the potency of Flyers' import
forwards. Some shrewd recruiting by Canadian
coach **Mark Morrison** had given his squad some of
the league's most dangerous attackers and they
scored six of Fife's eight goals.

The other tallies came from Scots **David Smith**
and **Steven King**. King, the playoffs' top British
scorer, played all three games despite sustaining a
fractured jaw when a puck struck him in the face in
game one. Another Scot, **John Haig**, had five
assists in the series.

There was more excitement in the early rounds
from which the cash-strapped Peterborough Pirates
and seventh-placed Solihull Blaze surprisingly
emerged to contest the semi-finals with Flyers and
Bison.

Pirates' 6-4 win in Hull and 4-3 home defeat of Fife
clinched a semi-final berth for the side that had
needed a one-to-one with their bank manager before
finishing the league schedule.

Mike Shewan was Solihull's hero after his winning
penalty shot at home to Slough helped to put Blaze
into a three-way tie in group B with Flames and
Bison.

Guildford lost out in the tie-break because they
were the only one of the three who needed to go to a
shootout to achieve their sole away win at Slough.
The league's tie-break system didn't take goals into
account, only victories.

*Editor's note - The BNL considers the league, play-
offs and Christmas Cup constitute their Grand Slam.
The Benson and Hedges Plate is a Superleague
competition in which BNL clubs are invited to play.*

nt: CHRISTMAS CUP

The third Christmas Cup campaign was open to the ten British National League clubs and played on a knockout basis over the Christmas and New Year period.

The draw for the quarter-finals was based on the league's final standings in 1998-99 with first playing eighth, second playing seventh and so on. The last placed sides, Edinburgh Capitals and Paisley Pirates, first played off against league newcomers, Milton Keynes Kings and Solihull Blaze, for the right to enter the competition proper.

The Cup was sponsored by telecoms and cable TV company, ntl:, the league's new partner.

QUALIFYING PLAYOFFS

4 Dec	Paisley-Edinburgh	3-4	)	**CAPITALS**
5 Dec	Edinburgh-Paisley	7-6	)	**win 11-9 agg**
11 Dec	M Keynes-Solihull	4-4	)	**KINGS**
12 Dec	Solihull-M Keynes	4-4ot*	)	**win 9-8 agg**
*Nick Poole scored game			)	
winning penalty shot			)	

QUARTER-FINALS

11 Dec	Bas'stoke-E'burgh	4-2	)	**BISON**
30 Dec	E'burgh-Bas'stoke	2-9	)	**win 13-4 agg.**
19 Dec	Peterboro'-Fife	2-4	)	**FLYERS**
28 Dec	Fife-Peterboro'	4-5	)	**win 8-7 agg.**
27 Dec	Guildford-Hull	4-3	)	**FLAMES**
29 Dec	Hull-Guildford	3-3	)	**win 7-6 agg.**
27 Dec	Slough-M Keynes	2-2	)	**KINGS**
28 Dec	M Keynes-Slough	5-3	)	**win 7-5 agg.**

SEMI-FINALS

2 Jan	Milton Keynes-Fife	3-6	)	**FLYERS**
4 Jan	Fife-Milton Keynes	5-1	)	**win 11-4 agg.**
3 Jan	Guildford-B'stoke	2-7	)	**BISON**
4 Jan	B'stoke-Guildford	7-4	)	**win 14-6 agg.**

FINALS

19 Jan	Fife-Basingstoke	3-3	(0-0, 2-2,1-1)
25 Jan	Basingstoke-Fife	2-3	(0-1, 2-1,0-1)

FIFE FLYERS win 6-5 on aggregate

LEADING SCORERS

	GP	G	A	Pts	Pim
Wayne Crawford BAS	6	10	6	16	8
Dru Burgess BAS	6	6	10	16	0
Jeff Daniels BAS	6	6	10	16	2
Nick Poole MIL	6	5	8	13	0
Derek Higdon MIL	6	4	6	10	2
Mark Morrison FIF	5	7	2	9	8
Russell Monteith FIF	6	5	4	9	0
Neil Donovan EDI	4	3	6	9	2
Ted Russell FIF	6	3	5	8	2
Todd Dutiaume FIF	6	2	6	8	8
Mike Ellis BAS	6	6	1	7	6
Frank Morris FIF	5	2	5	7	25
Gary Clark BAS	6	2	5	7	4

LEADING NETMINDERS

	GPI	Min	SoG	GA	Sv%
Stephen Murphy FIF	3	180	100	7	93.0
Joe Watkins BAS	6	317	146	14	90.4
Colum Cavilla HUL	2	120	64	7	89.1
Gavin Armstrong MIL	6	365	203	24	88.2
Ricky Grubb FIF	3	180	71	9	87.3

Qualification: 120 minutes

THE WINNING TEAM

FIFE FLYERS
Derek Downie, Ricky Grubb, Stephen Murphy; Frank Morris (capt), Ted Russell, Bill Moody, Derek King, Kyle Horne; Todd Dutiaume, Russell Monteith, Steven King, Mark Morrison, John Haig, Gary Wishart, Dean Edmiston, Andy Samuel, David Smith, Andy Finlay, Paddy Ward.
Manager: Chic Cottrell. *Coach:* Mark Morrison.

PAST WINNERS

1998-99	Peterborough Pirates
1997-98	Telford Tigers

FINAL GAME SUMMARIES

First leg, *Kirkcaldy, 19 January 2000*

FIFE FLYERS	3 (0-2-1)
BASINGSTOKE BISON	3 (0-2-1)

First Period
No scoring.
Pims: Fife 2, Basingstoke 4.
Second Period

1-0 FIF	S King (Morris, Dutiaume)	pp 0.44
1-1 BAS	Burgess (Daniels, Crawford)	6.02
1-2 BAS	Daniels (Burgess)	7.22
2-2 FIF	Morris (Monteith)	pp 12.19

Pims: Fife 2, Basingstoke 2.
Third Period

2-3 BAS	Crawford (Burgess, Newman)	8.10
3-3 FIF	Morrison (Morris)	19.27

Pims: Fife 6, Basingstoke 20 (Daniels ch/behind)
Shots on goal:
Murphy FIF   5-12- 6 23   *save percentage:* 86.9
Watkins BAS 11- 8-10 29 *save percentage:* 89.6
Men of Match: Russell FIF, Daniels BAS.
Referee: Graham Horner.
Linesmen: Allsopp, Smith.
Attendance: 1,386

Second leg, *Basingstoke, 25 January 2000*

BASINGSTOKE BISON	2 (0-2-0)
FIFE FLYERS	3 (1-1-1)

First Period

0-1 FIF	Samuel (Monteith, Russell)	19.39

Pims: Basingstoke 2, Fife 2.
Second Period

1-1 BAS	Daniels (Burgess, Crawford)	8.04
1-2 FIF	Morrison (Dutiaume)	13.20
2-2 BAS	Ellis (Grant, Carpenter)	14.19

Pims: Basingstoke 2, Fife 2.
Third Period

2-3 FIF	Russell (Moody)	pp 17.36

Pims: Basingstoke 4, Fife 4.
Shots on Goal
Watkins BAS 11-10-10 31 *save percentage:* 90.3
Murphy FIF   7-11-13 31 *save percentage:* 93.5
Men of the Match: Newman BAS, Russell FIF.
Referee: Dave Cloutman.
Linesmen: Gosden, Thompson.
Attendance: 1,600 (capacity)

Flying start

Fife Flyers began the 1999-2000 season as they finished the previous one - with a trophy.

The reigning BNL playoff champs defeated southern rivals Basingstoke Bison in the final by the narrowest of margins, one goal over two legs.

Canadian blueliner **Ted Russell** was credited with scoring the decider less than three minutes from time, though he insisted that his coach **Mark Morrison** had tipped it in.

Whatever, it meant that Bison had lost out in their second successive Christmas Cup final.

Flyers' victory in front of a packed house in Hampshire boosted their confidence and helped them to go on and win the league.

But their most inspirational victory had come a couple of weeks earlier on 28 December in the quarter-finals against Peterborough, the holders.

Leading 4-2 from the first leg in England, Flyers had a stinker at home, conceding five goals on nine shots in the first period.

But they staged a tremendous rally against the league leaders and goals from **Russell Monteith** (2) and **John Haig** levelled the aggregate score. That man Russell, who had played for Pirates the previous season, truly netted the winner this time with seven minutes left.

PUCK NAILED TO WALL

Afterwards, legend has it that manager **Chic Cottrell** nailed the puck to Flyers' dressing room wall, saying "that puck stays there to remind us what we can do."

Favourites Guildford Flames were well beaten by the Bison in the semis which they only reached after an epic tussle with Hull Thunder.

Flames had to overcome a three-goal first period deficit at home to win the first leg of their quarter-final 4-3. Then goals from **Norman Pinnington** and **Anthony Payne** knocked them 5-4 back early in the second period at Hull.

Flames **Ryan Campbell** and **Ricky Plant** scored within 77 seconds in the game's midpoint only for **Anthony Johnson** to tie it up again just before the interval. With time running out, Campbell struck the winner on a powerplay.

Milton Keynes Kings were the surprise packet in the early rounds, going as far as the semis, despite struggling in the league.

Nick Poole was Kings' hero. His penalty shot knocked out local rivals Solihull Blaze in the qualifiers and the former London Knight went on to score two of Kings' four goals before they lost out to Fife in the semis.

Basingstoke's forwards turned on the magic. **Wayne Crawford** scored the most goals in a game with four - twice - and **Jeff Daniels** had six assists against Edinburgh Capitals.

BENSON AND HEDGES CUP

COMPETITION FORMAT

The Benson and Hedges *(formerly Autumn) Cup* is the first major competition of the season.

For the third year running, the tournament was extended to include a Plate event for the British National League clubs.

Twenty teams - the most since 1995 - took part in the first round: all the Superleague and British National League (BNL) sides plus Whitley Warriors from the English League.

The First Round was played in five groups of four teams with the Superleague clubs making up two groups and the rest split geographically between the other three.

This was followed by a Challenge Round which matched the Superleague clubs against the BNL sides with the losing teams going into the Plate competition. (See later)

The Cup quarter-finals and the first round of the Plate were decided over home and away legs with the winners qualifying for the draw for the semi-finals which were also decided over two legs.

The total prize money for the Cup was £36,000 with the winner receiving £12,000. The Plate pot was worth £7,000

FIRST ROUND STANDINGS

Results were decided at the end of normal time, there was no overtime.

Group A	GP	W	L	D	GF	GA	Pts
Fife Flyers FIF	6	5	0	1	49	13	11
Edinburgh Capitals EDI	6	4	1	1	31	19	9
Paisley Pirates PAI	6	2	4	0	23	33	4
Whitley Warriors WHI	6	0	6	0	12	50	0
Group B							
Hull Thunder HUL	6	4	0	2	31	16	10
Peterborough Pirates PET	6	4	0	2	40	17	10
Milton Keynes Kings MIL	6	3	3	0	16	24	4
Telford Timberwolves TEL	6	0	6	0	11	41	0
Group C							
Basingstoke Bison BAS	6	3	1	2	23	12	8
Slough Jets SLO	6	2	1	3	17	13	7
Guildford Flames GUI	6	2	2	2	21	17	6
Solihull Blaze SOL	6	1	4	1	23	42	3
Group D							
Cardiff Devils CAR	6	2	2	2	18	14	6
Bracknell Bees BRK	6	2	2	2	27	26	6
London Knights LON	6	2	2	2	18	18	6
Sheffield Steelers SHE	6	2	2	2	17	22	6
Group E							
Manchester Storm MAN	6	5	1	0	29	15	10
Ayr Scottish Eagles AYR	6	4	2	0	24	16	8
Newcastle Riverkings NEW	6	2	4	0	14	26	4
Nottingham Panthers NOT	6	1	5	0	14	24	2

FIRST ROUND RESULTS

Group A	EDI	FIF	PAI	WHI
Edinburgh	-	1-6	3-2	7-1
Fife	3-3	-	9-4	9-1
Paisley	3-6	1-12	-	8-1
Whitley	4-11	3-10	2-5	-

Group B	HUL	MIL	PET	TEL
Hull	-	5-1	6-6	5-2
M Keynes	2-4	-	1-5	6-2
P'boro'	4-4	7-1	-	11-1
Telford	1-7	1-5	4-7	-

Group C	BAS	GUI	SLO	SOL
Bas'stoke	-	3-0	3-1	11-1
Guildford	5-1	-	1-1	9-2
Slough	1-1	1-1	-	7-4
Solihull	4-4	9-5	3-6	-

Group D	BRK	CAR	LON	SHE
Bracknell	-	4—3	7-2	3-4
Cardiff	6-2	-	2-3	3-1
London	5-5	1-1	-	1-3
Sheffield	6-6	3-3	0-6	-

Group E	AYR	MAN	NEW	NOT
Ayr	-	1-4	4-2	5-3
M'chester	5-3	-	6-1	5-2
Newcastle	1-6	3-7	-	4-1
Nott'ham	1-5	5-2	2-3	-

CHALLENGE ROUND

A complicated format was devised to create meaningful competition between the differing standards of Superleague and BNL clubs.

The First Round BNL group winners and the best BNL group runner-up met home and away in qualifying games.

The winners advanced to the Challenge Round - a single game at the BNL team's rink versus the two last placed Superleague sides.

The losers of the qualifying games entered the Frst Round of the Plate competition.

The winners of the Challenge Round entered the Cup quarter-finals. The losers joined the Plate competition along with the two best placed teams from the remaining BNL clubs in groups A, B and C.

The Challenge Round losers received a bye into the Plate semi-finals. If they had beaten their Superleague opponents they would have qualified for the Cup while the Superleague clubs would have dropped out altogether.

QUALIFICATION GAMES

21, 22, 23 September, home and away

Basingstoke -Hull 3-2h, 3-1a agg. **6-3**
Peterborough - Fife 2-1h, 4-3a agg. **6-4**
Hull and Fife enter the First Round of the Plate

NOT A LOT OF PEOPLE KNEW THIS

London coach **Chris McSorley** obviously keeps a copy of the IIHF rule book beside his bed.

In the controversial first leg of the Bees-Knights semi at Bracknell, the coach persuaded ref **Simon Kirkham** to check **Bruno Campese**'s stick not once but twice and Knights scored each time, both on 5-on-3 powerplays.

This took Knights' lead from 3-2 to 5-2 and virtually sewed up their place in the final.

But the good book says that Mac's second call should have been thrown out by Kirkham. The fine print under Equipment states that 'no measurement shall be allowed during the stoppage of play following a goal being scored'.

McSorley admitted afterwards that he reckoned the stakes - a place in the Cup final for the first time in Knights' short history - were worth him pushing his luck.

At least he knew the rule. Kirkham later accepted his blunder but Bees' coach **Dave Whistle** admitted he didn't know it existed.

CHALLENGE ROUND PROPER

29 September, one game at BNL rink

Basingstoke - **Sheffield**	**1-4**
Peterborough - **Nottingham**	**3-5**

Basingstoke and Peterborough earn a bye to the Plate semi-finals

QUARTER-FINALS

6, 9, 10 October, home and away

Bracknell - Newcastle	8-5*, 7-4h	agg. **15-9**
Cardiff - Nottingham	6-1a, 7-1h	agg. **13-2**
London - Ayr	0-1h, 7-0a	agg. **7-1**
Manchester - Sheffield	6-6h, 3-2ot/a	agg. **9-8**

* at Whitley Bay

SEMI-FINALS

26, 28, 29, 30 October, home and away

Manchester - Cardiff	4-0h, 0-0a	agg. **4-0**
London - Bracknell	5-3a, 5-3h	agg. **10-6**

SIN-BIN

Players' Penalties	GP	Pim	Ave
Norman Pinnington MIL	4	62	15.50
Graham Garden NOT	9	81	9.00
Nicky Chinn CAR	10	76	7.60

BENSON AND HEDGES CUP

FINAL

Sheffield Arena, 4 December 1999

MANCHESTER STORM   **3 (1-1-1-0)**
LONDON KNIGHTS   **3 (2-0-1-0)**
Storm won 4-3 after penalty shots

First Period
0-1 LON Hussey (Banks, Hoad)   1.52
0-2 LON Kenny (Duthie, Byce)   pp 11.20
1-2 MAN Allard (Morin, Wahlsten)   18.25
Pims: Storm 4, Knights 4.
Second Period
2-2 MAN Harding (Hurley, Campbell)   pp 1.28
Pims: Storm 4, Knights 14 (Banks 10-misc)
Third Period
3-2 MAN Jablonski (Livingston, Johnstone) pp 8.25
3-3 LON Scremin (Kenny, Bultje)   19.14
Pims: Storm 2, Knights 8.
Overtime
No scoring. No penalties.
Penalty Shots

1 LON	Hoad	save	0-0
2 MAN	Tomlinson	save	0-0
3 LON	Bultje	save	0-0
4 MAN	**Brebant**	**score**	**1-0**
5 LON	Byce	save	1-0
6 MAN	Krumpschmid	save	1-0
7 LON	Scremin	save	1-0
8 MAN	Wahlsten	save	1-0
9 LON	Burke	save	1-0

Shots on Goal (excluding penalty shots)
Pietrangelo MAN   9- 4- 9-4 26
save percentage: 88.46
Cavallin LON   8-11-10-3 32
save percentage: 90.62
Powerplay advantages
MAN - 7 (2 goals), LON - 4 (1 goal)
B&H Gold Award (Man of Match):
Rob Kenny LON
Referee: Andy Carson.
Linesmen: Matt Folka, Andy Craig.
Attendance: 6,500 est.

THE FINALISTS

MANCHESTER STORM

Frank Pietrangelo, Mark Bernard; Rob Robinson, Kevin Hoffman, Blair Scott, Scott Campbell, Kris Miller, Kevin Pozzo; Sami Wahlsten, Kelly Askew, Jeff Tomlinson (capt), Mike Morin, Norm Krumpschmid, Jeff Johnstone, Pierre Allard, Darren Hurley, Mike Harding, Jeff Jablonski, David Livingston, Rick Brebant.
Manager-coach: Kurt Kleinendorst.

LONDON KNIGHTS

Mark Cavallin, Gavin Armstrong*; Marc Hussey, Tim Murray, Tom Ashe, Neal Martin, Claudio Scremin, Greg Burke, Mike Ware; John Byce, Jeff Hoad, Ian Cooper, Mark Bultje, Rob Kenny (capt), Darren Banks, Ryan Duthie.
Chief Coach: Chris McSorley.
Asst coach: Scott Rex.
*guest from Milton Keynes Kings replacing the injured Trevor Robins.

The all-winners final

Manchester Storm won Superleague's 'dream final' between their big city clubs, but only on penalty shots. The teams' contrasting styles made the game the competition's most entertaining Cup final for years.

Manchester's first Cup came in the first final to go into overtime. **Rick Brebant** was the only one of nine shooters to convert his penalty shot.

The more skilful Storm iced 18 men but at least two, **Kris Miller** and **Rob Robinson**, were there only with the help of their physio. The defence-first Knights could put only 14 men out and their potent playmaker, **Paul Rushforth**, was especially missed.

There was little to choose between the teams after **Kurt Kleinendorst**'s men fought back from an early 2-0 deficit to tie the game 2-2 at 21.28.

After an action-packed but goalless middle period came the Big Brother penalty when the ref missed **Rob Kenny**'s elbow to the head of his former team-mate **Scott Campbell** and had to ask his linesmen what happened. Had they seen it 'live' or only via the replay on the big screen?

Whatever, it was a penalty against Knights and **Jeff Jablonski** made it 3-2 on the powerplay. But London's coach, **Chris McSorley**, let **Andy Carson**'s decisions - especially the Kenny one - get to him.

When Knights' argumentative **Darren Banks** was thrown out for delaying the game - during his team's powerplay - he returned to find McSorley haranguing Carson, and was promptly sacrificed for another two minutes.

The heated exchanges, however, appeared to inspire London. They killed the penalties and just as all seemed lost, their classy defender **Claudio Scremin** tied it up again.

After an even overtime period, the soft hands of Brebant - the only man on the night who knew how to take a penalty shot - settled the outcome.

■ London's **Jeff Hoad** was playing in a record fourth straight Cup final. He was on winning sides twice - with Nottingham Panthers (1996) and Ayr Scottish Eagles (1997). He was with Eagles again last year as they lost to Panthers.

■ Brebant quit Storm a week after the final and within days he was wearing Knights' colours.

-147-

LEADING SCORERS

including playoffs	GP	G	A	Pts	Pim
Kevin Riehl BRK	10	9	12	21	4
Rob Kenny LON	11	9	6	15	16
Colin Ward BRK	10	6	9	15	10
Jeff Jablonski MAN	11	8	6	14	4
Claudio Scremin LON	11	4	10	14	8
Rick Brebant MAN	11	3	11	14	10
Teeder Wynne SHE	8	5	7	12	2
Ed Courtenay SHE	9	5	7	12	2
Chris Brant BRK	10	4	8	12	41
Paxton Schulte BRK	10	4	8	12	43

LEADING NETMINDERS

including playoffs	GPI	Mins	SoG	GA	Sv%
Steve Lyle CAR	5	300	135	9	93.3
Frank Pietrangelo MAN	9	545	233	18	92.3
Derek Herlofsky CAR	5	300	198	11	94.4
Trevor Robins LON	10	562	256	23	91.0

FAIR PLAY

Team Penalties - Cup & Plate	GP	Pim	Ave
Newcastle Riverkings	8	98	12.25
Sheffield Steelers	9	122	13.55
Hull Thunder	10	138	13.80
Manchester Storm	11	153	13.91
Guildford Flames	6	90	15.00
Basingstoke Bison	12	214	17.83
Telford Timberwolves	6	109	18.17
Slough Jets	11	202	18.36
Whitley Warriors	6	114	19.00
Fife Flyers	12	235	19.58
Ayr Scottish Eagles	8	157	19.62
London Knights	11	236	21.45
Milton Keynes Kings	6	133	22.17
Bracknell Bees	10	231	23.10
Solihull Blaze	6	140	23.33
Nottingham Panthers	9	218	24.22
Peterborough Pirates	11	296	26.91
Paisley Pirates	6	211	35.17
Cardiff Devils	10	345	34.50
Edinburgh Capitals	8	322	40.25
CUP TOTALS	88	3764	21.39

Ingenious scheduling

Ice hockey's version of soccer's FA Cup avoided the Man Utd fiasco but it did have a major headache in sorting out a playing format.

Karen Earl Ltd, the agent for sponsor *Benson and Hedges*, had to negotiate long and hard with three leagues before they came up with an ingenious 88-game formula that accommodated 20 teams of very different abilities.

These included two clubs that will make answers to trivia questions in a few years' time.

The 1999 *B&H* Cup is the only tournament in which the short lived Telford Timberwolves competed and the only one to have a side, Whitley Warriors, from the third-tier English League.

Why so many teams? *B&H* are a generous sponsor. The prize money was £43,000 with the winners of the junior Plate competition receiving more than the Cup alone was worth in 1995. That was the last time the *B&H* had 20 teams and the jackpot then was a mere £6,000.

Despite all the scheduling rigmarole, the eight Superleague teams easily made it through to the Cup quarter-finals.

This was when **Chris McSorley** and his Knights really made their mark. After losing 1-0 at home to **Geoff Sargeant** and last year's finalists, Ayr Scottish Eagles, London and **Trevor Robins** returned the favour seven-fold in Scotland the next day.

Cup holders Nottingham Panthers, hamstrung by severe budget cuts, had a nightmare against Cardiff Devils. Only **Brent Bobyck** and **Calle Carlsson** scored for **Mike Blaisdell**'s squad.

Don McKee's Steelers went out to **Darren Hurley**'s OT goal for Manchester Storm in the thrilling second leg in Sheffield Arena.

In the semis, Manchester were involved in a minor classic at Cardiff's Ice House. With Storm leading comfortably 4-0 after the first leg, Welshman **Stevie Lyle** and Manchester's **Frank Pietrangelo** both had shutouts in one of the few 0-0 scores in the modern era.

PAST B&H CUP WINNERS

1998	Nottingham Panthers
1997	Ayr Scottish Eagles
1996	Nottingham Panthers
1995	Sheffield Steelers
1994	Nottingham Panthers
1993	Murrayfield Racers
1992	Cardiff Devils

PAST B&H PLATE WINNERS

1998	Guildford Flames
1997	Slough Jets

BENSON AND HEDGES PLATE

FIRST ROUND

5, 6, 12, 13 October, home and away

| Fife - Edinburgh | 5-2a, 4-4h | agg. | 9-6 |
| Slough - Hull | 3-7a, 5-0ot/h | agg. | 8-7 |

Peterborough and **Basingstoke** received byes

SEMI-FINALS

20, 23, 26, 31 October, home and away

| Slough - Peterboro' | 1-0a, 3-1h | agg. | 4-1 |
| Basingstoke - Fife | 5-3a, 3-3h | agg. | 8-6 |

FINAL

Sheffield Arena, 4 December 1999

| SLOUGH JETS | 1 | (1-0-0) |
| BASINGSTOKE BISON | 5 | (0-1-4) |

First Period
1-0 SLO Bicknell (Stefan)   6.56
Penalty minutes: Jets 2, Bison 2.
Second Period
1-1 BAS Baird   9.31
Penalty minutes: Jets 0, Bison 4.
Third Period
1-2 BAS Ellis (Crawford)   pp 6.18
1-3 BAS Ellis   pp 6.54
1-4 BAS Daniels (Burgess)   17.12
1-5 BAS Strachan (Paterson)   eng 18.43
Penalty minutes: Jets 4, Bison 14.
Shots on goal:
Gallace SLO 6-9-9 24
Watkins BAS 8-5-8 21
Referee: Dave Cloutman.
Linesmen: Thompson, Hankin.
Attendance: 3,000 est.

Gatto-Galazzi clash mars final

Basingstoke's first *B&H* Plate victory was marred by a nasty incident early in the second period of the final.

With Jets holding a narrrow 1-0 lead, Bison forward **Greg Gatto** tangled with Jet **Mark Galazzi**. The exact cause of Galazzi's injury may never be known but he collapsed in mid-ice and needed life-saving help from a paramedic.   Fortunately, he recovered after overnight hospital treatment.

This knocked the wind out of Jets. Minutes later, **Adam Bicknell** equalised for Bison and skipper **Mike Ellis** tallied two quick powerplay goals early in the last session to give Basingstoke a controlling 3-1 lead.

■ *More on this in our Review of the Season.*

THE WINNING TEAM

BASINGSTOKE BISON
Joe Watkins, Alex Field; Rick Strachan, Brian Mason, Adam Greener, Michael Knights, Wayne Crawford, Duncan Paterson, Joey Baird; Mike Ellis (capt), Greg Gatto, Jeff Daniels, Danny Meyers, Peter Romeo, Gary Clark, Tony Redmond, Mark Barrow, Dru Burgess.
Coaches: Charlie Colon, Rick Strachan.

Upsets galore

The big surprise of the 1999 competition was the failure of the defending Plate holders, Guildford Flames, to get past the first round of the Cup.

Unfortunately for **Stan Marple**'s team, they were drawn into the difficult Group C which produced the eventual Plate finalists, Basingstoke Bison and Slough Jets.

That said, Flames were the only BNL team to beat Bison, 5-1, on the first weekend of the season, a contest best remembered for Bison turning up without their strip and a mass brawl in the final minute.

Jets had the tougher route to the final as all seemed lost when they crashed 7-3 at Hull Thunder with six regulars missing.

But the return six days later produced perhaps the biggest comeback in their history. **Jason Reilly** tied the aggregate score 7-7 with 3.47 minutes left and player-coach **Joe Stefan** hit the winner 3.33 minutes into overtime.

They took an even bigger scalp when they knocked out high flying Peterborough Pirates in the semi-finals.

Slough's **Jason Kendall** scored the only goal of the game in Peterborough with **Richard Gallace** chalking up a 35-save shutout. After the sides met home and away in the league, Jets won their home leg 3-1 - the clubs' fourth meeting in seven days.

Two Scots clubs won through to the Plate with Fife Flyers knocking out their old rivals, Edinburgh Capitals, in the first round.

Goaltending was the key in the Bison-Flyers semi with first Englishman **Joe Watkins** having a blinder, then Scot **Stephen Murphy** putting up the shutters.

David Smith and **Steven King** gave Flyers a 2-0 first period lead at home in the first leg but the Hampshire team fought back to inflict a rare home reverse, 5-3, on the Kirkcaldy crew. Watkins turned away 23 of 26 shots on his net.

Murphy kicked out 30 of 33 shots in Basingstoke but **Mark Morrison**'s men had to settle for a 3-3 draw, 6-8 on aggregate. **Peter Romeo** returned from injury to hit the tying goal into the empty net in the dying seconds

ENGLISH LEAGUE

The English League, the sport's third tier, is split into a Premier Division and a regionalised Division One. The league was originally organised for clubs with low budgets whose chief aim is developing local players, but In 1997-98 an eight-team National division was introduced to accommodate the non-Superleague clubs who were unable to afford the increasing cost of competing in the British National League (BNL).

The National division was renamed Premier in 1998-99.

The low budget teams compete in Division One which also includes teams that act as reserve sides for higher league clubs.

There is no automatic promotion to the BNL from the English League.

In the Premier Division, teams met six times, three at home and three away, while the Division One sides played one home, one away in the North and two home, two away in the South.

LEADING SCORERS

Premier Division	GP	G	A	Pts	Pim
Mikko Skinnari INV	24	17	34	51	6
Duane Ward CHE	19	31	17	48	32
Andy Hannah CHE	23	23	25	48	26
Johan Larsson IOW	22	28	18	46	140
Lamonte Polet SWI	23	27	18	45	6

Div One North					
Paul Windridge BIL	18	25	58	83	49
Simon Leach	14	39	42	81	48
Tom Brown BIL	16	42	22	64	24
Mark Stokes FLI	17	28.	31	59	14
Stuart Potts SUN	18	20	28	48	4

Div One South					
Drew Campbell BAS	13	25	20	45	67
Zoran Kozic HAR	7	28	9	37	12
Adam Cathcart BAS	12	19	15	34	24
Leigh Baker SLO	16	17	15	32	4
Anthony Page BAS	12	7	24	31	4

FINAL STANDINGS

Premier Division	GP	W	L	D	GF	GA	Pts
Ch'ford Chieftains CHE	24	19	4	1	138	85	39
I of Wight Raiders IOW	24	13	8	3	141	103	29
Swindon Chill SWI	24	10	13	1	90	111	21
Invicta Dynamos INV	24	8	13	3	117	138	19
Romford Raiders ROM	24	5	17	2	78	127	12

Div One North							
Billingham Eagles BIL	18	15	3	0	170	75	30
Whitley Warriors WHI	18	12	4	2	163	59	26
Kingston Jets HUL	18	10	5	3	106	68	23
Altrincham Aces ALT	18	11	6	1	117	78	23
Sunderland Chiefs SUN	18	9	8	1	106	82	19
Flintshire Freeze FLI	18	8	8	2	109	86	18
Nottingham Lions NOT	18	8	9	1	82	88	17
Blackburn Hawks BLA	18	7	9	2	100	98	16
Sheffield Scimitars SHE	18	3	13	2	59	141	8
Bradford Bulldogs BRD	18	0	18	0	21	258	0

Div One South							
H'gey Greyhounds HAR	16	14	2	0	103	56	28
Bas'stoke Buffalo BAS	16	14	2	0	120	51	28
Bracknell Hornets BRK	16	4	11	1	62	104	9
Slough H. Hawks SLO	16	4	12	0	64	102	8
Telford Royals	16	3	12	1	48	84	7

The Basingstoke-Telford result on 12 September was awarded 5-0 to to Buffalo as Royals failed to travel. Solent Lightning withdrew from Div One South after games played on 9 January. All statistics relating to the team have been removed.

In Div One North, the Kingston-Flintshire game could not be arranged and the game was awarded 0-0.

LEADING NETMINDERS

Premier Division	GPl	Min	SoG	GA	Sv%
Ronald Bertrand SWI	21	1240	924	90	90.3
Simon Smith CHE	22	1306	733	77	89.5
Craig Wynn IOW	23	1358	838	91	89.1
Div One North					
Matthew Darlow SHE	7	354	291	27	90.7
Dave Clancy FLI	14	730	558	59	89.4
Alan Levers NOT	14	791	497	57	88.5
Div One South					
Andrew van					
Neutegem BAS	3	180	76	7	90.8
Rob Sheldrake HAR	14	693	362	38	89.5
Daniel Heslop TEL	14	829	656	71	89.2

Chiefs sweep the board

Chelmsford Chieftains won the English Premier League's first three-leg Grand Slam with successes in the league, playoffs and Millennium Cup.

Backed again by *PepsiCo* and with two of the league's top import forwards in **Kevin Conway** of Superleague and GB fame, and **Duane Ward** from Tulsa Oilers, Chiefs went one better than Solihull Blaze last year in scooping up all three trophies on offer.

In Division One, **Haringey Greyhounds** won their first major silverware taking the South title by one goal from Basingstoke Buffalo, and **Billingham Eagles** retained their crown in Div One North.

But the Premier League season was overshadowed by the mid-season withdrawals of two clubs - Cardiff Rage and Oxford Blades.

When Rage pulled out in February the problem was put down to internal troubles with stories circulating of the Cardiff dressing room being trashed after their 12-2 home loss to the Isle of Wight.

But the reported £30,000 cost of running the struggling and poorly supported side must also have forced the club to pull the plug early. Rage's owners went out of business at the end of the season.

Oxford Blades, too, ran out of money. Their last game came on 23 January after they had been pasted 16-3 at home by the Isle of Wight. Even EIHA chairman **Ken Taggart** could not save the club despite his repeated efforts.

continued on next page.....

FAIR PLAY

Premier Division	GP	Pims	Ave
Chelmsford Chieftains	23	341	14.8
Invicta Dynamos	24	465	19.4
Romford Raiders	23	547	23.8
Ise of Wight Raiders	24	874	36.4
Swindon Chill	24	925	38.5
Div One North			
Sunderland Chiefs	18	271	15.1
Flintshire Freeze	18	359	19.9
Kingston JetS	18	365	20.3
Bradford Bulldogs	18	376	20.9
Nottingham Lions	18	394	21.9
Billingham Eagles	18	505	28.1
Altrincham Aces	18	539	29.9
Sheffield Scimitars	18	559	31.1
Whitley Warriors	18	652	36.2
Div One South			
Haringey Greyhounds	16	469	29.3
Slough Harrier Hawks	16	507	31.7
Basingstoke Buffalo	15	586	39.1
Telford Royals	15	764	50.9
Bracknell Hornets	16	989	61.8

OFFICIAL EIHA WEBSITE
www.eiha.co.uk

PAST SCORING CHAMPIONS

Season	Player	GP	G	A	Pts
1998-99	Steve Chartrand SOL	32	79	86	165
1997-98	Steve Chartrand SOL	30	104	107	211
1996-97	Dan Sweeney WIG	22	50	44	94
1995-96	Slava Koulekov HUM	28	101	50	151
1994-95	Dan Sweeney WIG	23	61	74	135
1993-94	Dan Sweeney WIG	23	86	80	166
1992-93	Steve Chartrand SOL	34	135	146	281
1991-92	Luc Chabot MED	32	143	82	225
1990-91	Patrick Scott MIL	28	101	87	188
1989-90	Darin Fridgen BRK	24	106	54	160
1988-89	Rick Smith OXF	25	150	78	228

League only except includes playoffs.*

PREMIER RESULTS CHART

	CAR	CHE	INV	IOW	OXF	ROM	SWI
Cardiff	*****	2-4 18/9	3-7 2/10	1-11 11/12	7-7 11/9	3-9 15/1	3-20 26/9
Rage	*****	4-12 16/10	2-5 8/1	2-12 12/2			0-10 18/12
see Note	*****	0-8 5/2					
Ch'ford	12-4 17/10	*****	5-2 29/8	5-3 12/9	6-2 4/9	2-4 26/9	1-5 3/10
Chieftains	14-2 2/1	*****	12-3 23/1	12-3 16/1	13-3 30/10	7-4 24/10	6-5 31/10
		*****	10-6 12/3	6-1 6/2	12-3 28/11	6-5& 5/3	6-2 19/2
Invicta	12-3 5/9	2-4 19/9	*****	3-4 3/10	7-4 26/9	5-4 6/11	10-3 12/9
Dynamos	11-2 5/12	5-5 10/10	*****	9-3 31/10		3-6 16/1	2-2 17/10
	12-2 30/1	5-12 27/2	*****	3-3 19/2		7-3 6/2	6-1 9/1
Isle of Wight	9-5 25/9	7-2 23/10	9-3 11/9	*****	21-4 4/12	5-3 9/10	6-1 2/10
Raiders	17-5 30/10	5-6 18/12	10-7 15/1	*****	14-6 8/1	14-1 12/12	9-2 24/10
	3-8 26/2		13-4 4/3	*****		11-4 22/1	6-1 5/3
Oxford	9-3 10/10	1-7 9/1	6-5 24/10	3-9 19/9	*****	3-8 12/9	7-6 5/9
Blades			5-5 14/11	3-4 17/10	*****	5-3 25/9	
see Note				3-16 23/1	*****		
Romford	11-3 3/10	2-3 5/9	2-7 21/10	5-5 18/9	9-6 16/10	*****	8-2 19/9
Raiders	9-1 21/11	2-4 30/1	3-6 13/2	2-6 9/1	8-4 2/1	*****	1-5 10/10
		&	7-4 11/3	4-4 12/3		*****	5-4 23/1
Swindon	11-0 9/10	2-1 11/9	5-4 4/9	4-2 16/10	8-2 18/9	6-2 23/10	*****
Chill	16-3 22/1	2-5 15/1	8-5 25/9	6-5 29/1	11-2 11/12	7-1 8/1	*****
		7-10+ 12/2	4-6 18/2	2-4 11/3		4-0 5/2	*****

Second figure is date of game.
+ Also played for the Data Vision Millennium Cup final
& Chelmsford-Romford on 5 March played for four points.

NOTE
Cardiff Rage (12 February) and Oxford City Blades (23 January) withdrew from the league after games played on these dates. All league statistics involving these teams have been expunged. The results of their games have been shown here for the record.

Chiefs sweep the board, continued
If the remaining five teams were unhappy at this severe reduction of the Premier League, their irritation paled compared to the problems over the playoff structure.

Originally, the top four were to qualify for the post-season but with only five teams left, some clubs suggested that all five should take part.

This time, the Colorado, USA based Taggart left it to the clubs to decide among themselves. (Readers with long memories will recall that this was KT's approach to games when he was a referee - Ed.)

In the event, the fifth placed Romford, hardly the division's richest team, were unenthusiastic about the extra games and the four-team format remained in place.

Apart from a controversial decison to allow Invicta Dynamos to borrow Romford's goalie, **Matt van der Velden**, the playoffs themselves went off uneventfully.

Swindon's Link Centre did decide that urgent work was suddenly needed on the ice pad just as the games started, but then rinks do that sort of thing, don't they?

The ice was safe by the time Chieftains met Chill there in the first leg of the final. Too safe, Chill must have thought, as **Erskine Douglas**'s team, led by two goals from the playoffs' leading scorer, Englishman **Andy Hannah**, stormed to a 5-2 victory.

That win proved decisive as Chill forced a 2-2 draw in the return with both Swindon's goals coming from import, **Lamonte Polet**.

PLAYOFFS

At the end of the league games, the top four teams in the Premier Division qualified for the Playoffs when the league winner met the fourth place side and the runner-up played the third place team home and away.

The winning semi-finalists then played home and away for the playoff championship.

In Division One, all the teams in the South qualified, along with the top six in the North.

The eleven qualifying teams played a round-robin in four groups - regionalised two South and two North - with the winning team in each group contesting the two-leg semi-finals and final.

PREMIER PLAYOFFS

First semi-final

18 March	Invicta-Chelmsford	0-7
19 March	Chelmsford-Invicta	7-6

CHIEFTAINS won 14-6 on aggregate

Second semi-final

19 March	Isle of Wight-Swindon	1-5
22 March	Swindon-Isle of Wight	3-3

SWINDON won 8-4 on aggregate

LEADING SCORERS

Premier Division	GP	G	A	Pts	Pim
Andy Hannah CHE	4	5	4	9	6
Lamonte Polet SWI	4	5	3	8	0
Darren Cotton CHE	4	4	4	8	0
Darcy Cahill SWI	4	4	4	8	6
Duane Ward CHE	4	2	5	7	2
Kevin Conway CHE	4	3	3	6	0

LEADING NETMINDERS

Premier Division	GPI	Min	SoG	GA	Sv%
Ronald Bertrand SWI	4	240	189	11	94.2
Simon Smith CHE	4	240	116	10	91.4
Matthew van der Velden INV	2	120	111	14	87.4

PREMIER PLAYOFF FINAL
First leg, 25 March, Link Centre, Swindon

SWINDON CHILL	**2**	**(1-1-0)**
CHELMSFORD CHIEFTAINS	**5**	**(0-3-2)**

First Period
1-0 SWI	Cahill		1.11

Pims: Chill 6, Chieftains 8.
Second Period
1-1 CHE	D Cotton (Ward)		pp 1.24
1-2 CHE	Ward (Hannah, McFadyen)		pp 7.32
2-2 SWI	Josefsson (Forshee)		pp 18.30
2-3 CHE	J Cotton (Metcalf)		19.03

Pims: Chill 4, Chieftains 2.
Third Period
2-4 CHE	Hannah (Conway)		pp 12.18
2-5 CHE	Hannah (Conway, McFadyen)		pp 15.29

Pims: Chill 6, Chieftains 0.
Shots on Goal
Bertrand SWI	7-15-15 37	*save percent.*	86.5
Smith CHE	13- 9- 7 29	*save percent.*	93.1

Referee: Gary Plaistow.
Linesmen: Ashraff, Tottman.
Attendance: not rec.

Second leg, 26 March
Riverside Ice & Leisure Centre, Chelmsford

CHELMSFORD CHIEFTAINS	**2**	**(0-1-1)**
SWINDON CHILL	**2**	**(0-0-2)**

First Period
No scoring.
Pims: Chieftains 4, Chill 4.
Second Period
1-0 CHE	D Cotton (Ward)	15.59

Pims: Chieftains 6, Chill 2.
Third Period
1-1 SWI	Polet (Cahill, Johnston)	12.08
2-1 CHE	McFadyen (Rogers)	16.19
2-2 SWI	Polet (Johnston, Cahill)	17.03

Pims: Chieftains 0, Chill 0.
Shots on Goal
Smith CHE	8- 6-13 27	*save percent.*	92.6
Bertrand SWI	21-13-15 49	*save pecent.*	95.9

Referee: Gary Plaistow.
Linesmen: Ashraff, Tottman.
Attendance: 750

CHELMSFORD CHIEFTAINS champions,
7-4 on aggregate.

THE WINNING TEAM

CHELMSFORD CHIEFTAINS
Simon Smith, Paul Wilcox; Craig Metcalf, Peter Morley, Carl Greenhous, Andrew Clements, Karl Rogers, Richard Whiting, Darren Cotton, Jon Cotton, Tari Suwari, Kevin Conway, Dan Oliver, Jamie Randall, Jake French (capt), Billy Price, Duane Ward, Shaun Wallis, Shaun McFadyen, Andy Hannah, Craig Britton, Richard Gunn. *Head coach:* Erskine Douglas. *Asst. coach:* Andy Hannah.

DIVISION ONE PLAYOFFS

FIRST ROUND

Group A	GP	W	L	D	GF	GA	Pts
Billingham Eagles	2	2	0	0	10	5	4
Sunderland Chiefs	4	0	2	2	13	18	2
Kingston Jets	2	0	0	2	8	8	2
Group B							
Whitley Warriors	4	4	0	0	36	8	8
Flintshire Freeze	4	2	2	0	10	22	4
Altrincham Aces	4	0	4	0	10	26	0
Group C							
H'gey Greyhounds	4	4	0	0	24	10	8
Bracknell Hornets	4	1	3	0	18	23	2
Telford Royals	4	1	3	0	13	22	2
Group D							
Basingstoke Buffalo	2	2	0	0	23	8	4
Slough H Hawks	2	0	2	0	8	23	0

Billingham and Kingston unable to agree dates in Group A; their games were declared void. Whitley-Flintshire awarded 5-0 as Freeze refused to travel.

SEMI-FINALS

First Semi-Final
15 April   Basingstoke-Billingham   4-7
16 April   Billingham-Basingstoke   15-3
BILLINGHAM win 22-7 on aggregate
Second Semi-Final
16 April   Whitley-Haringey   11-3
23 April   Haringey-Whitley   2-7
WHITLEY win 18-5 on aggregate

LEADING SCORERS

	GP	G	A	Pts	Pim
Simon Leach WHI	7	18	13	31	16
Lee Baxter WHI	7	11	9	20	16
Adam Cathcart BAS	4	11	6	17	12
Tom Brown BIL	6	13	3	16	4
Karl Culley WHI	7	9	7	16	8
Paul Windridge BIL	6	1	15	16	2

LEADING NETMINDERS

	GPI	Mins	SoG	GA	Sv%
Chris Main ALT	2	120	88	8	90.9
Stephen Wall SUN	3	180	143	13	90.9
Anthony Markham WHI	7	375	203	21	89.7

FINAL

First leg, 30 April, Whitley Bay
WHITLEY-BILLINGHAM   7-4 (2-1,1-2,4-1)
Scoring: **Warriors** - Leach 3g; Baxter 2+2; Lonsdale 1+2; Willis 1+1; Bucas, Culley 1a.
Eagles - Brown 3g; Hehir 1g; Perry, Windridge 1a.
Penalty minutes: Warriors 8, Eagles 16.
Shots on Goal: Markham WHI 37, Flett BIL 29.
Referee: Kim Lawley.   *Attendance:* 1,659

Second leg, 14 May, Billingham
BILLINGHAM-WHITLEY   6-7 (2-2,2-2,2-3)
Scoring: **Eagles** - Brown 3g; Hehir 2g; Lewis 1g; Perry 3a; Windridge 2a; Richardson, Wallace 1a.
Warriors - Baxter, Leach 2+2; Bucas, Clish 1+1; Lonsdale 1g; Culley 1a.
Penalty minutes: Eagles 10, Warriors 16.
Shots on Goal: Flett BIL 35, Markham WHI 37
Referee: Mike Litchfield.   *Attendance:* not rec

WHITLEY WARRIORS *champions,*
14-10 on aggregate.

THE WINNING TEAM

WHITLEY WARRIORS
Anthony Markham, Gordon Ford; Andrew Clish, Bryan Dunn, Daniel Ord, Chris Taylor, Kevin Bucas, Lee Baxter, Simon Leach, Scott Taylor, Paul Willis, Paul McGinnety, Karl Culley, Bobby Bradley, Martin Gamsby, Paul Graham, Paul Sample, Nigel Bainbridge, Stuart Lonsdale.
Manager: Michael Winn. *Coach:* Peter Winn.

Warriors' delayed win

Whitley Warriors won their first major title for 25 years when they beat holders, Billingham Eagles, in the final of the Div One North playoffs.

The games did not lack for controversy. One of Flintshire Freeze's imports was almost thrown in the cells after a particularly rumbustious Warriors' visit in the first round and Freeze froze out the return in Whitley Bay.

Warriors' coach **Peter Winn** described as "an absolute disgrace" the EIHA's agreement to Billingham Eagles' request to delay the crucial second leg of their final at Billingham.

Eagles said their ice was unfit but Winn doubted the claim as Eagles had already failed to agree any dates for their first round games against Kingston Jets.

Warriors again attracted good crowds to their 3,000 seat arena, but their unwillingness to spend large sums on players like many of their opponents has resulted in their rapid decline from British League, Premier Division status only four seasons ago.

DATA VISION MILLENNIUM CUP

The Millennium Cup was competed for by the English Premier and Div One South teams, though all league teams were eligible.

The top team from each group met in a one-game final at Swindon's Link Centre, the home of the Chill whose sponsor, Data Vision, backed the Cup.

FIRST ROUND STANDINGS

Group A	GP	W	L	D	GF	GA	Pts
Ch'ford Chieftains	8	7	1	0	69	27	14
I of Wight Raiders	8	6	1	1	115	21	13
Invicta Dynamos	8	4	3	1	64	34	9
Telford Royals	8	2	6	0	32	95	4
Solent Lightning	8	0	8	0	14	117	0

Group B							
Swindon Chill	8	7	1	0	72	25	14
Romford Raiders	8	6	2	0	61	34	12
Oxford Blades	8	3	5	0	47	58	6
H'gey Greyhounds	8	2	5	1	42	57	5
Cardiff Rage	8	1	6	1	32	80	3

FIRST ROUND RESULTS

Group A	CHE	INV	IOW	SLT	TEL
Ch'ford Chieftains	-	4-1	3-5	*5-0	12-1
Invicta Dynamos	5-8	-	3-3	15-3	15-2
I of Wight Raiders	7-9	8-3	-	26-0	29-0
Solent Lightning	5-17	2-12	1-22	-	1-3
Telford Royals	3-11	4-10	2-15	17-2	-

Group B	CAR	HAR	OXF	ROM	SWI
Cardiff Rage	-	5-11	5-9	4-10	1-8
Haringey G'hounds	6-6	-	7-4	4-5	3-7
Oxford Blades	5-6	10-5	-	7-11	0-12
Romford Raiders	15-2	6-2	4-8	-	9-3
Swindon Chill	16-3	14-4	8-4	4-1	-

*Awarded score as Solent did not travel.

FINAL

12 February. Link Centre, Swindon

SWINDON-CHELMSFORD 7-10   (2-2,3-5,2-3)

Scoring

Chill - Forshee, Josefsson 2g; Mair 1+3; Cahill 1+2; Fiddes 1g; Polet 2a.

Chieftains - Ward 5g; D Cotton 1+2; J Cotton, Conway, Hannah 1+1; Randall 1g; French 3a; Morley, Rogers, Whiting 1a.

Shots on Goal: Bertrand SWI 61, Smith CHE 29.

Penalty minutes: Chill 46 (Davison 10, Armour GM), Chieftains 12.

Referee: Rene Ross.   *Attendance:* not recorded.

This game also counted towards English Premier League points.

THE WINNING TEAM

CHELMSFORD CHIEFTAINS

Simon Smith, Paul Wilcox; Craig Metcalf, Peter Morley, Carl Greenhous, Andrew Clements, Carl Rogers, Richard Whiting, Darren Cotton, Jon Cotton, Tari Suwari, Kevin Conway, Dan Oliver, Jamie Randall, Jake French (capt), Billy Price, Duane Ward, Shaun Wallis, Shaun McFadyen, Andy Hannah, Brian Biddulph, Craig Britton.

Head coach: Erskine Douglas.

Asst. coach: Andy Hannah.

First leg of Chiefs' Slam

Chelmsford Chieftains' star import, **Duane Ward**, a former Tulsa Oilers' centreman, went on a five-goal spree in a high scoring Millennium Cup final against the home side, Swindon Chill.

But Chieftains' victory in the *Data Vison* sponsored game - the first in their ultimate English Premier League Grand Slam - was achieved in controversial circumstances.

It seemed only natural that the one-leg final should be played at Swindon's Link Centre as this was the home of the team run by **Mike Kellond**, the owner of the sponsoring company.

Some English League clubs, however, believed that there were to be home and away semi-finals first between the top two teams in each group.

Romford and the Isle of Wight were miffed when they discovered that they had missed out on the chance to win the first prize of £1,000, a not inconsiderable sum for the small English League clubs

SCOTTISH CUP

Final, 4 March 2000, Fife Ice Arena

PAISLEY PIRATES	4 (1-2-1)
FIFE FLYERS	9 (2-3-4)

First Period

1-0	PAI Beveridge	pp2 2.15
1-1	FIF Monteith (Morrison)	8.48
1-2	FIF Russell (Monteith)	17.43

Pims: Paisley 6, Fife 16.

Second Period

2-2	PAI Beveridge (O'Neill)	0.20
2-3	FIF S King (Russell)	3.33
3-3	PAI Chalmers (Millar)	9.43
3-4	FIF Morrison (Smith)	pp 13.47
3-5	FIF S King (Edmiston)	18.04

Pims: Paisley 2, Fife 0.

Third Period

3-6	FIF Haig (Smith, Moody)	1.58
3-7	FIF Monteith (Morris)	3.36
4-7	PAI Beveridge (Hammill, Jamieson)	6.41
4-8	FIF Morris (S King, Dutiaume)	11.55
4-9	FIF Dutiaume (Haig, Monteith)	19.13

Pims: Paisley 0, Fife 4.

Shots on Goal

Grubb PAI   15-16-13 44   *save percentage:*   79.5
Murphy FIF   12-12-11 3   *save percentage:*   88.6

Men of Match: Jamieson PAI, Monteith FIF.

Referee: Andy Craig.   *Linesmen:* Cowan, Smith.

Attendance: 2,200.

THE WINNING TEAM

FIFE FLYERS

Ricky Grubb, Stephen Murphy, Frank Morris (capt), Ted Russell, Bill Moody, Derek King, Kyle Horne; Todd Dutiaume, Russell Monteith, Steven King, Mark Morrison, John Haig, Gary Wishart, Dean Edmiston, Andy Samuel, David Smith, Andy Finlay, Liam Grieg, Paddy Ward.

Manager: Chic Cottrell.   *Coach:* Mark Morrison.

PAST WINNERS

Fife Flyers	1998-2000 & 1994-95
Paisley Pirates	1996-97
Murrayfield Racers	1987-91 &1993
Whitley Warriors	1992
Dundee Rockets	1986

Fifth cup for Flyers

Fife Flyers won their third straight Scottish Cup and fifth since the competition began in 1986 with their home defeat of Paisley Pirates, the 1997 winners.

It was also Flyers' third trophy of the 1999-2000 season, squeezed in between winning their BNL title and 24 hours before they were due to open their defence of the playoff championship.

The game, which was sponsored by *Stella Artois*, was played in front of a near-capacity home crowd.

Flyers won all three periods even though Pirate **Matt Beveridge** opened the scoring in the third minute with the first goal of his hat-trick.

There was little to choose between the sides until the game's mid-point when Fife's player-coach **Mark Morrison** and Scot **Steven King** gave the home side a 5-3 lead.

When **John Haig** and **Russ Monteith** opened up a four-goal margin for Flyers early in the last session, it was all over for the plucky Pirates.

The teams had reached the final through an elongated qualifying process as only three Scots sides took part in the event.

As the defending champions, Fife took on and beat both the other contenders in two-leg affairs played after 10 p.m., while Paisley won the playoff against the third team, Edinburgh Capitals.

QUALIFYING GAMES

11 Jan	Paisley-Edinburgh	7-5
18 Jan	Edinburgh-Paisley	4-4

PAISLEY PIRATES win 11-9 on aggregate

1 Feb	Paisley-Fife	3-6
3 Feb	Fife-Paisley	8-10

FIFE FLYERS win 14-13 on aggregate

15 Feb	Edinburgh-Fife	5-5
17 Feb	Fife-Edinburgh	9-1

FIFE FLYERS win 14-6 on aggregate

YOUTH HOME INTERNATIONALS

Players born 1 January 1981 or later
MEN Arena, Manchester 2 April 2000

SCOTLAND under-19	4 (1-1-2)
ENGLAND under-19	3 (1-1-1)

Scorers: **Scotland** - Franklin 2g; Nelson 1+1; Hay 1g; Cowan 2a; Black, Johnston 1a.
England - Sample, Levers, Yardley 1g; Wojciak, Wales, Dodwell, Hardy, Thornton 1a.
Pims: Scotland 40, England 32.
Shots on Goal: Moffat (Scotland) 61 (95.1%), White/Wall (England) 20 (80.0%)
Men of Match: Black SCO, Phillips ENG.
Referee: Paul Shuttleworth. *Attendance:* 4,283.
Linesmen: Craig, Thompson.

Players born 1 January 1983 or later
Hull Ice Arena, 30 April 2000

ENGLAND under-17	7 (3-3-1)
SCOTLAND under-17	0 (0-0-0)

Scorers: Wallace 2g; Carr, Towalski, Moran, Plenty, Gunn 1g; Lake, Smith, Crinnion, Griffiths, Pope 1a.
Pims: **England** 65 (Lake 2+10, Hughes 5+GM), Scotland 39 (Heggie 2+2+2+10).
Shots on Goal: Cameron/Levers ENG 19 (100%), Cree/Kynoch SCO 45 (84.4%).
Referee: Paul Staniforth. *Attendance:* 1,223.
Linesmen: Litchfield, Chidley.

Marvellous Moffat

A remarkable 58-save performance from GB under-18 international keeper **Andy Moffat** was the key to a Scottish upset, their their first victory over the 'auld enemy' since 1994.

Two goals in under four minutes from **Derek Franklin** gave the Scots a 4-2 lead in the 48th minute with **Sean Yardley** beating Moffat for the consolation five minutes from time.

THE TEAMS

SCOTLAND UNDER-19
Matthew Davidge EDI, Andy Moffat FIF; Scott Edgar DUM, Steven Renton DUN, Graeme Walton (Dundonald, Belfast), Patrick Ward FIF, Craig Casement, Craig Gallagher (capt), Gordon Nelson PAI; Martin Connor, Scott Cowan, Gary Morris, Andy Watt AYR, Chris Black DUM, David Gibson, Mark Morrison (Dundonald, Belfast), Ross Hay EDI, Derek Franklin (Elgin), Liam Grieg FIF, Murray Johnson, John Wilson PAI.
Manager: Andy Nelson GLA. *Coach:* Colin Wilson GLA.

ENGLAND UNDER-19
Adam White SLO, Stephen Wall SUN; Richard Thornton BIL, Tyrone Miller GUI, Chris Bailey HUL, Michael Wales (capt) MIL, Darren Botha ROM, James Pease SOL, Andrew Munroe SUN, Chris McEwen SWI; Neil Leary BAS, Jonathan Phillips CAR, Mark Lovell FLI, Jason Moses GUI, Steffan Dodwell, Marc Levers NOT, David Clarke PET, Neil Hardy SHE, Shaun Yardley SOL, Stuart Potts SUN, Richard Wojciak SWI, Paul Sample WHI.
Manager: Dave Greenwood. *Coach:* Mick Mishner.

Punchless Scots

For the second year in a row at Hull, Scotland failed to score against England in a tempestuous game which saw ref Staniforth dish out over 100 minutes in penalties.

The win was the second in two months for the English who toppled Scotland 6-2 on 4 March in Kirkcaldy with a hat-trick from Nottingham's **Joe Wightman**. (No other details of this contest are available.)

THE TEAMS

ENGLAND UNDER-17
Alan Levers NOT, Matthew Cameron OXF; Gareth Crinnion BIL, Rhodri Evans CAR, Michael Plenty GUI, Nathan Hunt HUL, Adam Radmall NOT, Dan Hughes SHE; Tom Pope BAS, Tom Griffiths, Stephen Wallace BIL, Chris Deacon CAR, Richard Gunn CHE, Andrew Smith, Michael Timms GUI, Ryan Lake HUL, Paul Moran (capt), Paul Stanley, Joe Wightman NOT, Matt Towalski SLO, Gary Slevin SWI, Adam Carr SUN.
Manager: Mike Evans. *Coach:* Brian Smith.

SCOTLAND UNDER-17
Jamie Kynoch (Aberdeen), Alistair Cree AYR; Callum McEachran (Aberdeen), Ryan Telfer, Scott Welsh DUM, Michael Aird (capt), Andrew Hannah, Ewan Heeles DUN, Ross Young (Elgin), Neil Blair, Lawrie Clark, Mark McAndrew, Patrick Ward FIF, David Wylie (Inverness), Ross Findlay, Andy Heggie, Mark Ingram, Richard Murray PAI.
Manager: Duncan Clark. *Coach:* Allan Anderson.

WOMEN'S HOCKEY

FINAL STANDINGS

Premier League	GP	W	L	D	GF	GA	Pts
Nottingham Vipers	13	11	2	0	80	32	22
Slough Phantoms	14	9	3	2	56	37	20
Guildford Lightning	14	9	3	2	41	21	20
Sunderland Scorpions	13	8	3	2	57	25	18
Bracknell Queen Bees	14	7	7	0	46	33	14
Swindon Top Cats	14	5	8	1	53	86	11
Solihull Vixens	14	2	10	2	23	55	6
Basingstoke Lady Bison	14	0	13	1	13	90	1

Teams tied on points are separated by goal difference. Nottingham-Sunderland game could not be arranged.

LEADING SCORERS

Premier League	GP	G	A	Pts	Pim
Michelle Smith NOT	13	33	14	47	4
Louise Wheeler SLO	14	28	9	37	2
Nicola Bicknell SLO	14	14	10	24	0
Lynsey Emmerson SUN	13	17	7	24	2
Ruth Aspinall SWI	14	15	9	24	43

LEADING NETMINDERS

	GPI	Min	SoG	GA	Sv%
Vicki Robbins GUI	6	330	116	7	94.0
Beverley Kelland GUI	8	435	166	14	91.6
Clare Martin SLO	7	405	226	19	91

Qualification: 260 minutes.
(Some games were 45 minutes in length)

CHAMPIONSHIP PLAYOFFS

Hull Ice Arena, 27-28 May 2000

Chairman's Cup *(Premier League)*
Final	**SUNDERLAND** - Nottingham	4-0
3rd place	Slough - Guildford	1-2
Semi-finals	Slough - Sunderland	0-2
	Nottingham-Guildford	3-2

North/South Trophy *(Division One)*
Final	**Kingston** - Billingham	2-1
3rd place	Cardiff-Oxford	4-0
Semi-finals	Kingston-Oxford	4-2
	Cardiff-Billingham	0-2

Smith leads Vipers to first title

Nottingham Vipers, led by 33-goal super-scorer **Michelle Smith**, won the league title for the first time in their history.

But fourth-placed Sunderland Scorpions upset Vipers 4-0 in the final of the Championship Playoffs to take their sixth successive Chairman's Cup.

Smith repeated her scoring exploits in the World Championships when her nine goals and eleven points was the best in the tournament, the second time she has won this honour.

Britain's third place finish in Hungary was a big disappointment as their only defeat in four games came against the eventual champions, North Korea.

WOMEN'S WORLD CHAMPIONSHIPS

Pool B Qualifying, *Dunaujvaros & Szekesferhevar, Hungary, 22-26 March 2000*

Preliminary Group	GP	W	L	D	GF	GA	Pts
North Korea	3	2	0	1	14	5	5
Britain	3	2	1	0	14	7	4
Netherlands	3	1	1	1	6	7	3
Australia	3	0	3	0	2	17	0

BRITAIN'S RESULTS
22 Mar	Britain - N Korea	2-4 (1-1,0-2,1-1)
23 Mar	Britain - Australia	7-1 (2-0,1-1,4-0)
25 Mar	Netherlands - Britain	2-5 (1-2,0-1,1-2)

Third place playoff
26 Mar	Belgium - Britain	1-8 (0-2,0-4,1-2)

FINAL RANKING
1 N Korea, 2 Slovakia, **3 Britain**, 4 Belgium, 5 Netherlands, 6 Hungary, 7 Australia, 8 S Africa
North Korea promoted to Division 1 in 2001.

BRITAIN

Vicki Robbins GUI, Amy Johnson SWI; Vicky Burton BRK, Louise Fisher GUI, Susan Hemmerman KIN, Tonia Scialdone, Cheryl Smith NOT, Nicola Bicknell SLO; Natalie Arthur ALT, Zoe Bayne BIL, Laura Byrne, Samantha Cheetham BRK, Fiona King GUI (capt), Michelle Smith NOT, Emily Turner SHE, Louise Wheeler SLO, Debbie Palmer SWI, Claire Oldfield WHI. *Manager:* Teresa Fisher SWI. *Coach:* Laura Urquhart GUI.

HALL OF FAME

GARY STEFAN *left* and **VIC BATCHELDER** were inducted into the British Ice Hockey Writers' Association's Hall of Fame in March 2000 for 'distinguished service to the game of ice hockey in Britain'.
Photo: Mike Smith/Icepix

VIC BATCHELDER

Vic was the founding publisher and editor of Ice Hockey News Review, the sport's longest running magazine. His lively editorials entertained thousands of fans every fortnight for 18 years until ill-health forced his retirement in 1999.

It was the 1980 relaunch of Nottingham Panthers, not far from his home near Derby, that sparked Vic's love of ice hockey, though he recalled seeing a couple of games at Wembley as a youngster.

Believing that fans around the country would appreciate news of the sport, he came up with the idea of a regular newsletter. Starting in 1981 as an eight-page photocopied publication intended for insertion in club programmes, *IHNR* was soon selling in its own right.

As the sport grew rapidly in the Eighties, so did the *News Review,* Vic's crusading passion for the sport steering the magazine through several crises until it became a professional publication with colour photos.

Boasting 36 pages, *IHNR* was the magazine of record with loads of stats and reports, readers' letters, controversial opinion pieces and a variety of features. It was essential reading for fans, officials and players alike.

His publication's success had enabled Vic to give up his day job as a credit manager and in the late Eighties, he added the *Guardian* newspaper to his list of writing credits. He also did a long reporting stint on a telephone hotline, another 'must' for the dedicated fan.

His contributions to the sport did not end with journalism. For a spell in 1982-83 he was secretary of the Panthers and the assistant secretary of the Inter-City League which later expanded into the *Heineken* (British) League.

Though Vic has stepped down from his full-time commitment to *IHNR,* his love of the game is undimmed and he continues to write regularly for his old magazine as well as for the *Guardian.*

GARY STEFAN

The popular British-Canadian forward became known as 'Mr Slough Jets' after spending 13 seasons with the club as player and rink/team manager.

'Stef' scored over 1,000 league points for Jets and became one of the sport's all-time top scorers with more than 2,000 points in all competitions. He was capped 17 times for GB, twice helping his adopted country to gold medals.

Gary was born to be a hockey player. Raised in Brantford, Ontario, the heart of hockey's home land, his two brothers also played, goalie Greg with the NHL's Detroit Red Wings, and forward Joe who later joined Gary in Slough. The Gretzkys were family friends back in Brantford.

Knowing he was too small to join Greg in the big league, Gary came to London for a holiday with an aunt and signed with Richmond Flyers. One of the first Canadians to play here in the modern era, he made an immediate impact, earning a spot on the Inter-City League's All-Star team and lifting the top scorers' trophy.

Richmond's fierce rivals, Streatham Redskins, persuaded him to join them the next season. He formed a famous partnership with local man **Tony Goldstone** and won a second leading scorers' title and a Player of the Year award. In 197 games over five years he accumulated 436 goals and 670 points in all competitions.

His one Wembley appearance came in 1985 when Streatham lost to Fife Flyers in the *Heineken* Championship semi-final.

'Stef' was headhunted again when the Slough rink opened in 1986 and he was appointed Jets' hockey co-ordinator. He was also their first player signing and, fittingly, scored their first goal in the first minute of their first game.

He was coach for the 1993-94 season but did not particularly enjoy the experience. On his return to the ice, he helped Jets to the British League, Division One title for the third time and eventual promotion to the Premier Division.

Since his retirement after the 1998-99 season, 'Stef' has been far from idle. He was the colour commentator on the *Sky Sports* hockey broadcasts, was appointed a director of the governing body, Ice Hockey UK, and in summer 2000 he joined the British National League as their general manager.

■ Gary's scoring statistics are in *The Ice Hockey Annual 1997-98* (World Championships) and *1999-2000* (league and playoffs).

HALL OF FAME MEMBERS

The current Hall of Fame was established in 1986 by the British Ice Hockey Writers' Association.

In addition to the members profiled above, the Association have inducted the following: 1999 - Les Anning, Shannon Hope, Gordon Latto, Roy Shepherd. 1998 - Earl Carlson. 1997- John Lawless. 1996 - Johnny Murray. 1995 - Alex Dampier. 1994 - Mick Curry, Jack Wharry. 1993 - William (Willie) Clark, Nico Toemen, Ian Wight. 1992 - Frank Dempster, Alec Goldstone, Lawrie Lovell. 1991 - Jack Dryburgh, John Rost, Brian Glynne Thomas. 1990 - Alastair Brennan, Sir Arthur Elvin MBE, Willie Kerr Sr. 1989 - George Beach, William Walton (Bill) Booth, Art Hodgins, Peter Johnson, Alfie Miller. 1988 - Patricia Marian (Pat) Marsh, John Cumming (Johnny) Carlyle, *Percy H Nicklin, John Frederick James (Icy) Smith, Alan Weeks. 1987 - Ernest Sidney (Ernie) Leacock, Thomas (Red) Imrie, Terry Matthews, Derek Reilly, Les Strongman. 1986 - *John Francis (Bunny) Ahearne, Robert (Bobby) Giddens, Roy Halpin, Harvey (Red) Stapleford, Sam Stevenson.

British ice hockey's original Hall of Fame was created in 1950 by **Bob Giddens**, *the editor/ publisher of* Ice Hockey World, *the sport's only publication from 1935 to 1958.*

The members of the original Hall are: John Robert Louis (Lou) Bates, Joe Beaton, Keith William (Duke) Campbell, *John Gerald (Gerry) Davey, *Carl Erhardt, *Jimmy Foster, William John (Bill) Glennie, Gibson (Gib) Hutchinson, 'Doc' Kellough, George McNeil, Thomas (Tommy) Lauder, Robert J (Bobby) Lee, Walter (Wally) Monson, B M (Peter) Patton, Bert Peer, Gordon Arthur (Gordie) Poirier, Clarence (Sonny) Rost, Blane Sexton, Floyd Snider, *Archibald (Archie) Stinchcombe, Victor (Chick) Zamick.

* *In 1993 the Writers' Association elected the 1936 Triple Crown winning British team to the Hall. In addition to the members indicated, they are:* Alex Archer, Jimmy Borland, Edgar (Chirp) Brenchley, Jimmy Chappell, Arthur (Art) Childs, Johnny Coward, Gordon Dailley, Jack Kilpatrick, Bob Wyman.

■ *Biographies of all the Hall of Fame members inducted since 1986 are in* The Ice Hockey Annual *for the appropriate years*

OBITUARIES

ARCHIE CREIGHTON

The British playing career of **Archie Creighton** spanned the game's mid-1930's transition from the semi-pro English League (EL) to the professional English National League (ENL).

In 1933-34, Winnipeg-born Archie joined Queens who played out of London's Bayswater rink, north of Hyde Park. That year they finished runners-up in the seven-team English League.

Next winter he toured Europe with Winnipeg Monarchs before returning to Queens. But he was tempted away to the pro ranks when Harringay Arena opened in October 1936.

With Archie in the side, Racers won the London Cup and the league title the following year and were runners-up in both competitions in 1939-40, his last on this side of the Atlantic.

A shrewd and hard hitting left-winger, Creighton totalled 66 goals and 49 assists in his four years with Racers.

He died on 11 June 2000 in Ottawa, aged 77.

MURRAY DODD

A goalminder who won the Scottish playoffs by stopping a puck with his face died in March 2000 at his home in Calgary, Alberta, aged 68.

Dodd, a junior A player with Medicine Hat Tigers, crossed the Atlantic in 1951 to play with Falkirk Lions in the Scottish League. Lions made it to the playoffs and battled through the semi-finals to a home-and-away final against Perth Panthers.

In the first game at Falkirk, Dodd saved a sure-fire goal with his face. As the accident happened long before face masks became compulsory, he was in a bit of a state.

But after a 15-minute delay while he received attention, he bravely returned to the fray and helped Lions to a 6-4 victory. A 2-2 draw in the the second leg was enough to give Lions their third title in a row.

That wasn't Dodd's only moment of fame. He shared a shutout over Fife Flyers in his debut game and later in the season saved a penalty shot from **Andre Girard** of Ayr Raiders.

Tommy Grace (1934)

TOMMY GRACE

Tommy Grace, who died on 20 September 1999, aged 85, was one of the few English players to compete in the professional leagues before and after World War 2. He also played for Britain in the 1939 World Championship.

Born in London in 1914, Grace learned to play at Streatham and captained the team in season 1932-33. When Wembley Lions began play in the professional ENL in 1934, he was the only home-grown player they signed. He centred the second line alongside such greats as **Lou Bates, Gerry Cosby** and **Gordon Dailley.**

By 1936, however, with Lions relying entirely on imports, he moved to their 'second' team, the Olympics, though he turned out for Lions in challenge games.

He returned to the ENL with Southampton Vikings in 1937 but after seeing only limited ice-time he went back to his old rink and played for their intermediate side, the Royals.

Grace moved again in 1938-39, this time to Earls Court Marlboroughs who, like Royals, played in the London and Provincial League. This brought him to the attention of Britain's coach, **Percy Nicklin**, who invited him to play for the national team. In Zurich that February, he saw action on the second line in the 1-0 win over Hungary and the 2-0 defeat by Czechoslovakia.

Nicklin kept Tommy with him the next season on his ENL team, Harringay Racers, and succesfully converted him to a defenceman.

After the war, Grace enjoyed three years with the Brighton-based Sussex team in the Southern Intermediate League, finally hanging up his skates at the end of the 1951-52 season.

He died on 20 September 1999, aged 85.

NICK GREY

Nick Grey, a well respected linesman in both Superleague and the British National League, died on 11 April 2000, following a heart attack. He was 29.

Nick, born in Londonderry in 1971, battled tragedy all his short life. His father David, who played at the Billingham rink and introduced Nick to the game, died in 1999. Nick himself suffered from epilepsy and it was his dedication to hockey which helped him to overcome the debilitating illness.

In the Eighties, Nick and David settled in Telford where Nick played recreational hockey before joining Slough Jets in the British League, Division One. He played 54 games with Jets and later Telford Tigers before deciding in 1995 to turn his talents to officiating.

His quick reactions on the lines were recognised in November 1998 with a *Sekonda* monthly award for officials and he was assigned to the British National League finals at Hull the following March.

His fellow official, referee **Dave McGowan**, paid tribute to Nick. "He was a highly competent official who adored the game."

JOE WATTS

The youngest ever captain of Wembley Lions died on 28 September 1999, aged 74.

Watts was born in Rochester, N.Y. in 1925 but moved to Canada with his family six years later. He won the Ontario championship with the Kingston Locos before joining Tulsa Oilers of the US Hockey League.

The six foot-one defenceman jumped at the chance to cross the Atlantic in 1946 and so impressed Lions with his cool skills that he was made captain after only two months, at the age of 21.

After two seasons back in Canada with Maritime champions, Sydney Millionaires, he returned to Lions' blueline in the autumn of 1949. In all, he played 92 games in London, scoring 12 goals and 27 points and doing 201 minutes penalty time.

Settling back in Kingston, he played on two more Ontario championship winning teams. A popular citizen in later years, he was involved in numerous charities and regularly sang the National Anthem at Kingston's OHL games.

BUNNY WELSH

Bunny Welsh, who went from making the ice in the Empire Pool, Wembley to playing on it, died in 1999 at his home in Bammonsville, Ontario.

Welsh served in Europe with the Canadian Army in World War 2 and then settled in London. In 1946, he was employed at the Empire Pool on the crew responsible for the ice surface.

The first post-war English National League was about to begin and players were in short supply. In no time at all, Welsh found himself pulling on a Lions' sweater.

It was a successful conversion, as he played 92 games on left wing for Lions and their fellow Empire Pool inhabitants, the Monarchs, between 1946 and 1951, scoring 17 goals and 38 points.

He also tasted success with the Intermediate League Terriers, winning the league championship and the BIHA Knock-Out Cup. He was top scorer in 1949-50 with 25 goals and 40 points and runner-up in 1950-51.

MIKE WOLSTENHOLME

The Brighton-born centreman who played and coached in Southampton and Brighton between 1952 and 1965, died on 3 January 2000.

The highlight of Wolstenhome's chequered playing career was winning the Southern Intermediate League in 1952-53 with Southampton Vikings. He scored 12 goals and 14 points in 19 games.

He also made 14 appearances with Brighton Tigers but he will be best remembered as the driving force behind Tigers' second team, the Ambassadors, with whom he was player, coach and manager.

He topped Ambassadors' scoring with 13 goals and 24 points in the 1964 Church Motors tournament, while still finding time to write a regular column on the team's exploits for the monthly *Hockey Fan*.

Mike's career only ended when Brighton's famous Sports Stadium closed in 1965.

JONATHAN HAYNES

Aged 20, a youth player and popular coach with the Streatham junior club, in a street incident.

TAG TAYLOR

The chairman and driving force behind Milton Keynes junior club, one of the country's best organised youth systems.

---

*Tributes written by British historian **Martin C Harris** and former Ice Hockey World editor **Phil Drackett** with additional research by Canadian archivist **Bill Fitsell**.*

INTERNATIONAL ROUND-UP

HONOURS ROLL-CALL 1999-2000

World Championship
Pool A - CZECH REPUBLIC
Pool B - GERMANY
Pool C - HUNGARY
Pool D - ISRAEL

World Junior U20 Championship
Pool A - CZECH REPUBLIC
Pool B - BELARUS
Pool C - AUSTRIA
Pool D - CROATIA

World Junior U18 Championship
Pool A - FINLAND
Pool B - NORWAY

European Junior U18 Championship
Division I - KAZAKHSTAN
Division II - CROATIA

World Women's Championship
Pool A - CANADA
Pool B - KAZAKHSTAN

European League
Metallurg Magnitogorsk (Russia)

Continental Cup
AMBRI PIOTTA (Switzerland)

Stanley Cup
NEW JERSEY DEVILS

Magnitogorsk win Euro League

Russian club Metallurg Magnitogorsk successfully defended their *Skoda Auto* European Hockey League (EHL) title in Lugano, Switzerland.

Magnitogorsk's **Andrei Razine** scored both goals in his team's 2-0 defeat of Sparta Prague in the final on 6 February 2000. **Igor Karpenko** saved all 29 shots on Sparta's net.

The Lugano arena was barely half-full for the game which was watched by 4,536 fans. When Magnitogorsk won last year, there were 12,000 in Moscow's Luzhniki Sports Palace, an EHL record.

The league was won in its first two seasons by Finland's TPS Turku and VEU Feldkirch of Austria.

The last European League – for now

On 24 February 2000, two months after the European League's Final Four games, the governing International Ice Hockey Federation issued the following statement:

'Following consultation with our commercial partner, CWL Holding AG, the IIHF have decided to

suspend the running of the European Hockey League for the season 2000-01.

'Despite the conspicuous financial investment and the growing success of the league in terms of average calibre of the games and attention from the media and the spectators, the penetration through the network in the European territories cannot be regarded for the time being as satisfactory.

'In order to guarantee an optimal exposure of the league in the European territories starting from the 2001-02 season, the *IIHF* will begin immediate consultation with the European broadcasters.

'An international club competition, in the tradition of the previous European Cup, will be staged by in the 2000-01 season'.

This announcement did not come as a big surprise to Euro hockey watchers as the Swedish Elite League had come out publicly in December 1999 saying they were withdrawing from future EHL competition.

Some Finnish, Czech and Russian clubs had privately expressed reservations about their future participation

The problem for many countries was that crowds for EHL games were not as large as for their domestic league games.

Sweden also accused the EHL of 'bad planning', a situation that came to a head when MoDo of Ornskoldsvik, one of Sweden's two 1999-2000 EHL representatives, had to play their semi-final tie while several of their players were on national junior team duty.

It was only the threat of heavy fines that made the club think twice about withdrawing immediately.

THOSE IN FAVOUR...

"In its present format the [European] league is something of a burden to our club, but we wish to remain involved and be in it because in the future it could become something very big." *A director of Finnish club, TPS Turku. Ice Hockey News Review, October 1999.*

'The numbers the amount of TV exposure of the logo] show that Skoda branding at centre ice in the European Hockey League works very well.' *A spokesman for the league's sponsors.* SportVision *magazine.*

NHL in Europe - what's going on?

Phil Anschutz, 60, the multi-billionaire owner of Superleague's London Knights and the NHL's Los Angeles Kings, has been described in Fortune magazine as 'the richest American you've never heard of'.

His business empire was built on oil, railroads and the latest fibre-optic cabling. His hockey empire is built on new and renovated arenas and buying sports franchises.

Fans in Germany, Switzerland and the Czech Republic are joining those in Britain and America who are starting to hear the the the name of the publicity-shy tycoon who is reported to be worth a cool US$10 billion.

In June 2000 his company, Anschutz Sports Holdings (ASH), added Genéve-Servette (Red Eagles), in the Swiss capital, to his growing stable of European teams. ASH already own or hold substantial shares in Czech Elite League champs Sparta Prague and two German DEL clubs, Berlin Eisb<\d>ren (Ice Bears) and league winners Munich Barons, as well as the Knights.

Anschutz came close to adding a sixth European team in July 2000, but his bid for the struggling Swedish Elite Series club, AIK Stockholm, was beaten by **Harry Harkimo**, the wealthy Finnish businessman who owns Jokerit Helsinki in the Finnish Elite League and Superleague's Newcastle Riverkings.

Fortune magazine calls Anschutz 'a genuinely nice guy' and 'abnormally normal' for a billionaire. His teams, it says, 'appear designed to enhance the value of his investment in sports arenas rather than make him famous or fulfil some athletic fantasy'.

"He has no ego. He has never told me what athletes to hire," **Tim Leiweke**, the head of Anschutz's LA sports operation, told the magazine.

Be that as it may, his ownership of so many European teams caused some concern to the IIHF. Some leading nations feared that heavy North American involvement could lead to their teams becoming farm teams for the NHL.

"We lost 56 players last year who signed for the NHL," said IIHF president **Rene Fasel** in February 2000. "We have very good hockey in Europe, as good as the NHL. We are definitely not farm teams for the NHL."

At one time the dispute threatened the participation of NHL players in the 2002 Winter Olympics. The IIHF wanted a more effective agreement (read, more money) for the transfer of players from Europe to North America before allowing NHL players into the Olympics.

"Europe is our market and we'll fight anyone who comes over here and tries to steal our market," said Fasel. In December 1999, the Canadian weekly newspaper, The Hockey News, rated Anschutz as more influential than Fasel in international hockey.

The NHL's position is not as clear-cut as the IIHF's. Rumours persist that an NHL European division will be formed - the latest in March 1999 was reported in the last Annual - and just as regularly denied by the league.

Are Mr Anschutz's foreign adventures an embarrassment to the league, or is he being used by them as a stalking-horse? The sport's wealthiest man has never commented publically on these concerns. But all five of his European teams arranged a tournament among themselves in the German capital for August 2000.

See following article for more on the NHL/Europe tie-up.

NHL and European clubs are partners

Two NHL clubs agreed partnership deals with top European teams during 1999-2000.

The San Jose Sharks and Espoo Blues of the Finnish League signed a contract that includes player exchange, marketing consultation and financial co-operation. The contract will allow young players from San Jose to train and practice with Blues players to prepare for NHL games.

The contract was signed by **Dean Lombardi** general manager of the Sharks,and **Ilkka Sinisalo** Espoo's sport director. The agreement between Swedish champions jurgardens IF and Montreal

Canadiens also included a swap of rookie prospects plus the exchange of information about coaching techniques, player development, treatment of injuries and practice drills.

The teams have had informal ties for years and Canadiens' chief European scout **Dave King** expected to extend his contacts to include Djurgardens' large scouting network.

Ambri-Piotta Win Continental Cup

Swiss club HC Ambri-Piotta from the Alpine villages of Ambri and Piotta (total population 1,200), retained their Continental Cup trophy in the face of stiff opposition from hockey powerhouses Berlin Ice Bears and Russia's Ak Bars (White Cats) Kazan.

In the four-team round-robin final held in Berlin on 26-28 December 1999, Ambri beat HKM Zvolen from the Swiss National League B 7-3 in the decisive game. Three of their goals were scored by the **Celio** brothers, **Manuele** (2) and **Nicola.**

■ Although Ambri often draw capacity crowds to their 7,500-seat home arena, only a disappointing 1,050 fans watched their game against Zvolen. Last year when Ambri first captured the cup in Kosice, Slovakia, only 2,000 turned out for the deciding game.

Final Standings	GP	W	L	D	GF	GA	Pts
HC Ambri-Piotta	3	2	0	1	16	8	5
Berlin Ice Bears	3	1	0	2	7	6	4
Ak Bars Kazan	3	1	2	0	12	10	2
HKM Zvolen	3	1	2	1	5	16	1

Cup double for Ambri-Piotta

HC Ambri-Piotta, the big Swiss club from the small towns at one end of the Saint Gotthard Pass, pulled off a unique double when they added the 1999 European Super Cup to their Continental Cup title.

Ambri won the third Orbis Magnus Cup on 31 August 1999, beating Metallurg Magnitorsk, the EHL and Russian league champs 2-0. The game was held in Ambri's Valascia Arena in front of 4,580 fans.

Patrick Lebeau and **Ryan Gardner** were the scorers and Pauli Jaks had a 22-shot shutout.

The Super Cup is played annually between the winners of the EHL and the Continental Cup and this was the first time that the Continental Cup champion has come out on top.

The previous winners, Finland's TPS Turku and Austria's VEU Feldkirch, both held the EHL title.

IIHF president **Rene Fasel** hailed Ambri's victory: "This is a sign of how competitive the Continental Cup has become," he said. "The clubs in this tournament belong with the elite of European ice hockey."

In his moment of triumph, **Larry Huras**, Ambri's coach, was understandably ebullient. "We are the champions of Europe. It's a nice feeling. Now it would be nice to meet the Dallas Stars [the 1999 Stanley Cup champs] and play to become world champions."

Superleague, Swiss-style

The Swiss National A and B Leagues voted narrowly, 11-9, to create a 12-team professional league to begin play in 2000-01.

Most of the opposition to the proposal came from the B League where seven of the ten clubs voted against it.

At the end of 1999-2000 the NLA was to be expanded to 12 teams, all of.which had to be organised as share-holding companies or have a bank guarantee for a minimum of 100,000 Swiss francs (about £40,000).

NO CONTACT, PLEASE, WE'RE SWISS

A near capacity crowd of 10,087 watched the Swiss League's All-Star Game between a team of domestic players and one composed of imports. The local players beat the International Stars 6-4 in a game with only one penalty.

The contest was followed a skills competition, won by the imports, and the league's end-of-season awards ceremony.

To placate the NLB teams, it was agreed that promotion and relegation would continue between the two leagues and that any NLA side that finished last three seasons in a row would be immediately relegated without any playoff or qualification games.

The NLB will also consist of 12 teams and is expected to be regionalised into eastern and western divisions later.

The total number of clubs in the two leagues and the amount of foreign players (Switzerland are not part of the EU) was under discussion. Currently, Swiss teams are permitted three imports at any one time with a maximum of five per season.

St Petersburg hosts Worlds

The new St Petersburg Ice Palace in Russia, which was the main venue for the 2000 World Championships, cost around US$84 million (about £52 million), according to the International Ice Hockey Federation.

The building has 74 private VIP boxes, four of which are equipped with saunas. The cost of their construction alone was estimated at between $270,000 and $440,000.

The budget for the Championships was US$3.5 million. Revenue was expected to be $6.2 million and the profit $2.7 million.

St Petersburg is geographically well placed in the middle of a hockey hotbed. Every day at least 20,000 fans arrived from Finland, 3,500 from Sweden and 2,000 each from the Czech Republic and Latvia.

The Franco-Italian Cup

Nottingham's **Paul Adey** thought he would get away from it all in Italy by joining Milan in 1999-2000. But instead, he must have found the sport's politics there even more perplexing.

Due to a disagreement with the Italian Federation over import restrictions, Milan elected not to enter the Italian League and played instead in the new Franco-Italian Cup.

This was a league comprising Milan and the nine leading French sides with all the games not involving Milan counting towards the French championship.

Milan won the league comfortably and then hosted the finals where they finished runners-up. But there was more controversy in this tournament as their last game was abandoned.

Sharks win Spengler Cup

Leading German DEL club, Cologne Sharks, skated off with the 73rd Spengler Cup, one of Europe's oldest trophies, in December 1999.

Canadian **Lance Nethery** was the coach of Cologne who were the first German club to carry off the cup since EV Fussen in 1964.

Sharks beat off tough competition from the touring Team Canada, Sweden's Farjestad BK and Swiss hosts, Davos, but went down 3-2 to Russia's Metallurg Magnitogorsk.

Cologne, with over a dozen Canadians in their side, gained their revenge over the reigning EHL and Russian champions with a decisive 6-2 victory in the final.

The invitational tournament was first won by England's Oxford University in 1923.

Revolution in Sweden

Stockholm's Djürgardens IF have won more titles than any other Swedish club - 15, including the 1999-2000 championship. But their success hasn't come because they've played the same old way, year in, year out.

In the 1980s, Djürgardens survived heavy criticism of their extreme 1-3-1 tactics to win titles and see the brainchild of coaches **Putte Carlsson** and **Lasse Falk** adopted by NHL teams.

Last season, it was the turn of coaches **Hardy Nilsson** and **Mats Watlin** to devise another revolutionary system, one which called for four forwards and just one defender.

"The defenceman that disappears is transformed into another centreman," explained Watlin to the Swedish newspaper *Aftonbladet.* "So we have two centres, two very offensive forwards and one sweeper."

Some observers said that the aim of having a more creative attack and scoring more goals would leave too many gaps at the back. But such fears proved groundless.

"The centres have more responsibility all over the ice and both of them help out the lone defenceman when we defend," said Watlin.

The cynics also reckoned that Djürgardens had only adopted the idea because they were short of blueliners. But the new formation proved to be so effective that once more the NHL scouts came to Sweden to look and learn.

No Canada

The touring Canadian national team has been disbanded. With so many NHL players now competing for Canada in the World and Olympic championships, the team of college and minor league pros has passed its sell-by date.

The side was originally formed in 1963 by **Father David Bauer** to try and break the stranglehold of the Soviet Union and other top European nations. Canada had never iced a national team until then, and were represented at international level by their leading amateur club.

Announcing their decision, the Canadian Hockey Association said that it cost $490,000 (Canadian) to run the team and they felt the money would be better spent on grass-roots programmes.

Coach **Tom Renney** will remain as national team coach but his duties will be restricted to putting together sides composed of Canadians playing in Europe to compete in the Spengler Cup and other international tournaments.

OLYMPIC QUALIFICATION

Britain was one of 16 nations that entered the IIHF's four pre-qualifying tournaments for a place in the 2002 Winter Olympics in Salt Lake City, USA. The games were staged in four European cities in February 2000.

Britain played in group 3 where **France** qualified with three victories. **Germany** won group 1 in Ljubljana, Slovenia; the **Ukraine** qualified from group 2 in Talinn, Estonia; and **Denmark** went forward from group 4 on home ice in Copenhagen.

These four will meet **Belarus, Norway, Austria** and **Latvia** in the Olympic Qualification Round in February 2001 for the right to join the major hockey playing countries in Salt Lake City.

The Olympic Games will be contested by 12 or 14 teams, depending on whether or not the NHL agrees to release its players.

Group 3, Gdansk, Poland, 10-13 February 2000

FINAL STANDINGS

	GP	W	L	D	GF	GA	Pts
France	3	3	0	0	19	7	6
Poland	3	2	1	0	17	9	4
Britain	3	1	2	0	10	9	2
Romania	3	0	3	0	3	24	0

GB Player of the Tournament
ASHLEY TAIT, Nottingham
Selected by the GB Supporters Club

RESULTS

10 Feb	**Britain** - Romania	4-0
	Poland - France	2-5
11 Feb	France - Romania	9-1
	Britain - Poland	2-4
13 Feb	France - **Britain**	5-4
	Romania-Poland	2-11

BRITAIN'S POINTS SCORERS

	GP	G	A	Pts	Pim
Paul Adey	3	3	1	4	27
Scott Young	3	2	1	3	18
Darren Durdle	3	1	2	3	4
Rick Brebant	3	1	2	3	42
Steve Moria	3	1	1	2	4
Mike Harding	3	0	2	2	2
Darren Hurley	3	1	0	1	8
Merv Priest	2	1	0	1	2
Brent Bobyck	3	0	1	1	2
Vince Boe	3	0	1	1	2
David Longstaff	3	0	1	1	2
Rick Strachan	3	0	1	1	2

BRITAIN'S NETMINDING

	GPI	Mins	SoG	GA	Sav%
Stevie Lyle	3	180	52	9	82.69
TEAM TOTALS	3	180	52	9	82.69

BRITAIN

Stephen Foster AYR, Stevie Lyle CAR; Vince Boe, Scott Young AYR, Rick Strachan BAS, Matt Cote BRK, Darren Durdle CAR, Neil Liddiard PET, Andre Malo SHE, Jason Kendall SLO; Nicky Chinn, Darren Hurley, Steve Moria (capt), Merv Priest CAR, Rick Brebant LON, Mike Harding, Jeff Johnstone MAN, Brent Bobyck, Graham Garden, Ashley Tait NOT, David Longstaff SHE, Paul Adey (Milan).

Manager: Andy French CAR.
Head Coach: Peter Woods (ISL).
Asst coach: Dave Whistle BRK.

GB GAME SUMMARIES

10 February 2000

BRITAIN-ROMANIA   **4-0 (2-0,2-0,0-0)**

1-0 GBR Brebant (Bobyck)	pp 13.50
2-0 GBR Priest (Longstaff, Moria)	17.55
3-0 GBR Young (Harding)	22.05
4-0 GBR Adey (Brebant)	sh 31.20

Penalty minutes: Britain 18, Romania 14.
Shots on Goal:

Lyle GBR	9- 1 -2 12	(100.00%)
Laday ROM	14-21-21 56	(92.86%)

Powerplays/goals: Britain 6/1, Romania 8/0.
Britain's Man of Match: Boe.
Referee: Rejthar CZE.
Attendance: 100.

11 February 2000

BRITAIN-POLAND   **2-4 (0-1,1-2,1-1)**

0-1 POL Kwiatkowski (Piatek, Garbocz)	pp 2.14
1-1 GBR Hurley	23.09
1-2 POL Zamojski (Laskiewicz)	pp 27.08
1-3 POL Klisiak (Laskiewicz, Paryszek)	38.34
2-3 GBR Adey (Young, Durdle)	pp44.18
2-4 POL Garbocz	59.35

Penalty minutes: Britain 30, Poland 26.
Shots on Goal:

Lyle GBR	5- 5- 6 16	(75.00%)
Jaworski POL	9-14-17 40	(95.00%)

Powerplays/goals: Britain 9/1, Poland 10/2.
Britain's Man of Match: Garden.
Referee: Trainer GER.
Attendance: 3,500.

13 February 2000

FRANCE-BRITAIN   **5-4 (1-1,4-2,0-1)**

1-0 GBR Adey (Durdle)	12.38
1-1 FRA Rozenthal (Bozon, Briand)	15.26
2-1 FRA Briand (Barin) pp	22.05
3-1 FRA Bozon (Briand, Dewolf)	22.55
4-1 FRA Perez (Barin, Ouellet)	pp 27.07
4-2 GBR Young (Harding)	30.17
5-2 FRA Briand (Rozenthal, Meunier)	pp 35.09
5-3 GBR Durdle (Adey, Brebant)	pp 38.09
5-4 GBR Moria (Strachan, Boe)	pp 58.39

Penalty minutes: France 14, Britain 83 (Adey 5+game high-sticks, Brebant 10-misc + Game - abuse of official).
Shots on Goal:

Huet FRA	5-10- 6 21	(80.95%)
Lyle GBR	6- 5-13 24	(79.17%)

Powerplays/goals: Britain 7/2, France 14/3.
Britain's Man of Match: Strachan.
Referee: Radbjer SWE.
Attendance: 900.

Brits go out battling

With little left in the kitty after the World A Pool qualifiers, Britain's chances to progress in World and Olympic competition finally died on the ice in Gdansk. They won only one of their three games in Poland and finished a dismal third.

Peter Woods' men played like they were trying to win Superleague, but at this level in Europe, the refs see passionate, in-yer-face hockey as simply dirty hockey.

It was a makeshift team, too, with eight players missing from the side that so narrowly failed to win promotion to Pool A.

Due to injuries and club commitments - Superleague reluctantly cancelled most of their games but the BNL ran a full schedule - this was the first time since 1989 that no one called Cooper or Hand was in the national team.

Ian Cooper, Britain's most capped player with 73 internationals, had just joined the BNL's Guildford Flames who needed him for a crucial league game, and brother Stephen had to pull out with a knee injury as did **Tony Hand**, GB's all-time highest scorer.

With Woods having only 30 eligible Superleague players to call on, he brought in two BNL defencemen, **Neil Liddiard** (Peterborough) and dual national **Jason Kendall** (Slough).

But they saw little or no ice-time and, anyway, it was youth, discipline and goal-scoring forwards that the team desperately needed.

It was good to see **Paul Adey** back on form, **Brent Bobyck** overcome a mystery bug to excel himself against France, and a top form **Stevie Lyle** whose steady netminding prevented the defeats from being much wider.

Defencemen **Scott Young**, who still upset the refs too often, and **Darren Durdle** lent a much needed hand up front. But supporters' choice **Ashley Tait** was typical of the forwards who worked their whatsits off but lacked that killer touch around the net.

PAST OLYMPIC QUALIFYING RESULTS

1995-96, Venues in brackets.
Coach: **Peter Woods**

25 Oct	GB-Netherlands	4-1	(Milton Keynes)
3 Dec	GB-Denmark	1-1	(Milton Keynes)
20 Dec	Switzerland-GB	2-2	(Lausanne)
17 Jan	Slovenia-GB	4-5	(Ljubljana)
7 Feb	Denmark-GB	2-3	(Copenhagen)
12 Nov	GB-Slovenia	5-0	(Sheffield)
12 Dec	Netherlands-GB	2-8	(Heerenveen)
18 Dec	GB-Switzerland	3-3	(Sheffield)

1993, Sheffield Arena, 28 Aug-4 Sept
Coach: **Alex Dampier.**
Poland 2-2, Japan 2-4, Latvia 4-8, Slovakia 1-7.

WORLD CHAMPIONSHIPS

POOL A

St Petersburg, Russia, 27 April-14 May 2000

FINAL

14 May
SLOVAKIA-CZECH REP.   3-5 (0-3,1-0,2-2)

SEMI-FINALS

12 May
SLOVAKIA-FINLAND   3-1 (2-0,1-1,0-0)
CANADA-CZECH REP.   1-2 (1-1,0-0,0-1)

WORLD RANKINGS

1 CZECH REPUBLIC (World Champions), 2 Slovakia, 3 Finland, 4 Canada, 5 USA, 6 Switzerland, 7 Sweden, 8 Latvia, 9 Belarus, 10 Norway, 11 Russia, 12 Italy, 13 Ukraine, 14 Austria, 15 France, 16 Japan.

France relegated to Division I in 2001; Japan will compete in Far East qualifier.

LEADING SCORERS

	GP	G	A	Pts	Pim
Miroslav Satan SVK	9	10	2	12	14
Jiri Dopita CZE	9	4	7	11	16
David Vyborny CZE	9	4	6	10	6
Todd Bertuzzi CAN	9	5	4	9	47
Tomas Vlasak CZE	9	4	5	9	0

LEADING NETMINDERS

	GPI	Mins	SoG	GA	Sv%
Jose Theodore CAN	8	478	192	13	93.2
Reinhard Divis AUT	6	359	201	15	92.5
Roman Cechmanek CZE	8	480	212	16	92.4

ALL-STAR TEAM

Goal   R Cechmanek CZE
Defence   M Sykora CZE, P Nummelin FIN
Forwards   J Dopita CZE (C), M Satan SVK (R),
           T Vlasak CZE (L).

Hosts miss their own party

The Czech Republic successfully defended their World Championship title with a 5-3 final win over their surprising neighbours, Slovakia.

This was the first time since 1994 when the Czech and Slovak nations first entered the championships separately that the two countries had met in the gold medal game.

Slovakia's best finish since then was seventh in 1998 and 1999 so their appearance in the final was almost as big an upset as Russia's failure to reach the quarter-finals.

The Russians turned in their worst ever performance since their debut as the Soviet Union 46 years ago.

Alexander Yakushev's side won only two of their eight games - over Sweden and relegated France - despite having NHL superstars **Alexei Yashin** and **Pavel Bure** in their line-up.

Some suggested that it was just this influx of NHL players which had caused the team's disorganised play.

Ironically, it was the reluctance of many NHLers to travel to Russia that helped to make the championships one of the most competitive of recent years.

Only Japan failed to win a game. They qualified for Pool A as the best nation in the Far East, not an area of the world which has a large hockey following.

■ A capacity crowd of 12,350 watched the final.

POOL C

Beijing, China, 20-26 March 2000
1 Hungary, 2 China, 3 Croatia, 4 Lithuania, 5 S Korea, 6 Romania, 7 Spain, 8 Jugoslavia, 9 Bulgaria.

Hungary, China, Croatia and *Lithuania* will compete in Division I in 2001; remaining nations will compete in Division II.

POOL D

Reykjavik, Iceland, 10-16 April 2000.
1 Israel, 2 Belgium, 3 Australia, 4 South Africa, 5 Iceland, 6 New Zealand, 7 Mexico, 8 Luxembourg, 9 Turkey.
*All nations will compete in Division II in 2001, except **Luxembourg** and **Turkey** who will take part in a qualifying round.*

POOL A QUALIFYING GAMES

Britain's second place finish in the B Pool of the World Championships in April 1999 qualified them to compete with seven other nations for five places in the A Pool 2000.

The seven were **Denmark** and **Kazakhstan** who finished first and third in Pool B, plus the countries finishing 11th to 15th in Pool A - in order, **Latvia, Norway, Italy, Ukraine, France.**

(Japan, 16th, participated in a special Far East qualifier.)

The eight were split into two groups, based on their **1998** world rankings (see The Ice Hockey Annual 1998-99 for details).

Latvia, the highest placed, joined Kazakhstan (4th), Ukraine (5th), and Britain (8th) in Group A in Sheffield while the remaining four competed in Group B in Amiens, France.

After a round robin, the top two teams in each group were promoted to Pool A and the third-placed teams went to a one-game playoff at a neutral venue to decide the fifth and final place.

GROUP STANDINGS

GROUP A, Sheffield Arena, 11-14 Nov 1999

	GP	W	L	D	GF	GA	Pts
Latvia LAT	3	1	0	2	6	3	4
Ukraine UKR	3	1	0	2	5	4	4
Britain GBR	3	0	0	3	3	3	3
Kazakhstan KAZ	3	0	2	1	6	10	1

Latvia and *Ukraine* promoted to Pool A, *Britain* go to fifth place playoff.

GROUP B, Amiens, France, 11-14 Nov 1999

	GP	W	L	D	GF	GA	Pts
Italy ITA	3	2	1	0	11	7	4
France FRA	3	1	1	1	10	10	3
Norway NOR	3	1	1	1	7	8	3
Denmark DEN	3	1	2	0	9	12	2

Italy and *France* promoted to Pool A, *Norway* go to fifth place playoff.

GROUP RESULTS

11 Nov	Denmark-Italy	5-3
	Kazakhstan-Latvia	3-6
	France-Norway	3-3
	Ukraine-**Britain**	2-2
13 Nov	Italy-Norway	4-1
	Ukraine-Kazakhstan	3-2
	France-Denmark	6-3
	Latvia-**Britain**	0-0
14 Nov	**Britain**-Kazakhstan	1-1
	Norway-Denmark	3-1
	Italy-France	4-1
	Latvia-Ukraine	0-0

FIFTH PLACE PLAYOFF

Eindhoven, Netherlands
14 Dec   Norway-**Britain**   2-1
Norway promoted to Pool A, **Britain** remain in Pool B.

GB'S BEST PLAYERS

Goal	Stevie Lyle
Defence	Matt Cote
Forward	Rick Brebant

Selected by the organisers at Sheffield

BRITAIN'S GAME SUMMARIES

11 November 1999, Sheffield

UKRAINE-BRITAIN   **2-2 (1-0,0-1,1-1)**

0-1 UKR Oletskyy (Litvynenko, Butsenko) 13.57,
1-1 GBR Harding (Johnstone, Durdle) 26.46,
2-1 UKR Polkovnikov (Goncharenko) pp 47.59,
2-2 GBR Hand (Brebant, Harding) 54.41.
Penalty minutes: Ukraine 12, Britain 45 (Hurley: 5+game - roughing).
Shots on Goal: Karpenko UKR 23 (91.30%), Lyle GBR 42 (95.24%).
Powerplays/goals: Ukraine 7/1, Britain 3/0.
Britain's Man of Match: Cote.
Referee: Andersson.   *Attendance:* 1,406.

13 November 1999, Sheffield

LATVIA-BRITAIN   **0-0 (0-0,0-0,0-0)**

Penalty minutes: Latvia 6, Britain 12.
Shots on Goal: Naumovs LAT 21, Lyle GBR 32.
Powerplays: Latvia 5, Britain 2.
Britain's Man of Match: Lyle.
Referee: Vaisfeld.   *Attendance:* 2,011.

14 November 1999, Sheffield

BRITAIN-KAZAKHSTAN   **1-1 (1-0,0-0,0-1)**

1-0 GBR S Cooper (Thornton, Durdle) pp 13.25,
1-1 KAZ Raiskiy (Troshchinskiy, Dorokhin) pp
59.58
Penalty minutes: Britain 10, Kazakhstan 20
(Zarzhitskiy 10-misc.).
Shots on Goal: Lyle GBR 33 (96.97%),
Ogureshnikov KAZ 30 (96.77%)
Powerplays/goals: Britain 4/1. Kazakhstan 4/1.
Britain's Man of Match: Malo.
Referee: Lichtnecker.   *Attendance*: 1,998

14 December 1999, Eindhoven

NORWAY-BRITAIN   **2-1 (1-0,1-1,0-0)**

1-0 NOR Knutsen (Trygg) pp 19.51,
2-0 NOR Salsten (Knold, Skroder) 29.03,
2-1 GBR Durdle (S Cooper) pp 36.21.
Penalty minutes: Norway 10, Britain 12.
Shots on Goal: Schistad NOR 20 (95.00%),
Lyle GBR 38 (94.74%).
Powerplays/goals: Norway 6/1, Britain 5/1.
Britain's Man of Match: No award made.
Referee: Hellweg.   *Attendance*: 500.

BRITAIN

Stevie Lyle CAR, Wayne Cowley (Dayton,
ECHL), Joe Watkins BAS (reserve); Scott
Young AYR, Rick Strachan BAS, Matt Cote BRK,
Darren Durdle CAR, Paul Dixon GUI, Scott
Campbell MAN, Stephen Cooper NOT, Andre
Malo SHE; Tony Hand AYR, Steve Moria (capt),
Merv Priest & Steve Thornton CAR, Jeff
Johnstone LON, Rick Brebant, Mike Harding,
Darren Hurley & Jonathan Weaver MAN, Brent
Bobyck & Ashley Tait NOT, Paul Adey (Milan).
Manager: Andy French CAR. *Coach*: Peter
Woods (unatt.) *Asst coach*: Dave Whistle BRK.
Changes for Eindhoven playoff *Goal*: Stephen
Foster AYR replaced Cowley; *defence*: Vince
Boe AYR replaced Dixon; *forward*: Ian Cooper
LON replaced Brebant (injured).

ALL-STAR TEAM

Goal	**Stevie Lyle** GBR
Defence	**Oleg Polkovnikov** UKR
	Matt Cote GBR
Centre	**Harijs Vitolins** LAT
Right-wing	**Aleksandrs Belavskis** LAT
Left-wing	**Tony Hand** AYR

Selected by the Press at Sheffield

BRITAIN'S SCORERS

including Eindhoven	GP	G	A	Pts	Pim
Darren Durdle	4	1	2	3	8
Stephen Cooper	4	1	1	2	0
Mike Harding	4	1	1	2	0
Tony Hand	4	1	0	1	4
Rick Brebant	3	0	1	1	4
Jeff Johnstone	4	0	1	1	0
Steve Thornton	4	0	1	1	2
TEAM TOTALS	**4**	**4**	**7**	**11**	**79**

BRITAIN'S NETMINDING

inc. Eindhoven	GPI	Mins	SoG	GA	Sv%
Stevie Lyle	4	240	145	5	96.55
TEAM TOTALS	**4**	**240**	**145**	**5**	**96.55**

Two seconds from A heaven

It was worthy of the old sitcom line: "I do not
believe it!".

In the dying moments of GB's last game in
Sheffield, Kazakhstan pulled their goalie in an
all-out effort to equalise **Stephen Cooper**'s 14th
minute goal for GB.

Britain only needed to hold on to win
promotion to Pool A but **Andrei Raiskiy** scored
the equaliser just *two seconds from time*.

The scene was dreadfully reminiscent of GB's
3-3 draw with the Swiss in 1996 which knocked
them out of Olympic contention.

Embarrassingly, GB's two most skilful
forwards, **Tony Hand** and **Rick Brebant**, missed
the empty net. After Hand shot wide, Brebant
passed when he might have shot and then Tony
hit the near post.

But that's not to blame those two, or indeed
any of GB's hard-working squad for ultimately -
after an extra playoff in the Netherlands - failing
to win a game.

It might have helped had GB played
Kazakhstan as the late game on the Sunday so
that they would know exactly what they had to
do. Playing first to please the dear old Beeb was
playing blind, and it didn't give them enough rest,
either, after Saturday evening's superb but
gruelling encounter with top ranked Latvia.

The average crowd of 1,805 was enthusiastic
in its support but not loud enough in the
8,500-seat arena to help the home team.

Moreover, the low attendance exhausted the
GB Ice Hockey Board's limited funds and was a
severe setback to their ambition of staging Pool
A in this country in 2004.

POOL B

After failing to qualify for Pool A in Sheffield and Eindhoven, Britain competed in Pool B for the sixth successive year in 2000.

Katowice, Poland, 12-21 April 2000

FINAL STANDINGS

	GP	W	L	D	GF	GA	Pts
Germany GER	7	6	1	0	30	15	12
Kazakhstan KAZ	7	5	2	0	30	22	10
Britain GBR	7	4	2	1	31	23	9
Poland POL	7	4	2	1	28	19	9
Denmark DEN	7	2	3	2	22	19	6
Estonia EST	7	3	4	0	19	27	6
Slovenia SLO	7	0	5	2	16	31	2
Netherlands NED	7	0	5	2	13	33	2

Teams tied on points are separated by the results between them, then by goal difference.

GB'S WORLD RANKING: 19th

Germany are promoted to Pool A in 2001. Other nations will compete in the new Division I.

Britain's Best Players
Goal **JOE WATKINS**
Defence **STEPHEN COOPER**
Forward **TONY HAND**
Selected by The Ice Hockey Annual

RESULTS

	GER	KAZ	POL	DEN	EST	SLO	NED
GB	0-5	3-1	6-4	5-4	5-6	3-3	9-0
GER		5-2	2-6	3-2	3-2	7-2	5-1
KAZ			5-2	4-3	4-2	9-4	5-3
POL				3-3	5-1	3-1	5-1
DEN					4-0	4-2	2-2
EST						3-2	5-4
SLO							2-2

Best GB Players
'THE TEAM'
Awarded by the GB Supporters Club

BRITAIN'S NETMINDING

	GPl	Mins	SoG	GA	Sv%
Joe Watkins	5	300	181	14	92.3
Wayne Cowley	2	85	34	6	82.3
Jimmy Hibbert	1	35	16	3	81.2
TEAM TOTALS	7	420	231	23	90.0

BRITAIN'S SCORING

	GP	G	A	Pts	Pim
Steve Moria	7	6	4	10	2
Tony Hand	7	2	8	10	2
Rick Brebant	7	4	4	8	14
Paul Adey	7	3	5	8	14
Ashley Tait	7	3	4	7	10
Scott Young	4	3	3	6	20
Stephen Cooper	7	1	5	6	2
Merv Priest	7	2	3	5	8
David Longstaff	7	2	3	5	14
Ian Cooper	7	2	2	4	10
Darren Hurley	7	1	3	4	32
Mike Bishop	7	0	3	3	18
Mike Ellis	7	1	1	2	0
Rick Strachan	7	1	1	2	2
Paul Dixon	7	0	2	2	0
Shaun Johnson	7	0	1	1	0
David Clark	7	0	0	0	2
Glenn Mulvenna	7	0	0	0	18
TEAM TOTALS	7	31	52	83	168

Best Netminder of the Tournament
JOE WATKINS
GB
Selected by the IIHF

BRITAIN

Joe Watkins BAS, Jim Hibbert NEW, Wayne Cowley (Dayton, ECHL); Mike Bishop, Scott Young AYR, Rick Strachan BAS, Paul Dixon GUI, Glenn Mulvenna NEW, Stephen Cooper NOT, Neil Liddiard PET; Tony Hand AYR, Mike Ellis BAS, Darren Hurley, Steve Moria (capt), Merv Priest CAR, Ian Cooper GUI, Rick Brebant LON, Shaun Johnson NEW, Ashley Tait NOT, David Clarke PET, David Longstaff SHE, Paul Adey (Milan). *Manager:* Andy French CAR. *Coach:* Peter Woods (unatt.), *Asst. coach:* Dave Whistle BRK.

BRITAIN (Pool B in Katowice) *left to right back row:* Jason Ellery (equipment), Tom Blatchford (equipment), Rick Brebant, Glenn Mulvenna, Mike Ellis, Paul Dixon, Simon Harrs (doctor), Andy French (manager), Rachel Richardson (physio): *middle row :* Neil Liddiard, David Clarke, Ashley Tait, Ian Cooper, Mike Bishop, Darren Hurley, Scott Young, Merv Priest, David Longstaff; *front row:* Joe Watkins, Tony Hand, Shaun Johnson, Steve Moria, Peter Woods (head coach), Dave Whistle (coach), Rick Strachan, Paul Adey, Stephen Cooper, Wayne Cowley. *Inset:* Jim Hibbert.

BRITAIN'S GAME SUMMARIES

12 April, Satellite rink

ESTONIA-BRITAIN 6-5 (3-2,2-2,1-1)

GB scoring:

Priest (Hurley)	1.47	(0-1)
Strachan (Moria, Priest)	16.09 pp	(3-2)
Moria (Tait, Young)	30.46	(3-3)
I Cooper (Dixon, Hurley)	39.53 pp	(5-4)
Tait (Moria)	46.43 pp	(6-5)
Shots on Goal:	Terentjev EST	41	(87.8%)
	Hibbert/Cowley GB	22	(72.7%)

Penalty minutes: Estonia 18, Britain 38 (Young, Hurley 10-min. misconducts).
Goals/powerplays: Estonia 3/8, GB 3/10.
GB Man of Match: Longstaff.
Referee: Dunnett CAN. Attendance: 350
Not the start GB wanted. Already short on defence, Hibbert's back gave out halfway through and he was replaced with Cowley. Estonia went 4-3 up ten seconds later. Then Young was concussed and missed the rest of the contest.
This was GB's highest score since 1999 when they beat Estonia 6-3. "It's not often GB scores five and gets beaten," said Woods ruefully.

13 April, Satellite rink

SLOVENIA-BRITAIN 3-3 (1-1,2-1,0-1)

GB scoring:

Young (Tait, S Cooper)	10.11 sh	(0-1)
Longstaff (Young, Moria)	20.38 pp	(1-2)
Moria (Longstaff)	54.36 pp	(3-3)
Shots on Goal:	Simsic SLO	46	(93.5%)
	Cowley GB	28	(89.3%)

Penalty minutes: Slovenia 20, GB 40 (Mulvenna, Hurley 10-min. misconducts)
Goals/powerplays: Slovenia 1/6, GB 2/7.
GB Man of Match: Young.
Referee: Dahl NOR. Attendance: 340
With a less than sparkling defensive performance, especially from Cowley, GB needed a goal from their oldest player to scrape a draw against a nation that's only beaten them once in five meetings. Young's goal and assist showed that yesterday's knock fortunately had no lasting effects.

15 April, Satellite rink

BRITAIN-NETHERLANDS 9-0 (3-0,2-0,4-0)

Scoring:

Hurley (Adey, Bishop)	2.58	(1-0)
I Cooper (Priest, Young)	8.39	(2-0)
Brebant (Adey, Clarke)	12.01 pp	(3-0)
Brebant (Hurley, Adey)	27.51	(4-0)
Hand	30.41	(5-0)
Tait (I Cooper, Priest)	42.54	(6-0)
Brebant (Hand, Bishop)	49.58	(7-0)
Ellis (Dixon, Johnson)	51.43	(8-0)
Adey (S Cooper, Brebant)	59.02 pp	(9-0)
Shots on Goal:	Watkins GB	29	(100%)
	Nijland NED	34	(73.5%)

Penalty minutes: GB 12, Netherlands 10.
Goals/powerplays: GB 2/4, Netherlands 0/6.
GB Man of Match: Brebant.
Referee: Bergman BEL. Attendance: 500
GB's biggest win for seven years came in the nick of time to keep them in the promotion hunt. Better yet, goalie Watkins had a shutout on his international debut, probably a first for GB since World War 2.
Woods iced all his squad against the side that was in Pool C a year ago.

16 April, Spodek Arena

POLAND-BRITAIN 4-6 (1-1,2-1,1-4)

GB scoring:

Young (Brebant, Hand)	6.06 pp2	(0-1)
Young (Hand)	31.11 pp	(2-2)
Moria (Hand, Longstaff)	43.24	(3-3)
Hand (Tait, Brebant)	46.05 pp	(3-4)
S Cooper (Moria)	54.25	(4-5)
Brebant (Adey)	58.55	(4-6)
Shots on Goal:	Kieca POL	27	(77.8%)
	Watkins GB	41	(90.2%)

Penalty minutes: Poland 14, GB 22.
Goals/powerplays: Poland 2/8, GB 3/4.
GB Man of Match: Watkins.
Referee: Dunnett CAN. Attendance: 8,500
Watkins followed his shutout with a match-winning performance against the host nation and their huge support. He twice stopped NY Islander Czerkawski, Poland's best forward.
Hand gave the goalie a run for man of the match as he teed up GB's first three goals and fired home the fourth himself.

18 April, Satellite rink

DENMARK-BRITAIN 4-5 (3-2,1-1,0-2)

GB scoring:

Moria (Hand, S Cooper)	7.18	(3-1)
Moria (Bishop, Strachan)	15.41	(3-2)
Adey (Hand, S Cooper)	37.52 pp	(4-3)
Moria (Hand, Ellis)	48.42	(4-4)
Adey (Brebant, S Cooper)	55.51	(4-5)
Shots on Goal:	Hirsch DEN	40	(87.5%)
	Watkins GB	29	(86.3%)

Penalty minutes: Denmark 20, GB 18.
Goals/powerplays: Denmark 1/3, GB 1/4.
GB Man of Match: Moria.
Referee: Bergman BEL. Attendance: 500
One of Britain's finest displays of the modern era. A superb fight back after they fell 3-0 behind in the first seven minutes left them in third place one point behind Germany and Kazakhstan, their remaining opponents. "We control our own destiny now," said Woods.

19 April, Satellite rink

BRITAIN-KAZAKHSTAN 3-1 (1-0,1-0,1-1)

GB scoring:

Tait (Longstaff, Adey)	9.54	(1-0)
Longstaff	39.51	(2-0)
Priest (Tait, S Cooper)	57.52	(3-0)
Shots on Goal:	Watkins GB	45	(97.8%)
	Krivomazov KAZ	17	(82.3%)

Penalty minutes: GB 22, Kazakhstan 26.
Goals/powerplays: GB 0/6, Kazakhstan 0/9.
GB Man of Match: S Cooper.
Referee: Dunnett CAN. Attendance: 300
The win was sweet revenge for that two-seconds-from-time draw at Sheffield and it left GB needing both points from their last game to take the gold. A defensive contest in which Watkins only lost his shutout a little over two minutes from time.

21 April, Spodek Arena

BRITAIN-GERMANY 0-5 (0-0,0-3,0-2)

Shots on Goal:	Watkins GB	37	(86.5%)
	Seliger GER	25	(100%)

Penalty minutes: GB 18, Germany 14.
Goals/powerplays: GB 0/6, Germany 2/6.
GB Man of Match: Mulvenna.
Referee: Dunnett CAN. Attendance: 600
With gold for the taking, GB swarmed over the Germans outshooting them 14-6 in the first period. Then calamity! In the 25th minute, a deflected shot eluded Watkins. Eight minutes later, it was 2-0 and a weary GB couldn't recover.

'Joe Cool' blows hot

Coach **Peter Woods'** methods were called into question after Britain yet again failed to clinch victory when the chips were down.

Going into their final game against Germany, GB needed only a win to gain promotion to Pool A at the second, or counting Eindhoven, the third time of asking in 1999-2000. What's more, the Germans didn't need the points as they had a bye into the elite group as hosts in 2001.

Britain dominated the first period and the early part of the second but couldn't translate it into goals. Then the Germans struck twice in eight minutes. Kreutzer's goal went in off a defenceman and **Joe Watkins** was screened on Greilinger's shot.

Six energy-sapping games in eight days had taken their toll of the injury-hit squad and they just couldn't summon the strength to fight back in the remaining 27 minutes of the seventh contest.

> **QUOTES**
> "I felt I could play at this level but it was still the most nerve-wracking time I've ever had." *Joe Watkins on his international debut against the Netherlands.*
> "These guys are playing far better collectively than you might expect them to individually." *Peter Woods, delighted at his team's winning spirit.*

In truth, the tournament was lost after the opening two games. Forget the problems of lack of preparation, half the team being different from February's Olympic qualifiers and only expenses being available for the players.

There is scarcely any year when the team has had any sort of quality time together before important games. And paying players is only a recent phenomenon.

Goaltending is the key to winning and without the injured **Stevie Lyle**, Britain floundered against Estonia and Slovenia. Enter another native goaltending hero - Joe (Cool) Watkins.

Joe from Durham via Basingstoke, a protégé of Bison coach and GB defender **Rick Strachan**, was only 20-years-old and had no international experience. As the third choice of coach **Peter Woods**, he had every right to screw up on his ebut, which Woods presumably feared he might.

So what happened? He only whitewashed the Dutch in his first game and then led GB to a stunning 6-4 come-from-behind defeat of the host nation in front of 8,500 noisy patriots.

In his first two internationals...! Historian **Martin Harris** has yet to find any similar feat in the annals of British ice hockey history - at least, not since the epic triple of 1936.

But, of course, such a turn round of fortunes was not down to one man, however exceptional. After GB had unravelled the knots against the recently promoted Dutch, team spirit kicked in and their confidence soared.

> If you really want to upset yourself over Britain's so-near-yet-so-far attempts at winning promotion to Pool A, take a look at where some of the elite nations finished in 2000.
> 6th - Switzerland — GB drew 3-3 in 1996
> 8th - Latvia — GB drew 0-0 in 1999
> 9th - Belarus — GB won 4-2 in 1996
> 10th - Norway — GB lost 2-1 in 1999
> 13th - Ukraine — GB drew 2-2 in 1999

There was one hiccup when the Danes took a three-goal lead after only seven minutes of game five, but the Brits fought back brilliantly after a 30-second timeout.

Yes, this was a true team effort, one of the most spirited displays by Britain since 1993, the last time they won promotion. If Watkins had played in the first two games, who knows...?

It was even more remarkable coming from something of a makeshift team. Around a dozen players who had lined up in Sheffield missed out on the Poland trip, some with injuries but others for 'personal reasons', which usually meant they wanted more than just the challenge and the expenses on offer.

Woods' late additions from the BNL - **Neil Liddiard, David Clarke** and **Mike Ellis** - were used sparingly at this level, as was Newcastle's **Shaun Johnson** who had last competed internationally in 1992.

> **NOTHING CHANGES**
> 'League games have to be played and there has been no disposition in any quarter to relinquish players to the Olympic team for practice purposes.' *Report in the Montreal Gazette of 21 January 1936 on the British team's preparations for the Olympic Games. (GB won the gold medal - Ed.).*

With **Scott Young** (back) missing the last three games and **David Longstaff** (leg) parts of a couple, Woods iced only three lines - 15 players - in the big games.

The purists could be satisfied that of those 15 regulars, seven were Brits born and bred, and that Watkins' superb play gives GB three goalies under 21-years-old, assuming that Fife's teenager **Stephen Murphy** stays in Britain.

But these changes were forced on coach Woods. With 14 players aged over 30 on the squad and fewer eligible imports in the leagues, an overhaul in the selection process is long overdue. •

Britain's Record 1989-99

1999   Pool B, Katowice, Poland
Coach: **Peter Woods** (Superleague)
Slovenia 2-1, Kazakhstan 1-0, Germany 2-3,
Estonia 6-2, Poland 4-3, Hungary 4-2, Denmark 5-5.
World Ranking: 18th

1998   Pool B, Ljubljana/Jesenice, Slovenia.
Coach: Peter Woods (Superleague).
Ukraine 1-6, Denmark 7-1, Estonia 4-5, Slovenia 3-5,
Poland 4-3, Norway 3-4, Netherlands 10-3.
World Ranking: 22nd

1997   Pool B, Katowice/Sosnowiec, Poland
Coach: **Peter Woods** (Basingstoke)
Poland 3-4, Kazakhstan 2-4, Netherlands 8-2,
Denmark 9-1, Austria 2-2, Switzerland 2-3,
Belarus 2-6.
World Ranking: 18th

1996   Pool B, Eindhoven, Netherlands
Coach: **Peter Woods** (Basingstoke).
Latvia 5-6, Switzerland 2-7, Poland 4-2,
Netherlands 6-2, Japan 3-3, Denmark 5-1,
Belarus 4-2.
World Ranking: 16th

1995   Pool B, Bratislava, Slovakia.
Coach: **George Peternousek** (unatt.)
Slovakia 3-7, Romania 0-2, Netherlands 3-2,
Denmark 2-9, Japan 3-4, Poland 4-3, Latvia 4-8.
World Ranking: 19th

1994   Pool A in Bolzano, Italy.
Coach: **Alex Dampier** (Sheffield)
Russia 3-12, .Germany 0-4, Italy 2-10, Canada 2-8,
Austria 0-10, Norway 2-5.
World Ranking: 12th

1993   Pool B in Eindhoven, Netherlands.
Coach: **Alex Dampier** (Sheffield).
Poland 4-3, Denmark 4-0, Japan 5-4, Bulgaria 10-0,
Netherlands 3-2, Romania 10-4, China 14-0.
World Ranking: 13th

1992   Pool C in Hull, England.
Coach: **Alex Dampier** (Nottingham).
Australia 10-2, S Korea 15-0, Belgium 7-3,
N Korea 16-2, Hungary 14-3.
World Ranking: 21st

1991   Pool C in Copenhagen, Denmark.
Coach: **Alex Dampier** (Nottingham).
China 5-6, N Korea 7-2, Denmark 2-3, B elgium 11-0,
Hungary 3-3, Bulgaria 4-5, S Korea 7-1, Romania 6-5.
World Ranking: 21st

1990   Pool D in Cardiff, Wales.
Coach: **Alex Dampier** (Nottingham)
Australia 14-0, 13-3; Spain 13-1, 17-3.
World Ranking: 26th

1989   Pool D in Belgium.
Coach: **Terry Matthews** (Whitley Bay).
New Zealand 26-0, Romania 6-6, Belgium 5-6,
Spain 8-4.
World Ranking: 27th

SOMEONE UP THERE DOESN'T LIKE OUR PAUL

Paul Adey was GB's best forward in the Olympic qualifiers but he must have upset the officials.

First he was robbed of a goal by the scorekeeper who awarded his tally against Poland to **Darren Hurley**. That was bizarre because he put Adey's name on the arena scoreboard at the time.

Then the Milan forward was blamed by the Swedish ref for high-sticking a Frenchmen who was actually struck by an errant puck. That cost him a rare game misconduct which was bad enough but the scorekeeper obviously didn't think so and gave him 20 minutes for his five-minute high-sticking major.

Then in Pool B, no officials saw him score the ninth goal against the Dutch which was awarded to **Stephen Cooper**. But an eagle-eyed linesman was quick enough to spot his accidental high-stick on a German which was missed by the ref. and he got 2+2.

Stevie Lyle, on the other hand, must have buttered up the man with the pen and paper as he got his name on the scoresheet in Gdansk instead of **Steve Moria** for Britain's last goal against France.

Needless to say, the stats on these pages reflect the correct, if strictly unofficial goal scoring and penalties.

THE BRITISH SQUAD 1999-2000

The full roster of players who competed for Britain in their three tournaments in 1999-2000 - the World Pool A qualifying games, the Olympic qualifying games and World Pool B.

Name	GP	Pos	Birth Date (ft,in)	Hght (lbs)	Wght	Club	Birth Place
*Stephen Foster	0	G	1.7.74	6', 2"	187	Ayr	Durham
#*Joe Watkins	5	G	27.10.79	6', 1"	190	Basingstoke	Durham
*Stevie Lyle	7	G	4.12.79	5',10"	180	Cardiff	Cardiff
# Jimmy Hibbert	1	G	8.2.75	6', 2"	175	Newcastle	Etobicoke, Toronto
#Wayne Cowley	2	G	4.12.64	6', 0"	185	Dayton (ECHL)	Toronto
Mike Bishop	7	D	15.6.66	6', 3"	215	Ayr	Sarnia, Ontario
Vince Boe	4	D	23.12.70	6', 2"	198	Ayr	Fort Saskatchewan, Alberta
Scott Young	11	D	26.5.65	6', 1"	195	Ayr	Oakville, Ontario
Rick Strachan	14	D	27.3.63	5', 9"	183	Basingstoke	Winnipeg
Matt Cote	5	D	19.1.66	5', 9"	200	Bracknell	Vancouver
Darren Durdle	7	D	15.8.63	6', 3"	220	Cardiff	Gimli, Canada
*Paul Dixon	10	D	4.8.73	5',11"	188	Guildford	Sunderland
#Scott Campbell	4	D	22.1.72	6', 1"	190	London/Manchester	Glasgow
*Stephen Cooper	11	D	11.11.66	5',11"	190	Nottingham	Peterlee
#*Neil Liddiard	10	D	7.3.78			Peterborough	Swindon
Andre Malo	7	D	10.5.65	6', 1"	200	Sheffield	Hull, Quebec
#Jason Kendall	3	D	9.7.75			Slough	Winnipeg
*Tony Hand	11	F	15.8.67	5',10"	185	Ayr	Edinburgh
#Mike Ellis	7	F	21.5.73	5',10"	195	Basingstoke	Canada
Steve Moria	14	F	3.2.61	6', 0"	175	Cardiff	Vancouver
Merv Priest	13	F	2.8.73	6', 0"	189	Cardiff	Kirby Muxloe,England
Steve Thornton	4	F	8.3.73	5',11"	185	Cardiff	Edmonton
*Ian Cooper	8	F	29.11.68	6', 2"	196	London	Thorpe, England
Jeff Johnstone	7	F	21.9.75	6', 0"	195	London	Niagara Falls
Rick Brebant	13	F	21.2.64	5', 9"	182	Manchester	Elliot Lake, Ont.
#Mike Harding	7	F	24.2.71	6', 4"	220	Manchester	Edmonton
Darren Hurley	14	F	14.6.73	6', 2"	205	Manchester	Toronto
*Jonathan Weaver	4	F	21.1.77	5',11"	168	Manchester/ Mississippi	Sunderland
*Shaun Johnson	7	F	22.3.73	5',10"	175	Newcastle	Durham
# Glenn Mulvenna	7	F/D	18.2.67	6', 0"	190	Newcastle	Ottawa
#Brent Bobyck	7	F	26.4.68	5',10"	177	Nottingham	Regina, Sask.
*Ashley Tait	14	F	9.8.75	6', 1"	175	Nottingham	Toronto
#*David Clarke	7	F	5.8.81			Peterborough	Peterborough
*David Longstaff	10	F	26.8.74	6', 2"	101	Sheffield	Newcastle
Paul Adey	14	F	28.8.63	5',10"	185	Milan, Italy	Montreal

Head Coach: Peter Woods (ISL).   Asst coach: Dave Whistle (Bracknell).
Manager: Andy French (Cardiff).   Team captain: Steve Moria (Cardiff).

New cap (11).   * British trained (12).   Total players selected - 35.

GP - For goalies, this is games actually iced in.
Maximum games - 14 (Pool B - 7, Pool A qualifying - 4, Olympic qualifying - 3)

GREAT BRITAIN'S WORLD CHAMPIONSHIP and OLYMPIC PLAYER REGISTER 1989-2000
Forwards and Defencemen

ADEY Paul   b. 28-Aug-63

Club	Year	Comp	GP	G	A	Pts	PIM
Not	1995	OQ	3	1	0	1	0
Not	1996	WC	7	4	4	8	10
Not	1996	OQ	5	3	4	7	0
Not	1997	WC	7	5	1	6	4
Not	1998	WC	7	4	4	8	4
Not	1999	WC	7	3	3	6	2
Milan	1999	WCQ	4	0	0	0	0
Milan	2000	OQ	3	3	1	4	27
Milan	2000	WC	7	2	5	7	14
		Totals	50	25	22	47	61

BENNETT Ivor   b. 29-Jul-61

Club	Year	Comp	GP	G	A	Pts	PIM
Dur	1989	WC	4	0	1	1	2

BIDNER Todd   b. 5-Jul-61

Club	Year	Comp	GP	G	A	Pts	PIM
Una	1993	OQ	4	1	1	2	4

BISHOP Mike   b. 15-Jun-66

Club	Year	Comp	GP	G	A	Pts	PIM
Hum	1995	OQ	3	0	0	0	0
Hum	1996	WC	7	1	1	2	22
Not	1996	OQ	5	1	3	4	12
Not	1997	WC	7	2	1	3	45
Not	1998	WC	7	1	0	1	12
Ayr	2000	WC	7	0	3	3	18
		Totals	36	5	8	13	109

BOBYCK Brent   b. 26-Apr-68

Club	Year	Comp	GP	G	A	Pts	PIM
Not	1999	WCQ	4	0	0	0	0
Not	2000	OQ	3	0	1	1	0
		Totals	7	0	1	1	0

BOE Vince   b. 23-Dec-70

Club	Year	Comp	GP	G	A	Pts	PIM
Ayr	1999	WC	7	0	2	2	16
Ayr	1999	WCQ	1	0	0	0	4
Ayr	2000	OQ	3	0	1	1	2
		Totals	11	0	3	3	22

BREBANT Rick   b. 21-Feb-61

Club	Year	Comp	GP	G	A	Pts	PIM
Car	1994	WC	6	1	0	1	8
Dur	1995	OQ	1	0	0	0	0
Man	1998	WC	7	3	5	8	10
Man	1999	WCQ	3	0	1	1	4
Lon	2000	OQ	3	1	2	3	42
Lon	2000	WC	7	4	4	8	14
		Totals	27	9	12	21	78

CAMPBELL Scott   b. 22-Jan-72

Club	Year	Comp	GP	G	A	Pts	PIM
Lon	1999	WCQ	4	0	0	0	2

CHARD Chris   b. 22-Jun-71

Club	Year	Comp	GP	G	A	Pts	PIM
Bas	1995	OQ	1	0	0	0	0

CHINN Nicky   b. 14-Sep-72

Club	Year	Comp	GP	G	A	Pts	PIM
Car	1993	OQ	2	0	0	0	0
Car	1994	WC	6	0	0	0	0
Car	1995	WC	4	1	2	3	4
She	1995	OQ	1	0	0	0	0
She	1996	WC	3	1	0	1	2
She	1997	WC	7	1	1	2	29
She	1998	WC	7	1	2	3	31
Car	1999	WC	7	2	3	5	39
Car	2000	OQ	3	0	0	0	4
		Totals	40	6	8	14	109

CLARK David   b. 5-Aug-81

Club	Year	Comp	GP	G	A	Pts	PIM
Pet	2000	WC	7	0	0	0	2

CONWAY Kevin   b. 13-Jul-63

Club	Year	Comp	GP	G	A	Pts	PIM
Bas	1992	WC	5	13	10	23	6
Bas	1993	WC	7	8	11	19	8
Bas	1993	OQ	4	1	0	1	6
Bas	1994	WC	6	2	1	3	6
Bas	1995	OQ	3	2	1	3	6
Bas	1996	WC	7	3	2	5	6
Bas	1996	OQ	5	1	0	1	6
Bas	1997	WC	7	2	3	5	0
Bas	1998	WC	7	0	2	2	2
New	1999	WC	7	1	3	4	8
		Totals	58	33	33	66	54

COOPER Ian   b. 29-Nov-68

Club	Year	Comp	GP	G	A	Pts	PIM
Car	1989	WC	4	4	4	8	8
Car	1990	WC	4	6	5	11	8
Dur	1991	WC	8	4	2	6	16
Dur	1992	WC	5	3	6	9	8
Car	1993	WC	7	4	4	8	6
Car	1994	WC	6	1	0	1	4
Car	1995	WC	2	1	0	1	2
Car	1995	OQ	3	0	0	0	2
Car	1996	WC	7	0	2	2	10
Car	1996	OQ	5	1	2	3	2
Car	1997	WC	7	0	0	0	12
Car	1998	WC	7	3	2	5	38
Lon	1999	WC	7	1	2	3	2
Lon	1999	WCQ	1	0	0	0	0
Gui	2000	WC	7	2	2	4	10
		Totals	80	30	31	61	128

GREAT BRITAIN'S WORLD CHAMPIONSHIP and OLYMPIC PLAYER REGISTER 1989-2000
Forwards and Defencemen

COOPER Stephen   b. 11-Nov-66

Club	Year	Comp	GP	G	A	Pts	PIM
Car	1989	WC	4	3	4	7	4
Car	1990	WC	4	3	6	9	8
Dur	1992	WC	5	1	4	5	4
Car	1993	WC	7	0	4	4	6
Car	1993	OQ	4	1	0	1	2
Car	1994	WC	6	0	1	1	4
Car	1995	OQ	3	0	0	0	10
Car	1996	WC	7	0	3	3	6
Man	1996	OQ	3	0	0	0	4
New	1999	WC	7	0	0	0	2
Not	1999	WCQ	4	1	1	2	2
Not	2000	WC	7	2	4	6	2
		Totals	**61**	**11**	**27**	**38**	**54**

COTE Matt   b. 19-Jan-66

Club	Year	Comp	GP	G	A	Pts	PIM
Brk	1994	WC	6	0	0	0	8
Brk	1995	WC	7	0	1	1	4
Brk	1996	OQ	4	0	0	0	2
Brk	1996	OQ	4	0	0	0	2
Brk	1999	WC	7	0	1	1	2
Brk	1999	WCQ	4	0	0	0	0
Brk	2000	OQ	1	0	0	0	0
		Totals	**33**	**0**	**2**	**2**	**18**

CRAIPER Jamie   b. 29-Jan-60

Club	Year	Comp	GP	G	A	Pts	PIM
Brk	1990	WC	4	7	5	12	0
Brk	1991	WC	8	4	1	5	9
Brk	1992	WC	5	1	2	3	25
		Totals	**17**	**12**	**8**	**20**	**34**

CRANSTON Tim   b. 13-Dec-62

Club	Year	Comp	GP	G	A	Pts	PIM
She	1993	WC	7	3	1	4	41
She	1993	OQ	4	1	1	2	8
She	1994	WC	6	0	0	0	4
She	1995	OQ	3	0	2	2	6
She	1996	WC	7	4	4	8	14
She	1996	OQ	5	2	2	4	10
She	1997	WC	7	1	3	4	8
		Totals	**39**	**11**	**13**	**24**	**91**

DIXON Paul   b. 4-Aug-73

Club	Year	Comp	GP	G	A	Pts	PIM
Dur	1995	WC	5	1	1	2	2
Dur	1995	OQ	2	0	0	0	0
Dur	1996	WC	7	1	1	2	14
New	1996	OQ	2	0	1	1	0
New	1997	WC	7	0	1	1	0
New	1998	WC	4	0	2	2	2
New	1999	WC	7	0	1	1	0
Gui	1999	WCQ	3	0	0	0	2
Gui	2000	WC	7	0	2	2	0
		Totals	**44**	**2**	**9**	**11**	**20**

DURDLE Darren   b. 15-Aug-67

Club	Year	Comp	GP	G	A	Pts	PIM
Ber	1996	OQ	2	0	1	1	2
Ber	1998	WC	6	0	1	1	10
Ber	1999	WC	7	1	0	1	12
Car	1999	WCQ	4	1	2	3	8
Car	2000	OQ	3	1	2	3	4
		Totals	**22**	**3**	**6**	**9**	**36**

EDMISTON Dean   b. 12-Feb-69

Club	Year	Comp	GP	G	A	Pts	PIM
Pet	1991	WC	8	2	1	3	13
Med	1992	WC	4	1	3	4	2
		Totals	**12**	**3**	**4**	**7**	**15**

ELLIS Mike   b. 21-May-73

Club	Year	Comp	GP	G	A	Pts	PIM
Bas	2000	WC	7	1	1	2	0

FERA Rick   b. 13-Aug-64

Club	Year	Comp	GP	G	A	Pts	PIM
Bas	1993	WC	7	6	13	19	18
Tra	1993	OQ	4	0	2	2	12
Tra	1994	WC	6	1	2	3	4
		Totals	**17**	**7**	**17**	**24**	**34**

GARDEN Graham   b. 2-Jul-70

Club	Year	Comp	GP	G	A	Pts	PIM
Hum	1995	OQ	2	1	0	1	0
Hum	1996	WC	3	1	0	1	4
Deg	1996	OQ	5	0	0	0	2
Deg	1997	WC	7	1	0	1	10
Not	1999	WC	7	2	5	7	10
Not	2000	OQ	3	0	0	0	2
		Totals	**27**	**5**	**5**	**10**	**28**

HAND Paul   b. 24-Nov-65

Club	Year	Comp	GP	G	A	Pts	PIM
Mur	1989	WC	4	5	0	5	8
Fif	1990	WC	4	1	3	4	13
Fif	1991	WC	8	1	2	3	14
Mur	1992	WC	2	0	0	0	6
		Totals	**18**	**7**	**5**	**12**	**41**

HAND Tor.y   b. 15-Aug-67

Club	Year	Comp	GP	G	A	Pts	PIM
Mur	1989	WC	4	6	12	18	2
Mur	1990	WC	4	5	8	13	0
Mur	1991	WC	8	9	12	21	12
Mur	1992	WC	5	6	12	18	4
Mur	1993	WC	7	6	8	14	2
Mur	1993	OQ	4	0	2	2	4
Mur	1994	WC	6	0	0	0	0
Ayr	1999	WCQ	4	1	0	1	6
Ayr	2000	WC	7	2	8	10	2
		Totals	**49**	**35**	**62**	**97**	**32**

HARDING Mike   b. 24-Feb-71

Club	Year	Comp	GP	G	A	Pts	PIM
Man	1999	WCQ	4	1	1	2	0
Man	2000	OQ	3	0	2	2	4
		Totals	**7**	**1**	**3**	**4**	**4**

GREAT BRITAIN'S WORLD CHAMPIONSHIP and OLYMPIC PLAYER REGISTER 1989-2000
Forwards and Defencemen

HOPE Shannon — b. 25-Nov-62

Club	Year	Comp	GP	G	A	Pts	PIM
Car	1992	WC	2	0	0	0	0
Car	1993	WC	7	0	2	2	4
Car	1993	OQ	4	0	0	0	2
Car	1994	WC	6	0	1	1	14
Car	1995	WC	6	1	1	2	14
Car	1995	OQ	3	0	0	0	6
Car	1996	WC	7	0	1	1	8
Car	1996	OQ	4	0	1	1	28
Car	1997	WC	7	0	2	2	10
Car	1998	WC	7	0	0	0	2
		Totals	53	1	8	9	88

HUNT Simon — b. 16-Apr-73

Club	Year	Comp	GP	G	A	Pts	PIM
Not	1995	OQ	3	1	0	1	2
Not	1996	WC	7	2	1	3	24
Not	1996	OQ	1	0	0	0	0
		Totals	11	3	1	4	26

HURLEY Darren — b. 14-Jun-73

Club	Year	Comp	GP	G	A	Pts	PIM
Man	1999	WC	7	1	1	2	8
Man	1999	WCQ	4	0	0	0	29
Car	2000	OQ	3	1	0	1	8
Car	2000	WC	7	1	3	4	32
		Totals	21	3	4	7	77

IREDALE John — b. 8-Oct-66

Club	Year	Comp	GP	G	A	Pts	PIM
Whi	1989	WC	4	5	4	9	4
Whi	1990	WC	4	0	1	1	4
Whi	1992	WC	5	1	0	1	4
Whi	1993	WC	7	0	3	3	0
Whi	1993	OQ	4	0	0	0	0
		Totals	24	6	8	14	12

JOHNSON Anthony — b. 4-Jan-69

Club	Year	Comp	GP	G	A	Pts	PIM
Dur	1990	WC	4	6	3	9	2
Hum	1991	WC	8	1	1	2	10
Hum	1992	WC	5	5	5	10	0
Hum	1993	WC	7	3	4	7	4
Hum	1993	OQ	4	0	0	0	4
		Totals	28	15	13	28	20

JOHNSON Shaun — b. 22-Mar-73

Club	Year	Comp	GP	G	A	Pts	PIM
Hum	1992	WC	4	1	2	3	2
New	2000	WC	7	0	1	1	0
		Totals	11	1	3	4	2

JOHNSTONE Jeff — b. 21-Sep-75

Club	Year	Comp	GP	G	A	Pts	PIM
Brk	1999	WC	7	4	2	6	4
Lon	1999	WCQ	4	0	1	1	0
Man	2000	OQ	3	0	0	0	2
		Totals	14	4	3	7	6

JOHNSON Stephen — b. 19-Jun-67

Club	Year	Comp	GP	G	A	Pts	PIM
Dur	1990	WC	4	2	6	8	0
Hum	1991	WC	8	4	3	7	2
Hum	1992	WC	4	1	0	1	0
Hum	1993	WC	7	3	3	6	4
		Totals	23	10	12	22	6

KENDALL Jason — b. 9-Jul-75

Club	Year	Comp	GP	G	A	Pts	PIM
Brk	2000	OQ	3	0	0	0	0

KELLAND Chris — b. 22-Dec-57

Club	Year	Comp	GP	G	A	Pts	PIM
Mur	1990	WC	4	3	5	8	0
Mur	1991	WC	7	3	2	5	22
Not	1992	WC	5	4	1	5	4
Not	1993	WC	5	0	0	0	4
She	1993	OQ	4	0	0	0	6
She	1994	WC	6	0	0	0	8
		Totals	31	10	8	18	44

KIDD John — b. 22-May-63

Club	Year	Comp	GP	G	A	Pts	PIM
Ayr	1989	WC	4	2	1	3	0

KINDRED Mike — b. 26-May-71

Club	Year	Comp	GP	G	A	Pts	PIM
Mil	1995	WC	5	0	1	1	2

KURTENBACH Terry — b. 14-Mar-63

Club	Year	Comp	GP	G	A	Pts	PIM
Rom	1993	OQ	4	0	1	1	2
Rom	1994	WC	6	1	1	2	2
Gui	1995	WC	7	0	4	4	2
Gui	1995	OQ	3	0	1	1	0
Gui	1996	WC	7	0	0	0	0
Gui	1996	OQ	2	0	0	0	0
		Totals	29	1	7	8	6

LAMBERT Dale — b. 9-Oct-59

Club	Year	Comp	GP	G	A	Pts	PIM
Sol	1993	OQ	4	0	0	0	4

LARKIN Bryan — b. 2-Feb-67

Club	Year	Comp	GP	G	A	Pts	PIM
Swi	1997	WC	7	0	1	1	6

LATTO Gordon — b. 18-Dec-58

Club	Year	Comp	GP	G	A	Pts	PIM
Vas	1976	WC	4	0	0	0	0
Fif	1977	WC	6	0	1	1	2
Fif	1981	WC	7	0	0	0	2
Fif	1989	WC	4	2	1	3	6
		Totals	21	2	2	4	10

LAWLESS John — b. 8-Jan-61

Club	Year	Comp	GP	G	A	Pts	PIM
Car	1990	WC	4	4	8	12	0
Car	1991	WC	8	1	2	3	22
		Totals	12	5	10	15	22

LEE Phil — b. 22-Dec-65

Club	Year	Comp	GP	G	A	Pts	PIM
Sol	1989	WC	4	1	0	1	0
Sol	1990	WC	4	1	0	1	0
		Totals	8	2	0	2	0

LIDDIARD Neil — b. 7-Mar-78

Club	Year	Comp	GP	G	A	Pts	PIM
Pet	2000	OQ	3	0	0	0	0
Pet	2000	WC	7	0	0	0	0
		Totals	10	0	0	0	0

GREAT BRITAIN'S WORLD CHAMPIONSHIP and OLYMPIC PLAYER REGISTER 1989-2000
Forwards and Defencemen

LINDSAY Jeff — b. 5-Jul-65

Club	Year	Comp	GP	G	A	Pts	PIM
Pet	1995	WC	7	0	0	0	10
Man	1995	OQ	3	0	1	1	4
Man	1996	WC	7	0	0	0	6
Man	1996	OQ	5	0	0	0	2
		Totals	22	0	1	1	22

LITTLE Richard — b. 16-Sep-66

Club	Year	Comp	GP	G	A	Pts	PIM
Bas	1996	OQ	3	2	1	3	4
Bas	1997	WC	7	3	1	4	14
		Totals	10	5	2	7	18

LONGSTAFF David — b. 26-Aug-74

Club	Year	Comp	GP	G	A	Pts	PIM
Whi	1994	WC	6	0	0	0	6
Whi	1995	WC	7	6	1	7	8
New	1995	OQ	1	0	0	0	0
She	1996	WC	7	1	2	3	10
She	1996	OQ	5	1	3	4	6
She	1997	WC	7	1	2	3	8
She	1998	WC	7	4	3	7	8
She	1999	WC	7	2	2	4	4
She	2000	OQ	3	0	1	1	2
She	2000	WC	7	2	3	5	14
		Totals	57	17	17	34	66

MacNAUGHT Kevin — b. 23-Jul-60

Club	Year	Comp	GP	G	A	Pts	PIM
Med	1990	WC	4	4	4	8	4
Med	1991	WC	8	3	7	10	10
Med	1992	WC	5	7	5	12	2
		Totals	17	14	16	30	16

MALO Andre — b. 10-May-65

Club	Year	Comp	GP	G	A	Pts	PIM
Bil	1993	WC	7	1	2	3	6
Not	1993	OQ	4	0	0	0	8
Not	1994	WC	5	0	0	0	6
She	1997	WC	7	1	3	4	4
She	1999	WC	7	0	2	2	16
She	1999	WCQ	4	0	0	0	0
She	2000	OQ	3	0	0	0	0
		Totals	37	2	7	9	40

MARSDEN Doug — b. 13-Nov-64

Club	Year	Comp	GP	G	A	Pts	PIM
Pai	1997	WC	7	0	1	1	8

MASON Brian — b. 1-Apr-65

Club	Year	Comp	GP	G	A	Pts	PIM
Slo	1990	WC	4	4	3	7	2
Slo	1991	WC	8	2	2	4	6
Slo	1992	WC	5	3	4	7	29
Mil	1993	WC	7	1	1	2	0
Slo	1993	OQ	4	0	0	0	0
Slo	1994	WC	6	0	0	0	0
		Totals	34	10	10	20	37

McEWEN Doug — b. 2-Oct-63

Club	Year	Comp	GP	G	A	Pts	PIM
Car	1993	WC	7	2	4	6	6
Car	1993	OQ	4	2	1	3	4
Car	1994	WC	6	1	2	3	0
Car	1995	OQ	2	0	0	0	4
Car	1996	WC	7	2	0	2	2
Car	1996	OQ	4	1	1	2	0
Car	1997	WC	7	2	0	2	8
Car	1998	WC	7	2	5	7	4
		Totals	44	12	13	25	28

MORGAN Neil — b. 24-Dec-72

Club	Year	Comp	GP	G	A	Pts	PIM
Bla	1995	WC	7	1	2	3	2
Not	1995	OQ	2	0	0	0	0
Not	1996	WC	7	3	1	4	2
Not	1996	OQ	5	1	4	5	2
Not	1997	WC	7	0	1	1	6
Not	1998	WC	7	6	3	9	4
		Totals	35	11	11	22	16

MORIA Steve — b. 3-Feb-61

Club	Year	Comp	GP	G	A	Pts	PIM
Car	1995	OQ	2	0	0	0	0
Car	1996	WC	7	2	1	3	4
Car	1996	OQ	5	4	1	5	2
Car	1997	WC	7	4	2	6	4
Car	1998	WC	7	3	3	6	12
Car	1999	WC	7	2	1	3	2
Car	1999	WCQ	4	0	0	0	0
Car	2000	OQ	3	1	1	2	4
Car	2000	WC	7	6	4	10	2
		Totals	49	22	13	35	30

MORRIS Frank — b. 22-Mar-63

Club	Year	Comp	GP	G	A	Pts	PIM
Mur	1994	WC	6	0	0	0	8
Tra	1995	WC	7	1	1	2	2
		Totals	13	1	1	2	10

MORRISON Scott — b. 12-Aug-64

Club	Year	Comp	GP	G	A	Pts	PIM
Whi	1993	WC	7	10	4	14	2
Whi	1993	OQ	4	0	0	0	0
Whi	1994	WC	4	0	1	1	4
Hum	1995	WC	7	4	2	6	10
Bas	1995	OQ	3	1	1	2	0
		Totals	25	15	8	23	16

MULVENNA Glen — b. 18-Feb-67

Club	Year	Comp	GP	G	A	Pts	PIM
New	2000	WC	7	0	0	0	18

NEIL Scott — b. 1-Aug-62

Club	Year	Comp	GP	G	A	Pts	PIM
Mur	1981	WC	7	0	0	0	4
Mur	1989	WC	4	5	4	9	0
Mur	1990	WC	4	5	3	8	0
Mur	1991	WC	8	7	1	8	10
Mur	1992	WC	5	6	4	10	4
She	1993	WC	5	0	0	0	0
She	1993	OQ	4	0	0	0	0
		Totals	37	23	12	35	18

ORD Terry — b. 4-Dec-65

Club	Year	Comp	GP	G	A	Pts	PIM
Whi	1989	WC	4	0	1	1	0

GREAT BRITAIN'S WORLD CHAMPIONSHIP and OLYMPIC PLAYER REGISTER 1989-2000
Forwards and Defencemen

O'CONNOR Mike   b. 12-Dec-61

Club	Year	Comp	GP	G	A	Pts	PIM
Dur	1992	WC	5	3	1	4	10
Dur	1993	WC	7	0	3	3	16
Hum	1993	OQ	4	1	1	2	14
Hum	1994	WC	6	0	0	0	12
		Totals	**22**	**4**	**5**	**9**	**52**

PAYNE Anthony   b. 26-Jun-72

Club	Year	Comp	GP	G	A	Pts	PIM
Pet	1995	WC	6	1	0	1	0

PENNYCOOK Jim   b. 12-Jun-57

Club	Year	Comp	GP	G	A	Pts	PIM
Dun	1977	WC	5	1	0	1	0
Mur	1979	WC	7	3	4	7	0
Mur	1981	WC	7	3	1	4	4
Tay	1989	WC	4	3	4	7	0
		Totals	**23**	**10**	**9**	**19**	**4**

PENTLAND Paul   b. 11-Nov-64

Club	Year	Comp	GP	G	A	Pts	PIM
Mur	1989	WC	4	0	0	0	0

PLOMMER Tommy   b. 26-Aug-68

Club	Year	Comp	GP	G	A	Pts	PIM
She	1995	OQ	3	0	0	0	4
She	1996	OQ	4	3	0	3	0
		Totals	**7**	**3**	**0**	**3**	**4**

POUND Ian   b. 22-Jan-67

Club	Year	Comp	GP	G	A	Pts	PIM
Sol	1995	WC	7	0	0	0	10

PRIEST Merv   b. 2-Aug-73

Club	Year	Comp	GP	G	A	Pts	PIM
Bas	1996	WC	7	1	0	1	4
Bas	1996	OQ	3	1	2	3	4
Car	1999	WC	7	1	2	3	10
Car	1999	WCQ	4	0	0	0	2
Car	2000	OQ	2	1	0	1	2
Car	2000	WC	7	2	3	5	8
		Totals	**30**	**6**	**7**	**13**	**30**

REID Alistair   b. 15-Jul-63

Club	Year	Comp	GP	G	A	Pts	PIM
Ayr	1989	WC	4	1	2	3	0

RHODES Nigel   b. 19-Jul-67

Club	Year	Comp	GP	G	A	Pts	PIM
Not	1989	WC	4	2	0	2	2

ROBERTSON Iain   b. 2-Jun-69

Club	Year	Comp	GP	G	A	Pts	PIM
Fif	1991	WC	8	0	1	1	2
Fif	1992	WC	5	2	2	4	0
Fif	1993	WC	7	1	0	1	0
Fif	1995	WC	7	1	0	1	0
		Totals	**27**	**4**	**3**	**7**	**2**

SAUNDERS Lee   b. 3-Jun-70

Club	Year	Comp	GP	G	A	Pts	PIM
Bas	1995	WC	7	0	1	1	0
Mil	1996	OQ	1	0	0	0	0
		Totals	**8**	**0**	**1**	**1**	**0**

SCOTT Patrick   b. 12-Nov-66

Club	Year	Comp	GP	G	A	Pts	PIM
Mil	1993	OQ	4	2	0	2	0
Mil	1994	WC	6	2	0	2	2
Mil	1995	OQ	3	0	1	1	0
Mil	1996	WC	7	1	4	5	2
Bas	1996	OQ	4	1	1	2	2
Bas	1997	WC	7	4	3	7	18
		Totals	**31**	**10**	**9**	**19**	**24**

SMITH Damian   b. 8-Oct-71

Club	Year	Comp	GP	G	A	Pts	PIM
Dur	1992	WC	4	2	2	4	0
Dur	1993	WC	4	1	1	2	0
Dur	1995	WC	6	0	1	1	10
		Totals	**14**	**3**	**4**	**7**	**10**

SMITH David   b. 14-Feb-73

Club	Year	Comp	GP	G	A	Pts	PIM
Tra	1995	WC	5	1	0	1	0

SMITH Paul   b. 3-Jul-61

Club	Year	Comp	GP	G	A	Pts	PIM
Dur	1981	WC	7	0	0	0	11
Dur	1989	WC	4	0	1	1	2
		Totals	**11**	**0**	**1**	**1**	**13**

SMITH Peter   b. 29-Nov-61

Club	Year	Comp	GP	G	A	Pts	PIM
Pet	1989	WC	4	4	1	5	2
Pet	1990	WC	2	2	0	2	2
Car	1991	WC	8	1	1	2	6
		Totals	**14**	**7**	**2**	**9**	**10**

SMITH Stephen   b. 11-Apr-63

Club	Year	Comp	GP	G	A	Pts	PIM
Whi	1989	WC	4	2	1	3	2

STEFAN Gary   b. 23-Jun-59

Club	Year	Comp	GP	G	A	Pts	PIM
Slo	1990	WC	4	4	7	11	8
Slo	1991	WC	8	3	1	4	12
Slo	1992	WC	5	5	2	7	8
		Totals	**17**	**12**	**10**	**22**	**28**

STONE Jason   b. 30-Dec-72

Club	Year	Comp	GP	G	A	Pts	PIM
Car	1998	WC	6	0	0	0	0

STRACHAN Rick   b. 27-Mar-63

Club	Year	Comp	GP	G	A	Pts	PIM
Mil	1995	WC	7	0	0	0	2
Bas	1995	OQ	3	0	0	0	0
Bas	1996	WC	7	2	1	3	2
Bas	1996	OQ	5	1	1	2	2
Bas	1997	WC	7	1	4	5	2
Bas	1998	WC	6	0	2	2	2
Bas	1999	WC	7	1	0	1	0
Bas	1999	WCQ	4	0	0	0	2
Bas	2000	OQ	3	0	1	1	2
Bas	2000	WC	7	1	1	2	2
		Totals	**56**	**6**	**10**	**16**	**16**

TAIT Ashley   b. 9-Aug-75

Club	Year	Comp	GP	G	A	Pts	PIM
Not	1995	WC	2	0	0	0	4
Not	1995	OQ	3	1	1	2	0
Not	1996	WC	7	1	1	2	10
Kin	1998	WC	7	2	0	2	4
Not	1999	WCQ	4	0	0	0	4
Not	2000	OQ	3	0	0	0	6
Not	2000	WC	7	3	4	7	10
		Totals	**33**	**7**	**6**	**13**	**38**

GREAT BRITAIN'S WORLD CHAMPIONSHIP and OLYMPIC PLAYER REGISTER 1989-2000
Forwards and Defencemen

THOMPSON Paul   b. 6-May-68

Club	Year	Comp	GP	G	A	Pts	PIM
Gui	1998	WC	6	1	1	2	8

THORNTON Steve   b. 8-Mar-73

Club	Year	Comp	GP	G	A	Pts	PIM
Car	1999	WC	7	2	1	3	0
Car	1999	WCQ	4	0	1	1	2
		Totals	11	2	2	4	2

WEAVER Jonathan   b. 20-Jan-77

Club	Year	Comp	GP	G	A	Pts	PIM
New	1998	WC	7	1	5	6	0
Man	1999	WC	7	0	2	2	2
USA	1999	WCQ	4	0	0	0	2
		Totals	18	1	7	8	4

WEBER Randall   b. 2-Sep-68

Club	Year	Comp	GP	G	A	Pts	PIM
Not	1998	WC	7	0	2	2	6

WILSON Rob   b. 18-Jul-68

Club	Year	Comp	GP	G	A	Pts	PIM
She	1998	WC	7	1	4	5	10
She	1999	WC	7	1	3	4	6
		Totals	14	2	7	9	16

WAGHORN Graham   b. 31-Dec-72

Club	Year	Comp	GP	G	A	Pts	PIM
Not	1991	WC	8	0	2	2	10
Not	1993	WC	7	1	1	2	4
Not	1995	OQ	1	0	0	0	2
Not	1996	OQ	3	0	0	0	0
		Totals	19	1	3	4	16

YOUNG Scott   b. 26-May-65

Club	Year	Comp	GP	G	A	Pts	PIM
Ayr	1999	WCQ	4	0	0	0	10
Ayr	2000	OQ	3	2	1	3	18
Ayr	2000	WC	5	3	3	6	20
		Totals	12	5	4	9	48

THE CAT STOPS ANOTHER
STEVIE (the Cat) LYLE who was voted the Best Goaltender during Britain's ill-fated attempt to win promotion to the World A Pool at Sheffield Arena in November 1999.

Photo: Mike Smith/Icepix

GREAT BRITAIN WORLD CHAMPIONSHIP and OLYMPIC PLAYER REGISTER 1989-2000
Goalkeepers

COWLEY Wayne　　b. 4-Dec-64

Club	Year	Comp	GP	GPI	Mins	GA	GAA
Not	1999	WCQ	3	0	0	0	0.00
Not	2000	WC	7	3	160	10	3.75
		Totals	10	3	160	10	3.75

FOSTER Stephen　　b. 1-Jul-74

Club	Year	Comp	GP	GPI	Mins	GA	GAA
Dur	1995	WC	7	6	320	28	5.25
Dur	1995	OQ	2	0	0	0	0.00
Dur	1996	WC	5	3	180	11	3.67
New	1996	OQ	3	0	0	0	0.00
New	1997	WC	5	4	200	12	3.60
New	1998	WC	6	3	155	10	3.87
Ayr	2000	OQ	3	0	0	0	0.00
		Totals	31	16	855	61	4.28

GRAHAM David　　b. 24-Oct-59

Club	Year	Comp	GP	GPI	Mins	GA	GAA
Not	1989	WC	4	3	150	12	4.80
Not	1990	WC	3	1	60	1	1.00
Not	1991	WC	3	2	120	5	2.50
		Totals	10	6	330	18	3.27

GRUBB Ricky　　b. 3-Mar-77

Club	Year	Comp	GP	GPI	Mins	GA	GAA
Fif	1995	WC	1	1	40	5	7.50

HANSON Moray　　b. 21-Jun-64

Club	Year	Comp	GP	GPI	Mins	GA	GAA
Mur	1989	WC	2	1	60	4	4.00
Mur	1991	WC	3	2	120	11	5.50
Mur	1994	WC	4	3	137	17	7.45
		Totals	9	6	317	32	6.06

HIBBERT Jim　　b. 8-Feb-75

Club	Year	Comp	GP	GPI	Mins	GA	GAA
New	2000	WC	1	1	20	3	9.00

LYLE Stevie　　b. 4-Dec-79

Club	Year	Comp	GP	GPI	Mins	GA	GAA
Car	1995	OQ	1	0	0	0	0.00
Car	1996	WC	3	1	60	2	2.00
Car	1996	OQ	2	0	0	0	0.00
Car	1997	WC	6	2	120	8	4.00
Can	1998	WC	5	4	205	12	3.51
Car	1999	WC	7	5	300	12	2.40
Car	1999	WCQ	4	4	240	5	1.25
Car	2000	OQ	3	3	180	8	2.67
		Totals	31	19	1105	47	2.55

McCRONE John　　b. 26-Feb-63

Club	Year	Comp	GP	GPI	Mins	GA	GAA
Ayr	1989	WC	2	1	30	0	0.00
Ayr	1991	WC	4	4	240	9	2.25
Ayr	1992	WC	3	3	122	4	1.97
Fif	1993	WC	7	5	280	13	2.79
Fif	1993	OQ	3	3	180	13	4.33
Fif	1994	WC	4	3	105	18	10.29
		Totals	23	19	957	57	3.57

McKAY Martin　　b. 27-Apr-68

Club	Year	Comp	GP	GPI	Mins	GA	GAA
Mur	1990	WC	2	2	120	4	2.00
Mur	1992	WC	3	1	60	2	2.00
Mur	1993	WC	3	1	60	0	0.00
She	1993	OQ	3	1	60	8	8.00
She	1994	WC	4	3	118	14	7.12
		Totals	15	8	418	28	4.02

MORRISON Bill　　b. 27-Oct-64

Club	Year	Comp	GP	GPI	Mins	GA	GAA
Bas	1995	WC	6	1	60	2	2.00
Bas	1995	OQ	3	3	180	4	1.33
Bas	1996	WC	6	3	180	10	3.33
K/R	1996	OQ	5	5	300	11	2.20
Rat	1997	WC	3	2	100	2	1.20
Pai	1998	WC	3	1	60	5	5.00
Rod	1999	WC	7	2	120	4	2.00
		Totals	33	17	1000	38	2.28

O'CONNOR Scott　　b. 3-May-69

Club	Year	Comp	GP	GPI	Mins	GA	GAA
Pet	1992	WC	4	3	118	4	2.03
Pet	1993	WC	3	2	80	0	0.00
Mil	1993	OQ	2	0	0	0	0.00
		Totals	9	5	198	4	1.21

SMITH Jeff　　b. 11-Jul-63

Club	Year	Comp	GP	GPI	Mins	GA	GAA
Car	1990	WC	3	1	60	2	2.00

WATKINS Joe　　b. 27-Oct-79

Club	Year	Comp	GP	GPI	Mins	GA	GAA
Bas	1999	WCQ	1	0	0	0	0.00
Bas	2000	WC	6	4	240	10	2.50
		Totals	7	4	240	10	2.50

JUNIOR CHAMPIONSHIPS

WORLD CHAMPIONSHIP

World Junior u20 Championship, Pool C, Nagano, Japan, 30 Dec 1999-3 Jan 2000

Age *limit* is under 20 years on 1 January 2000

Eight nations competed in Pool C divided into two groups. After each country had played the others in its group, the top team in group A played off against the top team in group B for promotion to Pool B. The lower ranked teams similarly played off for the remaining pool places.

GROUP STANDINGS

Group B	GP	W	L	D	GF	GA	Pts
Slovenia	3	2	0	1	12	7	5
Britain	3	1	0	2	9	7	4
Japan	3	1	1	1	11	9	3
Lithuania	3	0	3	0	6	15	0

BRITAIN'S POINT SCORERS

	GP	G	A	Pts	Pim
Colin Shields	4	4	5	9	4
Rob Lamey	4	5	3	8	2
David Clarke	4	4	3	7	4
Greg Owen	4	1	1	2	4
Jake Armstrong	4	1	1	2	4
Stephen Murphy (N)	4	0	2	2	0
Kyle Horne	4	0	2	2	2
Anthony Childs	4	0	2	2	10
Joe Baird	4	1	0	1	4
Adam Bicknell	4	0	1	1	2

BRITAIN'S NETMINDER

	GPI	Mins	SoG	GA	Sv%
Stephen Murphy	4	239	173	9	94.8

BRITAIN UNDER-20

Stephen Murphy FIF, Alex Field BAS; Joe Baird & Anthony Childs BAS, Kyle Horne FIF, Dominic Hopkins GUI, James Morgan MIL, James Pease SOL; Gary Clark & Danny Meyers BAS, Jonathan Phillips CAR, Rob Lamey GUI, Rob Chalmers, James Clarke & Bryan O'Neil PAI, David Clarke PET, Adam Bicknell SLO, Jake Armstrong SOL, Greg Owen (Notre Dame, Canada), Colin Shields (Cleveland, USA). *Manager:* Jim Laing. *Coach:* Troy Walkington.

BRITAIN'S RESULTS

30 Dec Japan-**Britain**	2-2	(0-1,2-0,0-1)
31 Dec Slovenia-**Britain**	3-3	(0-1,1-2,2-0)
2 Jan **Britain**-Lithuania	4-2	(0-0,1-2,3-0)
Third Place Playoff		
3 Jan Hungary-**Britain**	2-7	(1-4,1-2,0-1)

FINAL RANKINGS

1 Austria (promoted), 2 Slovenia, **3 Britain**, 4 Hungary, 5 Japan, 6 Estonia, 7 Lithuania, 8 Jugoslavia (relegated).

Brits win bronze

A disciplined Britain took home a bronze medal for the first time since Rome in 1991-92 after going undefeated in all their four games.

In fact, with two contests ending tied, they were only a couple of goals away from winning promotion. Shades of the senior national squad!

They finished third in the Fair Play rankings, averaging a modest 18.50 minutes.

Scot **Colin Shields**, 19, who has four seasons' experience in North America and **Rob Lamey**, 20, of the BNL's Guildford Flames, were the team's top forwards, along with Peterborough's **David Clarke**, 18, who hit some important goals.

The anchor of the side was another Scot, **Stephen Murphy**, 18, of Fife Flyers. The tournament's leading netminder, he also found time to set up a couple of goals!

Murphy faced 173 shots on his net, twice as many as the runner-up, **Patrick Machreich**, of Pool champions, Austria.

EUROPEAN CHAMPIONSHIP

European Junior u18 Championship, Div 1,
Maribor, Slovenia, 20-24 March 2000

Age limit is under 18 years on 1 January 2000

FINAL STANDINGS

Prelim. Group B	GP	W	L	D	GF	GA	Pts
Kazakhstan	3	3	0	0	32	5	6
Slovenia	3	2	1	0	21	9	4
Britain	3	1	2	0	10	18	2
Romania	3	0	3	0	3	34	0

BRITAIN'S RESULTS

20 Mar **Britain**-Romania   7-2 (2-0,2-1,3-1)
21 Mar Kazakhstan-**Britain**   8-0 (2-0,3-0,3-0)
23 Mar **Britain**-Slovenia   3-8 (1-2,1-1,1-5)

Fifth place playoff
24 Mar Lithuania-**Britain**   4-5ot (2-1,1-2,1-1,0-1)

BRITAIN UNDER-18

Andy Moffat FIF, Adam White SLO; Richard Thornton BIL, Tyrone Miller, Michael Plenty GUI, Nathan Hunt HUL, Michael Wales MIL, Jon Fone NOT; Danny Meyers BAS, Jonathan Phillips CAR, Jason Moses GUI, Chris Markham HUL, Paul Moran, Paul Stanley NOT, Ross Jones ROM, Neil Adams, Shaun Yardley SOL, Russell Cowley, Richard Wojciak SWI, Paul Sample WHI. *Manager:* John Bailey. *Coach:* Darryl Easson.

FINAL RANKINGS

1 Kazakhstan, 2 Estonia, 3 Slovenia, 4 Hungary, **5 Britain**, 6 Lithuania, 7 Romania, 8 Spain.

BRITAIN'S POINT SCORERS

	GP	G	A	Pts	Pim
Jonathan Philips	4	2	4	6	4
Neil Adams	4	3	2	5	0
Paul Moran	4	2	1	3	4
Danny Meyers	4	2	1	3	8
Paul Stanley	4	2	0	2	0
Russell Cowley	4	1	1	2	0
Richard Thornton	4	1	1	2	10
Jon Fone	4	0	2	2	8
Chris Markham	4	0	2	2	27
Richard Wojciak	4	1	0	1	4
Paul Sample	4	1	0	1	31
Michael Wales	4	0	1	1	4
Shaun Yardley	4	0	1	1	4
Tyrone Miller	4	0	1	1	6

BRITAIN'S NETMINDERS

	GPI	Mins	SoG	GA	Sv%
Andy Moffat	1	60	23	4	82.6
Adam White	3	180	95	18	81.0

Out of the medals again

It was all too horribly familiar. Britain's fifth place finish, one place lower than in 1999, left them below four East European nations.

A lot of hard work had gone into preparing the team, highlighted by a trip to the French Alps at Christmas for the second successive year, a challenge match against a BNL team and a one-day training camp in Haringey.

Britain began their challenge in Slovenia with the best possible result, a 7-2 defeat of Romania with Britain's goals all coming from different scorers. Coach **Darryl Easson** couldn't help but sound optimistic afterwards. "Although our game against Kazakhstan will be very tough indeed, I'm sure we have enough about us to get out there and grab two points."

Unfortunately, there was a world of difference between the two East European opponents. The Kazakhs would end up being promoted while Romania would have to playoff to avoid relegation. Nevertheless, the 8-0 whitewash was demoralising, especially as the Kazakhs only outshot the Brits 39-29.

With a rest day before playing the host nation, GB recovered well. Slovenia needed four goals in the last five minutes for their win, and **Danny Meyers**' game-winning penalty shot brought victory over the tiny Baltic republic of Lithuania.

TOURNOI JUNIORS DE NOEL

Invitation Tournament, Pralognan, Meribel and Courchevel, France, 28-30 December 1999
Results and Scorers
28 Dec Britain-Denmark   3-5
29 Dec Britain-Slovenia   0-8
30 Dec Britain-France   3-5

Britain failed to win a game on their second successive trip to this four-team competition in the French Alps.

The opposition was very strong, however, with the French and Danish sides competing in Pool B of the European under-18 Championships. Britain were pleased to win the Fair Play award and **Paul Sample** was voted GB's best player.

CHALLENGE
8 Jan Chelmsford Chieftains-Britain 6-4

BRITAIN UNDER-16 team and coaching staff celebrate with the Chris Verwijst 2000 trophy.

YOUTH INTERNATIONALS

Gold for Britain's under-16s

It was the lucky 13th time for Britain's under-16s who won four of their five games and took the gold medal in the annual Chris Verwijst junior tournament in Tilburg, Netherlands.

Britain have entered this prestigious international competition every year since 1988 as there is no world championship for this age group.

CHRIS VERWIJST TOURNAMENT

Tilburg, Netherlands, 24-26 March 2000

GB RESULTS

24 Mar	Britain-Austria	1-4	(0-1,1-0,0-3)
25 Mar	Tilburg HOL-Britain	1-11	(1-3,0-5,0-3)
25 Mar	Romania-Britain	1-8	(0-2,1-5,0-1)
26 Mar	Britain-France	3-2	(1-2,1-0,1-0)
26 Mar	Britain-Bled SLV	6-5	(5-1,0-3,1-1)

FINAL RANKINGS

1 Britain, 2 Bled (Slovenia), 3 France, 4 Austria, 5 Denmark, 6 Netherlands, 7 Tilburg (N'lands), 8 Romania.

Billingham's **Stephen Wallace**, with 13 goals and 20 points, was voted the tournament's Most Valuable Player and Sunderland's **James Hutchinson** was selected to the All-Star team.

BRITAIN'S LEADING SCORERS

	GP	G	A	Pts	Pim
Stephen Wallace	5	13	7	20	4
Andrew Smith	5	1	5	6	4
Scott Ward	5	1	5	6	4
Matthew Towalski	5	4	1	5	4
Lee Hardy	5	3	2	5	8

BRITAIN UNDER-16

Alan Levers NOT, Geoff Woolhouse SHE; Gareth Crinnion BIL, Rhodri Evans CAR, Patrick Ward FIF, Daniel Hughes SHE, James Hutchinson SUN; Lee Hardy ALT, Scott Padwick, Tom Pope BAS, Shaun Buckley, Stephen Wallace, Scott Ward BIL, Neil Hay EDI, Andrew Smith GUI, Adam Radmall NOT, Matthew Towalski SLO, Adam Carr SUN, Dean Mills, Gary Slevin SWI. *Manager*: Bob Wilkinson. *Coach*: Allan Anderson

ENGLAND UNDER-14s

For the third year in a row, England's under-14 team entered the International Pee-Wee tournament in Quebec, Canada.

This tournament is the most highly rated in the world at this age level.

ENGLAND'S RESULTS

Quebec Colisee, February 2000.

Pro Lac, Quebec-England 6-4; **Laval-England 4-1**; **Montmangy-England 4-3**.

Semi-final: Quebec Champlain-England 4-0.

Team manager **Alan Moutrey** *told the Annual about the England team's trip which, as usual, attracted a lot of attention in Canada.*

'The season started with regional trials at Telford (Midlands), Whitley Bay (North) and Milton Keynes, followed by a final trial at Nottingham when 19 players were selected.

After a training weekend at the Lilleshall National Sports Centre, we played the Northern, Midland and South-West conference under-15 sides and twice against the GB women's team.

Once in Canada, before the big games in the Quebec Colisee, the lads warmed up with a 3-1 win over Japan and a fine 3-0 shutout against an American squad from Columbus, Ohio.

We reached the semi-final of the tournament proper but for some reason we just could not get into the game against Quebec and, to be honest, we deserved our 4-0 defeat.

We ended a marvellous trip with two more exhibitions - a 3-3 draw with Swiss club, Romande, and a 3-2 defeat by the Ukraine. In all, we played eleven games in 13 days and the lads really benefited from playing against quality international sides.'

ENGLAND UNDER-14

Nathan Craze CAR, David Wride BRK; Robert Simmonds BRK, James Parsons CAR, Kurt Reynolds GUI, Daniel Ramsden SHE, Barney Wood SLO, Stuart Bates TEL, Robert Wilson WHI; Peter Traynor ALT, Lance McDermott BLA, Robert Chamberlain, Lewis Day HUL, Oliver Bronnimann, Ashley Jackson INV, Simon Butterworth, Chace Farrand SHE, Thomas Carlon TEL, Ian Emerson WHI. *Manager*: Alan Moutrey. *Coach*: Tony Hall.

SKODA AUTO EUROPEAN LEAGUE

Sixteen teams, representing 11 countries, participated in the fourth season of the European Hockey League (EHL). The Czech Republic, Finland, Germany, Russia and Sweden each entered two teams. Skoda Auto returned for a second season as the league's sponsor.

Invitations were issued based on a combination of the clubs' national success and their facilities. The teams were seeded into four divisions of four teams each, with each team playing the other in its group twice, home and away, for a total of six games.

At the end of the first round, the top two teams in each division qualified for the semi-finals which were played over two legs, home and away. (Pairings were decided by a draw except that teams from the same country played each other.) The winning teams progressed to the Top Four Final. [See International Round-Up for results.]

Points are awarded as follows: win = three points, draw after 60 minutes = one point each, win in overtime or on game winning shots = one extra point. The team winning on game winning shots (better known in Britain as penalty shots) is credited with one extra goal.

With eight fewer clubs competing compared to 1998-99, only one British club gained entry, Superleague champions Manchester Storm.

This was the first season that Storm were awarded a place on merit. In the league's previous three seasons, Storm had earned a 'wild card' entry owing to their state-of-the-art, 17,250-seat arena, one of Europe's best facilities. They narrowly failed to get past the first round in 1997-98 and 1998-99.

In 1999-2000 Storm were drawn into probably the toughest group of all, Division B, which comprised teams from Finland, Sweden and the Czech Republic whose leagues are among the continent's strongest.

Helsinki were runners-up in the Finnish league, Brynas were fifth in Sweden, and Prague were fourth in the Czech league.

FINAL STANDINGS

DIVISION B	GP	W	L	OW	OL	GF	GA	Pts
IFK Helsinki FIN	6	5	1	0	0	29	25	15
Sparta Prague CZE	6	3	1	1	1	29	15	12
Brynäs IF SWE	6	1	3	2	0	19	24	7
Manchester Storm GBR	6	0	4	0	2	13	26	2

OW - overtime win, OL - overtime loss.
IFK Helsinki and Sparta Prague qualified for the semi-final round

DIVISION B RESULTS

28 Sep	Brynäs-Prague	5-4ot*
	Storm-Helsinki	3-5
12 Oct	Prague-Storm	2-1ot*
	Helsinki-Brynäs	5-0
26 Oct	Brynäs-Storm	4-1
	Helsinki-Prague	6-3
2 Nov	Storm-Prague	1-4
9 Nov	Brynäs-Helsinki	4-6
23 Nov	Prague-Helsinki	12-1
	Storm-Brynäs	4-5ot*
7 Dec	Prague-Brynäs	4-1
	Helsinki-Storm	6-3

* after game winning shots

STORM'S LEADING SCORERS

	GP	G	A	Pts	Pims
Jeff Jablonski	6	4	2	6	10
Dave Livingston	6	3	2	5	31
Rick Brebant	6	1	3	4	4
Kris Miller	6	0	3	3	4
Kelly Askew	5	1	1	2	4
Rob Robinson	6	1	1	2	2
Jeff Tomlinson	6	1	1	2	4
Mike Harding	6	1	1	2	8
Norm Krumpschmid	6	0	2	2	8

STORM'S NETMINDING

	GPI	Mins	SoG	GA	Sv%
Frank Pietrangelo	5	251	146	15	89.7
Mark Bernard	3	127	74	11	85.1

Europe 'never easy' - KK

Storm's fourth venture into Europe was their least successful since their first in 1996-97. **Kurt Kleinendorst**'s team failed to win any games, though they twice came heartbreakingly close.

KK admitted that Superleague's £500,000 wage ceiling was a big handicap. Some of Storm's opponents pay that sort of money to just one of their top players!

Before their home game against Swedish club, Brynas, when Storm were still mathematically in the hunt, the coach said: "For whatever reason, this is a group of players which has fallen short in Europe this season.

"After that first game against Helsinki, which we deserved to lose because we were not disciplined enough, we could easily have won any one of the games we have played since.

"From a coaching standpoint, the guys have given me their best and I can ask no more. I really believe we have done our best.

"But it's never easy playing in Europe. It's a compliment to be involved, but at the same time it's very time consuming and tiring."

STORM'S GAME SUMMARIES

28 September 1999, MEN Arena, Manchester

STORM-HELSINKI   3-5 (1-1,0-3,2-1)

Storm's opening game had everything - goals, emotion, fights, excitement - and despite their defeat, they went off to a standing ovation.

Coach Kleinendorst saw it slightly differently. "Slashing, hacking, whacking, elbowing and charging," he complained. "I don't mind honest penalties... I just don't like retaliation penalties."

Storm were frustrated by the powerful Finns, who were 4-1 up after two periods, with three Helsinki goals coming on powerplays. "Our penalty killing sucked," said KK. " Three of their goals came from the blue line. If you understood our system, we don't allow that."

Only in the last period did Storm's powerplay click for a couple of consolation goals.

The Finns were no angels, either. Two of their players were thrown out for roughing and the Dutch referee felt it necessary to talk to a few of the participants to try and calm things down.

"We didn't come out to play that physical," said Helsinki's GM **Frank Moberg**, "but we have a whole new team this year and all our skilled guys are gone, so we had to change our style. Also we knew from experience that Storm are a physical team so we were well prepared."

Frank Pietrangelo came off after the first period with a suspected broken rib and defenceman **Blair Scott** needed x-rays on a wrist injury.

First Period
1-0 MAN Harding (Miller, Brebant) 3.21
1-1 HEL Kultanen (Caloun, Pirjeta) pp 11.23
Second Period
1-2 HEL Hurme (Kuhta) pp 6.25
1-3 HEL Kuhta (Nieminen, Kultanen) sh 9.54
1-4 HEL Karalahti (Sihvonen, Kultanen) pp 17.29
Third Period
1-5 HEL Hurme (Nieminen, Zidlicky) 1.16
2-5 MAN Jablonski (Livingston, Robinson) pp 11.27
3-5 MAN Tomlinson (Krumpschmid) 14:49
Penalty minutes
Storm   49 (Gatto - game misc.)
Helsinki 70 (Nielikainen, Sihvonen - game misc.)
Shots on Goal
Pietrangelo/Bernard MAN 8-13-11 =32
save percentage: 84.37
Ahonen HEL 11-14-17 = 42
save percentage: 92.86
Referee: Bergman HOL.   *Spectators:* 4,239
Linesmen: Folka, Staniforth GBR.

MANCHESTER STORM
Frank Pietrangelo, Mark Bernard; Troy Neumeier (capt), Blair Scott, Kevin Hoffman, Kris Miller, Rob Robinson, Mike Morin; Mike Harding, Rick Brebant, Greg Gatto, Jeff Jablonski, David Livingston, Norm Krumpschmid, Darren Hurley, Jeff Tomlinson, Pierre Allard.
Manager-coach: Kurt Kleinendorst.

DIVISION B	GP	W	L	OW	OL	GF	GA	Pts
Helsinki	1	1	0	0	0	5	3	3
Brynäs	1	0	0	1	0	5	4	2
Sparta Prague	1	0	0	0	1	4	5	1
Storm	1	0	1	0	0	3	5	0

Prague, Czech Republic, 12 October 1999

PRAGUE-STORM   1-1ot   (1-0,0-0,0-1,0-0)
Prague won 2-1 after penalty shots

Despite a marvellous 40-save performance from recovered goalie **Frank Pietrangelo**, Storm lost in Prague on penalty shots.

But they maintained their unbroken record against Sparta and gained their first EHL point with a 1-1 tie after ten minutes of overtime.

Rick Brebant and **Jeff Tomlinson** converted their 'game winning shots' past Czech international goalie, **Petr Briza**. Prague got level but then Briza blocked **Jeff Jablonski**'s crucial fifth shot and **Frantisek Ptacek** beat Pietrangelo for the decider.

Prague, with eight internationals but without their sacked coach, bombarded Pietrangelo with 19 shots in the first period alone. Zelenka's goal was effectively a powerplay one as it came just as Storm's **Greg Gatto** returned from the sin bin.

"We were able to keep our crease clear and avoid dangerous situations for Pietrangelo," said Kleinendorst. "He did a tremendous job in stopping every puck".

Storm twice beat Prague two seasons ago: an historic 7-0 shutout in Manchester came after Jablonski netted the winner in Storm's 4-3 upset victory in the Czech capital.

First Period
1-0 PRA Zelenka (Hlinka, Chabada) 13.31,
Second Period
No scoring.
Third Period
1-1 MAN Livingstone (Hoffman, Jablonski) 13.43

EUROPEAN HOCKEY LEAGUE

Overtime
No scoring.
Game Winning Shots

1 MAN Weaver - save	0-0
2 PRA Zelenka - save	0-0
3 MAN Tomlinson - score	0-1
4 PRA Eiselt - score	1-1
5 MAN Brebant - score	1-2
6 PRA Hlinka - save	1-2
7 MAN Krumpschmid - save	1-2
8 PRA Nedved - score	2-2
9 MAN Jablonski - save	2-2
10 PRA Ptacek - score	**3-2**

Penalty Minutes Prague 8, Storm 12.
Shots on Goal (ex. Game Winning Shots)
Briza PRA   8-8- 4-1   21
save percentage 95.24
Pietrangelo MAN 19-9-11-3   41
save percentage 97.56
Referee: Bachelet FRA.   *Attendance*: 2,542
Linesmen: Blaha, Cizek CZE.

MANCHESTER STORM
As on 28 September with the addition of forwards Kelly Askew
and Jonathan Weaver.

DIVISION B	GP	W	L	OW	OL	GF	GA	Pts
Helsinki	2	2	0	0	0	10	3	6
Sparta Prague	2	0	0	1	1	6	6	3
Brynäs	2	0	1	1	0	5	9	2
Storm	2	0	1	0	1	4	7	1

Gävle, Sweden, 26 October 1999

BRYNÄS-STORM   4-1(1-0,1-0,2-1)

Storm were out-skated and fired only 14 shots on the Brynäs
goal. But the coach of the Swedish playoff champions, **Roger
Melin**, admitted: "Manchester were a big, positive surprise for
me. We were chased all the time and had big problems."

Storm went 2-0 down after 33 minutes but Jablonski pulled
them to within one with eleven minutes left. Then, pressing hard
for the equaliser, they took a few liberties and the Russian ref
dished out eight minors in under seven minutes.

With Storm forced to kill a five-on-three powerplay for four
minutes, including one when KK failed to have the Swedes
convicted for using an illegal stick, Brynäs scored twice for their
first outright EHL win of the campaign.

Jan Larsson, the highest scorer in the Swedish Elitserien,
had two goals for Brynäs.

Naturally, KK was upset at the officiating but for once he was
pleased with his team's effort. "There is not a single guy who
should walk out of the locker room hanging his head because
we played a great game," he said.

Storm now needed good results from their next two games,
both at home, before meeting leaders Helsinki in Finland.

First Period
1-0 BRY Olsson (Samuelsson) 2:07.
Second Period
2-0 BRY Larsson (Bissett) 13:44.
Third Period
2-1 MAN Jablonski (Livingston) 8:54
3-1 BRY Larsson (Olsson) pp 17:35
4-1 BRY Lundqvist (Larsson; Djoos) pp 19:43
Penalty Minutes
Brynäs 14, Storm 40.

Shots on Goal
Holmqvist BRY   6-5- 3 = 14
save percentage 92.86
Pietrangelo MAN 8-8-13 = 29
save percentage 86.21
Referee: Zaitsev RUS.   *Attendance*: 2,402
Linesmen: Lindgren, Takula SWE.

MANCHESTER STORM
As on 28 September with the addition of forwards Kelly Askew
and Jonathan Weaver but without defenceman Matt Hoffman
(shoulder).

DIVISION B	GP	W	L	OW	OL	GF	GA	Pts
Helsinki	3	3	0	0	0	16	6	9
Brynäs	3	1	1	1	0	9	10	5
Prague	3	0	1	1	1	9	12	3
Storm	3	0	2	0	1	5	11	1

MEN Arena, Manchester 2 November 1999

STORM-PRAGUE   1-4 (0-1,1-1,0-2)

Reduced to 15 out-players, including just four natural
defencemen, Storm left too many gaps at the back and crashed
virtually out of contention for the top two places in the division.

Martin Chabada scored a hat-trick for the Czechs who
outshot Manchester 39-25.

Storm had their moments, though, with **Greg Gatto** hitting
the crossbar and efforts from **Jon Weaver** (kicked in) and **Kelly
Askew** (after whistle) being ruled out. Had Askew's attempt
stood, it would have been 2-2 early in the last period.

Penalties took their toll, too, with Prague's first two goals
coming on powerplays.

A disappointed KK felt the team had not played with
sufficient intensity, but he singled out defender **Mike Morin**.
"He played the whole 60 minutes and was our unsung hero."

The coach attributed the team's problems to the Superleague
wage cap. "When you take £100,000 out of the kitty, it's bound
to affect the quality of player you can bring in," he said.

First Period
0-1 PRA Eiselt (Bros, Kratena) pp 16:06
Second Period
0-2 PRA Chabada (Nedved) pp 4:31
1-2 MAN Jablonski (Brebant, Miller) 10:17
Third Period
1-3 PRA Chabada (Vyborny) 7:49
1-4 PRA Chabada (Benysek) 11:11
Penalty Mniutes
Storm 18, Prague 14.
Shots on Goal
Pietrangelo MAN 9-19- 11 = 39
save percentage 89.74
Briza PRA   7- 4-14 = 25
save percentage 96.00
Referee: Lichtnecker GER.   *Attendance*: 3,859.
Linesmen: Folka, Staniforth GBR.

MANCHESTER STORM
As on 28 September with the addition of forwards Kelly Askew
and Jonathan Weaver but without defenceman Matt Hoffman
and Troy Neumeier (shoulders).

DIVISION B	GP	W	L	OW	OL	GF	GA	Pts
Helsinki	3	3	0	0	0	16	6	9
Prague	4	1	1	1	1	13	13	6
Brynäs	3	1	1	1	0	9	10	5
Storm	4	0	3	0	1	6	15	1

EUROPEAN HOCKEY LEAGUE

Blackburn Arena, 23 November 1999

STORM-BRYNäS   4-4ot (1-2,2-1,1-1,0-0)
Brynäs won 5-4 after penalty shots

Still mathematically in the hunt for a place in the semis, Storm went all out for a win and for the second time they came achingly close, eventually losing on a penalty shootout.

Mark Bernard made a creditable EHL debut with a better save percentage than his opposite number, NHL draftee **Johan Asplund**, 18.

"Any time you go to a shootout you can pretty much flip a coin," said Kleinendorst. "But the odds were stacked against us because they have so much skill among their forwards."

First Period
1-0 MAN Jablonski (Krumpschmid, Miller) 10:25;
1-1 BRY Hermansson (Petre) 13:53;
1-2 BRY Olsson D (Tuulola, Samuelsson) 16:15.
Second Period
1-3 BRY Sjödin (Luovi, Kyrö) pp 3:06;
2-3 MAN Brebant (Askew, Bernard) 16:08;
3-3 MAN Livingston (Jablonski) 16:48.
Third Period
3-4 BRY Rudslätt (Tuulola, Djoos) 4:00;
4-4 MAN Livingston (Scott, Pozzo) 8:58
Overtime
No scoring
Game Winning Shots

1	MAN	Tomlinson - score	1-0
2	BRY	Larsson - score	1-1
3	MAN	Krumpschmid -score	2-1
4	BRY	Djoos - save	2-1
5	MAN	Brebant - save	2-1
6	BRY	Bissett - score	2-2
7	MAN	Livingston - save	2-2
8	**BRY**	**Rudslätt - score**	**2-3**
9	MAN	Jablonski - miss	2-3

Penalty minutes: Storm 14, Brynäs 12
Shots on Goal (ex Game Winning Shots)
Bernard MAN 15 - 11 -10 - 6 = 42
save percentage 90.48
Asplund BRY 10 - 9 - 8 - 5 = 32
save percentage 87.50
Referee Schimm GER. *Attendance*: 1,174.
Linesmen: Folka, Staniforth GB.
MANCHESTER STORM
As on 28 September with the addition of forward Kelly Askew and defenceman Kevin Pozzo but without defenceman Troy Neumeier (shoulder) and forward Greg Gatto (released by club).

DIVISION B	GP	W	L	OW	OL	GF	GA	Pts
Helsinki	5	4	1	0	0	23	22	12
Prague	5	2	1	1	1	25	14	9
Brynäs	5	1	2	2	0	18	20	7
Storm	5	0	3	0	2	10	20	2

Helsinki, Finland, 7 December 1999

HELSINKI-STORM   6-3 (2-1,2-1,2-1)

Storm's final game will be recalled as the Battle of the Baltic as all 12 players on the ice were involved in a mass brawl at the end of the first period. An EHL record of 353 penalty minutes were called in total.

The Finns were leading 2-1 and Storm were killing a penalty at 18.35 when fighting broke out behind Manchester's goal. The trouble was caused when a Finn jabbed his stick into **Kevin Hoffman**. As the defenceman was still recovering from an eye injury, his teammates rushed to his aid.

After several minutes of fighting, the Swedish referee **Ulf Radbjer** ejected all the players, including both goalies. A 13th player, a Finn, was given a game misconduct 54 seconds into the second period.

The trouble was unexpected. Helsinki do have a reputation as a rough side but only by modest Finnish standards and Storm are hardly a 'physical' team. Both sides were playing for pride. Storm were out of contention for the next round while Helsinki had already clinched a semi-final place.

First Period
1-0 HEL Uusikartano (Lydman) 3.48;
2-0 HEL Kuhta (Nielikäinen) 6.02;
2-1 MAN Askew (Campbell) 13.14
Second Period
2-2 MAN Robinson (Harding, Tomlinson) 13.49;
3-2 HEL Makiaho (Uusikartano) 17.25
4-2 HEL Makiaho (Uusikartano, Hurme) 17.59
Third Period
5-2 HEL Uusikartano (Kalto) 2.30;
6-2 HEL Pirjeta 4.33
6-3 MAN Wahlsten (Morin, Brebant) 8.33.
Penalty minutes
Helsinki 183 (Ahonen, Nielikäinen, Kultanen, Tuominen, Kuhta, Rajala - GM for roughing at 18.35; Kuparinen - Match Penalty for fisticuffs at 20.54), Storm 170 (Livingston, Bernard, Hoffman, Hurley, Johnstone - GM for roughing, Campbell - Match Penalty for fisticuffs, all at 18.35).
Shots on Goal
Ahonen/Stromberg HEL 7- 4- 8 19
(save percentage 84.21)
Bernard/Pietrangelo MAN 7-18-12 37
(save percentage 83.78)
Referee: Radjer SWE. *Attendance:* 6,171
Linesmen: Tarko, Peltonen FIN.
MANCHESTER STORM
As on 28 September with the addition of forward Kelly Askew and defencemen Kevin Pozzo and Scott Campbell but without defenceman Troy Neumeier (shoulder) and forward Greg Gatto (released by club).

PAST BRITISH CLUB RESULTS

1998-99
AYR SCOTTISH EAGLES (coach **Jim Lynch**)
Group placing - 3rd

v Mannheim GER 3-6,	v Litvinov CZE 4-3,
at Kazan RUS 4-2,	v Kazan 3-1,
at Litvinov 4-5ot,	at Mannheim 5-6.

MANCHESTER STORM (coach **Kurt Kleinendorst**)
Group placing - 3rd

v Tampere FIN 4-2,	at Bolzano ITA 2-1,
at Leksands SWE 2-2ot*	v Leksands 2-3ot,
v Bolzano 2-5,	at Tampere 3-7.

* Storm won on game winning shots.

1997-98
MANCHESTER STORM (coach **Kurt Kleinendorst**)
*Group placing - 2nd. **Failed to progress by one-goal difference.***

at Bolzano ITA 5-6ot,	v Moscow Dyn RUS 2-3ot
at Prague CZE 4-3,	v Prague 7-0,
at Moscow 9-3,	v Bolzano 4-2.

1996-97
MANCHESTER STORM (coach **John Lawless**)
Group placing - 4th

v TPS Turku FIN 0-6,	at Lulea SWE 6-10,
v Berlin GER 2-4,	at Berlin 1-6,
v Lulea 0-11,	at Turku 1-2.

CONTINENTAL CUP

The Continental Cup was established in 1997 as a replacement for the European Cup. (The name was changed to avoid confusion with the European League (EHL).)

The Cup was devised for clubs and countries whose teams and/or facilities do not meet the strict standards of the EHL. Costs are kept down by gathering clubs together geographically as far as possible and allowing games to be played by groups of teams in one venue, rather than home and away.

Forty-nine clubs representing 28 countries participated in the 1999 Continental Cup.

The competition was played over three qualifying rounds in September, October and November, the teams being seeded according to the position of their national teams in the last World Championships.

In each of the first two rounds, 24 teams competed in six groups of four. There were 12 teams, three groups of four, in the Third Round. In each round, the teams played a round-robin over three days.

(At the end of each game, a shoot-out competition took place to decide the final rankings in case of equal placing.)

The winner of each group was promoted to the next round.

The winners of the Third Round qualified for the Final Round which was played in Berlin, Germany on 26-28 December 1999. [See International Round-Up.]

Britain's representatives were seeded into the Seond Round. They were Cardiff Devils, the 1999 Superleague Playoff Champions; Nottingham Panthers, the 1998 Benson and Hedges Cup winners; and Sheffield Steelers, the 1998-99 Challenge Cup title-holders.

This was Panthers' first ever venture into a major European competition.

Unusually, two British venues hosted games in Round Two - Cardiff's Ice House which was home to Group L (into which Nottingham Panthers were drawn as well as the Devils) and the Sheffield Arena where Group M was staged.

Group L at the Ice House, Cardiff

STANDINGS		GP	W	L	D	GF	GA	Pts
Lada Togliatti RUS		3	2	1	0	26	11	4
Nottingham Panthers GBR		3	2	1	0	16	14	4
Cardiff Devils GBR		3	2	1	0	16	13	4
Lyon Lions FRA		3	0	3	0	6	26	0

Lada Togliatti promoted to the Third Round.

COMPLETE RESULTS

22 Oct
Nottingham Panthers-Lada Togliatti   8-6
Cardiff Devils-Lyon Lions   9-2
23 Oct
Lyon Lions-**Lada Togliatti**   1-12
Cardiff Devils-Nottingham Panthers   5-3
24 Oct
Nottingham Panthers-Lyon Lions   5-3
Lada Togliatti-**Cardiff Devils**   8-2

DEVILS' AND PANTHERS' TOP SCORERS

	GP	G	A	Pts	Pim
Greg Hadden NOT	3	4	5	9	4
Steve Moria CAR	3	4	2	6	0
Brent Bobyck NOT	3	2	3	5	0
Steve Thornton CAR	3	1	4	5	2
David Struch NOT	3	2	2	4	4
Calle Carlsson NOT	3	2	2	4	2
Jamie Leach NOT	3	1	3	4	2
Vezio Sacratini CAR	3	2	2	4	0
Darren Durdle CAR	3	0	4	4	8

DEVILS' AND PANTHERS' NETMINDING

	GPI	Mins	SoG	GA	Sv%
Stevie Lyle CAR	2	66	27	2	92.59
Jordan Willis NOT	3	180	78	13	83.33
D Herlofsky CAR	2	114	61	10	82.26

CUP FACTS
- The crowds at the two venues just topped 15,000, with the biggest being the 3,633 who watched Steelers beat Omsk.
- Sheffield and Cardiff estimated that they lost between £20,000 and £50,000 in staging the games.

STANDINGS	GP	W	L	D	GF	GA	Pts
Storhamar Dragons NOR	3	1	0	2	11	5	4
Sheffield Steelers GBR	3	1	0	2	11	9	4
Avangard Omsk RUS	3	1	1	1	15	6	3
Angers Ducs FRA	3	0	2	1	4	21	1

COMPLETE RESULTS

21 Oct
Avangard Omsk-Storhamar Dragons 2-2
Sheffield Steelers-Angers Ducs 4-4
22 Oct
Angers Ducs-Avangard Omsk 0-11
Storhamar Dragons-**Sheffield Steelers** 3-3
24 Oct
Storhamar Dragons-Angers Ducs 6-0
Sheffield Steelers-Avangard Omsk 4-2

STEELERS' TOP SCORERS

	GP	G	A	Pts	Pim
Jason Weaver	3	2	5	7	4
Greg Clancy	3	1	2	3	0
Kip Noble	3	1	2	3	2
Ed Courtenay	3	3	0	3	0
Rob Wilson	3	1	1	2	6
Matt Hoffman	3	1	1	2	2
Dale Junkin	3	1	1	2	2
Dan Ceman	3	1	0	1	0

STEELERS' NETMINDING

	GPI	Mins	SoG	GA	Sv%
Shawn Silver	1	60	48	2	95.83
Grant Sjerven	2	120	69	7	89.86
TEAM TOTALS	3	180	117	9	92.31

CUP FACT
■ Former Ayr Scottish Eagles goalie **Vincent Riendeau** (he did a mid-season runner, remember?) played half of one Togliatti game, compiling a 90.91 save percentage against the weak French club, Lyon.

BRITISH TEAMS

CARDIFF DEVILS
Derek Herlofsky, Stevie Lyle; Aaron Boh, Alan Schuler, Jason Stone, Patrik Lundback, Darren Durdle, Daniel Jardemyr; Saku Eklof, Steve Thornton, Nicky Chinn, Steve Moria, John Brill, Ian McIntyre, Ivan Matulik (capt), Merv Priest, Vezio Sacratini, Todd Gillingham, Jonathan Phillips.
Manager: Andy French.   *Coach:* Paul Heavey.

NOTTINGHAM PANTHERS
Jordan Willis, Jarkko Kortesoja; Brent Pope, Steve Carpenter, Stephen Cooper, Calle Carlsson; David Struch, Greg Hadden, Simon Hunt, Marty Flichel, Curtis Bowen, Ashley Tait, Jamie Leach (capt), Graham Garden, Aaron Cain, Brent Bobyck.
Manager: Gary Moran.   *Coach:* Mike Blaisdell.

SHEFFIELD STEELERS
Grant Sjerven, Shawn Silver; Kip Noble, Rob Wilson (capt), Mark Matier, Andre Malo, Shayne McCosh, Kayle Short; Jason Weaver, Greg Clancy, Ed Courtenay, Matt Hoffman, Dale Junkin, Derek Laxdal, David Longstaff, Dan Ceman, Teeder Wynne, Tom Plommer.
Manager: Dave Simms.   *Coach:* Don McKee.

Brits bow out

Even with home ice advantage, Britain's three clubs all failed to win their second round groups in the Continental Cup.

The two Russian clubs, Lada Togliatti and Avangard Omsk, were the most feared sides and Togliatti duly won their event in Cardiff.

Their only loss, 8-6 to Nottingham Panthers, was one of the best British results, ranking alongside Sheffield Steelers' 4-2 defeat of Omsk.

Steelers' loss was Storhamar's gain as the Norwegian side won their closely-contested group only on goal difference after the two sides had drawn their game 3-3.

Cardiff's group was even closer with three teams tying on points and goal difference being needed again to decide the final placings.

Nottingham's **Greg Hadden** with nine points (four goals) was the top scorer among the British clubs' players, with **Jason Weaver** of Steelers the runner-up on seven points (two goals).

Devils' teenager **Stevie Lyle** was voted the Best Netminder in the Cardiff tournament, partly on the basis of his remarkable 100 per cent record in the shoot-out competitions which were staged as tie-breakers after each game.

NATIONAL HOCKEY LEAGUE

FINAL STANDINGS

EASTERN CONFERENCE	GP	W	L	D	OL	GF	GA	Pts
NORTHEAST DIVISION								
(3) Toronto Maple Leafs TOR	82	45	30	7	3	246	222	100
(6) Ottawa Senators OTT	82	41	30	11	2	244	210	95
(8) Buffalo Sabres BUF	82	35	36	11	4	213	204	85
(10) Montreal Canadiens MTL	82	35	38	9	4	196	194	83
(11) Boston Bruins BOS	82	24	39	19	6	210	248	73
ATLANTIC DIVISION								
(1) Philadelphia Flyers PHI	82	45	25	12	3	237	179	105
(4) New Jersey Devils NJ	82	45	29	8	5	251	203	103
(7) Pittsburgh Penguins PIT	82	37	37	8	6	241	236	88
(11) New York Rangers NYR	82	29	41	12	3	218	246	73
(13) New York Islanders NYI	82	24	49	9	1	194	275	58
SOUTHEAST DIVISION								
(2) Washington Capitals WSH	82	44	26	12	2	227	194	102
(5) Florida Panthers FLA	82	43	33	6	6	244	209	98
(9) Carolina Hurricanes CAR	82	37	35	10	0	217	216	84
(14) Tampa Bay Lightning TB	82	19	54	9	7	204	310	54
(15) *Atlanta Thrashers ATL	82	14	61	7	4	170	313	39

WESTERN CONFERENCE

	GP	W	L	D	OL	GF	GA	Pts
CENTRAL DIVISION								
(1) St Louis Blues STL	82	51	20	11	1	248	165	114
(4) Detroit Red Wings DET	82	48	24	10	2	278	210	108
(11) Chicago Blackhawks CHI	82	33	39	10	2	242	245	78
(13) Nashville Predators NSH	82	28	47	7	7	199	240	70
NORTHWEST DIVISION								
(3) Colorado Avalanche COL	82	42	29	11	1	233	201	96
(7) Edmonton Oilers EDM	82	32	34	16	8	226	212	88
(9) Vancouver Canucks VAN	82	30	37	15	8	227	237	83
(12) Calgary Flames CGY	82	31	41	10	5	211	256	77
PACIFIC DIVISION								
(2) Dallas Stars DAL	82	43	29	10	6	211	184	102
(5) Los Angeles Kings LA	82	39	31	12	4	245	228	94
(6) Phoenix Coyotes PHO	82	39	35	8	4	232	228	90
(8) San Jose Sharks SJ	82	35	37	10	7	225	214	87
(10) Anaheim Mighty Ducks ANA	82	34	36	12	3	217	227	83

OL - Overtime Losses, worth one point. (Introduced in 1999-2000 season)
Teams tied on points are separated by the number of victories.
Figure in brackets indicates overall Conference position.
The top eight teams in each conference qualify for the Stanley Cup playoffs.
Division leaders are seeded 1,2,3. Then seeding is determined by (a) points,
(b) wins, (c) points gained against tied teams, (d) goal difference. Top seed plays the
eighth seed, second plays seventh and so on.
* New franchise in 1999-2000

LEADING SCORERS

	GP	G	A	Pts	Pim
Jaromir Jagr PIT	63	42	54	96	50
Pavel Bure FLA	74	58	36	94	16
Mark Recchi PHI	82	28	63	91	50
Paul Kariya ANA	74	42	44	86	24
Teemu Selanne ANA	79	33	52	85	12
Owen Nolan SJ	78	44	40	84	110
Tony Amonte CHI	82	43	41	84	48
Mike Modano DAL	77	38	43	81	48
Joe Sakic COL	60	28	53	81	28
Steve Yzerman DET	78	35	44	79	34

LEADING NETMINDERS

	GPI	Mins	SoG	GA	Sv%
Ed Belfour DAL	62	3620	1571	127	91.9
Dominik Hasek BUF	35	2066	937	76	91.9
Jose Theodore MTL	30	1655	717	58	91.9
Brian Boucher PHI	35	2038	790	65	91.8
Olaf Kolzig WSH	73	4371	1957	163	91.7
Mike Vernon FLA	34	2791	1380	115	91.7

Qualifcation: 1,640 minutes

TEAM OF THE CENTURY

The Canadian national team that won the first Canada-Russia Summit Series in 1972 was voted the Team of the Century in a survey of editors and broadcasters conducted by the Canadian Press.

The staff of Canada's respected paper *The Hockey News* went with the Montreal Canadiens' Stanley Cup winning side of 1955-56.

SIN BIN

Players' Penalties	GP	Pim	Ave
Gordie Dwyer TB	24	135	5.62
Kelly Chase STL	25	118	4.72
Peter Worrell FLA	48	169	3.52

ALL STARS

Goal	**Olaf Kolzig** WSH
Defence	**Chris Pronger** STL
	Niklas Lidstrom DET
Centre	**Steve Yzerman** DET
Left-wing	**Brendan Shanahan** DET
Right-wing	**Jaromir Jagr** PIT

LEAGUE HIGHLIGHTS

Expensive players, cheap shots

St Louis Blues carried off the President's Trophy as the NHL's top team in a difficult season for the 83-year-old league.

The wonderful skills of the league's European contingent, led by Czech **Jaromir Jagr** and Russian **Pavel Bure**, only barely made up for the loss of superstars **Wayne Gretzky** (retired), Ottawa's **Alexei Yashin** (suspended all season in a contract dispute) and Philadelphia's **Eric Lindros** (three concussions).

Lindros, the league's highest paid player on US$8.5 million (£5.3 million), was controversially stripped of his captaincy in March after sustaining his fourth concussion in two seasons.

Coach **John Muckler** and GM **Neil Smith** were sacked after New York Rangers finished 23rd in the 28-team league despite splashing out a record $60 million on salaries. This level of spending continued to threaten the very existence of most of the NHL's Canadian teams.

Both Ottawa Senators and Montreal Canadiens were put up for sale, though Senators' owner, **Rod Bryden**, changed his mind after 87 per cent of the fans renewed their season tickets.

GRETZKY A COYOTE

Atlanta Thrashers made their debut in October (they finished last), Carolina Hurricanes drew a sell-out crowd of 18,730 to their first game in the new Raleigh Sports Arena, and Gretzky became part owner of Phoenix Coyotes.

The new four-on-four overtime system was declared a success but the referees continued to be criticised for not calling interference on the game's best players. Jagr's 96 points was the lowest total for years.

But **Brett Hull** scored his 610th goal to equal his father Bobby's NHL total and make the pair the only father-and-son duo in the 600-goal club.

The season was overshadowed by some of the most violent incidents in recent memory. By far the worst was **Marty McSorley**'s wild stick swing to the head of Boston Bruins' enforcer **Donald Brashear** in February.

McSorley, the brother of London Knights' coach Chris, was suspended for the rest of the season (23 games) and the playoffs and would need to meet with NHL Commissioner, **Gary Bettman** before being allowed to play again. He was later charged with 'assault with a weapon' and faced a trial in September 2000.

■ Toronto's **Tie Domi** was the league's best paid tough guy on US$1.55 million. Poor old Brashear earned only US$750,000.

The average player's salary in 1999-200 was $1.4 million.

STANLEY CUP 2000

All playoff series are decided over the best of seven games. Full details of the playoff system are in The Ice Hockey Annual 1996-97.

SERIES RESULTS

(Teams highest in standings first)

EASTERN CONFERENCE
Quarter-finals

Philadelphia-Buffalo	4-1
Washington-Pittsburgh	1-4
Toronto-Ottawa	4-2
New Jersey-Florida	4-0

Semi-Finals

Philadelphia-Pittsburgh	4-2
Toronto-New Jersey	2-4

Final

Philadelphia-New Jersey	3-4

WESTERN CONFERENCE
Quarter-finals

St Louis-San Jose	3-4
Dallas-Edmonton	4-1
Colorado-Phoenix	4-1
Detroit-Los Angeles	4-0

Semi-Finals

Dallas-San Jose	4-1
Colorado-Detroit	4-1

Final

Dallas-Colorado	4-3

STANLEY CUP FINAL

New Jersey-Dallas	4-2

7-3, 1-2, 2-1, 3-1, 0-1ot, 2-1ot

LEADING CUP SCORERS

	GP	G	A	Pts	Pim
Brett Hull DAL	23	11	13	24	4
Mike Modano DAL	23	10	13	23	10
Jason Arnott NJ	23	8	12	20	18
Patrik Elias NJ	23	7	13	20	9
Mark Recchi PHI	18	6	12	18	6
Peter Sykora NJ	23	9	8	17	10
Jaromir Jagr PIT	11	8	8	16	6

LEADING CUP NETMINDERS

	GPI	Mins	SoG	GA	Sv%
Ron Tugnutt PIT	11	746	398	22	94.5
Curtis Joseph TOR	12	729	369	25	93.2
Ed Belfour DAL	23	1443	651	45	93.1

CUP HIGHLIGHTS

Devils happy with Larry

New Jersey Devils won the Stanley Cup for the second time in five years after an epic six-game battle with defending champions Dallas Stars.

Games five and six of the 107th Cup final lasted an energy-sapping 3 hours, 14 minutes and 21 seconds. Though only four goals were scored in that time, both contests were highly entertaining and attracted the biggest TV audiences for the NHL in 20 years.

Jason Arnott's winner vindicated Devils' surprise decision in March to sack coach **Robbie Ftorek** and replace him with his assistant, former LA Kings mentor, **Larry Robinson**. And it was a great way for owner **John McMullen** to bow out after selling the team to the owners of basketball's Nets and baseball's Yankees for $175 million (about £120 million).

Overtime was not a big feature of the early rounds with only seven of 77 games failing to be settled in the usual 60 minutes. But game four between state rivals Philadelphia and Pittsburgh ground on for five overtime periods before **Keith Primeau's** goal ended the third longest OT ever.

GIANT-KILLING SHARKS

League runners-up Washington Capitals made their traditional early exit, but when President's Trophy winners, St Louis Blues, were knocked out by giant-killers San Jose Sharks, it was the first time in nine years that the regular season champs had gone out in the first round.

In the Conference finals, there were two questions - would superstar **Eric Lindros**, who had suffered his third concussion of the season, be fit and, if not, would his Philadelphia Flyers miss him?

Flyers faced the Devils in an epic seven-gamer in the East. Devils took the first game, 4-1, but when they dropped the next three the normally mild-mannered Robinson lost his cool. His tirade to his disorganised team could be heard through the dressing room walls.

Devils got the message, won game five in Philly, 4-1, and by the time Lindros returned New Jersey were on a roll, winning game six 2-1.

In his first shift of game seven - would you credit it? - Lindros was smacked in mid-ice by a huge, but clean, bodycheck from **Scott Stevens**. He had to be helped off the ice with another suspected concussion and his future was put in serious doubt. Devils went on to complete a rare three-game comeback with a 2-1 victory.

In the West, Colorado-Dallas also went the full distance with neither club going more than one game up. Game seven was all over by 5.31 when Stars took a 3-0 lead.

AWARD WINNERS

Art Ross Trophy (Most Points)
Jaromir Jagr, Pittsburgh Penguins

Maurice 'Rocket' Richard Trophy (Most Goals)
Pavel Bure, Florida Panthers

Hart Memorial Trophy (Most Valuable Player)
Chris Pronger, St Louis Blues

James Norris Mem'l Trophy (Best Defenceman)
Chris Pronger, St Louis Blues

Vezina Trophy (Best Goaltender)
Olaf Kolzig, Washington Capitals

William Jennings Trophy (Goaltending average)
Roman Turek/Jamie McLennan, St Louis Blues

Lester B Pearson Trophy (Players' Player)
Jaromir Jagr, Pittsburgh Penguins

Calder Memorial Trophy (Rookie of the Year)
Scott Gomez, New Jersey Devils

Lady Byng Mem'l Trophy (Most Sportsmanlike)
Pavol Demitra, St Louis Blues

Frank J Selke Trophy (Defensive Forward)
Steve Yzerman, Detroit Red Wings

Jack Adams Award (Coach of the Year)
Joel Quenneville, St Louis Blues

Conn Smythe Trophy (Playoff MVP)
Scott Stevens, New Jersey Devils

Bill Masterton Memorial Trophy (Most Dedicated)
Ken Daneyko, New Jersey Devils

King Clancy Memorial Trophy (Leadership)
Curtis Joseph, Toronto Maple Leafs

MINOR LEAGUE PLAYOFF WINNERS

American League (Calder Cup)
Hartford Wolf Pack

International League (Turner Cup)
Chicago Wolves

East Coast League (Kelly Cup)
Peoria Rivermen

Central League (Bill Levins Trophy)
Indianapolis Ice

United League (Colonial Cup)
Flint Generals

Western Pro League (President's Cup)
Shreveport Mudbugs

West Coast League (Taylor Cup)
Phoenix Mustangs

Canadian (Major Junior A) Hockey League
(Memorial Cup) **Rimouski Oceanic**

HALL OF FAME

The following were elected to the Hockey Hall of Fame in November 1999:

Wayne Gretzky

The Great One was elected to the Hall only months after his retirement in April 1999 following 21 record-shattering seasons, all bar one of them in the NHL.

The normal waiting period after retirement is three years. The Hall's board of directors decided that Gretzky will be last person to be 'fast-tracked' for entry.

The superstar was the NHL's leading scorer ten times and its most valuable player on nine occasions. He won four Stanley Cups with Edmonton Oilers, three Canada Cups with the national team, and set 61 NHL records.

Our tribute to him appeared in The Ice Hockey Annual 1999-2000.

Several times at his induction he told his huge audience: "I miss the game more than the game misses Wayne Gretzky."

Andy van Hellemond

Andy van Hellemond was the NHL's top ranked referee for 14 successive seasons and 18 in all. He worked a remarkable 19 Stanley Cup finals in a career that began in 1972-73. When he retired in 1996 he had refereed a record 1,475 league games and 227 playoff contests.

Now director of operations in the East Coast Hockey League, van Hellemond had a reputation for being the man to turn to for important games.

"You knew he was taking the game as seriously as the players were," said **Bill Torrey**, the former GM with New York Islanders. "He officiated with confidence, a bit of arrogance."

Ian 'Scotty' Morrison

Surely the only man to join the Hall while wearing a kilt in honour of his Scottish roots (Gretzky was heard to mutter 'thank God I'm Polish'), Scotty Morrison was elected as one of the game's builders.

He was the NHL's youngest ref. in 1954 at the age of 24 and in 1965 he became the league's referee-in-chief. In 1986 he was appointed president of the Hall of Fame and oversaw the Hall's move to its present site from the Canadian National Exhibition.

Russ Conway

Sports editor of the Eagle-Tribune newspaper of Lawrence, Massachusetts, who exposed the wrong-doing of **Alan Eagleson**, the disgraced former boss of the NHL Players Association.

Richard Garneau

Montreal Canadiens' radio and TV play-by-play commentator who called the action for nine Stanley Cup winning Canadiens' teams.

OBITUARIES

MAURICE 'ROCKET' RICHARD

The photo in the morning paper showed Montreal Canadiens' star forward, **'Rocket' Richard**, dazed and bloodied, shaking hands with Boston Bruins' goalie, **'Sugar' Jim Henry**.

Richard, the finest player of his era, had just scored his greatest goal which won the 1952 Stanley Cup semi-final against the Bruins. He had been knocked unconscious in the first period but insisted on going back out in the third.

With four minutes to go he leaped into the fray, gathered a loose puck, powered past two Bruins and beat Henry for the winner. He went into convulsions in the Canadiens' dressing room and had to be sedated. "That beautiful bastard," said a reporter, "he scored semi-conscious."

When Richard died in May 2000, age 78, almost 3,000 people attended his funeral in Montreal's Notre Dame Basilica which attracted a who's who of hockey and politics rarely seen together. Earlier, an estimated 115,000 had filed past his open casket in the Molson Centre.

Joseph-Henri-Maurice Richard was one of eight children of a mechanic on the Canadian Pacific Railway.

The first player in 1944-45 to score 50 goals in 50 games, the Montreal-born right-winger went on to score 544 goals in 978 league games spread over 18 seasons, more games and more goals than any other player at the time.

His astonishing speed and the aggressive determination of his attacks earned him the nickname of 'Rocket'. He was listed at fifth in the list of *100 Top NHL Players of All Time* compiled by *The Hockey News* of Canada; in his native Quebec he was revered like royalty.

When he was suspended for three games by NHL president **Clarence Campbell** in 1955 for striking a linesman who had tried to break up a fight, there were riots in the streets of Montreal. Some believe the trouble led directly to the growth of militant French-Canadian nationalism.

On his retirement in 1960, he held 17 scoring records and though some were beaten, the 50-goal mark would always remain Richard's. His achievements came when the NHL comprised only six teams and the competition was far more intense.

Once he wore Detroit Red Wings' defenceman, **Earl Seibert**, like a coat before scoring. Seibert's coach, **Jack Adams**, berated him on the bench but the blueliner held up a gloved hand. "Mr Adams," he said, "I'm 6ft, 2in. Any man who can carry me on his back from the blueline in deserves to score."

Richard and his wife, who died in 1994, had seven children.

Hall of Famer **SID ABEL**, who died in February 2000, aged 81, was the centreman on Detroit Red Wings' famous Production Line of the Forties and Fifties with **Gordie Howe** and **'Terrible' Ted Lindsay**.

The trio helped Red Wings to win three Stanley Cups; Lindsay, followed by captain Abel and Howe, were 1-2-3 in NHL scoring in 1949-50.

Abel won the Hart Trophy as the league's most valuable player in 1948-49, the year he led the NHL in goals with 28.

Detroit's Winged Wheel emblem went all the way through him as he coached the Red Wings for ten-and-a-half seasons, served as the team's broadcaster and coached or managed their farm teams.

ROY EDWARDS, age 62. NHL goalie with Detroit and Pittsburgh 1967-74. Won the World Championship with Canada (Whitby Dunlops) in 1958 with three shutouts and a 0.86 average.

'Cowboy' BILL FLETT, a colourful character who played 13 NHL seasons, died on 16 July 1999 after a failed liver transplant. He was 55.

He was best known as a member of the Philadelphia Flyers during their Broad Street Bullies days in the Seventies and he assisted **Bobby Clarke** on the 1974 Stanley Cup winning goal.

ED KEA, 51, a nine-year veteran of the NHL with Atlanta Flames and St Louis Blues, drowned at his summer cottage in Parry Sound, Ontario.

A rugged defenceman, in 1983 he hit his head on the ledge of the boards following a hard but clean hit while playing in the Central League and suffered irreparable brain damage.

BILL QUAKENBUSH, a member of the Hall of Fame and the first defenceman to win the Lady Byng Trophy for gentlemanly conduct, died in September 1999, aged 77.

He received the Byng Trophy in 1948-49 after a penalty-free 60 games with Boston Bruins. He admitted he was no good at body-checking. "I always tried to get the puck first," he said.

As well as Bruins, he played six seasons with Detroit Red Wings in his 13-year NHL career, scoring 62 goals and 284 points, with just 89 penalty minutes in his 774 games.

HOWIE YOUNG, one of pro hockey's most colourful characters, died in November 1999, aged 62. Known for his fun-loving nature, he played only three NHL seasons in a career marred by alcohol abuse and a bad boy image.

In 336 games in the Sixties, he scored 74 points and accumulated 851 penalty minutes.

USEFUL ADDRESSES

ICE HOCKEY UK LTD

Chairman: Jim Anderson.
Administrator: Gill Short, Galleries of Justice, Shire Hall, High Pavement, Nottingham NG1 1HN.
Tel: 0115-915-9204. Fax: 0115-915-1376.
e-mail: hockey@ukhockey.freeserve.co.uk
website: www.icehockeyuk.co.uk

ICE HOCKEY SUPERLEAGUE LTD

Chairman: David Davies.
Chief Executive: Ian Taylor.
League Secretary: Brian Storey, Grange Farm Business Park, Hugglescote, Leicester LE67 2BT. Tel: 01530-838899. Fax: 01530-830055.
e-mail: bstorey@btconnect.co.uk
website: www.iceweb.co.uk

BRITISH NAT. ICE HOCKEY LGE LTD

Chairman: Tom Muir.
General Manager: Gary Stefan.
Secretary: Stan Wiltshire, Henleaze House, 13 Harbury Road, Henleaze, Bristol BS9 4PN.
Tel/Fax: 0117-907-8783.
e-mail: admin@britnatleague.co.uk
website: www.britnatleague.co.uk

ENGLISH ICE HOCKEY ASSOCIATION

Chairman: Ken Taggart.
Secretary: Bill Britton, 7 Laughton Avenue, West Bridgford, Notts NG2 7GJ.
Tel/Fax No: 0115-923-1461.
website: www.eiha.co.uk

SCOTTISH ICE HOCKEY ASSN.

President: Frank Dempster.
Chairman: Jack Dryburgh.
Secretary: Joe Guilcher, 9 Morton Avenue, Clements Park, Dundee DD2 8NA.
Tel/Fax: 01382-523255.

N IRELAND ICE HOCKEY ASSN.

Chairman: Andrew Gibson.
Secretary: Barbara McCarter, 33 Hillsborough Drive, Belfast BT6 9DS.
Tel: 02890-283276. Fax: 02890-484049.

ENGLAND WOMEN'S ICE HOCKEY ASSOCIATION

Chairman: Bill Britton.
Secretary: Helen Ensor, 27 Wheatley Grove, Sheffield S13 8HZ.
Tel: 0114-269-8066.
website: www.eiha.co.uk

ICE HOCKEY PLAYERS ASSOCIATION (GB)

Secretary: Joanne Collins, 25 Caxton Avenue, Addlestone, Weybridge, Surrey KT15 1LJ.
Tel: 01932-843660. Fax: 01932-844401.
e-mail: ihpa@virgin.net
website: www.ihpa.co.uk

BRITISH ICE HOCKEY WRITERS' ASSOCIATION

Chairman: Andy Costigan.
Secretary: Tony Allen, Flat 3, 45 Rita Road, London SW8 1JX. Tel/fax: 0207-582-7747.
e-mail: idletonyallen@yahoo.co.uk
website: www.bihwa.co.uk

GB SUPPORTERS CLUB

Secretary: Annette Petrie, 65 Leas Drive, Iver, Bucks SL0 9RB. Tel/Fax: 01753-710778.
e-mail: gbsc@vossnet.co.uk
website: www.gbsc.co.uk/

ICE HOCKEY UK LTD

The Board of Directors of the sport's national governing body are:
Jim Anderson (chairman), **John Fisher, Neville Moralee, Gary Stefan, Richard Stirling**.
Further members were to be elected at the Board's AGM in Spetember.

CLUB DIRECTORY 2000-01

ABERDEEN

Rink Address: Linx Ice Arena, Beach Leisure Centre, Beach Esplanade, Aberdeen AB2 1NR. **Tel**: 01224-655406/7. **Fax**: 01224-648693. **Ice Size**: 184 x 85 feet (56 x 26 metres). **Spectator Capacity**: 1,200 **Club Secretary**: Colette Cowie, 18 Woodhill Terrace, Aberdeen AB. **Tel**: 01224-312250. **Senior Team**: Alligators (Scottish Nat League). **Colours**: *home*: Green, White & Black; *away*: Black, Green & White.

ALEXANDRA PALACE

Rink Address: The Ice Rink, Alexandra Palace, Wood Green, London N22 4AY. **Tel**: 0208-365-2121. **Fax**: 0208-444-3439. **Ice Size**: 184 x 85 feet (56 x 26 metres). **Spectator Capacity**: 1,250. **Club Secretary**: Harvey Wroe, 10 Firs Avenue, Muswell Hill, London N10 3LY. **Tel**: 020-888-5469. **Fax**: 0208-444-3439. **Senior Team**: Haringey Greyhounds (English Premier League). **Colours**: Blue & Gold.

ALTRINCHAM

Rink Address: Devonshire Road, Altrincham, Cheshire WA14 4EZ. **Tel**: 0161-926-8316. **Fax**: 0161-927-7632. **Ice Size**: 190 x 85 feet (58 x 26 metres). **Spectator Capacity**: 1,800. **Communications to**: Joe Torraca at the rink. **Senior Team**: Aces (English Nat Lge North). **Colours**: *Home*: White, Red & Black; *away*: Black, Red & White. **website**: www.alt-ice-rink.demon.co.uk/aces.htm

AYR

Arena Address: Centrum Arena, Ayr Road, Prestwick KA9 1TR. **Tel**: 01292-678822. **Fax**: 01292-678833. **Ice Size**: 200 x 103 feet (61 x 31.5 metres). **Spectator Capacity**: 2,745. **Senior teams**: Scottish Eagles (Superleague) and Bruins (Scottish National League). **Club Secretaries**: *Eagles* - Ken MacLeod at Centrum. **Tel**: 01292-281311. **website**: www.scottish-eagles.com *Bruins* - Adeline Andrews, 3 Hollybank, Viewpark, Ayr KA7 3PW. **Tel**: 01292-265800. **Colours**: *Eagles* - *Home*: White, Green, Orange & Gold; *away*: Green, Orange, Gold & Black.

BASINGSTOKE

Rink Address: Planet Ice Basingstoke Arena, Basingstoke Leisure Park, Worting Road, Basingstoke, Hants RG22 6PG. **Tel**: 01256-355266. **Fax**: 01256-357367. **Ice Size:** 197 x 98 feet (60 x 30 metres) **Spectator Capacity:** 1,600. **Communications to:** Charlie Colon at the rink. **Senior Team:** Bison (British National League). **Colours:** *home*: White, Red & Silver; *away*: Red & Silver. **website** www.bstokebison.co.uk

BELFAST

Arena scheduled to open in December 2000. Information available at press-time. **Arena Address**: Odyssey Arena, Queen's Quay, Belfast BT3. **Ice Size**: 197 x 98 feet (60 x 30 metres). **Spectator Capacity** (for ice hockey): 8,000. **Address**: Belfast Giants Ltd, Unit 2, Ormeau Business Park, 8 Cromac Avenue, Belfast BT7 2JA. **Tel**: 028-9059-1111. **Fax**: 028-9059-1212. **Team**: Giants (Superleague). **Colours**: *home*: White, Red & Teal; *away*: Teal, White & Red. **website** (unofficial): members.aol.com/hockeyni/belfast-giants/

DUNDONALD
Rink Address: Dundonald International Ice Bowl, 111 Old Dundonald Road, Dundonald, Co Down, N Ireland. **Tel**: 02890-482611. **Fax**: 02890-489604. **Ice Size:** 197 x 98 feet (60 x 30 metres). **Spectator Capacity**: 1,500. **Senior Team**: Goldwings (Scottish Nat. League) **Club Secretary**: David Gibson, 43 Rossdale Heights, Cairns Hill Road, Belfast BT8 4XZ. **Tel/fax**: 02890-403505.

BILLINGHAM

Rink Address: Billingham Forum Leisure Centre, Town Centre, Billingham, Cleveland TS23 2OJ. **Tel/Fax:** 01642-551381.
Ice Size: 180 x 80 feet (55 x 24 metres)
Spectator Capacity: 1,200.
Club Secretary: Brian McCabe, 7 Cranstock Close, Billingham, Cleveland TS22 5RS.
Tel: 01642-534458.
Senior Team: Eagles (English Nat Lge North).
Colours: Home: White/Red; away: Red/White.

BIRMINGHAM

Rink Address: Planet Ice Birmingham Arena, Pershore Street, Birmingham B5 4RW
Tel: 0121-693-2400. **Fax:** 0121-693-2401
Ice Size: 180 x 80 feet (55 x 24 metres)
Spectator Capacity: 300
Communications to: David Graham at the rink.
Senior Team: Rockets (English Nat Lge South)
Colours: Black, gold, red & blue.

BLACKBURN

Rink Address: Blackburn Arena, Lower Audley, Waterside, Blackburn, Lancs BB1 1BB.
Tel: 01254-263063/668686. **Fax:** 01254-691516.
Ice Size: 197 x 98 feet (60 x 30 metres)
Spectator Capacity: 3,200.
Communications to: Bobby Haig at the rink.
Senior Team: Hawks (English Nat Lge North)
Colours: Pacific Teal, Grey, Black & White.

BRACKNELL

Rink Address: John Nike Leisuresport Complex, John Nike Way, Bracknell, Berks RG12 4TN.
Tel: 01344-789000, **Fax:** 01344-789201.
Ice Size: 197 x 98 feet (60 x 30 metres)
Spectator Capacity: 3,100.
Club Secretary: Jane McDougall at the rink.
e-mail: bracknellbees@hotmail.com
Senior Team: Bees (Superleague).
Colours: home: White, Gold & Black; away: Black, Gold & White. **website:** www.bees.nu/

BRADFORD

Rink Address: Great Cause, Little Horton Lane, Bradford, Yorks BD5 0AE.
Tel: 01274-729091. **Fax:** 01274-778818.
Ice Size: 180 x 80 feet (55 x 24 metres)
Spectator Capacity: 700.
Club Secretary: Phil Lewis, Glendair, Gawthorpe Drive, Bingley, W Yorks BD16 4DH.
Tel: 01274-567735.
Senior Team: Bulldogs (English Nat Lge North).
Colours: White, Green & Black.

BRISTOL

Rink Address: John Nike Leisuresport Bristol Ice Rink, Frogmore Street, Bristol BS1 5NA.
Tel: 0117-929-2148. **Fax:** 0117-925-9736.
Ice Size: 180 x 80 feet (55 x 24 metres).
Spectator Capacity: 650.
Club Secretary: Mary Faunt, c/o the rink.
Juniors only 2000-01.

CAMBRIDGE UNIVERSITY

No home ice 2000-01. Recreational.
Communications to: Craig Steeves, Dept of Engineering, University of Cambridge, Trumpington Street, Cambridge
e-mail: icehockey@cus.cam.ac.uk
Colours: Light Blue & White.
website:
www.cam.ac.uk/CambUniv/Societies/cuihc/main.htm

CARDIFF

Rink Address: The BT Ice House, Hayes Bridge Road, Cardiff CF1 2GH.
Tel: 02920-397198, **Fax:** 02920-397160.
Ice Size: 184 x 85 feet (56 x 26 metres).
Spectator Capacity: 2,700.
Communications to: Andy French at the rink.
e-mail: cardiffdevils@www.cwtc.co.uk
Senior Team: Devils (Superleague).
Colours: home: White, Red & Black; away: Red, Black & White.
Website: www.cardiffdevils.co.uk

CHELMSFORD

Rink Address: Riverside Ice & Leisure Centre, Victoria Road, Chelmsford, Essex CM1 1FG.
Tel: 01245-615050. **Fax:** 01245-615056.
Ice Size: 184 x 85 feet (56 x 26 metres).
Spectator Capacity: 1,200.
Club Secretary: Sylvian Clifford, 14 Windrush Drive, Springfield, Chelmsford CM1 7QF.
Tel No: 01245-259181. **Fax:** 01245-352880.
Senior Team: Chieftains (English Premier Lge).
Colours: home: White/Blue/Red; away: Blue/White/Red.
Website: www.osts.co.uk/chieftains/

COVENTRY

Rink Address: Planet Ice at Skydome Arena, Skydome Coventry, Croft Road, Coventry CV1 3AZ. **Tel:** 024-7663 0693. **Fax:** 024-7663 0674
Ice Size: 184 x 92 feet (56 x 28 metres)
Spectator Capacity (for ice hockey): 3,000.
Communications to: Michelle Wilson, Blaze Promotions Ltd, Centre Court, 1301 Stratford Road, Hall Green, Birmingham B28 9HH.
Tel: 0121-702-2481. **Fax:** 0121-777-7298.
e-mail: blaze@charman.prestel.co.uk
Senior Team: Blaze (British National League).
Colours: *Home:* White & Navy Blue; *away:* Navy Blue & White.
website: www.blaze.clara.net

DUMFRIES

Rink Address: The Ice Bowl, King Street, Dumfries DG2 9AN.
Tel: 01387-251300, **Fax:** 01387-251686.
Ice Size: 184 x 95 feet (56 x 29 metres).
Spectator Capacity: 1,000.
Club Secretary: Sandra Edgar, 5 St Anne's Road, Dumfries DG2 9HZ. **Tel:** 01387-264010.
Senior Team: Solway Sharks (Scot. Nat. Lge).
Colours: blue, white & green.
website: www.solways.freeserve.co.uk

DUNDEE

Rink scheduled to open in September 2000. Information available at press-time.
Rink Address: Camperdown Leisure Park, Kingsway West, Dundee.
Ice Size: 197 x 98 feet (60 x 30 metres).
Spectator Capacity: 2,400.
Club Secretary: Joe Guilcher, 9 Merton Avenue, Clement Park, Dundee DD2 3NA.
Tel/fax: 01382-523255.
Senior Team: Tigers (Scottish Nat. League).
Colours: *home:* White, Gold & Black; *away:* Black, Gold & White.

EDINBURGH

Rink Address: Murrayfield Ice Rink, Riversdale Crescent, Murrayfield, Edinburgh EH12 5XN.
Tel: 0131-337-6933, **Fax:** 0131-346-2951.
Ice Size: 200 x 97 feet (61 x 29.5 metres).
Spectator Capacity: 3,800.
Communications to: Scott Neil at the rink.
Tel/fax: 0131-313-2977.
e-mail: edcapitals@aol.com
Senior Teams: Capitals (British National Lge) and Murrayfield Raiders (Scottish Nat Lge).
Colours: Capitals - *Home:* White, Red & Blue; *away:* Red, White & Blue.
website: members.aol.com/edcapitals/

FIFE

Rink Address: Fife Ice Arena, Rosslyn Street, Kirkcaldy, Fife KY1 3HS.
Tel: 01592-595100. **Fax:** 01592-595200.
Ice Size: 193.5 x 98 feet (59 x 30 metres).
Spectator Capacity: 3,280.
Communications to: Tom Muir at the Arena.
Tel: 01592-651076.
e-mail: fifeflyers@cableinet.co.uk
Senior Teams: Flyers (British National League) and Kirkcaldy Kestrels (Scottish Nat League).
Colours: Flyers - *Home:* White, Gold & Blue; *away:* Blue, White & Gold.
Website: www.fifeflyers.co.uk

FLINTSHIRE

Rink Address: Deeside Ice Rink, Leisure Centre, Chester Road West, Queensferry, Clwyd CH5 5HA.
Tel: 01244-814725. **Fax:** 01244-836287.
Ice Size: 197 x 98 feet (60 x 30 metres).
Spectator Capacity: 1,200.
Communications to: Mike Walshe at the rink.
e-mail: mstokes@compuserve.com
Senior Team: Freeze (English Nat Lge North).
Colours: *home:* White, Purple & Green; *away:* Green, Purple & White.

GILLINGHAM

Rink Address: The Ice Bowl, Ambley Road, Gillingham Business Park, Gillingham, Kent ME8 0PP.
Tel: 01634-377244. **Fax:** 01634-374065.
Ice Size: 184 x 85 feet (56 x 26 metres).
Spectator Capacity: 1,500.
Club Secretary: Jackie Mason, 17 Beckenham Drive, Maidstone, Kent ME16 0TG.
Tel/Fax: 01622-671065. **Fax:** 01622-754360.
e-mail: jackie@community-centre.demon.co.uk
Senior Team: Invicta Dynamos (Eng Prem Lge).
Colours: *Home:* White, Black, Green & Red; *Away:* Red, Green, Black & White.
website: www.cableinet.co.uk/david.trevallion/dynamos

GOSPORT

Rink Address: Forest Way, Fareham Road, Gosport, Hants. PO13 0ZX.
Tel: 02392-511217. **Fax:** 02392-510445.
Ice Size: 145 x 73 feet (44 x 22 metres).
Spectator Capacity: 800.
Club Secretary: Peter Marshall, 15 Islands Close, Hayling Island, Hants PO11 0NA.
Tel: 02392-466809.
Juniors only 2000-01

GRIMSBY

Rink Address: The Leisure Centre, Cromwell Road, Grimsby, South Humberside DN31 2BH. **Tel:** 01472-323100. **Fax:** 01472-323102.
Ice Size: 120 x 60 feet (36.5 x 18 metres).
Spectator Capacity: 1,300.
Club Secretary: Allan Woodhead, Weelsby Park Riding School, Weelsby Road, Grimsby, South Humberside DN32 8PL.
Tel: 01472-346127/355562.
Senior Team: Buffaloes (English Nat Lge North) **Colours:** *Home:* Red & White, *away:* Black, White & Red.

GUILDFORD

Rink Address: Spectrum Ice Rink, Parkway, Guildford GU1 1UP.
Tel: 01483-444777. **Fax:** 01483-443311.
Ice Size: 197 x 98 feet (60 x 30 metres).
Spectator Capacity: 2,200.
Communications to: Malcolm Norman at rink.
Tel: 01483-452244, **Fax:** 01483-443373.
e-mail: flames@guildfordflames.com
Senior Team: Flames (British National League).
Colours: *Home:* Gold, Red & Black; *away:* Black, Red & Gold.
website: www.guildfordflames.com

HULL

Rink Address: The Hull Arena, Kingston Park, Hull HU1 2DZ.
Tel: 01482-325252. **Fax:** 01482-216066.
Ice Size: 197 x 98 feet (60 x 30 metres).
Spectator Capacity: 2,000.
Communications to: Glenn Meier at the rink.
Tel/Fax: 01482-211983.
e-mail: mizey13@hotmail.com
Senior Team: Thunder (British National Lge).
Colours: *Home:* White/purple/black, *away:* Purple/black/silver.
Website: www.hullthunder.demon.co.uk

IRVINE

Rink Address: Magnum Leisure Centre, Harbour Street, Irvine, Strathclyde KA12 8PD.
Tel: 01294-278381. **Fax:** 01294-311228.
Ice Size: 150 x 95 feet (45.5 x 29 metres).
Spectator Capacity: 750.
Club Secretary: Jennifer Wilson, 18 Woodfield Road, Ayr KA8 8LZ. **Tel/Fax:** 01292-263739.
Senior Team: Magnum Flyers (Scottish Lge).
Colours: Red, White & Blue.

ISLE OF WIGHT

Rink Address: Planet Ice Ryde Arena, Quay Road, Esplanade, Ryde, I of Wight PO33 2HH.
Tel: 01983-615155. **Fax:** 01983-567460.
Ice Size: 165 x 80 feet (50 x 24 metres)
Spectator Capacity: 1,000.
Communications to: Mavis Siddons at the rink.
Senior Team: Raiders (English Premier Lge).
Colours: *Home:* White, Black & Purple; *away:* Black & Purple.
website: members.aol.com/wightraid/index.htm

KILMARNOCK

Rink Address: Galleon Leisure Centre, 99 Titchfield Street, Kilmarnock, Ayr KA1 1QY.
Tel: 01563-524014. **Fax:** 01563-572395.
Ice Size: 146 x 75 feet (44.6 x 23 metres)
Spectator Capacity: 200
Club Secretary: Mrs Alison Crockatt, 58 Main Street, Ochiltree, Strathclyde.
Tel: 01290-700550.
Team: Avalanche (Scottish Nat. League).

LEE VALLEY

Rink Address: Lee Valley Ice Centre, Lea Bridge Road, Leyton, London E10 7QL.
Tel: 0208-533-3156. **Fax No:** 0208-446-8068.
Ice Size: 184 x 85 feet (56 x 26 metres).
Spectator Capacity: 1,000.
Communications to: Mike Smith at the rink.
Juniors only 2000-01.

LONDON

Arena Address: London Arena, Limeharbour, London E14 9TH.
Tel: 0207-538-8880. **Fax:** 0207-538-5572.
Ice Size: 197 x 98 feet (60 x 30 metres).
Spectator Capacity: 10,000.
Communications to: Paula George, Anschutz Sports Holdings Ltd, 36 Harbour Exchange Square, London E14 9GE.
Tel: 0207-536-2604. **Fax:** 0207-536-2603.
Senior Team: Knights (Superleague).
Colours: *home:* White, Red, Blue & Gold; *away:* Red, Blue, White & Gold.
website: www.knightice.co.uk/

MANCHESTER

Arena Address: *Manchester Evening News* Arena, 21 Hunts Bank, Victoria Exchange, Manchester M3 1AR.
Tel: 0161-950-4000. **Fax:** 0161-950-6000.
Ice Size: 197 x 98 feet (60 x 30 metres).
Spectator Capacity: 17,250 (for ice hockey).
Communications to: Terry Christensen (x4002) or Joanne Houlcroft (x5335) at the Arena.
Senior Team: Storm (Superleague).
Colours: *Home:* White, Purple, Blue, Grey & Black; *away:* Black, Purple, Blue & Grey.
Website: www.manchesterstorm.com/

MILTON KEYNES

Rink Address: Planet Ice Milton Keynes Arena, The Leisure Plaza, 1 South Row, (off Childs Way H6), Central Milton Keynes, Bucks MK9 1BL.
Tel: 01908-696696. **Fax:** 01908-690890.
Ice Size: 197 x 98 feet (60 x 30 metres)
Spectator Capacity: 2,200.
Communications to: Mike Darnell, Milton Keynes Ice Hockey Ltd, PO Box 617, Milton Keynes MK6 2ZJ. **Tel/Fax:** 01908-662981.
e-mail: info@mk-kings.demon.co.uk
Senior Team: Kings (British National League)
Colours: *Home:* White & Blue; *away:* blue.
website: www.mk-kings.demon.co.uk

NEWCASTLE

Arena Address: *Telewest* Arena, Arena Way, off Railway Street, Newcastle-on-Tyne NE4 7NA.
Tel: 0191-260-5000. **Fax:** 0191-260-2200.
Ice Size: 197 x 98 feet (60 x 30 metres).
Spectator Capacity: 7,000 (for ice hockey).
Communications to: Mike O'Connor at Arena.
Tel: 0191-260-2327. **Fax:** 0191-260-2328
Senior Team: Jesters (Superleague).
Colours: *Home:* Light Blue, Red & Gold; *away:* Dark Blue, Red & Gold.
website *(to be changed):* www.riverkings.co.uk

NOTTINGHAM

Rink Address: National Ice Centre, Lower Parliament Street, Nottingham NG1 1LA.
Tel: 0115-853-3000. **Fax:** 0115-853-3034.
Ice Size: 197 x 98 feet (60 x 30 metres).
Spectator Capacity (for ice hockey): 7,500.
Communications to: Gary Moran/Simon Moor.
Panthers' Office Tel: 0115-941-3103.
Fax: 0115-941-8754. .
e-mail: office@panthers.demon.co.uk
Senior Team: Panthers (Superleague).
Colours: *Home:* White, Gold & Red; *away:* Black, Gold & Red.
Website: www.panthers.co.uk

OXFORD

Rink Address: The Ice Rink, Oxpens Road, Oxford OX1 1RX.
Tel: 01865-248076. **Fax:** 01865-243163.
Ice Size: 184 x 85 feet (56 x 26 metres).
Spectator Capacity: 1,025.
Club Secretary: Paul Ager, 18 Queen's Road, Kingston, Surrey KT2 7SN.
Tel: 0208-546-3828.
Senior Team: City Stars (Eng Nat Lge South)
Colours: Dark Blue & White.
website: www.crockett32.freeserve.co.uk

OXFORD UNIVERSITY

Home Ice: Oxpens Road, Oxford OX1 1RX.
Communications to: Jon Finer, OUIHC Captain, Balliol College, Oxford OX1 3BJ.
Tel: 01865-277777. **Fax:** 01865-277803.
e-mail: jonathan.finer@balliol.ox.ac.uk
Colours: Dark Blue and White.
website: users.ox.ac.uk/~crushtab/proto.html
Recreational.

PAISLEY

Rink Address: Lagoon Leisure Complex, Mill Street, Paisley PA1 1LZ.
Tel: 0141-889-4000. **Fax:** 0141-848-0078.
Ice Size: 184 x 85 feet (56 x 26 metres).
Spectator Capacity: 1,000.
Communications to: Alan Smith at the rink.
Tel/Fax: 0141-561-8007
Senior Team: Pirates (British National League) and Mohawks (Scottish National League).
Colours: *Home:* White/Red; *away:* Black/Red.
Website: www.paisleypirates.com

PERTH

Rink Address: Dewars Ice Rink, Glover Street, Perth PH2 0TH.
Tel: 01738-624188. **Fax:** 01738-637812.
Ice Size: 151 x 118 feet (46 x 36 metres).
Spectator Capacity: 500.
Club Secretary: Gillian Latto, 14 Ruthven Street, Auchterarder, Perth PH3.
Tel: 01764-664480.
Perth Panthers are playing their Scottish National League games away.

PETERBOROUGH

Rink Address: Planet Ice Peterborough Arena, 1 Mallard Road, Bretton, Peterborough, Cambs PE3 8YN.
Tel: 01733-260222. **Fax:** 01733-261021.
Ice Size: 184 x 85 feet (56 x 26 metres).
Spectator Capacity: 1,500.
Communications to: Doug McEwen at the rink.
Tel: 01733-331441. **Fax:** 01733-331322
Senior Team: Pirates (British National League).
Colours: *Home*: White, Orange & Black; *Away*: Orange, Black & White.
website: www.peterboroughpirates.freeserve.co.uk/

ROMFORD

Rink Address: Rom Valley Way, Romford, Essex RM7 0AE.
Tel: 01708-724731. **Fax:** 01708-733609.
Ice Size: 184 x 85 feet (56 x 26 metres).
Spectator Capacity: 1,500.
Club Secretary: Cathy Evans at the rink.
Senior Team: Raiders (English Premier Lge).
Colours: *Home*: White, Gold & Blue; *away*: Blue, White & Gold.
website: welcome.to/romfordraiders

SHEFFIELD

Arena Address: Sheffield Arena, Broughton Lane, Sheffield S9 2DF. **Tel:** 0114-256-5656.
Ice Size: 197 x 98 feet (60 x 30 metres).
Spectator Capacity: 8,500.
Communications to: Betty Wareing, Sheffield Steelers Ice Hockey Club Ltd, Stonerow Way, Parkgate, Rotherham S60 1SG.
Tel: 01709-514772. **Fax:** 01709-514775.
e-mail: steelers@ssihcl.demon.co.uk
Senior Team: Steelers (Superleague).
Colours: *Home*: White, Blue, Orange & Teal; *away*: Black, Blue, Orange & Teal.
website: www.steelers.co.uk.
NOTE **Sheffield Scimitars** play in English Nat Lge North at the Sheffield Ice Sports Centre, Queens Road, Sheffield S2 4DF. *Tel*: 0114-272-3037. *Club Secretary*: Keith Leland, 'Lyndene', Rotherham Road, Halfway, Sheffield S20 8GL. *Tel*: 0114-251-0663.

SLOUGH

Rink Address: The Ice Arena, Montem Lane, Slough, Berks SL1 2QG.
Tel: 01753-821555. **Fax**: 01753-824977.
Ice Size: 184 x 85 feet (56 x 26 metres).
Spectator Capacity: 1,500.
Communications to: Pauline Rost at the rink.
Tel: 01753-822658. **Fax**: 01753-823361.
Senior Team: Jets (British National League).
Colours: *Home*: White, Blue & Red; *away*: Blue, White & Red.
website: www.sloughjets.com

SOLIHULL

Rink Address: Hobs Moat Road, Solihull, West Midlands B92 8JN.
Tel: 0121-742-5561. **Fax**: 0121-742-4315.
Ice Size: 185 x 90 feet (56 x 27 metres).
Spectator Capacity: 2,200.
Communications to: Adrian Broadbelt at rink.
Senior Team: Barons (English Premier Lge).
Colours:.*home*: White, Red & Blue; *away*: Red, Blue & White.
website: under construction at press-time.

STREATHAM

Rink Address: 386 Streatham High Road, London SW16 6HT.
Tel: 0208-769-7771. **Fax**: 0208-769-9979.
Ice Size: 197 x 85 feet (60 x 26 metres).
Communications to: Hugh Carnegy, 13 Eynella Road, London SE22 8XF. **Tel**: 0208-693-7697.
Juniors only 2000-01.

SUNDERLAND

Rink Address: Crowtree Leisure Centre, Crowtree Road, Sunderland, Tyne & Wear SR1 3EL.
Tel: 0191-553-2600. **Fax**: 0191-553-2563.
Ice Size: 184 x 85 feet (56 x 26 metres).
Spectator Capacity: 1,200.
Club Secretary: Robert Laidler, 4 Victoria St, Seaham, Co. Durham. **Tel/fax**: 0191-581-8159.
Senior Team: Chiefs (English Nat Lge North).
Colours: *Home*: White, Red & Blue; *away*: Blue, Red & White.
website: www.123net.co.uk/sihc

CLUB DIRECTORY

SWINDON

Rink Address: Link Centre, White Hill Way, Westlea, Swindon, Wilts SN5 7DL.
Tel: 01793-445566. **Fax:** 01793-445569.
Ice Size: 184 x 85 feet (56 x 26 metres).
Spectator Capacity: 1,650.
Club Secretary: Phil Jefferies, 9 Pennycress Close, Swindon SN2 3RT.
Tel: 01793-729130. **Fax**: 01793-702856.
e-mail: PJefferies@compuserve.com.
Senior Team: Chill (English Premier League).
Colours: *Home*: White, Black & Blue; *away*: Blue, Black & White.
website:
ourworld.compuserve.com/homepages/PJefferies

TELFORD

Rink Address: The Ice Rink, Town Centre, Telford, Salop TF3 4JQ.
Tel: 01952-291511. **Fax**: 01952-291543.
Ice Size: 184 x 85 metres (56 x 26 metres).
Spectator Capacity: 2,250.
Club Secretary: Jackie Fielder, 7 Ironstone Close, St Georges, Telford TF2 9PH.
Tel: 01952-613433.
e-mail: admin@telford-royals.co.uk
Senior Team: Royals (Eng Nat Lge South).
Colours: *Home*: White, Orange & Black; *away*: Orange, Black & White.
Website: www.telford-royals.co.uk

WHITLEY BAY

Rink Address: The Ice Rink, Hillheads Road, Whitley Bay, Tyne & Wear NE25 8HP.
Tel/Fax: 0191-291-1000.
Ice Size: 186 x 81 feet (56.5 x 24.5 metres).
Spectator Capacity: 3,200.
Club Secretary: Tom Smith at the rink.
Senior Team: Warriors (Eng Nat Lge North).
Colours: *Home*: White, Gold & Maroon; *away*: Maroon, White & Gold.
Website: www.icewarrior.freeserve.co.uk

LEGEND

The abbreviations used in the *Annual* are -

LEAGUES

ISL	Ice Hockey Superleague Ltd
BNL	British National Ice Hockey League
E(P)L	English (Premier) League

SCORERS

GP	-	Games Played
G	-	Goals
A	-	Assists
Pts	-	total Points
Pim(s)	-	Penalties in minutes
(N)	-	Netminder

NETMINDERS

GPI	-	Games Played In
Mins	-	Minutes played
SoG	-	Shots on Goal
GA		Goals Against
SO	-	Shutouts
Sv%	-	Save percentage

TEAMS

S	-	Seasons
W	-	Won
L	-	Lost
D	-	Drawn
GF	-	Goals For
GA	-	Goals Against
Ave	-	points/games or points/pims average

PLAYERS

*	British born and trained (ISL only)
I	ITC holder (BNL & EL)
WP	Work Permit holder

ITC - INTERNATIONAL TRANSFER CARD
A signed International Transfer Card (ITC) is required by any player who has been a member of another national federation. There are two types of ITC - 'limited' for one season, and 'unlimited' for players who intend to remain in this country. Ice Hockey UK only keeps records for players needing 'limited' cards and these are the ones shown in the *Annual*.

SAVE PERCENTAGE - CALCULATION METHOD
Shots on goal less goals against, divided by shots on goal, multiplied by 100.
Example: 100 shots less 10 goals scored, equals 90, divided by 100, equals 90 per cent.